BIC.

An Insight into Management Accounting

Professor John Sizer was born in Grimsby, Lincolnshire, in 1938. He worked in the trawling, frozen food and dairy industries while studying for the examinations of the Chartered Institute of Management Accountants, of which he is now a Fellow; in 1961 he was awarded their Leverhulme Prize. He read Industrial Economics at Nottingham University from 1961 to 1964. After graduating he became a financial adviser in the Group Controller's Department at G.K.N. plc, and subsequently lectured at Edinburgh University and at the London Graduate School of Business Studies. Since 1970 he has been Professor of Financial Management at Loughborough University of Technology and was founding Head of the Department of Management Studies from 1971 to 1984. He was Dean of the School of Human and Environmental Studies from 1973 to 1976 and Senior Pro-Vice-Chancellor from 1980 to 1982.

In May 1984 John Sizer was appointed a member of the University Grants Committee and is Chairman of its Business and Management Studies Sub-Committee. He was a member of the Council of the Chartered Institute of Management Accountants from 1983 to 1988 and was Chairman of the Executive Bureau and Directing Group of the Programme on Institutional Management in Higher Education of O.E.C.D./C.E.R.I. from 1979 to 1984, and a member of the Research Advisory Group of the Leverhulme Programme of Study into the Future of Higher Education.

John Sizer is the author of *Case Studies in Management Accounting* (1974; Penguin, 1975, 1979); *Perspectives in Management Accounting* (1981); *Institutional Responses to Financial Reductions within the University Sector* (1987); and (jointly with J. Finnie) *Simplichange: Evaluating the Installation of NC Machine Tools*. He has edited *Readings in Management Accounting* (Penguin, 1980); *Resources in Higher Education* (jointly with Alfred Morris) (1982); and *A Casebook of British Management Accounting*, Volumes 1 and 2 (jointly with N. J. Coulthurst) (1984, 1985). He contributes frequently to the leading British and international accounting, management and educational journals. He undertakes consulting work and conducts seminars for national and international organizations and companies in the fields of management accounting, higher education policy and institutional management.

JOHN SIZER

An Insight into Management Accounting

THIRD EDITION

PENGUIN BOOKS

PENGUIN BOOKS
Published by the Penguin Group
27 Wrights Lane, London W8 5TZ, England
Viking Penguin Inc., 40 West 23rd Street, New York, New York 10010, USA
Penguin Books Australia Ltd, Ringwood, Victoria, Australia
Penguin Books Canada Ltd, 2801 John Street, Markham, Ontario, Canada L3R 1B4
Penguin Books (NZ) Ltd, 182–190 Wairau Road, Auckland 10, New Zealand

Penguin Books Ltd, Registered Offices: Harmondsworth, Middlesex, England

First published 1969
Reprinted with revisions 1975, 1977, 1978
Second edition 1979
Reprinted in Penguin Education 1980
Reprinted with revisions 1982
Reprinted with revisions in Pelican Books 1985
Third edition 1989
1 3 5 7 9 10 8 6 4 2

Copyright © John Sizer, 1969, 1975, 1977, 1978, 1979, 1982, 1985, 1989

To my parents

Contents

Preface to the First Edition

There are a large number of very weighty cost and management accountancy textbooks containing detailed descriptions of various accounting techniques. These books are primarily aimed at students preparing for the examinations of professional accountancy bodies. The questions set by these bodies frequently require complex calculations without any discussion of the limitations of the techniques employed. Many of these textbooks are inevitably technique-oriented and do not fully examine the role of the modern management accountant in the firm. At the other extreme some books on accountancy for managers treat the subject matter superficially. These books tend to assume that the reader has had no previous contact with accounting information. However, most managers have received financial data of one kind or another for a number of years. They require to know how the data is prepared and how to make maximum use of it. The objective has been to produce a book which falls between these two extremes and meets the needs of present and future managers.

It was my former colleague, Professor Edward Stamp, Professor of Accounting and Business Method at the University of Edinburgh, who brought to my attention Elbert Hubbard's description of a typical accountant:

A man past middle age, spare, wrinkled, intelligent, cold, passive, non-committal, with eyes like a codfish; polite in contact but at the same time unresponsive, calm and damnably composed as a concrete post or a plaster of Paris cast; a petrification with a heart of feldspar and without charm of the friendly germ, minus bowels, passion or a sense of humour. Happily they never reproduce and all of them finally to go Hell.

In Professor Stamp's opinion accountants don't have to be like this, even if most of them are. Certainly, Hubbard's description is still representative of many managers' images of their accountants. One of my objects has been to break down this nineteenth-century image. The modern management accountant was recently described by Joseph R. Dugan as:

A highly skilled technician – well educated, complex, confident, intelligent, optimistic – who abhors detailed direction. He expects to be influenced, persuaded and enlightened. He wants to be confronted with choices and alternatives, demanding freedom to structure his work, select his alternatives, present his solutions and speak for himself. He refuses to be considered an automaton who is supposed to respond eagerly to orders, edicts and ultimatums.

The book is concerned with the world of Dugan's modern management accountant, not Hubbard's typical nineteenth-century accountant.

An Insight into Management Accounting should provide executives in general management and in other management specialisms with an insight into the financial aspects of management and the techniques available to the management accountant. It is concerned with the information the accountant should provide management to assist in planning, decision-making and control. A detailed explanation of the mechanics of the techniques is not appropriate, but an adequate description is provided to form the basis for a critical examination of their strengths and weaknesses. Throughout, the subject matter is considered in the context of the environment of the firm. It is hoped that the book will encourage readers to ask their accountants the right questions. It is felt that some accountants, particularly in small and medium-sized firms, are not up-to-date in their thinking because they are not kept on their toes by management. The accounting techniques employed are all too often wrapped up in an aura of mystique.

As well as meeting the needs of managers, *An Insight into Management Accounting* is designed as an introductory text for postgraduate management students, and could also form the basis for a one-term course in management accounting for science or engineering students. Students preparing for the examinations of professional accountancy bodies will find the book integrates much of the material presented in the technique-oriented textbooks and relates it to other relevant disciplines, such as managerial economics, human relations, and operational research. It is hoped that the book will also be of interest to many qualified accountants, particularly those with a professional background, who wish to bring their thinking on management accounting up to date. While the book is primarily directed at general and specialist managers and management students, intelligent lay readers requiring an insight into management accounting will certainly not find the material beyond their comprehension.

A number of authors and publishers willingly gave permission to quote from their publications. In particular, parts of Chapters 8, 9, and 10 [in the first edition] appeared originally in articles I wrote for *Accountancy*, the *Accountant*, the *Accountant's Magazine* and the *Journal of Management Studies*.

The book is based on lectures given to post-graduate, post-experience, and in-plant management accountancy courses for management students and experienced managers during the three years I was a member of the Department of Business Studies at the University of Edinburgh. The participants on these courses constantly stimulated my thinking with their pointed questions. The lectures were, in part, based on my previous industrial experience. I am indebted to my former colleagues in industry who shared their experiences, in particular to Hugh Webster who guided my development as an accountancy student. Ninety-five per cent of the book was written during my last year at the University of Edinburgh, and I benefitted considerably from the interaction with my colleagues in the Department of Business Studies. In particular, my thanks are due to Professor Norman Hunt, Michael Knowles, Tom Milne, and Howard Thomas, who gave advice on particular points falling within their specialist fields. David Tweedie read the manuscript from the point of view of the potential reader and provided some useful comments. I am deeply indebted to my wife who has been a constant source of encouragement during the writing of this book and has helped in its preparation whenever possible.

Carpenders Park, Watford JOHN SIZER
December 1968

Preface to the Second Edition

During the decade since the first edition of *An Insight into Management Accounting* was written, dynamic changes have taken place in the external environment in which enterprises operate. They are required to make faster and more sophisticated adjustments than in the past. They have also had to learn to live with a high rate of inflation and serious liquidity problems. Management accountants have developed more sophisticated techniques in response to these conditions. Many of these developments are described in this second edition.

Changes have also been made to the structure of the book. They reflect the helpful comments of colleagues and students of the Department of Management Studies at the University of Technology, Loughborough; of lecturers at other institutions who have used the book; and of executives of companies for whom seminars and courses have been conducted. Many of the developments referred to in the first paragraph have been discussed with members of the Institute of Cost and Management Accountants at national and regional conferences, and at branch meetings. These discussions always prove to be both enjoyable and productive.

There are thirteen chapters in the second edition, compared with ten in the first. The former chapter on 'Costs for Decision-Making' has been divided into two ('Costs for Decision-Making' and 'Marginal Costing') and brought forward to a more logical point, prior to an examination of the various stages of the profit planning and control cycle. A new chapter has been written on 'Accounting Information for Marketing Management'. The examination of 'Accounting Information for Pricing Decisions' has been expanded and a new chapter added to cover pricing decisions in inflation and transfer pricing. Chapter 2, 'The Nature of Financial Statements',

Chapter 6, 'Profitability – Measurement and Analysis', and Chapter 9, 'Budgetary Planning and Control Systems', have been extensively rewritten to reflect recent developments. New material has been introduced into other chapters, but they remain substantially as in the first edition.

Since writing the first edition, my family and university responsibilities have increased with correspondingly greater demands on my time. This second edition has only been possible because of the sympathetic understanding of my family, and the exceptional support of my secretary, Lisa Thirlby, to whom I am enormously indebted.

Loughborough   JOHN SIZER
January 1979

Preface to the Third Edition

At the time of writing the second edition in the late 1970s, managements of British businesses faced considerable government constraints. Prices were set within criteria established by the government and policed by the Price Commission, and there were controls on wages and salaries, dividends and foreign exchange. Throughout the 1970s managements also had to live with high rates of inflation. To quote Richard Giordano, Chairman of B.O.C.:

> A fellow came to work in the morning. He could not fire anybody. He did not set the wages. He did not set the prices. His own pay was probably frozen. He was hardly managing the business.
>
> (*Financial Times*, 1 April 1987)

The election of a Conservative government in May 1979 under Mrs Thatcher's premiership led to the removal of many of the constraints on competitive business and had a dynamizing effect on British business management. Mrs Thatcher's cure for high rates of inflation was to administer a severe dose of recession, the brunt of which was borne by the manufacturing sector. Manufacturing output fell by nearly 16 per cent between the second quarter of 1979 and the final quarter of 1980.

For the first two to three years of the Thatcher government many groups of British companies were forced by necessity to concentrate on the disposal of loss-makers and the elimination of surplus capacity. Following the period of retrenchment a number of groups undertook more fundamental reviews of their policies and strategies. These strategic reviews frequently led to changes in structure and organizational philosophy involving greater decentralization of profit responsibility. The major revisions to the structure of the book reflect these developments.

There are twelve chapters in the third edition, compared with ten in the first. A new chapter has been written – 'Financial Control of Subsidiary Companies' (Chapter 10). It considers financial control in groups of companies and in divisionalized companies in the context of the strategic and structural changes that have occurred during the 1980s. The use of return on investment to measure the performance of divisions and subsidiaries (in Chapter 6 of the second edition), and the determination of transfer prices for goods and services sold by one autonomous profit centre to another (in Chapter 12 of the second edition), are also examined in this new chapter. The remainder of Chapter 12 of the second edition has been merged with Chapter 11, and some new illustrations added, to form Chapter 12, 'Accounting Information for Selling Price Decisions'. New material has also been introduced in Chapter 3, 'Basic Cost Accounting, Chapter 4, 'Costs for Decision-Making', Chapter 7, 'Long-Range Planning', and Chapter 8, 'Capital Investment Appraisal', reflecting developments during the 1980s.

In the first two editions, the text was illustrated as far as possible with examples taken from industrial and consulting experience. I have recently edited jointly with Nigel Coulthurst two unique case-books [1] as a contribution to bridging the wide gulf that many accountants believe exists between management accounting systems and methods recommended in textbooks and those systems and methods used in practice. They contain detailed descriptions of systems currently in use in a cross-section of twenty-two leading British companies and public corporations. I am grateful to the Institute of Chartered Accountants in England and Wales for permission to make extensive use of examples from these case studies. Each chapter is also cross-referenced to the relevant case studies. I am also indebted to the Open University for permission to use, in Chapters 9 and 10, extracts from an edited transcript of a discussion on audio cassette of budgetary planning and control systems with three senior members of the Council of the Chartered Institute of Management Accountants, which forms part of the Open University's Continuing Education Course, P671, 'Accounting and Finance for Managers'. In order to accommodate the new chapter on financial control of

1 John Sizer and Nigel Coulthurst, *A Casebook of British Management Accounting*, Volumes 1 and 2, Institute of Chartered Accountants in England and Wales, 1984, 1985.

subsidiary companies and the additional detailed examples of management accounting systems and methods in use in named companies and public sector organizations, the two Appendices to Chapter 6, together with Chapter 13 in the second edition, have been omitted.

I am deeply indebted to Lisa Thirlby who brought her usual efficiency, enthusiasm and patience to the task of successfully turning my untidy drafts and at times illegible writing into a polished manuscript. She was ably assisted by Olivia Fergus.

Woodhouse Eaves,   JOHN SIZER
Leicestershire
February 1988

NOTE

There are increasing numbers of female management accountants, but simply for convenience I have used 'he' rather than 'he/she' throughout the text. – J.S.

1

What is Management Accounting?

This book is concerned with management accounting. What is management accounting? In the broadest sense all accounting is management accounting. All financial and cost information generated by accountants is of some interest to management. But, in practice, where management accounting differs from financial accounting, cost accounting, budgetary control, and financial planning, is on the emphasis upon *purpose* rather than upon techniques. Management accounting may be defined as the application of accounting techniques to the provision of information designed to assist all levels of management in *planning*, in making *decisions*, and in *controlling* the activities of an organization. The management accountant should identify and satisfy, through effective communication, management's financial information needs. In satisfying these needs, the management accountant employs the techniques of financial accounting, cost accounting, budgetary planning and control and many others.

The term 'management accounting' came into use when accountants added to two existing functions:

1. Correctly determining a firm's profit or loss for a period and evaluating its assets and liabilities on the last day of the period, and
2. Generating information for controlling operations to maximize efficiency,
   a third one:
3. Assisting management in planning and decision-making.

Management accounting became fashionable in Britain following the visit of the Anglo-American Council of Productivity Management Accounting Team to the United States during April, May and June 1950. In the introduction to its report, entitled *Management Accounting* and published in November 1950, the team stated:

Management accountancy is the presentation of accounting information in such a way as to assist management in the creation of policy and in the day-to-day operation of an undertaking.' It recommended that industrial accountants should make greater efforts to acquaint themselves with the problems of management and the technical processes in their industry, and concentrate their efforts towards producing information which would serve as a guide to policy and action. Shortly after the publication of the report of the management accounting team, the Institute of Cost and Works Accountants decided in future to award its Fellowship (F.C.W.A) on the basis of an examination in management accountancy, and offered the Fellowship as a post-experience qualification to members of other professional accounting bodies in Great Britain. Today these examinations are part of the Institute's Associateship examinations.

In March 1972 the Institute of Cost and Works Accountants became the Institute of Cost and Management Accountants, because 'this title more accurately reflects the purpose of the Institute today and the qualifications and standing of its members'. Members of the Institute felt that management accounting achieved the highest possible confirmation of its status as a separate and distinct accountancy discipline when the Queen in Council approved the grant of a Royal Charter of Incorporation to the Institute in February 1975. An amendment to the Institute's Royal Charter was approved in January 1987 to change its name to the Chartered Institute of Management Accountants, which allowed members to describe themselves as 'Chartered Management Accountants'.

While accountancy provides the essential financial information system of business – the language of business – economists would argue that they provide its underlying logic. Therefore, it is useful to develop a classification of accountancy which makes the relationship between accountancy and economics clearer. A distinction can be made between:

Stewardship (including tax accounting), e.g. periodic financial statements for external users;

Decision accounting, e.g. estimates of costs and revenues associated with particular alternatives; and

Control accounting, e.g. information to assist management to plan and control effectively.

Financial accounting is concerned with stewardship. The task of the financial accountant is to produce profit-and-loss accounts and balance sheets that provide a true and fair view to the shareholders and meet the requirements of the law. Professional accountants in practice are concerned with the auditing of these financial accounts. While a knowledge of financial accounting is an essential prerequisite of any discussion of management accounting techniques, the management accountant is primarily concerned with decision accounting and control accounting. However, it is extremely important that the concepts underlying the preparation of company profit-and-loss accounts, balance sheets and cash flow statements are understood. Financial accounting is the subject of Chapter 2, and emphasis is placed in this chapter on explaining these basic concepts. High rates of inflation during the 1970s highlighted the inadequacies of the historical cost accounting system, which has been in use for many centuries. These inadequacies are considered in Chapter 2, together with a summary of the developments that have taken place within the British accounting profession as to how the impact of inflation should be reflected in financial statements. While disclosure in published company accounts is also an important topic, it is beyond the scope of this book. A specialized aspect of financial accounting is company taxation, both the computation of tax payable and the management of the company's affairs to legally minimize tax payable. The management accountant must take taxation into account when evaluating alternatives and preparing long-term and short-term financial plans. Many companies employ taxation specialists, and the management accountant will consult the specialist on taxation aspects of his work.

The management accountant is primarily concerned with *decision accounting* and *control accounting*. The questions considered by the accountant under these headings are also of interest to the behavioural scientist, the managerial economist and the operational researcher. It is important that the management accountant should be familiar with these disciplines, and they form an important part of his professional education. Firstly, he must remember at all times that a business is a human/organizational system, and that management involves people. People are subject to complex motives and attitudes. The management information system must take account of the human element; it must not simply be seen as something mechanistic. The management accountant must think carefully about how he is to communicate effectively with his customers. The systems he operates, whether manual or computer-based, can only aim at providing the most useful set of data to each manager; *responses* to the data and action on the data will be determined by the individual manager.

Effective communication will occur if the manager makes *positive* responses and takes *positive* actions. When generating information for decision-making, an appreciation of managerial economics is essential. The management accountant should also be familiar with operational research and quantitative techniques and know when to seek the advice of an operational research team or a statistician. He must work with these and other specialists, particularly in information technology, in the design and implementation of integrated management information systems.

Decision accounting is mainly concerned with *ad hoc* decisions. These *ad hoc* decisions require the analysis of the profitability of various allocations of resources. While these decisions may be repeated at intervals, it will probably be at irregular intervals. The task of *control accounting* is to produce data at regular intervals in a standard form, so that the firm's actual performance can be compared with plans, budgets and forecasts, and differences analysed by causes. Control accounting, by making possible such comparisons of planned and actual performance, and forecast and planned performance, enables a 'feedback' process to operate and guides the progress of the firm. The managerial economist is more likely to be interested in decision accounting than in control accounting. He will be particularly interested in pricing, marketing and investment decisions, but will obviously appreciate that control accounting is important. The operational researcher will be interested in the appraisal of all types of decisions and in the establishment of control systems and management information systems. The behavioural scientist, on the other hand, will probably be more interested in control accounting. For example, the motivational aspects of establishing standards and budgets and the subsequent reporting of actual compared with planned performance are within his sphere of interest.

Before an examination can be made of planning and control systems and the appraisal of long-term and short-term decisions, an understanding of the terminology of both cost and management accounting, types of costing systems, and decision cost concepts is necessary. Cost accounting is the subject of Chapter 3. Much of the cost information used by the management accountant flows from the cost accounting system. In Chapter 3 the classification of costs, overhead absorption, costing systems, and historical and standard costs are explained and illustrated, and the impact of developments in advanced manufacturing technology on costing systems is briefly considered. Certain limitations of absorption cost data are pointed out and these are further examined in subsequent chapters. The decision cost concepts which will be employed in later chapters are explained and illustrated in the first half of Chapter 4. A knowledge of cost-volume-profit relationships is often essential in the analysis of alternatives. The use of break-even analysis and charts to examine cost-volume-profit relationships is considered in the second half of Chapter 4, together with an explanation of the impact of cost inflation and recession on such relationships. Marginal costing is more appropriate than absorption costing to the analysis of cost-volume-profit relationships in multi-product, multi-market firms, and the whole of Chapter 5 is devoted to explaining and illustrating marginal cost-analysis and marginal costing systems.

The Planning and Control Cycle

It will be appreciated that limited liability companies raise finance from various sources: long-term finance from their shareholders in the form of share issues and retained earnings; secured and un-secured long-term loans mainly from institutional investors; short-term finance from banks, finance companies, hire-purchase companies; trade credit from suppliers, etc. Each of these sources of finance has a cost in terms of a rate of interest per annum, and the financial director's objective should be to raise finance in a form which will optimize the weighted average cost of this finance. Having raised the finance it is invested in assets, both fixed and current, which should be employed to generate an adequate return on the assets. This return should in the longer term be at least equal to the weighted average cost of the finance raised. In order to generate both increasing profits and a satisfactory return on assets employed, companies need to plan their growth in both the long term and the short term. If companies are to optimize the cost of financing this growth they must also plan when, how much, and from what source they are to raise the additional finance. In periods of high inflation, in rapidly expanding or seasonal businesses, short-term cash and working capital management are equally important. Thus financial planning and control, long- and short-term and working capital management, should be an integral part of a company's profit planning and control system. In such a system, planning is the basis of control, and the control process is broadly one of:

— analysing historical performance;
— examining the future environment in which the company will be operating;
— developing long-term objectives, including financial objectives;
— formulating a strategy to achieve the objectives;
— translating the strategy into operating plans for the next three to five years;
— developing more detailed action plans and budgets by responsible managers for next year;
— motivating people to achieve the plans and budgets; and continually comparing actual with planned performance and forecast with planned performance, and reporting to responsible management, as a basis for taking action to improve both performance and the effectiveness of the planning process.

There is therefore a continuous process which is illustrated in Figure 1.1.

Within this planning and control cycle companies must seek out and appraise investment (long-term) opportunities and make various tactical (short-term) decisions, such as pricing and product mix decisions. The essence of the difference between *investment decisions* and *tactical decisions* is *time*. Where, in choosing between alternative courses of action, the time factor is important, the decision is of an *investment* nature. It carries a cost, or interest, on the finance invested in the project during the years of its life. Tactical decisions have a short life and therefore do not normally attract such a cost. For tactical or short-term decisions the time factor is not important. It will be recognized that regardless of whether the decision under consideration is an investment or a tactical one, decision-making

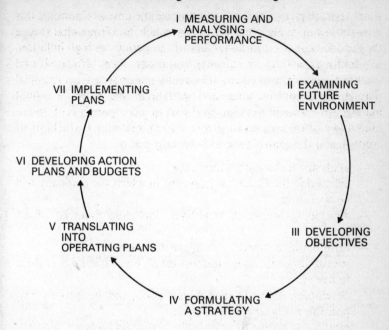

Figure 1.1. *Stages in profit planning and control cycle*

involves the evaluation of, and choice between, competing alternatives. Management therefore requires an answer to the question, 'Which is the most worthwhile alternative: A, B, C . . .?' Management requires the management accountant to measure the 'worthwhileness' of each alternative.

The various stages of the company profit planning and control cycle and the evaluation of investment and tactical decisions are considered in sequence. The use of accounting and financial ratios in the measurement of past performance, the diagnosis of the present position and the establishment of profitability objectives are considered in Chapter 6. The establishment of profitability objectives leads into a discussion of long-range planning, and, in particular, of financial planning in Chapter 7. Financial planning is an integral part of long-range planning. Therefore prior to the consideration of financial planning the establishment of corporate objectives, the development of a strategy to achieve the agreed objectives, and the translation of this strategy into an operational plan, are examined.

Long-range planning gives rise to the need to appraise capital investment decisions, and to plan and control in the short term. Capital
investment appraisal is the subject of Chapter 8. Within the framework of the financial plan, a budgetary planning and control system
should be operated to ensure that detailed budgets are prepared for
the current year of the financial plan. These budgets, supplemented
by periodic forecasts during the budget year, normally form the
basis for subsequent control. The introduction and operation of
budgetary planning and control systems in individual businesses or
operating units is considered in Chapter 9, and financial control of
subsidiaries and divisions in groups of companies and divisionalized
businesses in Chapter 10.

The dynamic changes that are continually taking place in the
environment in which companies operate have their greatest impact
in the market place. It is important that a system of accounting is
developed which satisfies the financial information needs of marketing management. This is the subject of Chapter 11. Selling price
decisions are key decisions in most companies and have to be taken
in the context of marketing and product policy. The accountant's
contribution to selling price decisions is examined in Chapter 12.

Companies are operating in an environment which requires fast
and sophisticated adjustments and reactions to the dynamic changes
that are occurring in the environment in which they operate. Immense problems of co-ordination and control are raised by complicated technology, shorter product life-cycles, the geographical scale
of operations in highly competitive international markets, large-scale
capital facilities, specialization within organizations by functional
specialists, and highly sensitive and interrelated management processes. While the rate of change has accelerated, operations have
become less flexible. Managements are preparing company long-
term plans against the background of an uncertain economic environment, and technological, ecological, political and sociological
unknowns obscure the horizon. The more sophisticated systems and
techniques the management accountant has had to develop and
employ in response to this situation are examined in the appropriate
chapters, including the use of information technology. Whenever
possible these developments are illustrated by real-world examples,
often from named companies.

Inevitably in an introductory text of this length which aims to give an insight into management accounting, it is not possible to develop in depth many aspects of particular topics. The number of illustrations of the application of techniques to practical problems and real-world examples is also limited, for the same reason. In order to minimize these two limitations, at the end of each chapter a list of Selected Readings and named case studies is provided. The case studies are published in John Sizer and Nigel Coulthurst, *A Casebook of British Management Accounting*, Institute of Chartered Accountants in England and Wales (Volume 1, 1984; Volume 2, 1985), from which many of the examples in the text are taken. The two volumes contain detailed descriptions of management systems in use in twenty-two leading British companies and public corporations.

Summary

It has been emphasized that management accounting is concerned with the *purpose* of accounting rather than with techniques. The management accountant should employ planning, control and decision-making techniques to provide information to assist all levels of management in planning, decision-making and controlling the activities of the firm. He must have an understanding of the nature of decision problems and the information needed to solve them, as well as appreciating that any business is a complex of interlocking sets of 'systems'. In many businesses these systems have been integrated into unified computer-based management information systems. All this implies that a management accountant, in addition to his specialized training in accounting and financial management, must have a fairly thorough understanding of basic disciplines such as mathematics, statistics, economics, human and organizational behaviour, etc. He must be familiar with developments in information technology and be able to work closely not only with marketing, production and personnel managers, etc., but also with other specialists in the management team. While he has employed information technology to develop more sophisticated planning and control systems and decision-making techniques in response to an increasingly complex and uncertain environment, the ultimate test of the management accountant's effectiveness within an organization depends on an ability to identify and satisfy, through effective communication, management's financial information needs. In the absence of effective communication, all the information technology revolution can produce is data.

2

The Nature of Financial Statements

A knowledge of financial accounting is an essential prerequisite for any discussion of the techniques and concepts employed by the management accountant. In this chapter the concepts underlying the preparation of financial statements are examined including a summary of the developments that have taken place within the British accounting profession as to how the impact of inflation should be reflected in financial statements. The inadequacies of the existing historical cost accounting (H.C.A.) system have been acknowledged but the accounting profession has been slow in moving towards a new system of current cost accounting (C.C.A.). The traditional historical cost accounting system is considered first, leading into an analysis of the impact of inflation on this system, and an examination of the current cost accounting system.

Financial accounting is concerned with the *external* requirements of shareholders, prospective investors, financial analysts, creditors, trade unions, the Registrar of Companies, the Inland Revenue, and persons outside the management, as well as with the *internal* requirements of the management of a company. Accountants record the revenue received and expenditure incurred by a company so that its *overall* performance over a period of time and its financial position at a point in time can be ascertained. The financial accounting system, which is frequently integrated with the management accounting system, classifies, records, and interprets in terms of money, transactions and events of a financial character. These facts and figures are summarized and presented to management and outside parties in the form of periodic financial reports and statements. The following periodic financial statements will normally be prepared for the management of a manufacturing company:

Balance sheet;
Manufacturing and trading account;
Profit-and-loss account;
Profit-and-loss appropriation account;
Cash flow or funds flow statement.

These financial statements are illustrated in Tables 2.1–2.6. A further statement, the value added statement, which may increase in importance with the movement towards greater disclosure of financial information to employees, is illustrated in Table 2.7.

Balance Sheet

The *balance sheet* (Table 2.1) is a statement on the *last day* of the accounting period of:

1. The *assets* or *resources* of the company, e.g. fixed assets such as buildings, plant and machinery, vehicles, etc., and current assets such as stocks, debtors, cash, etc.
2. The *liabilities* or *obligations* of the company, e.g. long-term liabilities such as debentures and future taxation, and current liabilities such as creditors, current taxation, proposed dividends, etc.
3. The *share capital and reserves* or *shareholders' investment* in the company, e.g. ordinary share capital, preference share capital (if any), capital reserves, and revenue reserves.

In the balance sheet the company's assets are equal to liabilities plus share capital and reserves. The reason for this is explained later in this chapter.

Limited liability companies raise finance from various sources: long-term finance from their shareholders in the form of share issues and retained earnings; secured and unsecured long-term loans mainly from institutional investors; and short-term finance from banks, finance companies, and hire-purchase companies. Each of these sources of finance shown in the balance sheet has a cost in terms of rate of interest per annum, and the finance director's objective should be to raise finance in a form which will optimize the company's weighted average cost of capital.

Having raised the finance it is invested in assets or resources, e.g.

THE E.D. COMPANY LTD
Balance Sheet as at 31 December 1989

	£	£		Cost	Accumulated Depreciation	£	£
Authorized Capital			*Fixed Assets*				
500,000 Ordinary Shares of £1 each	500,000						
			Freehold Land	75,000	—		75,000
			Freehold Buildings	125,725	30,253		95,472
Issued Capital			Plant and Machinery	172,240	95,368		76,872
300,000 Ordinary Shares of £1 each fully paid		300,000	Fixtures and Fittings	10,640	5,614		5,026
			Motor Cars	1,200	1,000		200
				£384,805	£132,235		252,570
Revenue Reserves			*Investments*				
General Reserve	20,000		Quoted				21,483
Profit-and-loss Account	24,764	44,764	(Market Value £21,234)				
Total Shareholders' Interests		344,764					
Long-term loan		50,000	*Current Assets*				
Deferred Taxation		28,000	Stocks in Hand and Work-in-progress		165,560		
		422,764	Sundry Debtors		97,855		
			Short-term Deposits		10,000		
Capital Employed			Cash at Bank		5,874		
Current Liabilities							279,289
Sundry Creditors	100,578						
Current Taxation	15,000						
Proposed Dividend	15,000	130,578					
		£553,342					£553,342

fixed assets which have a long but nevertheless limited life, such as buildings, plant and machinery, vehicles, etc.; and current assets which change from day to day, such as stocks, debtors, cash, etc. Therefore in addition to showing shareholders' investment and liabilities, the balance sheet also contains a statement of *assets* or *resources* of the company on the last day of the accounting period. These assets should be employed by the company to generate a return on capital employed greater than the company's weighted

Table 2.2

THE E. D. COMPANY LTD

Manufacturing Account for the year ended 31 December 1989

	£	£
Raw Materials		42,000
Opening Stock		
Purchases		250,307
		292,307
Less Closing Stock		30,000
Costs of Materials Consumed		262,307
Production Wages		220,000
Prime Cost of Production		482,307
Factory Overhead:		
Packing Wages	10,000	
Factory Rates	435	
Factory Insurance	895	
Packing Materials	13,600	
Factory Repairs	7,020	
Factory Gas, Water, and Electricity	6,556	
Non-productive Wages	180,458	
Works Salaries	33,140	
Depreciation of: Plant and Machinery	15,224	
Fixtures and Fittings	532	
Freehold Premises	4,784	272,644
		754,951
Less Increase in Work-in-progress		2,520
Factory Costs of Production		752,431
Less Stock of Finished Goods in Factory		20,000
Cost of Goods to Warehouse to Trading Account		£732,431

average cost of capital. Return on capital employed is fully considered in Chapter 6.

Manufacturing, Trading, and Profit-and-Loss Accounts

The return generated from the employment of assets is shown in a company's manufacturing, trading and profit-and-loss accounts. The *manufacturing and trading accounts* (Tables 2.2 and 2.3)[1] show the cost of goods manufactured during the period of the accounts, the cost of goods sold during the period of the accounts, the sales for the period, and the gross profit. The gross profit is transferred to the *profit-and-loss account* (Table 2.4). Marketing and distribution costs, administrative costs, and any research and development expenditure are deducted to determine the company's *trading or operating profit* for the period. To this, investment income is added and interest payable deducted to give *profit before taxation* from which corporation tax is deducted to give the *net profit or loss* for the period. The *profit-and-loss appropriation account* (Table 2.5) indicates the profit available for appropriation to shareholders in the form of dividends, and for transfer to reserves, and for carrying

Table 2.3

THE E. D. COMPANY LTD

Trading Account for the year ended 31 December 1989

	£
Finished Goods in Warehouse	
Opening Stock	65,000
Factory Production transferred	732,431
	797,431
Less Closing Stock	45,000
Cost of Sales	752,431
Gross Profit to Profit-and-loss Account	103,285
Sales	£855,716

1 In practice the manufacturing and trading accounts may form a single account, as may the profit-and-loss account and the profit-and-loss appropriation account. They have been shown as separate accounts to simplify presentation.

Table 2.4

THE E. D. COMPANY LTD

Profit-and-loss Account for the year ended 31 December 1989

	£	£	£
Gross Profit from Trading Account			103,285
Selling and Distribution Cost			
Carriage Outwards	4,300		
Salesmen's Travelling Expenses	1,763		
Sales Office Salaries	2,000		
Salesmen's Salaries	10,620	18,683	
Advertising		2,075	
General Expenses		2,012	
Administration Expenses			
Office Salaries		12,005	
Depreciation: Freehold Premises	252		
Fixtures and Fittings	532		
Cars	300	1,084	
Directors' Salaries		18,000	
Audit Fees		500	
Provision for Bad Debts		2,765	
Bank Interest		2,427	
		59,551	
Less Discounts Received		2,030	57,521
Operating Profit			45,764
Investment Income			2,000
Profit before Interest and Taxation			47,764
Less Loan Interest			5,000
Profit before Taxation			42,764
Taxation			18,000
Net Profit for year to Appropriation Account			£24,764

forward to the next account. The profit available for appropriation is represented by the balance brought forward from the previous account, plus or minus the net profit or loss for the period. Retained profit is an important source of capital for financing future growth. The relationship between the balance sheet and the profit-and-loss

Table 2.5

THE E. D. COMPANY LTD

Profit-and-loss Appropriation Account for the year ended
31 December 1989

	£	£
Balance brought down from previous year		20,517
Net Profit for year		24,764
Available for Appropriation		45,281
Interim Dividend of 1.5 pence per share	4,500	
Proposed Final Dividend of 5 pence per share	15,000	19,500
		25,781
Transfer to General Reserve		14,500
Balance carried forward to next year		£11,281

account, under the historical cost accounting system, is illustrated in a simplified form in Figure 2.1. A more detailed analysis of the relationship between these statements will be undertaken in Chapter 6.

Sources and Applications of Cash or Funds Statements

The profit-and-loss account of a company shows the amount of profit made during a period, and serves as a link between the balance sheet at the beginning of the period and the end of the period. The *cash flow* or *funds flow statement* (Table 2.6) shows the link between successive balance sheets from a different point of view. It identifies the movements in assets, liabilities and capital which have taken place during the period and the resultant effect on cash or net liquid funds. It describes the sources from which additional cash (funds) was derived and the applications to which this cash (funds) was put. A distinction is made in the statement between *internal sources* of funds generated by the company, such as profit before depreciation and investment income, and *external sources* of funds raised from outside the company, such as share capital and debenture loans.

A distinction is also made in the statement between applications arising from increases or decreases in *working capital*, such as

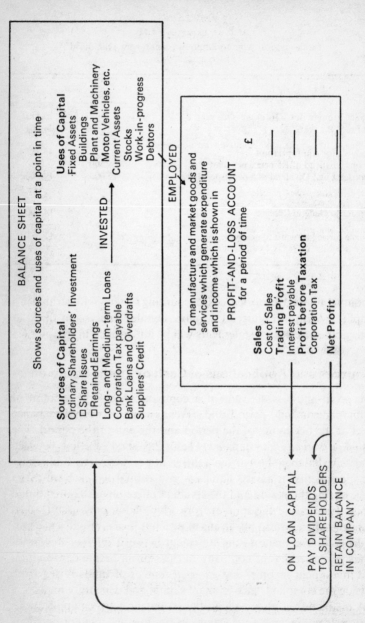

Figure 2.1. *Relationship between balance sheet and profit-and-loss account under Historical Cost Accounting*

Table 2.6

THE E. D. COMPANY LTD

Sources and Applications of Funds year ending
31 December 1989

	£	£
Sources of Funds		
Profit before Taxation		42,764
Adjustments for items not involving the movement of funds:		
Depreciation		21,624
Total generated from Operations		64,388
Funds from other Sources		
Sale of Fixed Assets		1,200
Issue of Shares for Cash		100,000
		165,588
Application of Funds		
Dividends paid	21,000	
Taxation paid	12,000	
Purchase of Fixed Assets	53,358	86,358
		79,230
Increase/Decrease in Working Capital		
Decrease in Stocks	(9,480)	
Increase in Debtors	20,000	
Increase in Trade Creditors	(15,000)	
Increase in Cash Balances	83,710	£79,230

increases in stocks and debtors, and purchases of fixed assets, such
as plant and machinery. Thus sources and applications of cash or
funds statements show the movements in the permanent and working capital cycle illustrated in Figure 2.2. In studying Figure 2.2 it is
important to note that a credit sale, and the profit or loss arising
from a credit sale, appear in the profit-and-loss account when the
sale is made, *not* when the customer subsequently pays.

Value Added Statement

Value added statements rarely appear in company annual reports
and accounts. However, with the growing trend towards increasing

disclosure of financial information to employees, and the recognition that, in the long run, if Britain is to compete in international markets and at the same time increase the real disposable incomes of its population, it must sustain a high rate of growth of productivity, the value added statement may become a standard company financial statement. For example, Kalamazoo plc (*A Casebook of British Management Accounting*, Vol. 2), a co-partnership company whose founders were Quakers, employs a value added presentation to inform employees monthly on the performance of the company and to involve them in improving it.

Value added is represented by a company's sales income during a period less bought-in materials and services. Value added is the wealth the company has been able to create by its own and its employees' efforts during a period. It is out of the 'value added cake' that a company rewards its various stakeholders, i.e. shareholders, directors, managers, employees, Inland Revenue, etc. Value added is more than a measure of shop-floor productivity, it is also a function of good design, efficient purchasing, effective terotechnology, good industrial relations, ability to differentiate products in the market place, and all the other factors that make for an efficient organization.

The value added statement shows the size of the 'value added cake' and how the 'cake' has been divided amongst the various stakeholders. In its discussion paper, *The Corporate Report*, the Accounting Standards Steering Committee envisage value added statements in the format similar to that shown in Table 2.7. How investment income should be treated is not discussed in *The Corporate Report*.

Published Accounts

British companies are required to prepare a summarized profit-and-loss account and a balance sheet in accordance with the requirements of the Companies Acts of 1948, 1967, 1976 and 1981. The 1981 Act sets out two alternative formats for the balance sheet and four alternative formats for the profit-and-loss account. Disclosure in company annual reports and accounts has received considerable attention during the last two decades. In particular, the leading accounting bodies established the Accounting Standards Steering Committee, which has issued a series of Statements of Standard Accounting Practice. These lay down minimum standards of disclosure.

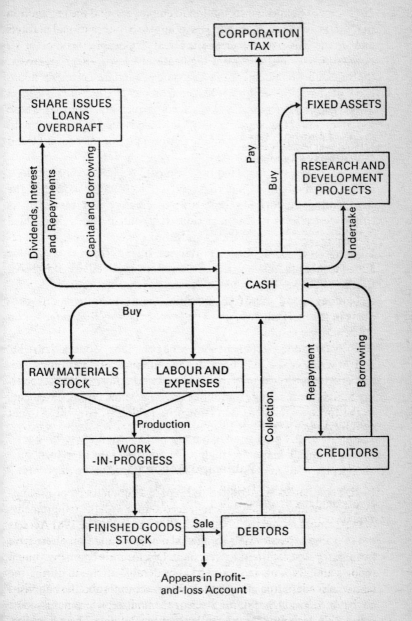

Figure 2.2. *Permanent and working capital cycle of manufacturing firm*

Table 2.7

THE E. D. COMPANY LTD

Statement of Value Added, year ending 31 December 1989

	£	£
Sales		855,716
Bought-in Materials and Services		302,105
Value Added generated by the Company		553,611
Add Investment Income, i.e. share of value added		
generated by other companies		2,000
		£555,611
Applied in the following way:		
To pay Employees		
Wages, Pensions, and Fringe Benefits		486,223
To pay Providers of Capital		
Interest on Loans	5,000	
Dividends to Shareholders	19,500	24,500
To pay Government		
Taxation		18,000
To provide for Maintenance and Expansion of Assets		
Depreciation	21,624	
Retained Profits	5,264	26,888
		£555,611

The main concern of this chapter is the examination of financial accounting principles and concepts. This knowledge is an essential prerequisite of any discussion of management accounting techniques such as financial planning, budgetary control, rate of return on capital employed, and ratio analysis. It is particularly important that readers should appreciate the concepts underlying the preparation of company financial statements. A full discussion of published accounts will be found in Selected Readings 6, 7, 10, 11 and 12.

Double-entry Accounting

To build up the trading and profit-and-loss accounts and the balance sheet, the financial accounting department classifies and records receipts and payments, assets and liabilities, and debtors and creditors in ledgers or in computer files using a *double-entry* accounting system. To fully understand financial accounting concepts and principles the double-entry system must be mastered.

The resources owned by a business are called *assets*, and the claims of various parties against these assets are either liabilities or capital. *Liabilities* are claims of creditors, everyone other than the owners of the business. *Capital* is the claim of the owners of the business and represents their investment in the business. A company has a legal identity separate from that of its shareholders, and the shareholders' investment in the company represents a potential claim on the company. Since all the assets of a company are claimed by someone (either by the shareholders or by the creditors), and since these claims cannot exceed the amount of assets available to be claimed, it follows that: ASSETS = CAPITAL + LIABILITIES   and   CAPITAL = ASSETS − LIABILITIES. Therefore, any changes in one of these items must result in an equal change in one of the others. For example, if assets are increased by the introduction of £1,000 additional cash from shareholders, then capital must increase by an equal amount. Accounting systems are designed to record the two aspects of every event (transaction) of a financial character in the activities of the company, i.e. changes in assets and changes in liabilities or capital. It follows that every event that is recorded in the ledgers, normally computer based, affects at least two items; there is no conceivable way of making a single-item change in the accounts. Accounting is therefore called a double-entry system. In this system one entry is the creditor or *credit entry* and the other the debtor or *debit entry*. In any transaction the creditor *gives* and the debtor *receives*. Thus, in the introduction of further capital the shareholders *give* £1,000 and the cash account *receives* £1,000. This transaction is recorded in the ledger as follows:

Dr	*Share Capital A/c*		Cr
		Cash	£1,000

	Cash A/c		
Share Capital	£1,000		

It will be seen that any increase in capital or liabilities is recorded with a credit entry, any increase in assets with a debit entry, and with a decrease the entries are reversed. In addition to assets and liabilities a company has expenses and revenue. If £100 wages are paid by cash, cash *gives* and wages *receives*, and the entries in the ledger would be:

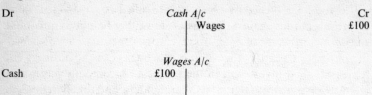

In the case of sales for cash the entry would be the opposite, sales *gives* (credit entry) and cash *receives* (debit entry). It follows then that expenses are *debit entries* and revenues are *credit entries*. In summary, increases in assets, decreases in liabilities or capital, and expenses appear as *debit entries*; increases in liabilities or capital, decreases in assets, and sales appear as *credit entries*.

A Simple Illustration

A. Trader & Co. Ltd commenced business on 1 September with the issue of 750 £1 shares for cash. The company's transactions for the month of September are summarized in Table 2.8. It will be seen that for the first ten transactions the account that *receives* (the debit entry) and the account that *gives* (the credit entry) are indicated. Readers are invited to complete columns four and five. Each transaction has been numbered to enable the reader to trace the double entry for each transaction in the ledger accounts (Table 2.9). The reader's completion of Table 2.8 can also be checked. Having traced each transaction into the ledger accounts, the next stage is to prepare the trading account and the profit-and-loss account.[2] The balances of expense and revenue accounts have to be transferred to the trading and profit-and-loss accounts for September, that is sales, purchases, and wages. Gross profit is determined by deducting from sales the cost of goods sold. In order to arrive at the cost of goods sold, it is necessary to deduct from the purchases during September the stock

2 In practice, before the trading account and profit-and-loss account are prepared, a trial balance would be taken out to ensure that the transactions have been correctly entered in the ledgers, and that the total of the debit entries equals the total of the credit entries.

Table 2.8

A. TRADER & CO. LTD
Transactions – September

Date	Transaction	£	Receives (Debit)	Gives (Credit)	No.
1st	Issued 750 £1 shares for cash	750	Cash	Share Capital	1
2nd	Purchased goods from A. Peters on credit	250	Purchases	A. Peters	2
3rd	Purchased second-hand van for cash	100	Motor Vehicles	Cash	3
4th	Purchased goods for cash	27	Purchases	Cash	4
5th	Sold goods for cash	25	Cash	Sales	5
8th	Sold goods to W. Trainer on credit	50	W. Trainer	Sales	6
9th	Sold goods to R. Roberts on credit	27	R. Roberts	Sales	7
11th	Purchased goods from H. Morton on credit	100	Purchases	H. Morton	8
12th	Paid A. Peters cash	150	A. Peters	Cash	9
15th	Received cash from W. Trainer	30	Cash	W. Trainer	10
18th	Bought goods from A. Peters on credit	50			11
19th	Received cash from R. Roberts	17			12
23rd	Sold goods to W. Trainer for cash	125			13
25th	Sent cash to A. Peters	100			14
26th	Paid wages	37			15
30th	Paid cash to H. Morton	50			16

on hand at 30 September of £290. How does this appear in the ledger? Stock is an asset and the stock account must therefore be debited and the trading acount credited (shown by a deduction on the debit side). The entry is therefore:

	Dr	Cr
Stock Account	£290	
Trading Account		£290
Stock on Hand at 30 September		

It will be seen that the balance of the stock account is carried down to become the opening stock of the next period.

Table 2.9

A. TRADER & CO. LTD

Ledger

Dr   Cr

Share Capital A/c

		£			£
Sept. 30 Balance	c/d	750	Sept. 1 Cash	(1)	750
			Oct. 1 Balance	b/d	750

Motor Vehicles A/c

		£			£
Sept. 3 Cash	(3)	100	Sept. 30 Provision for Depreciation		5
			30 Balance	c/d	95
		£100			£100
Oct. 1 Balance	b/d	95			

Cash A/c

		£			£
Sept. 1 Share Capital	(1)	750	Sept. 3 Motor Vehicles	(3)	100
5 Sales	(5)	25	4 Purchases	(4)	27
15 W. Trainer	(10)	30	12 A. Peters	(9)	150
19 R. Roberts	(12)	17	25	(14)	100
23 Sales	(13)	125	26 Wages	(15)	37
			30 H. Morton	(16)	50
			30 Balance	c/d	483
		£947			£947
Oct. 1 Balance	b/d	483			

Stock A/c

	£		£
Sept. 30 Trading A/c	290	Sept. 30 Balance	c/d 290
Oct. 1 Balance	b/d 290		

Table 2.9 – continued

Dr			Cr

Sales A/c

	£			£
Sept. 30 Trading A/c	227	Sept. 5 Cash	(5)	25
		8 W. Trainer	(6)	50
		9 R. Roberts	(7)	27
		23 Cash	(13)	125
	——			——
	£227			£227

Purchases A/c

		£		£
Sept. 2 A. Peters	(2)	250	Sept. 30 Trading A/c	427
4 Cash	(4)	27		
11 H. Morton	(8)	100		
18 A. Peters	(11)	50		
		——		——
		£427		£427

Wages A/c

		£		£
Sept. 26 Cash	(15)	37	Sept. 30 Profit-and-loss A/c	37

Provisions for Depreciation A/c

	£		£
Sept. 30 Motor Vehicles	5	Sept 30 Profit-and-loss A/c	5

W. Trainer A/c

		£			£
Sept. 8 Sales	(6)	50	Sept. 15 Cash	(10)	30
			30 Balance	c/d	20
		——			——
		£50			£50
Oct. 1 Balance	b/d	20			

R. Roberts A/c

		£			£
Sept. 9 Sales	(7)	27	Sept. 19 Cash	(12)	17
			30 Balance	c/d	10
		——			——
		£27			£27
Oct. 1 Balance	b/d	10			

Table 2.9 – continued

Dr				Cr
CREDITORS		*A. Peters A/c*		
	£			£
Sept. 12 Cash	(9) 150	Sept. 2 Purchases		(2) 250
25 Cash	(14) 100	18 Purchases		(11) 50
30 Balance	c/d 50			
	———			———
	£300			£300
	≡≡≡			≡≡≡
		Oct. 1 Balance		b/d 50

H. Morton A/c

	£			£
Sept. 30 Cash	(16) 50	Sept. 11 Purchases		(8) 100
30 Balance	c/d 50			
	———			———
	£100			£100
	≡≡≡			≡≡≡
		Oct. 1 Balance		b/d 50

Trading and Profit-and-loss Accounts – September

	£		£
Purchases	427	Sales	227
Less Closing Stock	290		
	———		
Cost of Goods Sold	137		
Gross Profit	c/d 90		
	———		———
	£227		£227
	≡≡≡		≡≡≡
Wages	37	Gross Profit	b/d 90
Depreciation	5		
Net Profit	c/d 48		
	———		———
	£90		£90
	≡≡≡		≡≡≡
		Oct. 1 Balance	b/d 48

The second-hand van has a long but nevertheless limited life, and the cost of the van must be systematically reduced over its life by the process called *depreciation*. The purpose of the depreciation process is gradually to remove the cost of the asset from the motor vehicles account and show it as an expense. The depreciation charge on the van for September is £5 and is recorded in the ledger with the following entry:

	Dr	Cr
Provision for Depreciation	£5	
Motor Vehicles Account		£5
Motor Vehicle Depreciation for September		

The balance of the provision for depreciation account is then transferred to the profit-and-loss account like any other expense. It is important to appreciate that the provision for depreciation does not provide a fund to replace the asset at the end of its life. No cash is involved in accounting for depreciation, merely book entries. However, it does reduce the profit available for distribution to shareholders, and, therefore, the potential outflow of cash from the business in the form of dividends.

The balance of the profit-and-loss account represents the profit for the period, and it will be seen that it is a *credit* balance. Profit is net revenue and revenue is a credit entry. Profit earned is payable to shareholders and any profit retained in the business represents an additional investment in the company by the shareholders. Thus, retained profit forms part of the capital of the company and increases in capital appear as credit entries. The other capital, liability, and asset accounts are now balanced. The balances are carried down to the next period because they represent the capital, liabilities, and assets at the commencement of the next period. The balance sheet (Table 2.10) which is a *statement* of the company's assets, liabilities, and capital on the last day of the period, is then prepared.

It will be appreciated that this is a very simple illustration, but by systematically working through the entries in the ledger accounts the reader should be able to grasp the principles of double-entry accounting.

Accruals and Prepayments

In the A. Trader & Co. Ltd illustration it was assumed that all expenses for the period had been paid when the trading and profit-and-loss accounts for September were prepared, and also that no expenses had been paid in advance. In a normal business at the end of the accounting period some expenses have not been paid and have to be *accrued*, and others have been paid in advance and have to be treated as *prepayments*. How are accruals and prepayments handled in double-entry accounting?

Accruals are liabilities which have become due or are accruing at

Table 2.10

A. TRADER & CO. LTD

Balance Sheet as at 30 September

	£			£
Capital and Reserves		*Fixed Assets*		
750 £1 Ordinary Shares	750	Motor Vehicles at cost		100
		Less Provision for Depreciation		5
Profit-and-loss Account	48	Written down Value		95
	798	*Current Assets*	£ £	
		Stocks	290	
Current Liabilities		Sundry Debtors		
Sundry Creditors	£	W. Trainer	20	
A. Peters	50	R. Roberts	10 30	
H. Morton	50 100			
		Cash on Hand	483 803	
	£898			£898

the end of the accounting period but have not been recorded in the ledger accounts. These may include such items as charges for gas, water, electricity, or telephone, or similar items consumed or expenses incurred during the period, for which no invoice has yet been received. For example, if the electricity account of a manufacturing concern has a balance of £1,250 at the end of the accounting period (31 December) and there is an outstanding electricity charge of £150 for December, the amount to be transferred to the profit-and-loss account is £1,400. The balance of the electricity account is carried down to the next period as a liability in the same way as a balance due to a creditor. The electricity account would appear as follows:

Electricity A/c

Dr				Cr
Dec. 31 Expenses paid (detailed)	£ 1,250	Dec. 31 Profit-and-loss A/c		£ 1,400
31 Balance: December Charge outstanding c/d	150			
	£1,400			£1,400
Jan. 15 Expense paid	150	Jan. 1 Balance		b/d 150

The credit balance on 31 December would appear in the balance sheet as an accrued charge under current liabilities. Frequently, accrued charges are lumped in the balance sheet with sundry creditors as sundry creditors and accrued charges. When the outstanding amount is paid in January it cancels out the accrued charge.

Prepayments arise when payments for expenses such as rent, rates, insurances, etc. made during an accounting period refer wholly or partly to a succeeding period. The treatment is similar to that for accruals. For example, if the rent and rates account of a manufacturing concern has a balance of £1,000 at the end of the accounting period (31 December), and the sum of £80 for local rates for the half-year ending 31 March following was paid on 1 December, the amount to be transferred to the profit-and-loss account is £960 (i.e. £1,000 minus £40 rates paid in advance). The balance of the rent and rates account is carried down to the next period, in the same way as a balance due to a debtor, and would appear in the balance sheet as a payment in advance under the heading of current assets. The prepayment of one period becomes an expense of the next period. The ledger account would appear as follows:

Rent and Rates A/c

Dr		£				Cr £
Dec. 31 Expenses paid (detailed)		1,000	Dec. 31 Balance: one quarter's rates paid in advance	c/d		40
			31 Profit-and-loss A/c			960
		£1,000				£1,000
Jan. 5 Balance	b/d	40				

Financial Accounting Concepts

There are a number of broad basic assumptions and concepts that underlie the periodic financial statements of business enterprises. When presenting accounting statements to management, accountants do not always fully explain these assumptions and concepts.

1. *The Money Measurement Concept.* In accounting a record is made of those facts and events that can be expressed in monetary

terms. This concept imposes severe limitations on the scope of accounting statements. The accounts of a company do not reveal, for example, that a competitor has introduced a new product which is technologically superior to the company's product. The money measurement concept is a common denominator concept and is clearly an essential one. While money is probably the only practical denominator, the use of money implies homogeneity, a basic similarity between one pound and another. In periods of inflation this homogeneity does not in fact exist. This problem is returned to later in this chapter.

2. *The Business Entity Concept.* Accounts are maintained for business entities as distinct from the persons who own them, operate them, or are otherwise associated with them. There follows from this distinction between the business entity and the outside world the idea that an important function of financial accounting is *stewardship*. The directors of the company are entrusted with the finance supplied by the shareholders, debenture holders, banks, and creditors. Financial accounting systems are in part designed to produce reports to indicate how effectively this responsibility, or stewardship, has been undertaken.

3. *The Going Concern Concept.* Accounting assumes that the business will continue to operate for an indefinitely long period in the future. Accounting does *not* attempt to measure at all times what a business is currently worth to a potential buyer. Accounting does *not* produce balance sheets which show the value of the assets of the company should it go into voluntary liquidation. A business is viewed as an economic/financial system for adding value to the resources it uses, and its success is measured by comparing the value of its output with the cost of the resources used in producing that output. Profit is the term used to describe the difference between the value of its output and the costs of the resources it uses. Resources which have been acquired but not yet employed in producing output are called assets. Unless the company has revalued its assets, at the present time, they are shown in an historical cost accounting system in the accounting records *not* at their current replacement cost or at their current value to an outside buyer, but rather at their original cost. The current value may be above or below the cost shown in the accounting records.

4. *The Cost Concept.* A fundamental concept of accounting, closely related to the money measurement and going concern con-

cepts, is that an asset is ordinarily entered in the accounting records at the price paid to acquire the asset, and that cost is the basis of all subsequent accounting for the asset. The accounting measurement does *not* normally reflect the worth of assets except at the moment they are required. The going concern concept and the cost concept may result, particularly in a period of rapid inflation, in the production of accounting statements which make it difficult to measure how efficiently the directors have carried out their stewardship function.

The cost concept does not mean that all assets remain in the accounting records at their original cost for as long as the company owns them. The cost of a fixed asset, such as a boiler, that has a long but nevertheless limited life, is systematically reduced over the life of the asset by the process of *depreciation*. The purpose of depreciation is gradually to remove the cost of the asset from the accounting records by showing it as a cost of the operations in the profit-and-loss account. The depreciation charge to the profit-and-loss account is intended to represent the portion of the cost of the resource utilized during the accounting period; and the written down value of the asset, the proportion of the cost of the resources unused at the end of the period. It is important to appreciate that the depreciation process does *not* provide a fund to replace the asset at the end of its useful life. It does reduce the profit available for distribution to shareholders and, therefore, the potential outflow of cash from the business in the form of dividends to shareholders. The depreciation process has no clear relationship to changes in the market value of the asset or its real worth to the company; nor is there any clear relationship with the cost arising from a decision to replace at the end of the asset's useful life.

Another important consequence of the cost concept is that if the company pays nothing for an item it acquires, this item will usually not appear in the accounting records as an asset. The knowledge, skill and expertise of an electronic company's research and development team does not appear in the company's balance sheet as an asset. The failure of accounting statements to reflect the value of a company's human assets can give rise to significant differences between the book value of a company's assets, the break-up value of a company's assets, the value of the company if sold as a going concern, and the market value of its shares.

5. *The Accruals Concept.* In accounting, revenue and costs are

accrued. They are recognized as they are earned or incurred, not as money is received or paid. Revenue and costs are matched with one another so far as their relationship can be established or justifiably assumed, and dealt with in the profit-and-loss account of the period to which they relate.

6. *The Consistency Concept*. The Companies Acts require companies to apply accounting policies consistently from one financial year to the next. Without this rule, it would be difficult to ensure comparability from year to year, or to prevent companies manipulating results. It would be possible for a company, by changing the accounting policies, to increase or decrease profits.

7. *The Concept of Prudence*. Accountants are always conservative when preparing financial statements. Revenue and profits are *never* anticipated and only included in financial statements when they are realized, but provision is made for *all* known liabilities (expenses or losses).

Accounting Bases and Policies

It is important to appreciate that difficulties can and do arise in applying the fundamental accounting concepts. The main difficulty arises from the fact that many business transactions have financial effects spreading over a number of years. Accountants have to make decisions on the extent to which expenditure incurred in one year can reasonably be expected to produce benefits in the form of revenue in other years and should be carried forward in whole or in part; in other words, to what extent the expenditure should appear in the profit-and-loss account of the current year, as distinct from appearing in the balance sheet as a resource at the end of the year. It will be appreciated that all such decisions require consideration of future events of uncertain financial effect, and an element of *commercial judgement* is unavoidable in the assessment. Significant matters which require judgement include depreciation of assets, valuation of stocks and work-in-progress, repairs and renewals, research and development expenditure, and long-term contracts.

Accounting bases are the methods which have been developed for expressing or applying fundamental accounting concepts to financial transactions and items. *Accounting policies* are the specific accounting bases judged by business enterprises to be most appropriate to their circumstances and adopted by them for the purpose of preparing financial accounts. In the areas where judgement is required the choice of accounting bases may have a material effect on the reported results and financial position of a company. For example, Associated Electrical Industries (A.E.I.) incurred a loss before tax of £4.5 million in 1967 compared with a forecast of £10 million profit before tax made on 1 November 1967 by the Board of Directors, during A.E.I.'s battle to fight off a successful takeover bid by the General Electric Company. Two firms of accountants, Price Waterhouse & Co. and Deloitte Plender & Griffiths & Co., compared the A.E.I. results for 1967 with forecasts made on 1 November, and in a letter to Lord Aldington, Chairman of G.E.C., stated:

You will appreciate that the appraisal of stocks, contracts, and a number of other matters involve the exercise of judgement; they are not matters of precision. Broadly speaking, of the total shortfall of £14.5 million we would attribute roughly £5m. to adverse differences which are matters substantially of fact rather than of judgement and the balance of some £9.5m. to adjustments which remain matters substantially of judgement.

In order to reduce the choice of accounting bases the accounting profession in the United Kingdom has published a series of Statements of Standard Accounting Practice. However, the complexity and diversity of business renders total and rigid uniformity of bases impracticable. An element of judgement will always remain. Companies are required to disclose, by way of a note to their published accounts, the accounting policies followed for dealing with items which are judged material or critical in determining profit or loss for the year and in stating the company's financial position. They are expected to observe the Statements of Standard Accounting Practice; although these are not legally binding on companies, if they are not observed a company's accounts will be qualified by its auditors.

The Problem of Inflation

Since the end of the Second World War accountants have become increasingly aware of the problems and impact of changing price levels on accounting records and statements. A full examination of the heated argument and protracted debate that has taken place, and continues, is beyond the scope of this book. The nature of the problem is explained, and various proposals for dealing with it and the current position in the United Kingdom are briefly summarized. Many of the management accounting implications of inflation accounting will be considered in later chapters. Full details of the various proposals will be found in Selected Readings 1, 2, 3, 4 and 9.

Accountants measure profit by finding the difference between the net assets at the beginning and end of the accounting period. They match the *actual* revenues of the period with the *actual* expenses of the period, and to the extent that revenue exceeds expenses, there is a profit. However, under the historical cost accounting system, the matching process may be of revenue of the period with costs of an earlier period; they do not necessarily match current values. Furthermore, the balance sheet is made up of a mixture of pounds of different periods, depending upon the mix of assets, the age structure of the assets, and depreciation policies.

An overstatement of *profit* and an understatement of *assets employed* will occur in times of rising prices if any input costs of one date are matched with output revenues of a later date, and if assets are shown in the balance sheet at their historical cost. In particular, this will arise in the case of:

1. *Depreciation* in the *profit-and-loss account* and *fixed assets* in the *balance sheet*;
2. The charge for *stocks and work-in-progress* consumed in the *profit-and-loss account* and *stocks and work-in-progress* in the *balance sheet*.

If the assets are depreciated on the basis of historical cost and stocks and work-in-progress on a first-in-first-out (F.I.F.O.) or similar basis, part of what accountants calculate as profit will be required to maintain the capital of the business intact. Part of the profit will be required to cover the increased cost of replacing fixed assets, and stocks which were bought or produced at prices considerably lower than those ruling at the date of consumption. If a company distributed as dividends the whole of its historical cost profit, it would have insufficient cash left to maintain its present level of stocks and work-in-progress and replace its fixed assets.

It will be appreciated that if, as a result of inflation, profit is seriously overstated, the burden of taxation on the business will be greater than that implied by the nominal rate of taxation. If reported profits, which result merely from a change in the value of money, or capital gains arising for the same reason, are taxed as if they are real income to the business, then the ability of the company to maintain the capital of the business intact and sustain real growth will be diminished. Furthermore, if historical cost profits are the basis for profit margin control under price legislation, a company's ability to generate adequate cash during a period of a high rate of inflation will be seriously impaired.

A Simple Illustration of the Inflation Problem

In order to illustrate how inflation can lead to an overstatement of profits, assume a company operating in a tax-free world with a share capital of £100. The company's only asset is a machine purchased at the commencement of Year 1 for £100. It was estimated that the machine would have a ten-year life and no residual value. The machine was depreciated at the rate of 10 per cent per annum of original cost, i.e. £10 per annum. The company generated a profit before depreciation, i.e. cash flow, in Year 1 of £30. Assume that the company distributed all its profits to shareholders in the form of dividends on the last day of the year. All costs and prices, and therefore profits, increased at an annual rate of 3 per cent per annum, i.e. there was a rate of inflation of 3 per cent per annum.

The company's balance sheet at the commencement of Year 1 was:

	£		£
Share Capital	100	Machine – Cost	100

The profit for Year 1 distributed to shareholders was:

	£
Profit before Depreciation	30
Less Depreciation	10
Profit paid as Dividend	£20

The balance sheet at the end of Year 1, assuming the dividend had been paid to the shareholders, was:

	£		£
Share Capital	100	Machine – Cost	100
		Less Depreciation	10
		Written down Value	90
		Cash	10
	£100		£100

The £10 cash in the balance sheet is the difference between the cash flow for the year and the dividend paid to shareholders. The profits for Years 2–10, assuming 3 per cent annual inflation, were:

	2	3	4	5	- - - -	10
	£	£	£	£		£
Profit before Depreciation	31	32	33	34		39
Less Depreciation	10	10	10	10		10
Profit paid as Dividend	£21	£22	£23	£24		£29

Because depreciation was based on the *original cost* of the asset, the depreciation charge remained constant over the period. Each year £10 of the cash flow was retained in the business. The cash flow and, therefore, the profit paid as dividends increased with the inflation. The dividend increased at a rate in excess of 4 per cent per annum because the depreciation charge was based on the original cost of the asset. Over the ten-year period the share capital remained constant at £100 and the asset side of the balance sheets for Years 2–10 appeared as follows:

	2	3	4	5	- - - -	10
	£	£	£	£		£
Machine – Cost	100	100	100	100		100
Less Depreciation	20	30	40	50		100
Written down Value	80	70	60	50		—
Cash	20	30	40	50		100
	£100	£100	£100	£100		£100

At the end of Year 10 the machine is written down to nil, it is completely worn out, and it is decided to replace it. £100 is available in the bank to replace the machine, i.e. the internally generated cash flow not distributed to the shareholders. An identical machine can be purchased, but, because of the 3 per cent inflation during the period, its cost has risen to £134. Thus, assuming accounts are based on the premise that the business is a going concern, part of the profit distributed to shareholders should have been retained in the business in order to replace the machine. Part of the distributed profit was required to maintain the capital of the business intact.

If the depreciation charge had been calculated on the basis of the *assumed current cost* of the machine, the depreciation charges to the nearest pound would have been:

	1	2	3	4	5	----	10
Assumed Current Cost	£103	£106	£109	£113	£116		£134
Accumulated Depreciation	10%	20%	30%	40%	50%		100%
Amount	£10	£21	£33	£45	£58		£134
Additional Depreciation	£10	£11	£12	£12	£13		£17

Using these additional depreciation[3] figures the profit-and-loss accounts for Years 2–10 would have been:

	2	3	4	5	----	10
	£	£	£	£		£
Profit before Depreciation	31	32	33	34		39
Less Depreciation	11	12	12	13		17
Profit paid as Dividend	£20	£20	£21	£21		£22

The cash flow retained in the business, i.e. the depreciation charge, would have been higher, and the asset side of the balance sheets would have shown cash balances equivalent to the accumulated depreciation. £134 would have been available in cash to replace the machine at the end of Year 10. With this approach the depreciation in excess of that based on original cost (£34) would be shown in the balance sheet under capital reserves. The balance sheet at the end of Year 10 would appear as follows:

3 The additional depreciation charge can be divided between the annual depreciation for the current period and *backlog* depreciation representing additional provisions in respect of earlier periods.

	£		£
Share Capital	100	Machine – Assumed Current	
Replacement Reserve	34	Cost	134
	——	*Less* Depreciation	134
			——
Total Shareholders' Interest	134	Written down Value	—
		Cash	134
	——		——
	£134		£134

Thus, by basing depreciation on the assumed current cost of the machine, the dividend paid to shareholders would have been lower, and the cash would have been available to replace the machine. The capital of the business would have been maintained intact.

Accounting for Inflation – from C.P.P. to S.S.A.P.16

How should the effects of inflation be reflected in accounting statements? In its Provisional Statement of Standard Accounting Practice No. 7, issued in May 1974, the United Kingdom Accounting Standards Steering Committee recommended that companies should employ the current purchasing power method (C.P.P.) to produce for their shareholders a *supplementary* statement in terms of the *value of the pound* at the end of the period to which the accounts relate. The provisional standard was issued pending the report of the independent Committee of Inquiry (the Sandilands Committee) established in July 1973 to consider the various methods of adjusting company accounts and whether, and if so, how, company accounts should allow for changes in costs and prices. In its Report (see Selected Reading No. 9) the Sandilands Committee rejected the C.P.P. method, largely on the basis of its application of general indices to specific assets, but also because it involves expressing accounts in terms of 'purchasing power units' rather than money. It recommended the current cost accounting system (C.C.A.) which is based on maintaining the value to the company of its existing assets. The main features of C.C.A. are:

1. money is the unit of measurement;
2. assets and liabilities are shown in the balance sheet at a valuation;

3. 'operating profit' is struck after charging the 'value to the business' of assets consumed during the period, thus excluding holding gains (i.e. differences between original cost and 'value to the business') from profit and showing them separately.

The Consultative Committee of Accounting Bodies (C.C.A.B.) informed the Government that the C.C.A. system proposed by the Sandilands Committee could prove to be an acceptable and practical method of accounting, and an Inflation Accounting Steering Group was established by the Accounting Standards Steering Committee in January 1976. Its 93-page Exposure Draft (E.D.18), *Current Cost Accounting*, was published at the end of November 1976, together with a 278-page manual (see Selected Reading 2) to provide guidance not just on the preparation of published accounts using C.C.A. principles, but also on the implementation and operation of a complete C.C.A. system. The Group proposed a phased introduction of an accounting standard for accounting periods beginning on or after 1 July 1978.

The system of C.C.A. proposed in E.D.18 to replace historical cost accounts distinguished between:

Operating Profit. Revenue less current expenses, including in those expenses the *value to the business of the physical assets consumed during the year*.

Extraordinary Items. Losses and gains arising not in the normal course of the business.

Holding Gains and Losses. The surpluses or deficits for the year arising from *revaluing physical assets to their current value to the business*.

Operating profit and *extraordinary items* would appear in the *profit-and-loss account* and *holding gains or losses* in a *profit-and-loss appropriation account*.

In the *balance sheet* physical assets (fixed assets and stocks and work-in-progress) would appear at their *current value to the business*. The E.D.18 proposals contained imprecise recommendations on how account should be taken in the C.C.A. system of the effect of inflation on monetary items, which partially offset the effects of inflation on operating profits. It was also proposed that the published accounts should include a statement, by way of a note, setting out prominently the gain or loss for the period of account in the shareholders' net equity interest after allowance has been made for the change in the value of money during the period. A full examination of the E.D.18 proposals is beyond the scope of this book. E.D.18 was widely criticized by accountants in the profession, in industry, and in commerce. The criticism culminated in a resolution being passed at a Special Meeting on 6 July 1977, 'that the members of the Institute of Chartered Accountants in England and Wales do not wish a system of current cost accounting to be made compulsory'. In the light of this rejection of E.D.18, the Accounting Standards Steering Committee accepted the need for a 'substantial simplification and modification' of the E.D.18 proposals. They requested the Inflation Accounting Steering Group to make a careful assessment of comments on the proposals and to prepare a new exposure draft. As an interim measure they established a new group (under the chairmanship of Mr William Hyde) to prepare simple *guidelines* for *supplementing* historical cost results with a C.C.A. profit-and-loss account wherever practical for the year to 31 December 1977.

The Hyde Group Guidelines were approved and published by the Accounting Standards Steering Committee in November 1977 (see Selected Reading 3). The Committee recommended that the published financial statements of companies listed on the Stock Exchange should include a prominent statement showing the financial results as amended by three adjustments, each shown separately:

1. *Depreciation.* An adjustment should be made for the difference between depreciation based upon the *current* cost of fixed assets and the depreciation charged in computing the *historical* cost result. Where other appropriate methods have not been developed, the charge for current cost depreciation may be computed by use of an appropriate index of price movements.
2. *Cost of Sales.* An adjustment should be made for the difference between the *current* cost of stock at the date of sale and the amount charged in computing the *historical* cost result.
3. *Gearing or Monetary Items.* It is recognized in the Guidelines that there are differing views on the question of how monetary items should be dealt with in inflation-adjusted accounts, but argued that an adjustment must be made if an incomplete and

potentially misleading picture is not to be given to shareholders and other users of the accounts. They recommend the following approach to the calculation of the gearing[4] adjustment unless another method is preferred:

(a) Where the total *liabilities* of the business, including preference share capital, exceed its total monetary assets, a calculation should be made of the proportion of the net balance of monetary assets to the net balance of monetary liabilities plus equity and share capital. An amount equal to this proportion of the depreciation and cost of sales adjustments should be *credited* as a separate adjustment in the statement.

(b) Where the total *monetary assets* of the business exceed its total liabilities, an adjustment should be calculated by applying to the net balance of monetary assets the percentage *change* in an appropriate index during the accounting year. This adjustment should be *charged* as a separate item in the statement.

Despite the crudeness of the gearing adjustment, the interim Guidelines were welcomed by the auditing profession, accountants in industry and commerce and by the Stock Exchange as a workable step towards a more comprehensive system of current cost accounting. The Inflation Steering Group continued its work on the development of such a system and produced a further exposure draft (E.D.24) in April 1979.

Unlike E.D.18, E.D.24 was a brief document which contained a statement both of the principles and the disclosure requirements of the system of current cost accounting it proposed. Like the Hyde Guidelines it was based on the concept of 'maintaining the capital of the business intact', but included monetary working capital as well as physical assets in its definition of capital. *Monetary working capital* requires an adjustment (MWCA) separate from the *gearing* adjustment. It represents the amount of additional (or reduced) finance needed for monetary working capital as a result of changes in input prices of goods and services used and financed by a business.

---

4 The term 'gearing' is used to define the proportions of debt and equity capital in the balance sheet. It will be examined more fully in Chapters 6 and 7.

Together the cost of sales adjustment and MWCA allow for the impact of price changes on the total amount of working capital used by the business in its day-to-day operations. In addition to requiring an MWCA, E.D.24 went further than Hyde in two respects:

1. It required listed companies to disclose the current cost earnings per share; and
2. It proposed that the supplementary current cost accounts should include a current cost balance sheet.

In contrast to E.D.18, E.D.24 received a wide degree of support, and an accounting standard (S.S.A.P.16) was issued on 31 March 1980 to be operative for accounting periods beginning on or after 1 January 1980. S.S.A.P.16 closely followed E.D.24 with some changes in definitions and terminology. The Standard applied to most listed companies and other large entities. It required them to publish current cost accounts in addition to historical cost accounts *or* historical cost information. A simplified illustrative example of current cost accounts for a manufacturing company, based on the example in S.S.A.P.16, is shown in Tables 2.11 and 2.12. The relationship between the C.C.A. profit-and-loss account and the balance sheet is illustrated in Figure 2.3.

Following a review of S.S.A.P.16, a new Exposure Draft (E.D.35) was issued in August 1984 which proposed a revised standard that required a single set of accounts, with information about the effect of changing prices shown in a note to the accounts where it was not given in the accounts themselves. Current cost balance sheets were not required by the proposed revised standard. Instead, only the current cost of fixed assets and stocks were required to be shown. In June 1985 S.S.A.P.16 was made non-mandatory by all the C.C.A.B. bodies, and in October 1986 five of the six C.C.A.B. bodies agreed that S.S.A.P.16 be formally withdrawn. At the same time the Accounting Standards Committee published *Accounting for the Effects of Changing Prices: A Handbook* (Selected Reading 4). The introduction includes the following statement:

Inflation has imposed a severe test on historical cost accounting as a reliable basis for reporting results and financial positions of companies. Indeed it is widely considered that where a company's results and financial position are materially affected by changing prices, historical cost informa-

Table 2.11

Y Limited and Subsidiaries
Summarized Group Current Cost Balance Sheet
as at 31 December 1984

	1984 £'000	£'000
Assets employed:		
Fixed assets		19,530
Net current assets:		
Stock	4,000	
Monetary working capital	800	
Total working capital	4,800	
Proposed dividends	(430)	
Other current liabilities (net)	(570)	
		3,800
		23,330
Financed by:		
Share capital and reserves:		
Share capital	3,000	
Current cost reserve (see Note)	14,404	
Other reserves and retained profits	3,926	
		21,330
		2,000
Loan Capital		
		23,330

Note on Current Cost Reserve

	£'000	£'000	£'000
Balance at 1 January 1984			12,350
Revaluation surpluses reflecting price changes:			
Land and Buildings	200		
Plant and Machinery	1,430		
Stocks and work-in-progress	490		
		2,120	
Monetary working capital adjustment		100	
Gearing adjustment		(166)	
			2,054
Balance at 31 December 1984			14,404
of which: realized[a]			2,494
unrealized			11,910
			14,404

[a] The realized element represents the net cumulative total of the current cost adjustments which have been passed through the profit-and-loss account, including the gearing adjustment.

Table 2.12

Y Limited and Subsidiaries

Group Current Cost Profit and Loss Account
for the year ended 31 December 1984

		1984 £'000
Turnover		20,000
Profit before interest and taxation on the historical cost basis		2,900
Less: Current cost operating adjustments:		
Cost of Sales	460	
Monetary working capital	100	
Depreciation	950	1,510
Current Cost Operating Profit		1,390
Gearing adjustment	(166)	
Interest payable less receivable	200	34
Current cost profit before taxation		1,356
Taxation		730
Current cost profit attributable to shareholders		626
Dividends		430
Retained current cost profit of the year		196
Current cost earnings per share		20.9p
Operating profit return on the average of the net operating assets		6.0%

tion alone is insufficient. In these circumstances, the A.S.C. considers that information on the effects of changing prices is important for a proper appreciation of a company's results and financial position.

Despite this statement, after fifteen years of long and at times heated debate, there is no requirement for companies to publish current cost accounts or any other form of accounts reflecting changing price levels.

Clearly great care must be taken in interpreting profit-and-loss accounts and balance sheets prepared on an historical cost basis and which take no account of inflation. The use of rates of return on capital employed to measure efficiency, for the discernment of trends in performance, and for both internal and external comparisons, can be hindered by the effects of accounting concepts, policies and bases used

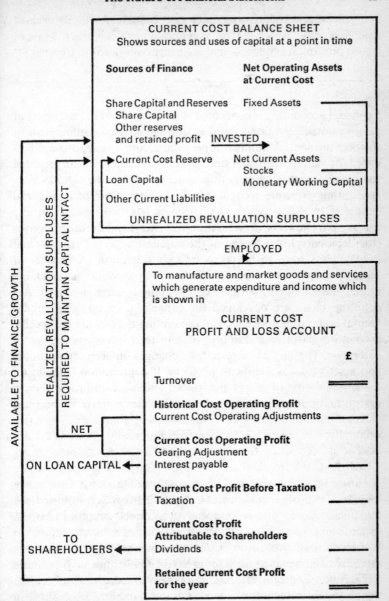

Figure 2.3. *Relationship between current cost balance sheet and profit-and-loss account under S.S.A.P.16*

in the preparation of financial statements. In particular the problem of changing price levels has to be recognized in calculating the rate of return on capital employed, and is further considered in Chapter 6.

Summary

Financial accounting is concerned with the external requirements of persons outside the firm as well as with the internal requirements of the management. A number of periodic accounting reports are prepared for management, and summarized annual reports are prepared for outside parties. Accounting systems employ the double-entry accounting principle recognizing that every event of a financial character in the activities of a business has two aspects. In any transaction one account gives (the credit entry) and the other receives (the debit entry). At the end of the accounting period accruals and prepayments have to be taken into consideration. A number of basic concepts are employed in financial accounting, including money measurement, business entity, going concern, and cost. Accounting bases are developed for expressing or applying fundamental accounting concepts, and accounting policies are the specific accounting bases judged appropriate to their circumstances by an enterprise. The impact of price-level changes on accounting profits and asset values is a difficult problem. If depreciation is based on the original cost of assets and stocks and work-in-progress on a first-in-first-out basis, there is a danger that the capital of the business will *not* be maintained intact. The Accounting Standards Committee originally recommended the Current Purchasing Power (C.P.P.) system of accounting for inflation. The Sandilands Committee rejected the C.P.P. method and recommended the Current Cost Accounting (C.C.A.) system. The Accounting Standards Committee issued an exposure draft on C.C.A. (E.D.18) which followed the Sandilands Committee recommendations closely, except in respect of monetary items. The complex proposals proved unacceptable to the accounting profession. Consequently, the Hyde Group was established and issued an interim set of Guidelines in November 1977. A new Exposure Draft (E.D.24) proved more acceptable leading to the introduction of an accounting standard (S.S.A.P.16) in March 1980. It is based on the concept of maintaining the capital of the business intact, both physical and monetary capital. S.S.A.P.16

was made non-mandatory in June 1985 and withdrawn in October 1986. Companies are still encouraged to take account of changing price levels but are under no obligation to do so.

Selected Readings

1. Accounting Standards Steering Committee, *Current Cost Accounting*, Exposure Draft 18, November 1976; Exposure Draft 24, April 1979; Statement of Standard Accounting Practice 16, March 1980; and Exposure Draft 35, August 1984.
2. Accounting Standards Steering Committee, *Guidance Manual on Current Cost Accounting*, Toller, London, 1976.
3. Accounting Standards Steering Committee, *Inflation Accounting – An Interim Recommendation*, 1977.
4. Accounting Standards Committee, *Accounting for the Effects of Changing Prices: A Handbook*, 1986.
5. John Arnold, Tony Hope and Alan Southworth, *Financial Accounting*, Prentice-Hall International, London, 1985.
6. Peter Bird, *Understanding Company Accounts*, Pitman, London, 1983.
7. John Blake, *Company Reports and Accounts*, Pitman, London, 1987.
8. Claude Hitching and Derek Stone, *Understanding Accounting*, Pitman, London, 1984.
9. *Inflation Accounting* (The Sandilands Report), H.M.S.O., London, 1985.
10. R. H. Parker, *Understanding Company Financial Statements*, Penguin, Harmondsworth, 1982.
11. Walter Reid and D. R. Myddelton, *The Meaning of Company Accounts*, Gower Press, Epping, 1982.
12. Arthur Young, *Companies Act 1985: Model Reports and Accounts*, Institute of Chartered Accountants of Scotland, Edinburgh, 1986.

CASE STUDY

In John Sizer and Nigel Coulthurst, *A Casebook of British Management Accounting*, I.C.A.E.W., 1985.

'Kalamazoo plc' (Volume 2) – a description of the value added presentation employed by a co-partnership business systems and services company to inform employees, monthly, of the company's performance.

3

Basic Cost Accounting

Cost accounting is primarily concerned with meeting the cost information requirements of management. The cost accountant classifies, records, allocates, summarizes and reports to management on past, current and future costs. The following activities are usually the responsibility of the cost accountant:

1. The design and operation of cost systems and procedures.
2. The determination of costs by departments, functions, responsibilities, activities, products, geographical area, periods, and other cost centres and cost units. The costs may be historical or actual costs, or future or predetermined standard costs.
3. The comparison of costs of different periods, of actual costs with estimated and standard costs, and costs of different alternatives.
4. The presentation and interpretation of costing information as an aid to management in controlling the current and future operations of a company.

There are three main purposes for which cost may be useful in the *control* of current operations:

— as a communication device;
— as a device for motivation;
— as an appraisal device.

As a *communication* device, cost data assists management in directing individuals within an organization to carry out plans, including the objectives the management wishes to achieve, the methods to be used to achieve these objectives, and the limitations to which the organization is expected to adhere. As a device for *motivation*, if cost data is properly constructed and is accompanied by proper management action and attitudes, it may serve as a significant incentive for attaining planned objectives. It should improve both the direction and strength of employee motivation. As an *appraisal* device, two types of preparation of costs for control purposes can be distinguished: *before* the fact (standards and/or budgets), and *after* the fact (performance reports). While performance reports are useful to avoid repeating previous mistakes, the knowledge that appraisals are being made may provide a strong incentive for good performance. This belief is based on the view that targets (standards and/or budgets) agreed by a manager and his subordinates are in themselves an incentive to good performance. They can form a yardstick against which a subordinate can measure and control his performance and against which his performance can be measured by his manager. This type of accounting, *responsibility accounting*, is considered in Chapter 9.

Cost data is also essential for planning purposes, both for period planning and for project planning. *Period planning* is the process whereby management systematically develops an acceptable set of plans for the total future activities of the firm, or some sub-division thereof, for a specified period of time. Long-term period planning is considered in Chapter 7. *Project planning*, on the other hand, is the process whereby management, confronted by a specific problem, evaluates each alternative in order to arrive at a decision as to the course of future action. The appraisal of capital expenditure projects is considered in Chapter 8.

In this chapter the classification of costs, overhead absorption, costing systems, and historical and standard costs are considered. The impact on costing systems of developments in advanced manufacturing technology is also briefly considered. The uses which can be made of the cost data produced are critically examined. Certain limitations, particularly when developing cost data for decision-making, are highlighted. This leads into the consideration of costs for decision-making in Chapter 4.

The Classification of Costs

The classification of costs is the basis of all cost accounting systems. Classification of costs is the identification of each item of cost and the systematic placement of like items of cost together according to their common characteristics. The classification of costs is an essential step in the summarization of detailed costs.

Costs are classified by *functions*:

production;
marketing/sales;
administration; and
research and development

Within functions costs are allocated by cost centres and within cost centres by cost units. A *cost centre* is a location such as a department or part of a department, a person or groups of persons, or an item or group of items of equipment, for which costs are ascertained for purposes of control. When a system of budgetary planning and control is in operation, cost centres will be planned so that results by responsibilities flow directly from them. Responsibility cost centres will be fully considered in Chapter 9.

The costs incurred by a cost centre have to be compared with a yardstick of activity, which is called a cost unit, in order to measure efficiency. A *cost unit* is a unit of product, service or time (or a combination of these) in relation to which costs may be ascertained or expressed. The cost unit may be a job, batch, contract, or product group, depending upon the nature of the production in which the firm is engaged. Examples of commonly used cost units are provided in Table 3.1, and of cost centres and cost units in the coke-making plant of an iron and steel works are shown in Table 3.2. Ultimately in an *absorption costing system* all cost centre costs are allocated to, apportioned to, or absorbed by cost units. Costs are first classified to cost centres for purposes of cost control. In a *marginal costing system* only the *variable costs* are related to cost units. Absorption costing systems are examined in this chapter and marginal costing in Chapter 5.

Within cost centres and cost units, costs are further classified into *cost elements*:

Material cost, which is the cost of commodities supplied to an undertaking;
Labour cost, which is the cost of remuneration (wages, salaries, bonuses, commissions, etc.) of the employees of an undertaking;
Expenses, which are the cost of services provided to an undertak-

Table 3.1
Examples of commonly used Cost Units

Industry or activity	Cost Unit
Manufacturing Industries	
Abattoirs	1,000 head of cattle handled
Brewers	Barrel/hectolitre
Brick-making	1,000 bricks
Coal mining	Ton/tonne
Electricity	K W H
Gas	Therm
Iron/Steel	Tonne/ton/cwt./sheet (a) Rolled
	(b) Cast
	(c) Extruded
Paper	Ream
Sand and gravel	Cubic yard/metre
Timber	100ft./standard/stere
Weaving	100,000 picks
Service Industries	
Hospitals	(a) Bed occupied
	(b) Out-patient
Local Authority	£ of rateable value
Schools	1 Number of enrolled students
	2 Number of successful students
	3 Number of school meals
Swimming baths	Number of bathers
Professional service (accountants, auditors, lawyers, surveyors)	Chargeable man-hour
Individual Organizations	
Personnel department and welfare	Employee
Materials storage/handling	(a) Requisition
	(b) Units issued/received
	(c) Values issued/received
Heating, lighting, rates, rent	Square feet/metres
Power	K W H
Salesmen's expenses	(a) £ of turnover
	(b) Calls made
	(c) Miles travelled
	(d) Orders taken (a) Number
	(b) Value
Sales ledger	Account maintained
Steam raising	1,000 pounds
Telephones	(a) Calls made
	(b) Number of extensions

(*Source:* Chartered Institute of Management Accountants: Official Terminology)

Table 3.2

Cost centres and cost units for coke-making plant

Cost Centre	Description	Cost Unit
Coal Preparation		
(a) Handling	The conveying of coal to coal preparation plant or stock yard	One ton of coal handled
(b) Stocking	The stocking of coal	One ton of coal handled
(c) Large coal crushing	The crushing of large coal to a size suitable for blending with other coals	One ton of coal crushed
(d) Washing/ blending/oiling	The washing/blending/oiling of coal	One ton of coal prepared
(e) Shale disposal	The disposal of shale from the coal washing	One ton of shale
Coal carbonization	The carbonizing of coal to produce disposable coke and by-products	One ton of disposable coke
Coke handling and screening	The handling and screening of quenched coke	One ton of coke screened
Crude gas-exhausting and cooling	The exhaustion and cooling of gas prior to the recovery of by-product	One ton of disposable coke
By-product recovery		
(a) Crude tar	The recovery and disposal of crude tar	One ton of dry crude tar
(b) Sulphate of ammonia	The production and disposal of sulphate of ammonia from am-moniacal liquor	One ton of sulphate of ammonia
(c) Crude benzole	The recovery and disposal of crude benzole	One gallon of crude benzole
(d) Gas storage and distribution	The storage and disposal of stripped gas received from benzole scrubbers	One net therm of stripped gas

ing, such as water and electricity, and the notional cost of the use of owned assets, such as depreciation of plant and machinery.

These cost elements are classified according to whether they are direct costs or indirect costs, i.e. direct or indirect material, direct or indirect labour, and direct or indirect expense.

A *direct* cost is one which can be allocated directly as a whole item to a cost centre or a cost unit. The cost can be directly associated with the production of a cost unit or with the activity of a cost centre. Cost allocation is, therefore, defined as the allotment of whole items of cost to cost centres or cost units. An *indirect* cost cannot be directly associated with the production of a cost unit or with the activity of a cost centre, but has to be apportioned to the cost centre or absorbed by the cost unit on a suitable basis. Thus, one *allocates* direct expenditure which can be directly identified with a cost centre or cost unit, but one *apportions* and *absorbs* indirect expenditure. For example, in a firm of printers the paper used in the production of a job can be allocated directly to a cost unit (i.e. the job), but oil used to lubricate printing machinery cannot be directly associated with a particular job. The paper used is a direct material cost, and the oil used an indirect material cost. The wages of a printing-machine operator can be allocated directly to the jobs printed by the machine, but the wages of a maintenance fitter who repairs printing and other machinery cannot be directly associated with a particular job. Similarly, the rent of factory premises has to be apportioned amongst cost centres and absorbed by cost units on a suitable basis.

As illustrated in Figure 3.1, direct materials, direct labour and direct expenses are *prime expenses*, and are traceable directly to the production of a cost unit or the activity of a cost centre. The sum of these direct costs for the production of a cost unit or the total production for a period is called the *prime cost of production*. The indirect costs of production, and all selling costs, distribution costs, research and development costs, and administration expenses are called *overheads*. Ultimately in an *absorption costing system* all overheads that have been apportioned to cost centres have to be absorbed by cost units. Overhead *absorption* is usually achieved by the use of one or a combination of overhead rates, for example, labour hour rate, machine hour rate, direct material cost percentage. These are illustrated later in this chapter.

Individual overhead costs may be either fixed costs or variable costs, though some have fixed and variable elements and are called semi-variable. *Fixed costs* or period costs are costs of *time* in that they accumulate with the passage of time irrespective of the volume of output, for example rent and rates, office salaries, insurance, etc. This does not mean that a fixed cost is always fixed in amount, for there are other forces, such as price-level changes, market shortages, etc., which can cause fixed costs to change in amount from period to period. Of course, if a sufficiently long time period is considered,

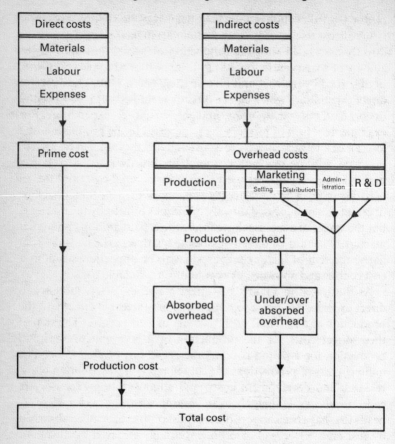

Figure 3.1. *Cost classification under absorption costing systems*

almost all costs become variable through changes in the scale of the
company's operations. For decision-making purposes, whether a
cost is fixed or variable will depend upon the decision under consideration. A *variable overhead cost* is one which tends to vary with
variations in the volume of output, but which cannot be allocated
directly to a cost unit and has to be absorbed on a suitable basis. It
will be appreciated that, in theory, all prime costs are variable costs
because their distinguishing characteristic is the very fact that they
can be associated with particular cost units. In practice, as will be

explained in Chapter 4, this may not necessarily be the case when classifying costs for decision-making purposes.

Total cost is the sum of prime costs and overheads attributable to the cost unit under consideration. The unit may be the whole undertaking, a job, batch, contract, or product group; it may be a process or a service. The cost classification, which has been outlined above, makes up total cost as follows:

	£	£
DIRECT COSTS		
Direct Material	5	
Direct Labour	6	
Direct Expense	1	
Prime Cost		12
OVERHEAD COSTS[1]		
Production Overheads:		
Indirect Material	1	
Indirect Labour	1	
Indirect Expense	3	
		5
Cost of Production		17
Selling and Distribution Cost	2	
Research and Development Cost	1	
Administration Expenses	1	
		4
TOTAL COST		£21

An Illustration – Cost Classification

The classification of costs is best understood by a simple illustration. The costs incurred by the Odd Job Engineering Co. during the year ended 31 December 1989 are listed in Table 3.3. Readers are invited to complete the column headed 'Classification', indicating whether

1 Individual items of overhead cost may be either fixed, variable, or semi-variable in nature.

Table 3.3

ODD JOB ENGINEERING COMPANY

Costs for the year ended 31 December 1989

Cost	£	Classification
Wages traceable to Jobs	45,000	Direct Labour
Wages paid to Maintenance Men	12,250	
General Manager's Car Expenses	150	
Hire of Cranes for Jobs 530–531	50	
Power for Factory	5,200	
Materials used on Jobs	47,350	
Lighting (Factory)	600	
Salesmen's Salaries	3,500	
Office Expenses	570	
Rent, Rates, and Taxes (Factory)	2,200	
Oils for lubricating Machines	150	
Machinery Depreciation	6,520	
Office Wages and Salaries	2,450	
Machinery Repairs	725	
Lighting (Office)	25	
Maintenance Materials	600	
Storekeepers' Wages	1,200	
Factory Management Salaries	5,300	
Delivery Costs	330	
Office Rent	150	
Advertising	220	
Depreciation of General Manager's Car	80	
Salesmen's Travelling Expenses	170	
General Manager's Salary	2,400	
Special Tools for Jobs 527–528	75	
Factory Premises Depreciation	270	
Agent's Commission	55	
Office Cleaning	200	

an item of cost is direct material, direct labour, or indirect expense, etc. The reader's classification of the costs can be checked in Table 3.4.

An Illustration – Overhead Absorption Rates

The calculations of overhead absorption rates may also be explained by way of a simple illustration. Bang-Bang Manufacturing Ltd operates a factory whose annual budget includes the budgeted trading account for the year ended 31 March 1989 shown in Table 3.5.

Table 3.4

ODD JOB ENGINEERING COMPANY

Classification of Costs for the year ended 31 December 1989

	£	£	£
Direct Materials			47,350
Direct Labour			45,500
Direct Expenses			
Hire of Cranes		50	
Special Tools		75	
		—	125
PRIME COST			92,975
Production Overheads			
Indirect Material			
Lubricating Oils	150		
Maintenance Materials	600		
	—	750	
Indirect Labour			
Maintenance Wages	12,250		
Storekeepers' Wages	1,200		
Factory Management Salaries	5,300		
		18,750	
Indirect Expenses			
Factory Power	5,200		
Factory Lighting	600		
Factory Rent, Rates, and Taxes	2,200		
Machinery Depreciation	6,520		
Machinery Repairs	725		
Factory Premises Depreciation	270		
		15,515	
Total Production Overheads			35,015
COST OF PRODUCTION			127,990
Selling and Distribution Costs			
Salesmen's Salaries		3,500	
Salesmen's Travelling Expenses		170	
Agents' Commission		55	
Advertising		220	
Delivery Costs		330	
		—	4,275
Administration Expenses			
General Manager's Salary		2,400	
General Manager's Car Depreciation		80	
General Manager's Car Expenses		150	
Office Wages and Salaries		2,450	
Office Expenses		570	
Office Lighting		25	
Office Rent		150	
Office Cleaning		200	
		—	6,025
TOTAL COST			£138,290

Table 3.5

BANG-BANG MANUFACTURING LTD
Budgeted Trading Account for the year ending 31 March 1989

	£	£
SELLING VALUE OF GOODS PRODUCED		300,000
Cost of Production		
Direct Wages		70,000
Direct Materials		90,000
PRIME COST		£160,000
Indirect Wages and Supervision		
Machine Dept A	3,800	
Machine Dept B	4,350	
Assembly Dept	4,125	
Packing Dept	2,300	
Maintenance Dept	2,250	
Stores	1,150	
General Dept	2,425	
		20,400
Maintenance Wages		
Machine Dept A	1,000	
Machine Dept B	2,000	
Assembly Dept	500	
Packing Dept	500	
Maintenance Dept	500	
Stores	250	
General Dept	450	
		5,200
Indirect Materials		
Machine Dept A	2,700	
Machine Dept B	3,600	
Assembly Dept	1,800	
Packing Dept	2,700	
Maintenance Dept	900	
Stores	675	
General Dept	400	
		12,775
Power		6,000
Rent and Rates		8,000
Lighting and Heating		2,000
Insurance		1,000
Depreciation		20,000
PRODUCTION OVERHEADS		£75,375
COST OF PRODUCTION		£235,375
BUDGETED FACTORY PROFIT		£64,625

The following operation information is also available:

| Departments | Effective h.p. | Area occupied (sq. ft) | Book Value of Machinery and Equipment | Productive Capacity (normal) | | |
				Direct Hours	Labour Cost	Machine hours
			£		£	
Productive						
Machine A	40	1,000	30,000	100,000	28,000	50,000
Machine B	40	750	40,000	75,000	21,000	60,000
Assembly	—	1,500	5,000	75,000	14,000	
Packing	10	750	5,000	50,000	7,000	
Service						
Maintenance	10	300	15,000			
Stores		500	2,500			
General		200	2,500			
		5,000	£100,000			

The general department consists of the factory manager and general clerical and wages personnel.

It will be noted that in the budgeted trading account the production costs are analysed into direct costs and production overheads. The direct costs can be charged directly to cost units as they arise, but the production overheads will have to be absorbed by cost units using some suitable basis of absorption. There are three stages in the calculation of hourly rates of overhead absorption for each productive department:

1. The various production overheads are first analysed to the seven cost centres, i.e. four productive departments and three service departments. The first stage is shown in Table 3.6. It will be seen that for some costs the figures for each department are shown separately in the budget and for other costs some suitable basis of apportionment has to be used. For example, power has been apportioned to departments on the basis of effective horse power available in each department.

2. The costs of each service department are apportioned to the productive departments using some suitable basis in Table 3.7. For

Table 3.6

BANG-BANG MANUFACTURING LTD
Overhead Analysis for the year ending 31 March 1989

Expense	Basis	Total	Productive Departments				Service Departments		
			Machine A	Machine B	Assembly	Packing	Maintenance	Stores	General
Indirect Wages and Supervision	Actual	20,400	3,800	4,350	4,125	2,300	2,250	1,150	2,425
Maintenance Wages	Actual	5,200	1,000	2,000	500	500	500	250	450
Indirect Materials	Actual	12,775	2,700	3,600	1,800	2,700	900	675	400
Power	Effective h.p.	6,000	2,400	2,400	—	600	600	—	
Rent and Rates	Area Occupied	8,000	1,600	1,200	2,400	1,200	480	800	320
Lighting and Heating	Area Occupied	2,000	400	300	600	300	120	200	80
Insurance	Book Values	1,000	300	400	50	50	150	25	25
Depreciation	Actual	20,000	6,000	8,000	1,000	1,000	3,000	500	500
TOTAL		£75,375	£18,200	£22,250	£10,475	£8,650	£8,000	£3,600	£4,200

Table 3.7
Appointment of Service Departments

Service Department	Basis		Productive Departments			
		Total	Machine A	Machine B	Assembly	Packing
Maintenance	Maintenance Wages	8,000	2,000	4,000	1,000	1,000
Stores	Indirect Materials	3,600	900	1,200	600	900
General	Direct Labour hours	4,200	1,400	1,050	1,050	700
		15,800	4,300	6,250	2,650	2,600
Add. Total from above		59,575	18,200	22,250	10,475	8,650
Production Department Totals		£75,375	£22,500	£28,500	£13,125	£11,250

Table 3.8
Hourly Cost Rates

Machine A $\dfrac{£22,500}{50,000 \text{ hrs}}$ = £0.45 per machine hour

Machine B $\dfrac{£28,500}{60,000 \text{ hrs}}$ = £0.475 per machine hour

Assembly $\dfrac{£13,125}{75,000 \text{ hrs}}$ = £0.175 per direct labour hour

Packing $\dfrac{£11,250}{50,000 \text{ hrs}}$ = £0.225 per direct labour hour

example, the maintenance department costs have been apportioned to the four productive departments on the basis of the maintenance wages budgeted for each department.[2]

3. Having apportioned the total production overheads to the four productive departments, the final stage is the calculation of separate hourly cost rates of overhead absorption for each productive department. The calculation appears in Table 3.8. It will be seen that in the

2 To simplify the illustration, the apportionment of service department costs among service departments has been ignored. In practice, this simplification may not be justified.

case of machine departments A and B, machine hour rates have been calculated by dividing the overhead cost by the normal productive capacity of the departments (normal capacity being defined as full capacity less normal unavoidable time). Similarly, direct labour hour rates have been calculated for the assembly and packing departments.

It is important to appreciate that *there is no one way of apportioning overhead costs and calculating overhead absorption rates*. There are a number of possible bases and the cost accountant has to decide which is the most suitable in the circumstances. It is quite possible for two equally competent accountants to arrive at different overhead absorption rates from the same basic data.

Uses of Overhead Absorption Rates

When these hourly overhead absorption rates have been calculated, how are they used by the cost accountant? They have a number of uses:

1. They are used for charging overhead costs to operations, processes, or products when *absorption costing* is employed, i.e. the practice of charging all costs, both fixed and variable, to operations, processes, or products. The overhead which, by means of rates of overhead absorption, is charged to cost units is called *absorbed overhead*. For example, if one unit of Product A requires 2 hours' machining in Machine Department A, 2 hours' machining in Machine Department B, 2 hours' direct labour in the Assembly Departments, and 1 hour of direct labour in the Packing Department, the overhead absorbed by producing one unit of Product A will be:

		£
Machine Dept A	2 hours at £0.45	0.900
Machine Dept B	2 hours at £0.475	0.950
Assembly	2 hours at £0.175	0.350
Packing	1 hour at £0.225	0.225
		£2.425

The difference between the total overhead absorbed by cost units produced during a period and the actual overhead incurred during a period is called *under-* or *over-absorbed overhead*. For example, if 48,000 machine hours' production for Machine Department A of the Bang-Bang Manufacturing Co. was charged to cost units during the year ended 31 March 1989, the absorbed overhead for the department would be £21,600, i.e. 48,000 × £0.45. If the actual overhead incurred during this period amounted to £23,000, then the overheads for Machine Department A would be *under-absorbed* by £1,400. If the actual overhead incurred amounted to £21,000, then the overheads for Machine Department A would be *over-absorbed* by £600. Normally, if actual production is *less* than normal capacity there will be *under-absorption*, and if actual production is *greater* than normal capacity there will be *over-absorption*. This is because certain overheads are fixed in nature and others variable and, therefore, the total production overhead does not change in proportion with changes in the level of production. Furthermore, because certain of Machine Department A's costs are fixed, the overhead absorption rate per machine hour is *only valid for normal capacity machine hours*, i.e. it is only £0.45 per machine hour for 50,000 hours. In particular, the machine hour rate for normal capacity hours is unsuitable for cost control purposes. Flexible budgets should be used, i.e. a series of static budgets for various forecast levels of activity. Flexible budgets are explained later in this chapter.

2. Overhead absorption rates are also used for valuing work-in-progress and finished stocks. For stock valuation purposes, overheads are usually charged to production on the basis of normal capacity. For example, product A may be valued for stock purposes as follows:

		£	£
Direct Material			5.500
Direct Labour			5.000
Production Overhead:			
Machine Dept A	2 hrs at £0.45	0.900	
Machine Dept B	2 hrs at £0.475	0.950	
Assembly	2 hrs at £0.175	0.350	
Packing	1 hr at £0.225	0.225	
			2.425
Cost of production			£12.925

It will be recognized that the production overhead is £2.425 and the cost of production £12.925 only when the actual production is the same as normal capacity. The effect of using absorption costing on stock valuation and reported profits is considered in Chapter 5, when absorption costing will be contrasted with stock valuation under marginal costing. However, it should be noted that the British Accounting Standards Committee requires, in Statement of Standard Accounting Practice 9, 'Stocks and Work-in-Progress', that cost of conversion for valuing stocks and work-in-progress includes production overheads based on the normal level of activity, taking one year with another. In its Standard 2, 'Valuation and Presentation of Inventories in the Context of the Historical Cost System', the International Accounting Standards Committee states that the historical cost of manufactured inventories should be based on absorption costing.

3. In many instances the overhead absorption rates are used in developing costs for decision-making, including pricing decisions, though this may not be the most suitable form of cost information for this purpose. Costs for decision-making are considered in the next chapter and costs for pricing purposes in Chapter 12. It is important to appreciate that overhead absorption rates are *not* suitable for calculating the effects of changes in volume and type of output, because they are only valid for normal capacity output. They do not represent the additional, the *incremental*, overhead costs of increasing or decreasing production by one unit. If one more unit of Product A is produced, the additional cost incurred in producing that unit will *not* be £12.925, because the production overhead in the above calculation includes fixed costs which will not change with changes in the volume of production in the short run. If one additional unit is produced the factory rent and rates will not increase, because rent and rates are a fixed cost.

Costing Systems

The methods of production and the problems faced by management differ from industry to industry and within industries from company to company. The costing system employed by a particular company must be designed to provide the management with the information required to meet its information needs. The two basic types of costing systems are *specific order* and *continuous operation/process costing*, and the system used will depend upon a number of factors. Some manufacturing companies produce one or more standard products for stock. Their manufacturing processes are firmly established, and work flows through a sequence of continuous operations or repetitive operations or processes. Such companies wish to know the production costs for each operation or process. They employ a *continuous operation/process costing* system to generate this information. Other manufacturing companies are not engaged in producing goods for stock; they are employed in production only when they receive an order from a customer. No two orders are necessarily alike, nor do all orders pass through the same manufacturing processes. Consequently, cost information must be accumulated for each order, job, or contract. The system of accounting that provides information in this way is called a *specific order costing system*. *Job costing, contract costing* and *batch costing* systems are types of specific order costing systems. *Job costing* is employed where work is undertaken to customers' special requirements and each order is of comparatively short duration. *Contract costing* systems also aggregate costs relative to a single order, but the contracts are usually major long-term ones. Some companies produce standard products but manufacture their products in separate, clearly distinguishable, batches or lots. When the cost of producing each batch is important to management, the company may decide to employ a specific order costing system, *batch costing*.

SPECIFIC ORDER COSTING SYSTEMS – JOB COSTING

When job costing is employed, costs are compiled for a specific quantity of product, equipment, repair, or other service. The cost unit, i.e. the specific quantity of product, etc., remains an identifiable unit as it passes through processes and operations, and costs directly associated with the production of that job, and usually a calculated portion of overheads, are charged to it. Each job is given a code number, known as a job number. With a manually operated system the costs relating to each job number are recorded on a job cost card or sheet for that job number. An example is provided in Table 3.9. Normally, computer-based job costing systems are in use, and the costs for each job are stored in the computer. The important consider-

Table 3.9
Example of a Job Card

Item: Small widgets					*Job Order No.:* 263		
					Quantity:	100	
Date ordered: 4 April				*Date started:* 16 April			
Date due: 30 April				*Date finished:* 2 May			

MATERIALS AND (RETURNS)

Date	Req. No.	Item	Quantity	Price	Amount	Cost Summary	£
16/4	2075	Material C	100	1.50	150.00	Materials	163.75
20/4	2103	Material D	10	1.00	10.00	Labour	570.00
22/4	2207	Material M	15	0.25	3.75	Overhead	255.00
					£163.75		
						TOTAL COST	£988.75
						UNIT COST	£9.89

	LABOUR				OVERHEAD	
Date	Department	Hours	Rate	Amount	Rate	Amount
20/4	Department X	20	12.00	240.00	5.00	100.00
27/4	Department X	15	12.00	180.00	5.00	75.00
2/5	Department Y	10	15.00	150.00	8.00	80.00
				£570.00		£255.00

ation, therefore, for the use of a job costing system is that individual jobs or batches can be separately identified in the operating departments. Among the industries using job costing are construction, printing, heavy engineering and shipbuilding.

A job costing system does compile data in a manner that is most useful in the administration of certain kinds of business. However, it is an expensive system to operate because it involves recording detailed information about each job. It is important that job costing is used only in situations where it is appropriate.

Batch and contract costing systems employ methods similar to those of job costing. Detailed illustrations are beyond the scope of this chapter, but examples are provided in *A Casebook of British Management Accounting*. The Boots Co. plc case study (Volume 2) describes the procedures adopted by the Industrial Division to plan and control production, direct and overhead costs, and to identify such costs with individual products, many of which are produced in batches. Brush Electrical Machines Ltd (Volume 2) produce a variety of electrical machines and associated control gear on a contract basis. The case study describes how costs and revenues are monitored against individual long-term contracts. The costing of a contract for a 51/2 M W diesel-driven generator is provided as an example. Table 3.10 is an extract from a typical contract cost file. The main entries to a cost file are derived from suppliers' invoices, stores requisitions and operatives' piecework tickets. For example:

Line 1   A purchase invoice – invoice 27 of batch 978, purchase order (GRN) number 401, delivery 01. Purchase ledger entries may be traced via the invoice or the purchase order. Actual cost, £2,321.94.

Line 7   An item drawn from stores – a casting (identified by code) drawn from Main (R M D) Stores, bin card line 296, quantity 1, requisition stored in batch 19 of period 7 1982 paperwork. Standard cost, £19.72.

Line 15   A piecework ticket issued for an operation carried out at cost centre 23-050 (Coil Shop Diamond Winding) worth 43 piecework hours, the ticket being stored in batch 136 of week 30. Cleared in cost, £42.65.

    (*Cleared in cost* is a composite cost rate per piecework hour which recovers both direct labour and overhead costs.)

CONTINUOUS OPERATIONS/PROCESS COSTING

Process costing is used in those industries where large quantities of homogeneous or very similar units of product are produced by continuous or mass production methods. In such industries it is not possible to identify the successive jobs or batches of production for cost accounting purposes. Unlike job costing, where costs are re-

Table 3.10

Extract from a Contract Cost File

```
*1058********** MASTER PRINT    1 ***************CONTRACT NUMBER
MAIN DIVISION----------CONTRACT COST RECORD  19/08/82
```

TRNS	TYPE	BOOKING REFERENCE		DATE	MATERIAL VALUE	LABOUR VALUE
		BROUGHT FORWARD BALANCE			0.00	0.00
1	400	INVOICE 9780027 P.O.	40101	0682	2321.94	0.00
2	400	INVOICE 9780030 P.O.	40200	0682	379.95	0.00
3	400	INVOICE 40144 P.O.	1234539	0682	74.60	0.00
4	400	INVOICE 40145 P.O.	1234556	0682	240.00	0.00
5	400	INVOICE 120019 P.O.	40102	0682	2115.57	0.00
6	400	INVOICE 120023 P.O.	40103	0682	634.55	0.00
7	100	RMD 05382-802 296	1	19:0782	19.72	0.00
8	100	RMD 1993064/72 275	2	19:0782	30.64	0.00
9	100	RMD 6134318/68 786	207	18:0782	384.32	0.00
10	100	RMD 6165261/03 649	1000	12:0782	79.90	0.00
11	100	RMD 6185718/05 370	1500	18:0782	146.55	0.00
12	100	RMD 6185718/87 726	1500	18:0782	96.00	0.00
13	100	RMD 6185718/98 777	1600	12:0782	152.00	0.00
14	100	RMS 21864-217 142	3	17:0782	0.96	0.00
15	150	SHOP 23/050 136	43.0	30:0782	0.00	42.65
16	150	SHOP 23/050 136	80.3	30:0782	0.00	79.65
17	150	SHOP 23/041 136	20.2	30:0782	0.00	16.74
18	150	SHOP 23/042 64	3.4	30:0782	0.00	3.32
19	150	SHOP 27/062 21	85.5	30:0782	0.00	75.47
20	150	SHOP 27/062 21	21.4	30:0782	0.00	18.69
21	150	SHOP 39/209 23	0.2	30:0782	0.00	0.27
22	150	SHOP 39/209 137	0.3	30:0782	0.00	0.41
23	150	SHOP 39/209 23	0.3	30:0782	0.00	0.41
24	150	SHOP 43/013 129	1.2	30:0782	0.00	3.03
25	150	SHOP 43/013 12	0.1	30:0782	0.00	0.25
		CARRIED FORWARD BALANCE			6677.10	241.09

corded separately for each job or order going through the plant, the emphasis in process costing is on the accumulation of costs for all work units during a given period of time. At the end of each period the cost per unit of goods produced is determined as an *average* unit cost for the period. The average cost per unit is used to value completed units and work-in-progress. The conditions for the use of process costing are continuous or mass production, loss of identity of individual items or lots, and complete standardization of product or process. Manufacturers using process costing may be classified as follows:

1. Production of a single product, e.g. cement or sugar;
2. Production of a variety of products using some basic production facilities, e.g. brick, tile and ceramic products;
3. Production of a variety of products using separate facilities, that is, a separate plant for each product (for example, a dairy

firm may have separate milk, orange drink, and cream bottling lines).

With a process costing system:

1. Costs are computed periodically, usually at the end of the month;
2. Average costs are calculated easily, provided the product is homogeneous; and
3. Less clerical effort and expense are involved than in job costing.

However, there can be problems, including:

1. Where the process costs are historical or actual costs they are not determined until after the end of the cost period;
2. Average costs are not always accurate because the units are not fully homogeneous; and
3. Where different products are manufactured using common processes, the proration of joint costs is necessary and the computation is made more difficult, often extremely difficult.

An Illustration of Process Costing

XYZ Ltd produces a single product and the costs incurred for the month of January for process 1 are as follows:

Process 1	£
Material	4,000
Labour	1,800
Overhead	1,700
	£7,500
Units completed and transferred	800 units
Work-in-progress 31 January	200 units

The production and costing departments estimate that the state of completion of the units in progress is:

1. Fully completed – material
2. Half completed – labour
3. Quarter completed – overhead.

There were no uncompleted units in progress at the beginning of the month. It is necessary to calculate average unit cost for January's production, the transfer cost to process 2, and the work-in-progress valuation at the end of the month.

To ascertain the transfer cost and work-in-progress valuation, the uncompleted units must be converted into equivalent production in terms of finished units. Thus, the units of work-in-progress in terms of completed units will be as follows:

Material = 200 (200 units completed)
Labour   = 100 (200 units half completed)
Overhead = 50 (200 units quarter completed)

If the equivalent production figures are added to the completed units and divided into the respective cost totals, the result will be an average unit cost in respect of materials, labour, and overhead costs. Thus:

	Per unit £
Material (800 + 200) = 1,000 units which divided into £4,000 =	4
Labour (800 + 100) = 900 units which divided into £1,800 =	2
Overhead (800 + 50) = 850 units which divided into £1,700 =	2
Average unit cost for January	£8

The work-in-progress valuation may be calculated as follows:

	£
Material 200 equivalent units × £4	800
Labour 100 equivalent units × £2	200
Overhead 50 equivalent units × £2	100
	£1,100

The transfer cost to process 2 may be calculated by multiplying the number of completed units by unit cost, i.e. 800 × £8 = £6,400.

The transfer cost and the valuation of work-in-progress together equal the month's total cost £7,500. The process account in the cost ledger would appear as follows:

		Process 1 A/c		
Dr				Cr
Jan. 31	£	Jan. 31		£
Stores Control A/c	4,000	Process 2 A/c		6,400
Labour Control A/c	1,800	Balance c/d		1,100
Overhead Control A/c	1,700			
	£7,500			£7,500
Feb. 1				
Balance b/d	1,100			

It will be seen that the cost of the completed unit has been transferred to the process 2 account. In the final process the transfer is made to the finished goods account. Thus, the finished goods of one process become the raw materials of a later process. Many simplifying assumptions have been made in this example; by-products, units lost in process, wastage, etc., have been ignored. A discussion of these aspects of process costing is beyond the scope of this book, but they are considered fully in Selected Readings 4, 6, 7 and 9.

HISTORICAL COSTING

The job costs and process costs calculated may be either *historical* or *standard* costs. With a historical costing system, actual costs are accumulated *after* operations have taken place. Historical costs are ascertained after the costs are incurred; standard costs are calculated *before* the costs are incurred. Historical costs are of limited value in themselves but are an essential part of a standard costing system. The historical costs are compared with the predetermined standard costs and the differences are analysed for control purposes. The principal disadvantages of using historical costs in isolation are:

1. The accuracy of the costs is open to doubt, so limited reliance can be placed on them.
2. Sound interpretation of costs, because of all the 'unknowns', is virtually impossible.

3. There is no yardstick against which efficiency can be measured. For this purpose, past actual costs are of limited value as they are a mixture of high and low efficiency.
4. Delays in taking action are inevitable, so inefficiencies are not likely to be minimized.

STANDARD COSTING

In a standard costing system, predetermined costs are carefully computed and later contrasted with actual costs to aid in cost control. Standard costs are scientifically predetermined costs of materials, labour, and overheads chargeable to a product or service. They represent a carefully planned method of producing a product or providing a service. A specimen standard product costing, from the Coloroll Ltd case study in Volume 1 of *A Casebook of British Management Accounting*, for a Wall-Covering and Textile Division product 'New Look' vinyl is shown in Table 3.11.

The differences between the actual costs and the predetermined standard costs are called *variances*. The cost accountant analyses these variances by causes, and inefficiencies are promptly notified to the persons responsible for them. For example, a *material cost variance*, i.e. the difference between standard material cost and actual material cost, may be analysed into a *material price variance* and a *material usage variance*. An unfavourable material cost variance may have arisen because the price paid for the material used was higher than the standard price, and/or because the quantity of material used was in excess of the standard quantity specified. A buyer may be responsible for a price variance and a departmental supervisor for a usage variance. Table 3.12 illustrates the calculation of these material variances. In process industries the usage variance may be further analysed into a *mixture variance* and a *yield variance*. The actual material usage may be above or below standard material usage because the mix of materials processed is different from the standard mix, and/or because the actual yield from materials processed is above or below the standard yield.

Similarly, a *direct wages variance*, i.e. the difference between actual direct wages and standard direct wages, may be analysed into a *wage rate variance* and a *labour efficiency variance*. Rates of pay above or below the standard rate may have been paid, and/or the efficiency

Table 3.11
Budgeted Costings

Run length = 2,500 rolls

R.P. Vinyl – New Look (own)

Pence/roll Waste	*Flexo* 19.1%	*Gravure* 19.1%
Std 80/90 (at .581/piece)	71.800	71.800
Adhesive	10.150	10.150
Reduced ink (4 colours, medium ink coverage)	8.443	9.046
Carton: 230 × 180 × 535 (194/1,000)	1.698	1.698
2′ buff vinyl tape – 66m coil (.76/coil)	.252	.252
Labels 5.25/1000	.597	.597
S wrap film	.646	.646
TOTAL MATERIAL COST	93.586	94.189
Labour		
Pre-paster	3.593	3.593
Printing	4.487	4.812
Converting	8.519	8.519
Duplexing		
S wrap and packing		
Label printer	.225	.225
TOTAL LABOUR COST	16.824	17.149
NET FACTORY COST	110.410	111.338
Overhead		
Pre-paster	7.466	7.466
Printing	8.438	7.258
Converting	11.105	11.105
Duplexing		
S wrap and packing		
Label printer	.032	.032
TOTAL FACTORY OVERHEAD	27.041	25.861
PRODUCTION COST	137.451	137.199
Origination	11.303	15.294
Warehousing costs	3.881	3.881
Distribution expenses	7.426	7.426
Selling expenses	22.733	23.264
Royalties at 2% E.S.P.	4.85	4.85
Admin. expenses	12.719	13.017
TOTAL COST	200.363	204.931

Table 3.11—continued

N.S.P. at 10% margin	222.626	227.701
N.S.P. at 15% margin	235.721	241.095
BUDGETED SALES PRICE Less 3% mkt. rebate	242.500	242.500

(*Source:* 'Coloroll Ltd', in Sizer and Coulthurst, *A Casebook of British Management Accounting*, Volume 1, I.C.A.E.W., 1984)

of the direct operatives may have been above or below standard efficiency. The computation of wages variances is illustrated in Table 3.13. A third group of variances are the *overhead variances*, i.e. the difference between the actual manufacturing overhead incurred and the standard overhead charged to production during the period. Overhead variances can be further analysed into *volume*, *expenditure* and *efficiency variances*. The computation of these variances is considered later in this chapter, following an explanation of fixed and flexible budgets. The principal cost variances calculated by comparing actual and standard costs are illustrated in Figure 3.2.

Standard costing may, therefore, be defined as: the preparation and use of standard costs, their comparison with actual costs and the analysis of variances to their causes and points of incidence. With a standard costing system, the standard costs are usually entered into the books of account to facilitate the comparison with actual costs. Although standard costs are generally incorporated in the accounts, some concerns prefer to use them for statistical purposes only.

It will be appreciated that the meaning of the variances between

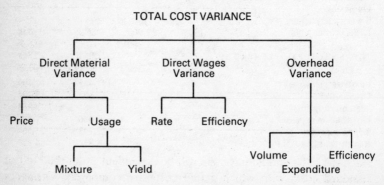

Figure 3.2. *Principal cost variances*

Table 3.12
Computation of Material Variances

Material Cost Variance = standard cost − actual cost, i.e. standard quantity × standard price − actual quantity × actual price. May be analysed into:

1 *Material Price Variance* = actual quantity × standard price − actual quantity × actual price
   or
   actual quantity (standard price − actual price)
2 *Material Usage Variance* = standard quantity × standard price − actual quantity × standard price
   or
   standard price (standard quantity − actual quantity)

Example

The standard raw material mix for a ton of finished product is:

Material A	1,200 lb. at £0.05 lb.
B	500 lb. at £0.10 lb.
C	500 lb. at £0.03 lb.
D	100 lb. at £0.15 lb.

Material used during an accounting period was as follows:

Material A	2,900 lb. at £0.06 lb.
B	1,300 lb. at £0.12 lb.
C	1,350 lb. at £0.02 lb.
D	260 lb. at £0.12 lb.

Production during the period was 5,600 lbs. Identify and calculate the material cost variances.

| | STANDARD | | | ACTUAL | | |
Material	Quantity (a)	Price (b)	£ (c)	Quantity (d)	Price (e)	£ (f)
	lbs.	per lb.		lbs.	per lb.	
A	3,000	£0.05	150.0	2,900	£0.06	174.0
B	1,250	£0.10	125.0	1,300	£0.12	156.0
C	1,250	£0.03	37.5	1,350	£0.02	27.0
D	250	£0.15	37.5	260	£0.12	31.2
			£350.0			£388.2

(*Table 3.12 continued overleaf*)

standard costs and actual costs will be dependent upon the kind of standard costs with which actual costs are compared. Variances resulting from careless standards will not have the same significance

Table 3.12 – continued

| | VARIANCES | | |
Material	Total c–f	Price d(b–e)	Usage b(a–d)
	£	£	£
A	(24.0)	(29.0)	5.0
B	(31.0)	(26.0)	(5.0)
C	10.5	13.5	(3.0)
D	6.3	7.8	(1.5)
	£(38.2)	£33.7	£(4.5)

Note: Brackets indicate variance is unfavourable

as variances from rigorous or 'tight' standards. A loose standard, as an incentive to better performance, may be completely useless. On the other hand, an ideal standard which is attainable only under the most favourable conditions would be impossible to achieve. An ideal standard probably will not motivate employees to improve their performance. An expected standard which it is anticipated can be attained during a future specific period is usually set. Such a standard takes into account human rates of work, normal machine breakdowns, and other unavoidable inefficiencies. It is a consistent, reliable standard, is attainable, and should provide an incentive to improve performance.

Assuming the existence of proper standard costs for the product of an operation, function, or department, the management can concentrate upon the discrepancies between actual and standard costs. The usefulness of this comparison between actual and standard costs is based upon the *principle of exceptions*, which makes it possible for the cost accountant to sift from the great mass of his cost data the essential facts needed by management. However, there is a danger that, with so much attention being focused on the 'exceptions', insufficient attention will be paid to the standards. If the standards become out-of-date or unreliable they may not be taken seriously by operating management. In a period of rapid cost inflation, such as that which occurred in Britain in the 1970s, this can happen very quickly. The standards must be constantly under review if the variances arising from the effects of inflation are to be segre-

Table 3.13
Computation of Wage Variances

Wages Variance = standard cost − actual cost, i.e. standard hours × standard rate − actual hours × actual rate.

May be analysed into:

1 *Wage Rate Variance* = actual hours × standard rate − actual hours × actual rate

or

actual hours (standard rate − actual rate)

2 *Labour Efficiency Variance* = standard hours × standard rate − actual hours × standard rate

or

standard rate (standard hours − actual hours)

Example

A company manufactures a standard model based on the following direct labour specification:

Standard Direct Labour Hours	20
Standard Direct Labour Hourly Rate	£0.25

During the month 250 models were produced, and direct labour amounted to £1,500 for 5,600 hours worked. Calculate the wages variances.

		£
1 *Wages Variance*		
Standard Cost (20 × 250 × £0.25)		1,250
Actual Cost		1,500
	Variance (adverse)	(£250)
2 *Wage Rate Variance*		
Standard Cost of Actual Hours (5,600 at £0.25)		1,400
Actual Cost of Actual Hours		1,500
	Variance (adverse)	(£100)
3 *Labour Efficiency Variance*		
Standard Hours for Actual Production (250 × 20)		5,000
Actual Hours for Actual Production		5,600
	Variance (adverse)	(600)
	at £0.25 per hr	(£150)

Note: Brackets indicate variance is unfavourable

gated from those arising from factors within the control of management. There must be confidence in the standards. If there is not, the use of standard costing can develop into a ritual which loses sight of the problem at issue. At the same time the 'cost of costing' must always be borne in mind. While a sophisticated standard costing system may reveal large inefficiencies in the early years of its use, there is always the possibility that the variances will eventually become insignificant in relation to the cost of operating the system.

The cost accountant must promptly draw the attention of operating management to the existence of *controllable* variances from standard. This requires that where a significantly large cost variance arises, the cost accountant should be able to present an analysis to management making it possible to determine:

Where the variance occurred;
Who was responsible; and
Why it happened.

The cost accountant must be able to present reports to management which highlight the essentials and point out particular variances and possibilities for improvement. For example, reports to departmental supervisors should:

1. Show the supervisor what his costs should have been;
2. Show him how closely he came to meeting these costs;
3. Show him whether his performance in this respect is improving;
4. Explain the causes of variances so that the knowledge of their causes can be used to achieve improvements in his performance.

Standard costs and budgets complement each other in various ways. The development of standard costs will provide a sound basis for budgetary control. The use of standards will tend to enhance the accuracy of budgets and will facilitate their preparation. Ideally, standard costs should be made an integral part of the budgetary control system, both in the preparation of budgets and in their use as a control device. For this reason, accounting for control involving the use of standards and budgets is considered more fully in Chapter 9 under the title 'Budgetary Planning and Control Systems'.

Fixed and Flexible Budgets

Factory overheads include both fixed or period costs and variable costs. For control of factory overheads it is necessary to compare actual costs with budgeted costs for each cost centre. The actual cost must be compared with the budgeted cost for the *actual* level of activity, and this budgeted cost may be derived from a *fixed* or static budget or from a *flexible* budget.

A factory overhead budget which is developed for a specific estimated level of production and specific operating conditions, and which is used for measurement without change during the budget period, is a *fixed* budget. It is designed to remain unchanged irrespective of the level of activity attained. In most companies, operating conditions and levels of activity vary from month to month; therefore the fixed budget for a period divided by the months in the period does not provide a fair allowance for overheads for any one month. Neither is it likely that monthly variations in conditions will average out so as to make the fixed budget a fair allowance for the full period. Frequent revision of a fixed budget is necessary to make it a useful control tool, but this is both time-consuming and costly. For these reasons, the flexible budget is more satisfactory and more widely used. A *flexible* budget is a series of static budgets for various forecast levels of activity. By recognizing the difference between fixed, variable and semi-variable costs, it is designed to change in relation to the level of activity attained. An illustration of a flexible budget for a cost centre which has a normal capacity of 1,000 hours is given in Table 3.14. It will be seen that some costs vary proportionately with changes in the level of activity and others are semi-variable or fixed in nature.

It is preferable to ascertain the budget for *actual* activity by interpolation of flexible budget figures, which show the true behaviour of the various items of cost in relation to changes in volume, rather than to attempt to adjust a fixed budget by use of a normal overhead rate. For example, if the actual level of activity for Cost Centre 501 for January 1990 is 1,200 hours and the total actual costs incurred £7,200, using a *fixed budget* the total cost variance would be:

Actual Cost − (Actual hours at Normal Overhead Rate)
= £7,200 − (1,200 hours at £6.025 per hour)
= £7,200 − £7,230
= £30 favourable.

However, as explained previously, because certain of the cost centre's costs are fixed and semi-variable in relation to changes in volume, the normal overhead rate per direct labour hour is only valid for 1,000 hours normal capacity. If the actual cost is compared with the *flexible budget* for 1,200 hours there is an *unfavourable* variance of £232, that is, £7,200 − £6,968. The difference between

Table 3.14

An Example of a Flexible Budget

Capacity	Cost Centre 501 0hr 0% £	200hr 20% £	400hr 40% £	600hr 60% £	Month ....19... 800hr 80% £	1,000hr 100% £	1,200hr 120% £
Costs							
Supervision	600	600	600	1,050	1,050	1,050	1,500
Indirect Labour	300	600	900	1,200	1,500	1,800	2,100
Maintenance	100	120	140	160	180	200	220
Depreciation	1,000	1,000	1,000	1,000	1,000	1,000	1,000
Supplies	37	50	62	75	87	100	112
Power	1,073	1,233	1,394	1,554	1,715	1,875	2,036
	£3,110*	£3,603	£4,096	£5,039	£5,532	£6,025	£6,968

* Stand-by cost

Normal Overhead Rate per direct labour hour:

$$\frac{£6,025}{1,000} = £6.025$$

the actual hours at normal overhead rate and the flexible budget of £262 (£7,230 − £6,968) is called a *volume variance*. The unfavourable variance of £232 for Cost Centre 501 for January 1990 is the *controllable variance*, i.e. the difference between the actual expenditure incurred and the expected cost for the actual level of activity, and may be analysed into *expenditure* and *efficiency variances*. The computation of overhead variances is explained in detail in the next section of this chapter.

The key to the difference between a fixed and flexible budget is that cost performance should be measured by the difference between actual cost and the cost budgeted for actual activity. To obtain a clear picture of cost performance, actual cost at actual activity must be compared with budgeted (expected) cost at actual activity. For purposes of determining standard unit product cost, using an absorption costing system, the budgeted costs for a single level of activity must be used. Hence the calculation of a normal overhead rate per direct labour hour for Cost Centre 501.

Overhead Variances

Having considered flexible budgets, the computation of overhead variances can now be considered.

An *overhead variance* is the difference between the manufacturing overhead incurred during a period and the standard overhead charged to production (standard hours produced × standard cost per hour) during that period. The overhead variance can be analysed into three general causes:

1. Variance of actual overhead incurred from overhead budgeted for actual production, which is called an *overhead expenditure variance*. The overhead budgeted for actual capacity is determined from a flexible budget. If actual overhead incurred is more or less than the amount that should have been incurred for the actual production, there will be an overhead expenditure variance.

2. Variances in activity from the normal capacity used for the determination of standard overhead cost per hour, which gives rise to a *volume variance*. The volume variance is the difference between the standard cost of actual hours production and the flexible budget for actual hours production. If actual production is less than normal capacity, an unfavourable volume variance may be thought of in terms of fixed capacity provided, giving rise to fixed costs, but not used.

3. Variance of actual hours from standard hours specified for actual production, which is called an *overhead efficiency variance*. This variance is similar to a labour efficiency variance (considered earlier in this chapter). The actual hours required to produce the actual production are greater or less than the standard hours specified for that level of production.

Assuming all the variances are unfavourable, the various overhead variances may be illustrated as in Figure 3.3.

The computation of overhead variances is illustrated in Table 3.15. In this illustration the overhead incurred was £470 greater than the standard overhead for actual production based on normal capacity. £74.75 of the £470 unfavourable *overhead variance* arose because the overhead incurred was greater than it should have been for the level of activity achieved, which resulted in an unfavourable *overhead expenditure variance*. A further £425.25 of this *overhead*

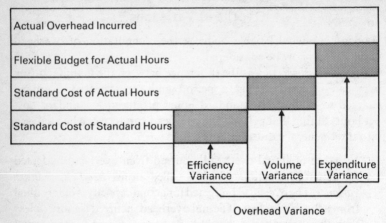

Figure 3.3

variance arose because the actual hours worked (790) were 210 hours less than the normal capacity on which the standard was based. This gave rise to an unfavourable *volume variance*, because production facilities had been provided but not used. The unfavourable *volume variance* (£425.25) and *overhead expenditure variance* (£74.75) were partly offset by the favourable overhead *efficiency variance* (£30). The company produced 800 standard hours' production during the 790 actual hours worked.

It should be noted that the *volume variance* (£425.25) equals the variance in actual hours worked from normal capacity hours (210 hours) multiplied by the fixed cost per hour in the standard overhead cost per hour (£2.025). It arises from the unitizing of fixed costs in an absorption costing system, and gives rise to the expression 'fixed costs provided but not used' for an unfavourable volume variance. In Chapter 5 we shall note that when a marginal costing system is in use fixed costs are not unitized and no volume variances arise when analysing overhead variances.

There is no general agreement on how the overhead variance should be analysed into volume, expenditure and efficiency variances;[3] many companies do not calculate a separate overhead

3. For an examination of the various methods of analysing overhead variances, see David Solomons, 'The Analysis of Standard Cost Variances', in D. Solomons (ed.), *Studies in Cost Analysis*, Sweet & Maxwell, London, 1968, pp. 426–43.

Table 3.15

Computation of Overhead Variances

Overhead Variance = standard overhead for actual production − actual overhead incurred

  May be analysed into:

Overhead Expenditure Variance = flexible budget for actual hours worked − actual overhead

Volume Variance = standard costs of actual hours − flexible budget for actual hours worked

Efficiency Variance = standard overhead for actual production − standard costs of actual hours

Example Compute overhead variances from the following data:

	£
Standard Cost Data	
Budgeted fixed overhead at normal capacity	2,025
Budgeted variable overhead at normal capacity	975
Budgeted overhead at normal capacity	£3,000
Standard allowed hours at normal capacity	1,000

	£
Standard fixed overhead per hour	2.025
Standard variable overhead per hour	0.975
Standard overhead per hour	£3.000

Period Information	
Standard allowed hours for actual production	800
Actual hours worked	790
Actual overhead incurred	£2,870
Flexible overhead budget for actual hours, i.e. £2,025 + (790 × £0.975)	£2,795.25
Standard overhead for actual production (800 × £3)	£2,400

Overhead Expenditure Variance
Flexible budget for actual hours worked − actual overhead incurred
£2,795.25 − £2,870   (74.75)

Volume Variance
Standard cost of actual hours − flexible budget for actual hours
(790 × £3) − £2,795.25   (425.25)

Efficiency Variance
(Standard hours − actual hours) × standard rate
(800 − 790) × £3   30

Overhead Variance
Standard overhead for actual production − actual overhead incurred
£2,400 − £2,870   (£470)

Note: Brackets indicate variance is unfavourable

efficiency variance. One method of calculating these variances has been given. From the manager's point of view, it is important that he recognizes that the overhead variance arises from these three general causes. The accountant should clearly explain to management the method he uses to calculate overhead variances.

The Impact of Advanced Manufacturing Technology

The future success of many manufacturers will depend upon their ability to introduce innovative, custom-designed, high-quality products for niche markets, produced efficiently in small batches, using automated manufacturing equipment. This recognition has arisen from two related sets of developments:

1. Investment in flexible manufacturing systems including CAD/CAM (Computer Aided Design/Computer Aided Manufacture), NC/CNC machine tools, and robots, is shifting the emphasis from large-scale, repetitive manufacturing processes producing standard products to a highly automated job shop environment.
2. Companies are also making fundamental changes to their organization of manufacturing operations, including 'just-in-time' scheduling, zero defect and zero inventory production systems, and flexible manning arrangements.

These developments have led companies to examine critically their costing systems. Many systems are based on factory-wide overhead absorption rates, using direct labour hour rates which assume a one machine/one man relationship. Such factory-wide overhead absorption rates are inappropriate for a factory which contains a variety of work stations with different technologies, man-machine relationships and cost structures. There is a need to develop separate cost rates for different types of work stations, including:

- hand operations, e.g. fitting, inspection;
- conventional machine operations with a one man/one machine relationship;
- multi-machines;
- group manning;
- manufacturing cells;

– automated flow lines;
– flexible manufacturing systems.

Each type has its own cost structure and therefore should be a separate cost centre with its own overhead absorption rate. Furthermore, as the man/machine interface breaks down, i.e. as computers replace direct operatives, direct *labour overhead rates* need to be replaced by *machine cycle time* rates, i.e. the time required to complete the process on a component/part/job, including loading and unloading times, when absorbing overheads, determining standard product costs, deriving costs for decision-making and measuring machine capacity utilization and efficiency. A full discussion of these developments will be found in Selected Readings 7 and 8. The Rolls-Royce Derby Manufacturing case study (in Volume 2 of *A Casebook of British Management Accounting*) describes the standard costing systems employed by a large gas turbine engine manufacturer for determining the standard cost of each component part of an engine type, leading to the establishment of the standard cost of each engine type. It also describes the impact of the introduction of new advanced manufacturing technology systems, including, for example, CAD/CAM, robot-controlled turbine blade production, and automated furnaces for precision casting of single crystal blades, on the company's standard costing systems. The introduction of *machine cycle times* as a basis for costing and for planning and control of group- and multi-manning work stations (i.e. more than one operator and several machines, automatic flow lines, robotics and flexible manufacturing systems) is described.

Summary

Cost accounting is concerned primarily with meeting the information requirements of management for decision-making and control. The classification of costs is the basis of all cost accounting systems. Costs are classified by functions, within functions by cost elements, and within cost elements according to whether they are direct or indirect costs. Individual indirect costs may be variable, semi-variable, or fixed in relation to short-run changes in volume. Direct costs can be allocated directly to cost units; indirect costs have to be absorbed by cost units. There are a number of alternative methods

Table 3.16
Product Profitability Statement – Absorption Costing

	Product A 100,000		Product B 500,000		Product C 200,000		Total
	£ per unit	£'000	£ per unit	£'000	£ per unit	£'000	£'000
Sales Units							
Value	20	2,000	5	2,500	5	1,000	5,500
Cost of Goods Sold							
Materials	3	300	0.8	400	1	200	900
Labour	5	500	1.2	600	2	400	1,500
Overhead	6	600	1.6	800	2.5	500	1,900
TOTAL	£14	£1,400	£3.6	£1,800	£5.5	£1,100	£4,300
Gross Margin	6	600	1.4	700	(0.5)	(100)	1,200
Selling and Admin. Expenses	3	300	0.8	400	0.75	150	850
Product Profits	£3	£300	£0.6	£300	£(1.25)	£(250)	350
Unabsorbed overhead							200
Operating Profit							£150

of overhead absorption. Overhead absorption rates and absorption or full cost profit statements are *not* suitable for calculating the effects of changes in volume and type of output. Consider the product profitability statement shown in Table 3.16. If Product C was withdrawn from the product range, would the operating profit increase by £250,000? If 1,000 additional units of Product A were sold, would the operating profit increase by £3,000? The answer to both questions is 'no', because Table 3.16 does not distinguish between variable costs and fixed costs. There are two basic costing systems: job costing and process costing. The system employed will depend upon the type of production and the information requirements of management. Job costing is expensive to operate and should be used only when essential. Job costs and process costs calculated may be either historical or standard costs. Historical costs in isolation are of limited value, but are an essential part of a standard costing system. The principle of exceptions is utilized in a standard costing system, management's attention being focused on the variances from standard. For control of overhead costs, flexible budgets are preferable to fixed budgets. The overhead volume variance arises from the unitizing of fixed costs in an absorption costing system. Budgets and standards complement each other, and ideally standard costs should be an integral part of a budgetary control system. Developments in advanced manufacturing technology have led companies to examine critically their costing systems as a result of the breakdown of the one man/one machine relationship.

Selected Readings

1. J. Arnold, B. Carsberg and R. Scapens, *Topics in Management Accounting*, Philip Allan, Oxford, 1983.
2. John Arnold and Tony Hope, *Accounting for Management Decisions*, Prentice-Hall International, London, 1983.
3. Chartered Institute of Management Accountants, *Management Accounting: Official Terminology*, London, 1982.
4. R. I. Dickey (ed.), *Accountants' Cost Handbook*, Ronald Press, New York, 1960.
5. Nicholas Dopuch, Jacob C. Birnberg and Joll S. Demski, *Cost Accounting*, Harcourt, Brace & Jovanovich, New York, 1982.
6. Colin Drury, *Management and Cost Accounting*, Van Nostrand Reinhold (U K), Reading, 1985.

7. Charles T. Horngren and George Foster, *Cost Accounting: A Managerial Emphasis*, Prentice-Hall, Englewood Cliffs, N.J., 1987.

8. Robert S. Kaplan, 'Measuring Manufacturing Performance: A New Challenge for Managerial Accounting Research', *Accounting Review*, October 1983, pp. 686–703; and 'Accounting Lag: the Obsolescence of Cost Accounting Systems', in Kim B. Clark, Robert H. Hayes and Christopher Lorenz (eds.), *The Uneasy Alliance*, Harvard Business School Press, Boston, 1985.

9. Gordon Shillinglaw, *Managerial Cost Accounting*, Irwin, Homewood, Illinois, 1982.

CASE STUDIES

In John Sizer and Nigel Coulthurst, *A Casebook of British Management Accounting*, I.C.A.E.W., 1984, 1985.

Coloroll Ltd (Volume 1) – the budgetary planning and control system and standard costing system and monthly accounts package in a wall-coverings and household textiles business.

The Boots Co. plc (Volume 2) – the planning and control of production costs in the Industrial Division producing a wide range of pharmaceutical and chemical products.

Brush Electrical Machines Ltd (Volume 2) – contract costing in a large engineering company.

Rolls-Royce Ltd, Derby Manufacturing (Volume 2) – a review and further development of the standard costing system employed in a gas turbine engine business as a result of the introduction of new manufacturing technology.

Spicers Ltd (Volume 2) – the implementation of a project on the computerization of production planning and control procedures in a paper converting factory using a standard costing system.

4

Costs for Decision-Making

The term 'cost' has many meanings in many different situations. Costs suitable for control purposes, which have been considered in Chapter 3 and will be considered further in Chapter 9, are not necessarily suitable for decision-making. The relevant decision cost concept to be employed in a particular situation depends upon the business decision being appraised. It is important to understand the different cost concepts available to the accountant for decision-making. In this chapter these concepts are explained and illustrated. The use of break-even analysis and charts to examine cost-volume-profit relationships is also considered. It concludes with an examination of the impact of cost inflation and recession on cost-volume-profit relationships.

Differential Cost and Incremental Cost

It will be recognized that the process of decision-making is essentially a process of choosing between competing alternatives, each with its own combination of income and costs. Problems of choice include capital expenditure decisions, make or buy decisions, the length of production runs, selection of the right product mix, selection of sales areas, selection of distribution channels, adoption of new products and abandonment of old products. Whatever the decision under consideration the problem can be expressed in similar terms, viz.: 'Which will be the most worthwhile, alternative A, B, C . . .?' Worthwhileness should be expressed in terms of effect on profitability. Management requires information in a form which enables it to choose correctly which alternative to accept. Management requires information which measures worthwhileness.

Differential costing is concerned with the effect on costs and revenues if a certain course of action is undertaken. The term *differential cost* is generally used by accountants to describe the same costs that the economist calls *incremental costs*. Differential costs may be defined as the increases or decreases in total cost, or the change in specific elements of cost that result from any variation in operations. Incremental costs have been defined as the additional costs of a change in the level or nature of activity. Any cost that changes as a result of a contemplated decision is a differential cost or incremental cost relating to that decision. Differential cost is therefore a useful and important cost concept when considering the worthwhileness of different alternatives.

Differential costing eliminates the residual costs which are the same under each alternative, and therefore irrelevant to the analysis. Differential cost is a simple concept, yet it is an essential one in decision-making. However, there are practical difficulties in applying the concept. It is not always a straightforward operation gathering the costs of each alternative in order to determine the differential costs. It is frequently difficult to derive the relevant cost information from an accounting system which employs absorption costing. It has been shown in Chapter 3 that such a system provides average unit cost on a full cost basis, and produces information for control purposes and for valuation of stocks. In making decisions, the costs which are of importance are those which will be incurred as a result of the decision, i.e. future costs. Past costs should be ignored. In considering alternatives, past or sunk costs are not relevant to decisions about the future, because these costs have already been incurred. Average unit costs produced by an absorption costing system include such past costs. The *relevant costs* are future differential or incremental costs – the costs which will be different under each alternative. Similarly, differential or incremental profit consists of differential revenue based on estimates of future revenue, less differential costs.

Differential costing can be applied to two types of decisions:

1. Short-run or tactical decisions;
2. Long-run or investment decisions.

The essence of the distinction is *time*. Where, in choosing between alternative courses of action, the time factor is important and carries costs or interest with it, the problem is of an investment nature. In this situation the time value of money has to be recognized and discounting techniques employed. Investment decisions will be considered in Chapter 8. This chapter is concerned with short-run or tactical decisions.

It should be appreciated that decisions are taken by management in an increasingly dynamic and uncertain environment. It is not possible in many instances to measure precisely the worthwhileness of the alternatives under consideration. This chapter is concerned with decision cost concepts and, in order to concentrate the reader's attention on these concepts, certainty will be assumed in all the illustrations. In later chapters the use of probability and sensitivity analysis will be considered and introduced into the discussion.

Illustration of Relevant Costs

Relevant cost concepts are best understood by way of an example. In the machining department of the Odd Job Engineering Co. there are two machines, 'A' and 'B', each capable of performing approximately the same type of work. Machine A is a slow-running machine and requires one operator, whereas Machine B, which runs more quickly, requires two operators. The following information was available for the two machines:

	Machine A	Machine B
Expected Normal Operating Hours	2,000	1,800
Hourly Rate of each Operator	£0.90	£0.90
Variable Operating Costs per hour operated	£1.65	£2.45
Fixed Overheads:		
Directly allocated per annum	£1,500	£3,600
Proportion of General Factory Overheads apportioned to machines per annum	£2,400	£4,050

A cost clerk has prepared a statement (Table 4.1) showing the comparative machine hour rates for the two machines. It will be noted that the clerk has employed absorption costing principles in calculating the machine hour rates. He has divided the fixed overheads by the expected normal operating hours.

Job XYZ can be produced on Machine A at the rate of 30 units per hour, or on Machine B at 50 units per hour. Materials cost £0.05 per unit. The management requires a statement of the comparative costs of the two machines for a batch of 300 units (Job XYZ), and a

Table 4.1

ODD JOB ENGINEERING COMPANY

Statement of Comparative Machine Hour Rates

		Machine A £		Machine B £
Operator's Wages at £0.90 per hour		0.90		1.80
Operating Costs per hour		1.65		2.45
Variable Cost per hour		2.55		4.25
Fixed Costs				
Directly allocated	(£1,500 ÷ 2,000 hrs)	.75	(£3,600 ÷ 1,800 hrs)	2.00
Apportioned	(£2,400 ÷ 2,000 hrs)	1.20	(£4,050 ÷ 1,800 hrs)	2.25
Total Cost per hour		£4.50		£8.50

Table 4.2

ODD JOB ENGINEERING COMPANY

Comparative Cost of Job X Y Z

	Batch size: 300 units	
	Machine A	Machine B
Units per hour	30	50
Hours required	10	6
Absorption Cost Approach	£	£
Materials at £0.05 per unit	15.00	15.00
Machine Costs	45.00	51.00
	£60.00	£66.00

recommendation as to which machine should be used. The clerk prepares a comparative cost statement (Table 4.2) and recommends the use of Machine A because the total cost would be £6 less than with Machine B. However, has the clerk taken into consideration only the differential costs – the costs which differ under each alternative? He clearly has not. His calculation includes material costs which are the same for both machines and fixed costs which will be incurred regardless of whether the machines are used or not. The fixed costs are sunk costs and are not relevant to the decision under consideration. They will be incurred regardless of which machine is used for Job XYZ. The only costs which vary between the alternatives are the variable machine costs. If Machine A is chosen, will it be used for 10 additional hours at a variable cost of £2.55 per machine hour and a *differential cost* of £25.50? Similarly, if Machine B is selected, will it be used for 6 additional hours at a variable cost of £4.25 per hour, resulting in a *differential cost* of £25.50? Thus, is the differential cost of the two machines the same, and has neither machine a cost advantage for Job XYZ? If the company is in a limited capacity situation, should the management consider the alternative work that could be carried out on the two machines? On the other hand, the company may be working below full capacity and labour costs may be fixed in the short run. The company may hoard skilled labour when it is temporarily working below capacity. Illustrations of surplus capacity and full capacity situations will highlight the need to recognize that different cost concepts are required for different situations.

Assume that further investigation in the machining department of the Odd Job Engineering Co. reveals that the company has spare capacity, and that the machine operators receive a guaranteed hourly wage of £0.70 per hour. This means that they receive an extra £0.20 per hour when they are operating the machines. A revised statement of relevant costs (Table 4.3) shows that Machine A has an incremental machine hour rate of £1.85, and Machine B a rate of £2.85. The incremental cost for Job XYZ is £1.40 lower for Machine B, and in a surplus capacity situation the machine should be employed for Job XYZ. Before considering a limited capacity situation, the concept of *opportunity cost* is explained.

Opportunity Cost

Opportunity cost is another important cost concept which should be employed in decision-making. It has been emphasized that decision-making is essentially a process of choosing between competing alternatives, each with its own combination of income and costs.

Table 4.3

ODD JOB ENGINEERING COMPANY
Revised Relevant Costs
Incremental Machine Hour Rates

	Machine A £	Machine B £
Rate per hour		
Operator's Wages	0.20	0.40
Running Costs	1.65	2.45
	£1.85	£2.85
Number of hours	10	6
Incremental Cost of Job X Y Z	£18.50	£17.10

Opportunity cost is concerned with the best alternative forgone. For example:

1. A choice has to be made between three alternatives, and calculations indicate that the three proposed alternatives would increase profit by £10,000, £6,000 and £3,000 respectively. If the first alternative is not accepted its opportunity cost is £4,000, the profit forgone by choosing the next best alternative, i.e. £10,000 − £6,000.

2. A company holds in stock 2,000 lbs of Raw Material A, for which it paid £500, and the scrap value of the material is £50. If the company uses this material to produce Product X, and it has no other use, the cost of using the material for Product X is £50, *not* £500. This is the opportunity cost because the best alternative use of the material is to scrap. The £500 original cost is a past cost and not relevant to the decision.

3. If a company retains increased profits to finance growth rather than pay higher dividends to its shareholders, the opportunity cost of this additional finance is the alternative return the shareholders would have earned if the retained profits had been distributed as dividends and the shareholders had invested them elsewhere.

4. If a research and development project is justified on the grounds

of potential reductions in production costs if the project is successful, it must still compete with other prospective investment opportunities in the business, such as the replacement of machinery, advertising outlays and new investments. All these prospective investments must justify tying up capital when compared with the alternative earnings from investing the capital outside the business, or the interest cost which would be avoided by not having to borrow.

Thus, opportunity cost should be measured by the profit forgone under the best available alternative. Although it is frequently difficult to measure, opportunity cost is an important concept and one that is increasingly used by the management accountant. It does make the accountant and the management think about the alternatives forgone, which they sometimes fail to do.

If the Odd Job Engineering Co. is in a limited capacity situation, in deciding whether or not to undertake Job XYZ and on which machine, the management must consider the alternative work that could be carried out on the two machines. Assume that if Job XYZ is undertaken, it will have to forgo Job CDF if Machine A is used for Job XYZ, and forgo Job ABC if Machine B is used for Job XYZ. The following additional information is available:

	Job CDF	Job ABC
Machine	A	B
Hours required	10	6
Materials	£25	£10
Selling Price	£80	£50

Should the Odd Job Engineering Co. undertake Job XYZ, and if so, on which machine? As the management is concerned with choosing between different jobs as well as between machines, selling prices must be taken into account. The selling price of Job XYZ is £75.

Two approaches to evaluating the alternatives will be considered: the incremental cost approach and the opportunity cost approach. In the first the incremental profit arising from each alternative is calculated (see Table 4.4) and the best combination of jobs and machines is determined. It will be noted that Job XYZ gives the highest incremental profit of the three jobs regardless of which machine is used. However, Job XYZ should be undertaken on Machine B because the combination of Jobs XYZ and CDF gives

Table 4.4

ODD JOB ENGINEERING COMPANY
Incremental Profit Approach

Job	XYZ	ABC	XYZ	CDF
Machine	A	B	B	A
Hours required	10	6	6	10
	£	£	£	£
Materials Cost	15.0	10.0	15.0	25.0
Incremental Machine Costs (from Table 4.3)	18.5	17.1	17.1	18.5
Total Incremental Costs	33.5	27.1	32.1	43.5
Selling Price	75.0	50.0	75.0	80.0
Incremental Profit	£41.5	£22.9	£42.9	£36.5

£64.4

£79.4

£59.4

an incremental profit of £79.4 (£42.9 + £36.5), against an incremental profit of £64.4 (£41.5 + £22.9) for Jobs XYZ and ABC, and £59.4 (£22.9 + £36.5) for Jobs ABC and CDF.

A second method of evaluating the alternatives is the opportunity cost approach, which is shown in Table 4.5. Consider carefully this table. With this approach, the opportunity cost of undertaking Job XYZ on a particular machine is taken into account. If Job XYZ is undertaken on Machine A the company forgoes the opportunity of undertaking Job CDF and earning an incremental profit of £36.5, as in Table 4.4. As shown in Table 4.5, this incremental profit is more than the incremental costs (materials plus machine costs) that will not be incurred if Job XYZ is not undertaken on Machine A. Therefore, the best alternative forgone is the £36.5 incremental profit on Job CDF that would no longer be earned if Job XYZ is undertaken on Machine A. In the case of Machine B, the opportunity cost of undertaking Job XYZ is the £32.1 incremental costs that will no longer be incurred if Job XYZ is not undertaken on Machine B, because these are higher than the incremental profit (£22.9) that would be forgone if Job ABC was not undertaken on Machine B. As the opportunity cost is higher for Machine A, and as the job

Table 4.5

ODD JOB ENGINEERING COMPANY
Opportunity Cost Approach

	Machine A £	Machine B £
Alternatives to Job X Y Z		
Job C D F not undertaken		
Incremental Profit forgone	36.5	—
Job A B C not undertaken		
Incremental Profit forgone	—	22.9
Job X Y Z not undertaken		
Incremental Costs not incurred *	33.5	32.1
Opportunity Cost of undertaking Job X Y Z	36.5	32.1
Selling Price	75.0	75.0
Additional Profit	£38.5	£42.9

* Material cost plus incremental machine costs

therefore shows a higher additional profit (£42.9) on Machine B
(see Table 4.5), Job X Y Z should be undertaken on Machine B and
Job C D F on Machine A, as indicated by the incremental profit
approach. The additional profit for the combined jobs (X Y Z and
C D F) is £79.4 (£42.9 + £36.5), as previously calculated. In practice,
most management accountants would use, and the author recommends, the more straightforward incremental profit approach.

After considering the concepts and illustrations of differential
cost, incremental cost, sunk cost and opportunity cost, it will be
appreciated that in determining decision-making costs the following
are required:

1. A precise picture of the alternatives available;
2. An understanding of different cost concepts; and
3. A flexible classification of accounting records on several alter-
    native bases, which computer-based accounting systems have
    made possible.

The management accountant must be able to ask the right questions of himself and of managers, and be able to select the data
which are relevant in answering them. The manager must be able to

ask the right questions of accountants and have sufficient understanding of decision cost concepts to know whether he has received
the right answers.

Differential Costing, Break-Even Analysis and Marginal Costing

A knowledge of cost–volume–profit relationships is often essential
in differential cost analysis of decisions of choice, because the alternatives frequently differ in total volume and in composition of
volume. Marginal costing and break-even analysis are concerned
with the effect on costs and profit of changes in the volume and type
of output. Break-even analysis is considered in this chapter, and
marginal costing in Chapter 5. It is sometimes contended that marginal costing is the same as differential costing or incremental costing. But cost–volume–profit relationships are not the only decisions
dealt with in differential costing, while marginal costing is essentially
a study of the effect of cost–volume–profit relationships based on a
classification of costs as fixed or variable. Differential costs and
incremental costs include many that are normally classified as fixed
or semi-fixed in the short run, and may be regarded as a general
class of which marginal costs are a narrow part, for marginal costs
refer to a single kind of increment only, i.e. the addition of another
unit to fixed plant. Marginal costing is essentially a short-run concept, and differential costing and incremental costing deal with
short-run and long-run decisions. The alternatives under consideration frequently involve cost–volume–profit relationships, but this is
not always the case, as for example when studying the desirability
for a proposed change in material specifications to reduce spoiled
work or rework costs, or when deciding when to replace machinery
or motor vehicles. The applications of marginal costing presented in
Chapter 5 are, therefore, examples of the application of differential
costing to short-run decisions. Long-run decisions are considered in
Chapter 8.

Break-Even Analysis

The simplest method of illustrating the relationship between cost,
volume of output, and profit is the break-even chart. The *break-even
chart* is a graph showing the amount of fixed and variable costs and

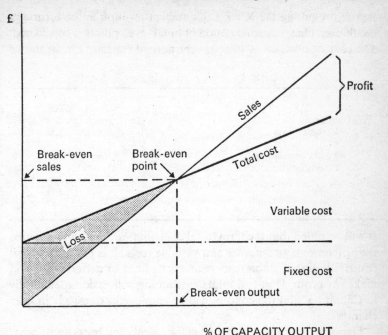

Figure 4.1. *Break-even chart*

the sales revenues at different volumes of output. A simple break-even chart is illustrated in Figure 4.1. It has been described as a condensed master flexible budget showing the normal profit for any given sales volume. It will become apparent that this description overrates its usefulness; however, it is a useful device for exploring the impact of volume changes, the increasing ratios of fixed to variable costs, and continuing cost inflation on profits.

A Simple Illustration

The XYZ Co.'s current costs and sales at 100 per cent normal capacity are:

	£'000
Annual Sales at 100% normal capacity	240
Fixed Costs	80
Variable Costs	120

Before presenting the X Y Z Co.'s current position in the form of a break-even chart, the calculation of break-even points is considered. The current position at 100 per cent normal capacity can be shown as follows:

	£'000
Sales	240
Variable Costs	120
Total Contribution	120
Fixed Costs	80
Profit	£40

It will be noted that the term 'total contribution' is used to describe the difference between sales and variable costs. It is out of this total contribution that a company recovers its fixed or period costs, and makes its profit. Unit and total contribution will be considered fully in Chapter 5, and the concept will be employed extensively in later chapters.

There are a number of formulae for calculating break-even capacity and sales value, i.e. the capacity and sales at which total costs equal total sales:

$$\text{Break-even Capacity} = \frac{\text{Total Fixed Cost}}{\dfrac{\text{Total Sales} - \text{Total Variable Cost}}{\text{Units of Capacity}}}$$

This formula can be used for X Y Z Ltd as follows:

$$\frac{80}{\left(\dfrac{240 - 120}{100\%}\right)} = 80 \times \frac{100\%}{120} = 66\tfrac{2}{3}\%$$

In this example units of capacity are measured in terms of percentage of normal capacity.

$$\text{Break-even Sales Value} = \frac{\text{Total Fixed Cost}}{1 - \left(\dfrac{\text{Total Variable Cost}}{\text{Total Sales}}\right)}$$

$$\text{X Y Z Ltd} = \frac{£80}{1 - \left(\tfrac{120}{240}\right)} = \frac{£80}{.5} = \underline{\underline{£160}}$$

In X Y Z Ltd's current position its break-even capacity is $66\tfrac{2}{3}\%$ and £160,000 sales, i.e. $66\tfrac{2}{3}\%$ of £240,000.

A useful ratio which can be employed to calculate break-even capacity and sales, and also the effect of changes in volume on profit, is the *profit–volume ratio* (P.V. ratio) or *contribution ratio*. The P.V. ratio is the rate at which profit increases/decreases with an increase/decrease in volume, and is given by the formula:

$$P.V. = 1 - \frac{\text{Variable Costs}}{\text{Sales}}$$

$$\text{or } P.V. = \frac{\text{Sales} - \text{Variable Costs}}{\text{Sales}}$$

$$\text{or } P.V. = \frac{\text{Total Contribution}}{\text{Sales}}$$

$$XYZ \text{ Ltd} = \frac{£120}{£240} = \underline{\underline{.5}}$$

This ratio indicates that for every £1 of sales, the XYZ Co. generates £0.5 (i.e. $0.5 \times £1$) contribution towards fixed costs and profits. P.V. ratio can be used to calculate break-even capacity and volume as follows:

$$\text{Break-even Sales} = \frac{\text{Fixed Costs}}{\text{P.V. Ratio}}$$

$$XYZ \text{ Ltd} = \frac{£80}{.5} = \underline{\underline{£160}}$$

Thus £160,000 sales will generate £80,000 contribution (i.e. $0.5 \times £160,000$) which is equal to the fixed costs.

$$\text{Break-even Capacity} = \frac{\left(\dfrac{\text{Fixed Costs}}{\text{P.V. Ratio}}\right)}{\text{Sales}} \times 100$$

$$XYZ \text{ Ltd} = \frac{\left(\dfrac{80}{.5}\right)}{240} \times 100 = 66\tfrac{2}{3}\%$$

A break-even chart for XYZ Ltd's current position appears in Figure 4.2. It should be noted that while break-even sales and capacity, fixed costs and sales, and total costs for different levels of capacity utilization can be read directly from a break-even chart,

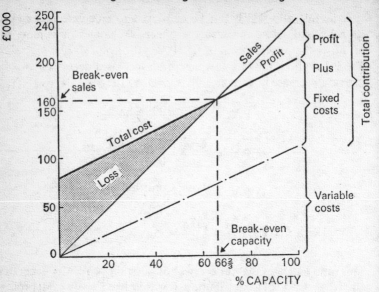

Figure 4.2. *X Y Z Ltd. Break-even chart*

profit cannot be read directly. Profit is the *difference* between two lines. An alternative form of presenting the same information is the *profit–volume chart* (see Figure 4.3). Profit can be read directly from a profit–volume chart. Thus at 70 per cent capacity a profit of £4,000 is expected, and at 80 per cent capacity a profit of £16,000.

The *profit–volume chart* recognizes that with no sales a company has a loss equivalent to its fixed costs. When it commences producing and selling it generates sales and incurs variable costs, which produces a contribution out of which fixed costs are recovered. Eventually it reaches the point where sales minus variable costs – i.e. total contribution – equals fixed costs, and this is the so-called 'break-even point'. Beyond this point, total contribution is greater than fixed costs and a profit is made. The *P.V. ratio* represents the slope of the profit line on the profit–volume chart (0.5 on Figure 4.3); the higher the P.V. ratio, the steeper the slope and the lower the break-even point. Thus if X Y Z's P.V. ratio was 0.6 its break-even sales would fall to £133,333 (£80,000 ÷ 0.6) or 55.6 per cent of normal capacity. Using a profit–volume chart it is possible to determine the

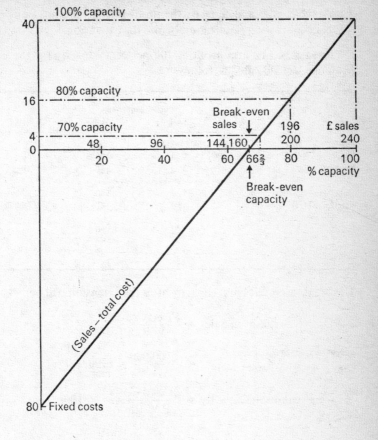

Figure 4.3. *X Y Z Ltd. Profit–volume chart*

change in profit that will result from a given change in volume, *provided other factors remain static.*

Let us consider further the X Y Z Co. example. It is proposed to increase the capacity of the company by the acquisition of $33\frac{1}{3}$ per cent additional space and plant. Fixed costs are expected to increase by £20,000 per annum. On the assumption that production efficiency, variable costs and selling prices remain unchanged, the management wishes to know:

1. The break-even sales and capacity after the expansion; and

2.   At what sales and capacity the profit will be the same as at 100 per cent capacity utilization before the expansion.

The sales, costs, and profit at 100 per cent capacity for the new plant can be calculated as follows:

| | 100% Capacity | | Change |
	Old	New	
	£'000	£'000	
Sales	240	320	+ 33⅓%
Variable Costs	120	160	+ 33⅓%
Total Contribution	120	160	
Fixed Costs	80	100	+ £20,000
Profit	£40	£60	
P.V. Ratio	.5	.5	

The break-even sales and capacity after the extension will be:

$$\text{Break-even Sales} = \frac{\text{Fixed Costs}}{\text{P.V. Ratio}}$$

$$= \frac{£100,000}{.5} = \underline{\underline{£200,000}}$$

$$\text{Break-even Capacity} = \frac{\left(\dfrac{\text{Fixed Costs}}{\text{P.V. Ratio}}\right)}{\text{Sales}} \times 100$$

$$= \frac{\dfrac{(£100,000)}{.5}}{£320,000} \times 100 = 62.5\%$$

It should be noted that because the fixed costs have increased by £20,000 the company has to generate an additional £40,000 sales in order to stand still. Thus if there is no change in the P.V. ratio an increase in fixed costs will result in an increase in break-even sales.

It will be recognized that sales to give a required profit can be calculated by the formula:

$$\frac{\text{Fixed Costs} + \text{Required Profit}}{\text{P.V. Ratio}}$$

The level of sales at which the extended plant will give the same profit (£40,000) as at 100 per cent capacity for the old plant is:

$$\frac{£100,000 + £40,000}{0.5} = £280,000$$

which is 87.5 per cent of capacity of the extended plant, i.e.

$$\frac{£280,000}{£320,000} \times 100$$

Because of the increase in fixed costs, an increase in sales of £40,000 is required if the same profit is to be made.

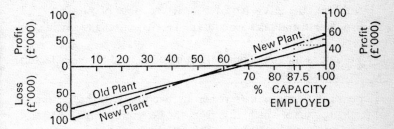

Figure 4.4. *X Y Z Ltd. Profit–volume chart*

The break-even points for the old and new plants are presented graphically in Figure 4.4. The fixed costs are plotted at 0 per cent capacity and the profit figures at 100 per cent capacity. The lines joining the 0 per cent and 100 per cent capacity points show the loss or profit at different levels of capacity, the break-even points being where the lines intersect the horizontal axis, i.e. $66\frac{2}{3}$ per cent for the old plant and 62.5 per cent for the new plant. The capacity utilization of the new plant, which gives the same profit as 100 per cent capacity utilization of the old plant, can be read from the chart as indicated. At 87.5 per cent capacity utilization the new plant will generate a profit of £40,000.

Limitations of Break-even Analysis

The break-even chart is a useful device for presenting a simplified picture of cost–volume–profit relationships as an aid to illustrating the effects of changes in various factors, such as volume, price and costs. However, for profit forecasting, the break-even chart with its *static* relationships has serious limitations which should not be ignored. Because of the many restrictive assumptions that must be made in order to compute a break-even chart, the break-even point is only an approximate best. For example, it is assumed that:

1. Costs are either fixed or variable, or at least they can be so classified for purposes of break-even charts.
2. Fixed and variable costs are correctly separated over the whole range of output.
3. Either selling price per unit is constant regardless of the level of output, or the demand curve for the product is known.
4. There is one product, or, if there is more than one product, a constant sales mix exists over the whole range of output.
5. Production and sales are equal and there is no change in finished products stock.
6. Volume is the only factor affecting costs, and all other factors remain constant.

Since profits are residuals, the profit function bears the full impact of the inaccuracies which arise from the determination of the *static* cost and revenue functions derived on the basis of the above assumptions. Usually the relationship will be valid only within a limited range of activity above and below the level of capacity for which the data is computed. The word *point* carries the connotation of great exactness. A better term would be break-even *area*, to indicate that the precise location of the break-even point is not known and can be estimated only roughly. To dramatize this, the cost and revenue lines should perhaps be drawn on the chart as wide bands with intersections over a wide area. It should also be recognized that, because of the many assumptions underlying the break-even chart, the analysis is only relevant over a limited range of output. Outside this range the chart is not meaningful. A break-even chart in the form shown in Figure 4.5 would be more realistic than that shown in Figure 4.1.

These limitations of break-even charts do not mean they are completely useless. Provided the assumptions on which the analysis is made are clearly stated, break-even analysis provides valuable information for the guidance of management, and the break-even chart is a simple means of presentation. The greatest value comes from the analysis of the underlying relationships of volume, costs

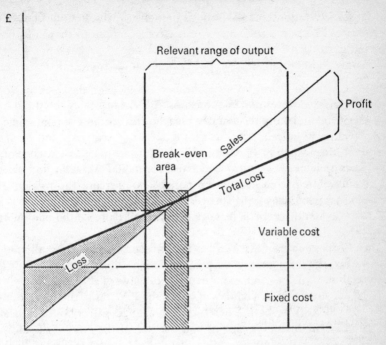

Figure 4.5. *Break-even area chart*

and profits revealed, and *not* from the location of the break-even point. The break-even point itself is of limited significance. It provides neither a standard of performance nor a guide for executive decisions. No business should be conducted in order to break even. The proximity of the break-even point may influence management's attitudes towards costs and risks, or towards the urgency for cost reduction efforts. One measure of the proximity of the break-even point is the so-called *margin of safety*.

Sales in excess of the break-even sales are said to represent a *margin of safety* (M/S).

$$\text{M/S} = \frac{\text{Actual Sales} - \text{Sales at Break-even Point}}{\text{Actual Sales}}$$

Thus, if the actual sales of the X Y Z Company remained at £240,000 per annum *after* the extension of the plant, the margin of safety would be:

$$\frac{£240,000 - £200,000}{£240,000} \times 100 = 16\tfrac{2}{3}\%$$

Therefore, given *static* relationships, X Y Z Ltd's sales could fall by $16\tfrac{2}{3}$ per cent before the company reached its break-even point. Since break-even volume depends on the level of fixed costs and on the P.V. ratio, margin of safety will change as a result of changes in sales volume, P.V. ratio and fixed costs. If P.V. ratio and sales volume are stable, it may be possible to increase the margin of safety by reducing fixed costs. If the P.V. ratio and total fixed costs are constant, increases in sales volume will increase the margin of safety.

Break-even point, P.V. ratio and margin of safety are all *static* rather than dynamic concepts. As will be illustrated in the next section, shifts in volume, particularly downward shifts, are likely to be accompanied by changes in either the P.V. ratio, or the amount of fixed costs, or both. Therefore such changes affect both the location of the break-even point and the size of the margin of safety. The margin of safety is a rather theoretical concept and is not likely to hold if conditions occur which cause it to be invaded. However, a substantial margin of safety does indicate that a company or a unit of a company is less vulnerable to a decline in sales than one which has a narrow margin of safety.

Some Underlying Relationships

It has been emphasized that the greatest value of break-even analysis comes from the analysis of the underlying relationships of volume, costs and profits revealed. In particular, managers should be familiar with:

1. The increasing ratio of fixed or period costs to total costs in many companies and its influence on profit–volume ratios and break-even areas; and
2. The impact of cost inflation on profit–volume ratios, break-even areas and profits.

INCREASING RATIO OF FIXED COSTS TO TOTAL COSTS

It will be recognized that in many companies costs are becoming increasingly fixed in relation to short-run changes in activity. Labour costs are assuming the characteristics of fixed or period costs, and in some companies material costs are the only truly variable costs. What influence does this trend have on a company's underlying cost–volume–profit relationships? Consider the following simple illustration.

X Ltd and Y Ltd each anticipate sales turnover amounting to £2,500,000, representing 100 per cent normal capacity. 10 per cent of turnover is expected to be profit if each achieves 100 per cent normal capacity. The variable costs at 100 per cent normal capacity are £1,350,000 for X Ltd and £2,000,000 for Y Ltd. Using the formula developed earlier in this chapter the following analysis can be undertaken:

	100% Capacity	
	X Ltd	Y Ltd
	£'000	£'000
Sales	2,500	2,500
Variable Costs	1,350	2,000
Total Contribution	1,150	500
Fixed Costs	900	250
Profit	£ 250	£ 250
Ratio of Fixed Costs to Total Cost	.40	.11
P.V. Ratio	.46	.20
B/E Sales	£1,956.5	£1,250
B/E Capacity	78.3%	50%

The information is presented graphically in a single profit–volume chart in Figure 4.6. It will be noted that X Ltd, which has the higher ratio of fixed costs to total costs, has the higher P.V. ratio, break-even sales, and percentage capacity utilization. What observations can be made regarding the effects of increased and decreased business for X Ltd and Y Ltd in the future? Provided all other factors remain *static*, the effect of a 10 per cent change in capacity utilization will be:

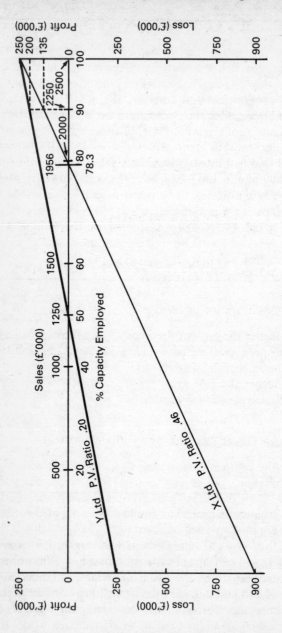

Figure 4.6. X Ltd and Y Ltd. Profit–Volume Chart

	X Ltd £'000	Y Ltd £'000
Change in Sales	250	250
P.V. Ratio	.46	.2
Change in Total Contribution and Profit	115	50

Thus, as illustrated in Figure 4.6, if sales fell from 100 per cent to 90 per cent of normal capacity to £2,250,000, X Ltd's profit would fall to £135,000 and Y Ltd's to £200,000. At the lower level of sales, *margins of safety* are:

$$\text{X Ltd: } \frac{£2,250,000 - £1,956,500}{£2,250,000} \times 100 = \underline{\underline{13.0\%}}$$

$$\text{Y Ltd: } \frac{£2,250,000 - £1,250,000}{£2,250,000} \times 100 = \underline{\underline{44.4\%}}$$

This simple illustration highlights:

1. The higher the ratio of fixed costs to total costs the higher will be the profit–volume ratio and break-even sales, and the lower will be the margin of safety; and
2. The higher the P.V. ratio the more volatile will profits be to changes in capacity utilization.

THE IMPACT OF COST INFLATION

Periodically, companies have had to learn to live with high rates of cost inflation. The impact of cost inflation on the profitability of a plant or company is influenced by its underlying cost–volume–profit relationships. Consider the case of the Cardboard Box Co.

Cardboard Box Co. operates two box plants and a sheet-board mill. One box plant (the long-run plant) has long runs of light boxes with no trimmings. The work is fast-moving and the plant operates on three eight-hour shifts per day. The other box plant (the short-run plant) has short runs of heavier boxes which are of complex designs, including quality printing and fitted pack work. The work

Table 4.6

CARDBOARD BOX CO.

Cost–volume–profit Profiles

	Long-Run Plant		Short-Run Plant		Sheet Plant	
Annual Sales Volume	60 m.s.m.*		30 m.s.m.		3 m.s.m.	
	£	£/t.s.m.†	£	£/t.s.m.	£	£/t.s.m.
Sales	4,800,000	80	3,600,000	120	600,000	200
Materials/Carriage	2,800,000	47	1,800,000	60	210,000	70
Total Contribution	2,000,000	33	1,800,000	60	390,000	130
P.V. Ratio	(.42)		(.50)		(.65)	
Period Costs	1,500,000	25	1,300,000	43	250,000	83
Profit	£500,000	£8	£500,000	£17	£140,000	£47
Break-even Sales						
Volume	45.454 m.s.m		21.667 m.s.m.		1.923 m.s.m.	
Value	£3,600,355		£2,600,000		£384,600	
% of Capacity	75%		72%		64%	

* m.s.m. = million square metres

† t.s.m. = thousand square metres

is slower-moving and the plant operates on two eight-hour shifts per day. The board mill undertakes very short runs of specialist work which sells at high prices. This mill offers a twenty-four-hour service, undertakes any type of work, and operates on a single-shift basis. Cost–volume–profit profiles for the three plants are summarized in Table 4.6.

The effect of 10 per cent cost inflation on the short-run plant of Cardboard Box Co. is illustrated in Table 4.7. It will be noted that without any price increase the company would require a 19.2 per cent increase in volume to recover a 10 per cent increase in costs. A comparison with other plants shows:

		To recover 10% Increase in Costs	
Plant	*P.V. Ratio*	*Volume Increase*	*or Price Increase*
Long-run	0.42	21·3%	9.0%
Short-run	0.50	19.2%	8.6%
Sheet plant	0.65	11.8%	7.7%

It will be noted that the lower the P.V. ratio the greater the impact of cost inflation on plant profitability.

Table 4.7

CARDBOARD BOX CO. SHORT-RUN PLANT
Effect of 10% Cost Inflation

	Before	Increase	After
Annual Sales Volume	30 m.s.m.	—	30 m.s.m.
	£	£	£
Sales	3,600,000	—	3,600,000
Materials/Carriage	1,800,000	(+) 180,000	1,980,000
Total Contribution	1,800,000	(−) 180,000	1,620,000
P.V. Ratio	(.50)		(.45)
Period Costs	1,300,000	(+) 130,000	1,430,000
Profit	£500,000	(−) £310,000	£190,000

Additional sales required to recover increase in costs:

$$\frac{\text{Required Additional Profit}}{\text{P.V. Ratio}} = \frac{£310,000}{.45} = £690,000 = 19.2\% \text{ of Sales}$$

% Price increase required to recover increase in costs:

$$\frac{\text{Required Additional Profit}}{\text{Sales}} = \frac{£310,000}{£3,600,000} \times 100 = 8.6\%$$

In Britain in the early 1980s many companies faced the prospect of falling demand, increasing costs and strong price competition. Let us consider the effect on the short-run plant of a 10 per cent fall in demand combined with a 10 per cent cost inflation. The effects on the profitability of the short-run plant are illustrated in Figure 4.7. It will be noted that the break-even volume has increased from 21.7 m.s.m. to 26.5 m.s.m. It will be seen from Table 4.8 that the company would have to increase prices by 14.57 per cent, or reduce period costs by 33 per cent, in order to maintain the profit of the short-run plant. A comparison with other plants shows:

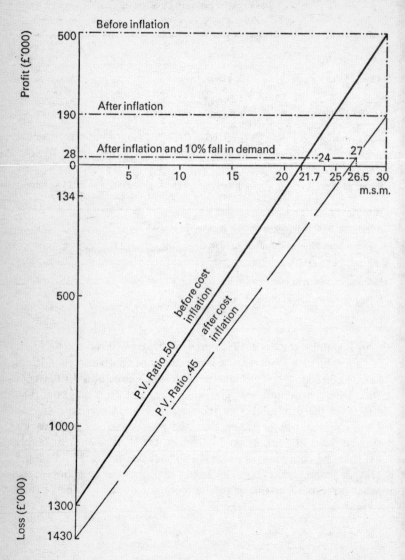

Figure 4.7. *Cardboard Box Co., profit–volume chart. Effect of 10 per cent cost inflation on short-run plant*

Plant	P.V. Ratio Before	P.V. Ratio After	Profit/(Loss) Before	Profit/(Loss) After	Change to maintain Profit Prices	Change to maintain Profit Period Costs
			£	£	%	%
Long-run	.42	.38	500	(8)	(+) 11.4	(−) 29.8
Short run	.50	.45	500	28	(+) 14.6	(−) 33.0
Sheet plant	.65	.62	140	57	(+) 15.4	(−) 30.2

In a highly competitive, stagnant or declining market, it is unlikely that the company will be able to achieve the increases in selling prices required to maintain profits. These are circumstances in which

Table 4.8

CARDBOARD BOX CO. SHORT-RUN PLANT
Effect of 10% Cost Inflation and 10% Fall in Demand

	After 10% Cost Inflation	Fall in Demand*	After Fall
Annual Sales Volume	30 m.s.m.	3 m.s.m.	27 m.s.m.
	£	£	£
Sales	3,600,000	(−) 360,000	3,240,000
Materials/Carriage	1,980,000	(−) 198,000	1,782,000
Total Contribution	1,620,000	(−) 162,000	1,458,000
P.V. Ratio	(.45)		(.45)
Period Costs	1,430,000	—	1,430,000
	£190,000	(−) £162,000	£28,000

* Assumes selling prices are not eroded by fall in demand

Price Increase required to maintain £500,000 Profit

$$\frac{£472,000}{£3,240,000} \times 100 = 14.57\%$$

Reduction in Period Costs required to maintain £500,000 Profit

$$\frac{£472,000}{£1,430,000} \times 100 = 33.01\%$$

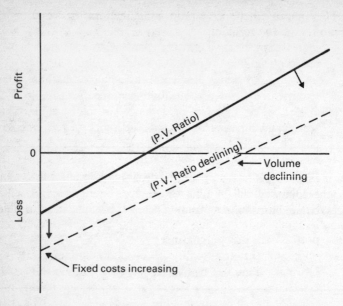

Figure 4.8. *Impact of inflation and recession on profit–volume chart*

management should take a long, hard look at all costs – particularly period costs.

Managing Cost–*Volume*–*Profit Relationships in Recession*

During the early 1980s British manufacturing industry went through a period of great trauma; the output of manufacturing industry fell by nearly 16 per cent between the second quarter of 1979 and the last quarter of 1980, and was very slow to recover. Not only did the recession create severe liquidity and profitability problems, but major structural changes also took place. The impact on cost–volume–profit relationships is summarized in Figure 4.8. What actions were taken by company managements that survived the recession and rebuilt their profitability?

1. They reduced the level of fixed costs to bring them into line with anticipated volumes so as to reduce break-even volume and improve profit/loss for a given volume. Levels of fixed costs were critically examined in all areas.

2. They improved the P.V. ratio and therefore the slope of the profit line, as a result of:
    - increased productivity through plant-wide incentive schemes;
    - shedding old plant (which also reduced period costs);
    - improved working practices, including combining jobs, team working, interchangeability between semi-skilled and skilled tasks, blurring of 'blue-collar' and 'white-collar' work, and building on positive attitudes to technological change;
    - employing advanced manufacturing technology (see the Rolls-Royce case study) and Japanese manufacturing management techniques;
    - reducing material costs through improved product design, handling and processing methods, material substitution, and professionalizing purchasing;
    - reviewing the profitability of products and markets (see Chapters 7 and 11) by rationalizing the product range, increasing emphasis on improved product design, quality and reliability, and at the same time reducing further fixed costs so as to bring them into line with rationalized product range.

In addition to these actions at the operating company/unit level, in groups of companies additional questions were asked: Is the group's organization structure appropriate to the reduced level of activity and anticipated growth? Are we occupying too many buildings and, in particular, too many expensive city-centre properties? Are we incurring excessive administrative costs because of the trappings of a large company, e.g. a secretary for everyone? Are we incurring excessive selling and marketing costs because we have failed to recognize that we are no longer selling in growth markets?

Summary

Costs obtained for control purposes are often not suitable for decision-making. Management requires information in a form which enables it to choose correctly between alternatives. To provide this information the management accountant must understand and employ the concepts of differential or incremental cost and opportunity cost. Marginal costing and break-even analysis are concerned with the effect on costs and profits of changes in volume and type of output. Break-even analysis can be a useful device provided too much emphasis is not placed on the break-even point, and the underlying relationships are examined carefully. The break-even chart, or the profit–volume chart, can be used as a means of presenting these relationships over a limited range of output. Managers should be familiar with the influence of the increasing ratio of fixed or period costs to total costs on profit–volume ratios and break-even areas; and the impact of cost inflation and of recession on profit–volume relationships. Actions can be taken to improve relationships and rebuild profitability.

Selected Readings

1. L. R. Amey and D. A. Egginton, *Management Accounting: A Conceptual Framework*, Longman, London, 1973.
2. Robert N. Anthony and James S. Reece, *Management Accounting: Text and Cases*, Irwin, Homewood, Illinois, 1983.
3. John Arnold and Tony Hope, *Accounting for Management Decisions*, Prentice-Hall International, London, 1983.
4. Colin Drury, *Management and Cost Accounting*, Van Nostrand Reinhold (U.K.), Reading, 1985.
5. Charles T. Horngren and George Foster, *Cost Accounting: A Managerial Emphasis*, Prentice-Hall, Englewood Cliffs, N.J., 1987.
6. Magnus Radke, *Manual of Cost Reduction Techniques*, McGraw-Hill, Maidenhead, 1972.
7. Gordon Shillinglaw, *Managerial Cost Accounting*, Irwin, Homewood, Illinois, 1982.
8. John Sizer, *Perspectives in Management Accounting*, I.C.M.A./Heinemann, London, 1981.
9. John Sizer, 'Managing Liquidity and Profitability in Recession', *Accountant's Magazine*, September, October and November 1981.
10. Spencer A. Tucker, *Profit Planning Decisions with Break-Even Analysis*, Gower, Farnborough, 1980.

5

Marginal Costing

Break-even analysis is of limited value when examining product profitability in a multi-product, multi-market business. Marginal costing is a more useful technique for studying the effects of changes in volume and type of output.

Marginal costing is an accounting technique which ascertains marginal cost by differentiating between fixed, or period, and variable costs. It is primarily concerned with the provision of information to management on the effects on costs and revenues of changes in the *volume* and *type* of output in the short run, although it may be applied to long-run problems. Marginal costing may be incorporated into the system of recording and collecting costs or it may be used as an analytical tool for studying and reporting the effects of changes in volume and type of output. Where it is incorporated into the system of recording and collecting costs, stocks are valued at variable cost, and fixed costs are treated as period costs in profit statements. The principles of marginal costing are explained in this chapter. Further applications and examples are provided in later chapters.

The Ascertainment of Marginal Cost

Marginal cost may be defined as the aggregate of increasing or decreasing the volume of output of a component, product, or service by *one unit* at a given level of output. The marginal cost of any given unit of output consists of the sum of the *additional* or incremental costs which are incurred as a result of its production and distribution. The additional costs are often the sum of the prime costs and variable overheads resulting from the production of one unit of output. It will be recalled that prime costs are the aggregate of direct material costs, direct wages, and direct expenses, a direct cost being

Table 5.1.

Marginal Cost of Product X

Level of Output	5,000 units
Additional Costs for one unit	£
Direct Material	0.50
Direct Labour	0.25
Direct Expense	0.25
Prime Cost	0.80
Variable Overhead	
Production	0.15
Selling and Distribution	0.10
Administration	0.03
MARGINAL COST	£1.08

a cost which can be allocated directly to a cost unit, as opposed to one which has to be apportioned to or absorbed by a cost unit. Variable overheads are the aggregate of variable production overheads, variable selling and distribution cost, and variable administration cost. A variable overhead cost is one which tends to vary directly with the volume of output but which cannot be allocated directly to a cost unit. Therefore, in order to ascertain the marginal cost of a given unit of product at a given level of output, the addition shown in Table 5.1 is frequently made.

When a system of standard costing is employed the marginal cost calculated will frequently be the standard marginal cost. The use of the prime cost plus variable overhead classification to calculate marginal cost, together with the frequent use of standard costing, tends to lead cost accountants to assume that the cost of the marginal unit is constant over a wide range of output. While marginal cost and variable cost per unit may be the same at a given level of output, the economist clearly distinguishes between marginal cost and average variable cost per unit. Accountants, on the other hand, recognize a distinction in concept, but tend to assume that average variable cost is equal to marginal cost at all levels of output and that both are constant for relevant portions of the output range in which they are operating.

The Effects of Changes in Volume and Type of Output

In order to simplify the illustrations of the use of marginal costing techniques for examining the effect of changes in volume and/or type of output, the following assumptions are made:

1. Selling price of products remains unchanged with a change in the level of output.

2. Demand for the product is assumed, i.e. a market price has been accepted, and marginal costing is not being used to determine the selling price. The application of marginal costing techniques to selling price decisions is considered in Chapter 12.

3. Marginal cost is constant for all products over the range of output under consideration.

Contribution

The difference between the marginal cost of the various products manufactured and their respective selling price is the *contribution* which each product makes towards fixed or period costs and profit. Contribution may be defined as the difference between the selling price of a unit and its marginal cost.

In order to determine the effect of short-run changes in volume on the profit of a company, it is necessary to multiply the additional sales of each product by the contribution per unit to arrive at the additional operating profit or reduced operating loss that will result from the increase in volume. This calculation assumes that there is idle capacity and there will be no increase in fixed or period costs. Any increase in fixed costs can be deducted separately from the additional contribution. For example, if A B C Co. received the following order:

Product	Units	Price per unit £
A	800	0.50
B	500	0.75
C	200	0.40
D	1,600	0.20

given the marginal cost per unit for each product, the additional profit can be calculated as follows:

Product	Selling Price per unit £	Effect on Profit of Increased Output Marginal Cost per unit £	Contribution per unit £	Additional Units	Profit £
A	0.50	0.40	0.10	800	80
B	0.75	0.60	0.15	500	75
C	0.40	0.35	0.05	200	10
D	0.20	0.10	0.10	1,600	160
					£325

Any increase in fixed costs which would result if the order was accepted should be deducted from £325.

The Limiting Factor Concept

Every company has one or more limiting factors, i.e. a factor in the activities of an undertaking which at a particular point in time or over a period will limit the volume of output. It is frequently market demand, but it may also consist of a certain class or type of raw material, or raw materials in general, a specific item of plant, skilled labour, floor space, or liquid resources. It is not a constant; it may vary from time to time within an undertaking and from one firm to another, depending upon the general economic conditions and the specific circumstances applying to the firm. In some instances there are a number of constraints operating simultaneously. The limiting factor concept is concerned with the single constraint situation. Some consideration will be given to multiple constraint situations later in this chapter.

Where the demands for a company's products exceed its present productive capacity, in the short run, it has to decide which is the best type of output to employ its limited capacity. If the company's aim is to secure maximum profit in the short run it should produce the combination of products or jobs which result in the highest possible contribution towards fixed or period costs and profit. By calculating the contribution which each product or job makes in relation to the limiting factor, the order of preference in which products or jobs should be manufactured can be decided.

For example, assuming that the factor which limits the volume of production of XYZ Company is plant hours, the contribution per hour of plant usage for the five products the company manufactures can be calculated as follows:

Product	Contribution per unit £	Limiting Factor Usage (hours of plant)	Contribution per hour of plant usage £
R	28	4	7
S	15	$2\frac{1}{2}$	6
T	16	2	8
W	16	4	4
X	15	5	3

Thus, if one additional unit of Product R was produced it would give £28 additional contribution to fixed costs and profit, and, because it requires four plant hours to manufacture, £7 additional contribution per hour of plant usage. In order to produce maximum contribution and maximum profit, XYZ Company should first concentrate on Product T. The order of priority after Product T is R, S, W, and finally X.

Assuming the plant capacity is 50,000 hours per month, and the following monthly demand exists for the various products:

Product	Number of Units	Equivalent Plant Hours
R	3,000	12,000
S	4,000	10,000
T	2,500	5,000
W	4,000	16,000
X	3,000	15,000
		58,000

The demand exceeds the plant capacity by the equivalent of 8,000 plant hours production. If period costs are £100,000 per month, the most desirable combination of products to produce and the highest attainable profit can be calculated as shown in the next table. The calculation assumes that it is feasible to market 1,400 units of Product X when the market demand is 3,000 units.

In Chapter 4, when considering the Odd Job Engineering Co.'s limited capacity situation, it was assumed that if Job XYZ was undertaken, the company would forgo Job CDF if Machine A was used for Job XYZ, and would forgo Job ABC if Machine B was

Most Desirable Combination of Products

Product	Plant Hours per unit	Units	Total Plant Hours	Contribution per plant hour	Total
				£	£
T	2	2,500	5,000	8	40,000
R	4	3,000	12,000	7	84,000
S	2½	4,000	10,000	6	60,000
W	4	4,000	16,000	4	64,000
X	5	1,400	7,000	3	21,000
			50,000	Total contribution	269,000
				Less Period Costs	100,000
				Profit per month	£169,000

used for Job X Y Z. Jobs A B C and C D F conveniently required the same number of machine hours as Job X Y Z, and were the only alternatives available. In practice in a limited capacity situation, there may be a large number of alternative jobs each requiring a different number of machine hours. For example, assume Machine C has a capacity of 300 machine hours per month and the company has to choose between the following jobs which could be undertaken in a particular month:

Job No.	Contribution £	Machine Hours required
601	500	125
602	350	140
603	400	40
604	600	30
605	275	55
606	550	50
607	375	25
608	700	100
Total	£3,750	565

Table 5.2

ODD JOB ENGINEERING CO.

Ranking of Jobs to be undertaken on Machine C

| Order of Preference | Job No. | Contribution | | | Machine Hours | |
		Per machine hour	Total	Cumulative Total	Total	Cumulative Total
		£	£	£	hrs	hrs
1	604	20	600	600	30	30
2	607	15	375	975	25	55
3	606	11	550	1,525	50	105
4	603	10	400	1,925	40	145
5	608	7	700	2,625	100	245
6	605	5	275	2,900	55	300
7	601	4	500	3,400	125	425
8	602	2.5	350	3,750	140	565

By dividing the contribution each job makes by its usage of the
limiting factor (machine hours) the jobs can be ranked in order of
profitability. As illustrated in Table 5.2 the Odd Job Engineering
Co. should reject Jobs 601 and 602 if Machine C has a capacity of
300 hours per month.

Linear Programming

In situations where there are a large number of limiting factors and
interacting variables, *linear programming* provides an efficient mathematical search procedure for selecting the optimum plan, viz. for
selecting the combination which maximizes total contribution. A
full examination of linear programming and illustrations of its
applications to accounting problems is beyond the scope of this
book, but basically it involves:

1. Constructing a set of simultaneous linear equations, which
represent the model of the problem and which take into consideration all the variable factors; and

2. Solving the equations, usually with the aid of a computer.
Simple linear programming problems can be expressed graphically

and an example is given below.[1] The role of the accountant is to assist the operational researcher in the construction of the model of the problem. He should assist in specifying the objectives, the constraints, and the variables. The solution of the equations can be left to the mathematician. The accountant should be able to recognize the type of problems which are suitable to analysis by linear programming techniques. He should know when to call in the operational researcher.

X Y Z Company markets two products which are produced in two successive departments. The contribution per unit of the two products and the weekly production capacity of the two departments are:

	Product A £		Product B £
Selling Price	15		16
Marginal Cost	10		12
Contribution	£5		£4
Production Capacity:			
Department Y	150	or	225
Department Z	200	or	200

A further constraint on the production of Product A is that demand is only 115 units per week.

The objective is to determine the combination of products which maximizes the total contribution to period costs and profit, taking into consideration the various constraints. This is called the *objective function* and can be expressed in the equation: £5A + £4B, where A and B equal the number of units of Product A and Product B. This equation is subject to the following inequalities:

Production Capacity:

Department Y	$1.5A + B \leqslant 225$
Department Z	$A + B \leqslant 200$
Demand for Product A	$A \leqslant 115$

Because production must be positive $\qquad A \geqslant O$ and $B \geqslant O$

---

1 For an introduction to linear programming and the class of problem to which it is applicable, see David Johnson, *Quantitative Business Analysis*, Butterworth, London, 1986; or Geoffrey Gregory, *Decision Analysis*, Pitman, London, 1988.

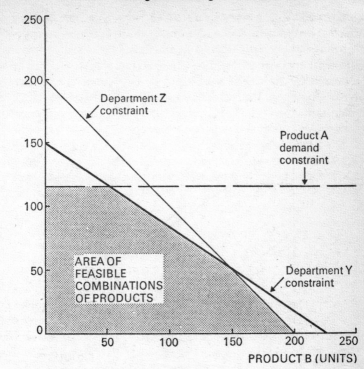

Figure 5.1

The various constraints on production are shown graphically in Figure 5.1.

The feasible solution to the problem must be within the shaded area in Figure 5.1. Within this area the objective function, 5A + 4B, must be maximized. These are quantities of Product A and Product B which lead to the same profit. For example, a total contribution of £400 would be obtained for all pairs of values of A and B satisfying the equation 5A + 4B = 400. This objective function line is shown in Figure 5.2. Any combination of products on this line will produce a total contribution of £400. The objective function of any other total contribution would be a line parallel to the one drawn for the equation 5A + 4B = 400. The maximum value of the objective function is determined by finding that line which lies parallel to the objective function line and at the furthest point from the origin, but within the

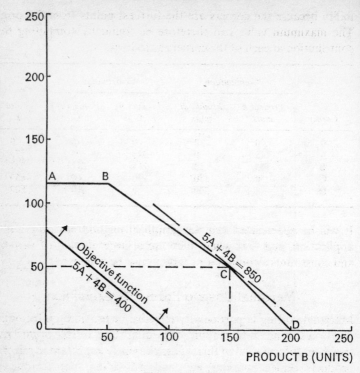

Figure 5.2.

feasible area. This line is $5A + 4B = 850$, which lies within the area of feasibility at corner C in Figure 5.2. The combination which maximizes the total contribution is 50 units of Product A, giving a contribution of £250, and 150 units of Product B, giving a contribution of £600. This combination meets the production constraints and fully utilizes productive capacity of both departments in that

$$1.5\,A + B = 1.5\,(50) + 150 = 225$$
$$A + B = \quad 50 \; + 150 = 200$$
$$A = \quad 50 \quad\quad \leqslant 115$$

It will be seen that the maximum value of the objective function lies on corner C of the area of feasibility O A B C D in Figure 5.2 and does not lie on any other part of the area of feasibility. In fact, the maximum value must lie on one of the corners of the area of feasibility because the corners are the furthest points from the origin. The maximum value can therefore be found by computing total contribution at each of the corners as follows:

Corner	Combination Product A units	Combination Product B units	Contribution Product A £	Contribution Product B £	Total £
0	0	0	0	0	0
A	115	0	575	0	575
B	115	53	275	212	787
C	50	150	250	600	850
D	0	200	0	800	800

It will be appreciated that the graphical method has only limited application, and that when there are a large number of variables and constraints a computer program must be employed.

Marginal Costing Form of Presentation

Marginal costing is particularly effective in providing information and presenting information regarding *cost-volume-profit relationships*. Information of this type is extremely important in selecting products, outlets, markets, etc., and in deciding upon relative emphasis where two or more products are manufactured. In the United States the marginal costing form of presentation is called *direct costing*.

It has been shown how the contribution per unit each product makes towards fixed or period costs and profit can be calculated. Similarly, a statement can be prepared to show the total contribution each product class has made towards the recovery of period costs. The important point is to determine how much contribution exists, and whether the total contribution from all product classes is sufficient to cover period costs, and leave an adequate profit. In some cases certain period costs, such as annual tooling and product advertising, are so directly involved with each product line that they presumably would be avoided if the product line were dropped. These fixed costs are called *separable* period costs. Other period costs, such as the managing director's salary and the insurance of his Bentley, are *common* period costs and cannot be directly associated with any one product line. A better measure of the profit contribution from each product group may be the profit or loss after deducting any *separable* period costs from the total product contribution.

These two points of view, i.e. total product contribution before and after deducting separable period costs, can be reconciled. Total product contribution *before* charging separable period costs is appropriate where the company is already committed to the retention of a product class, or is committed to such an extent that the period costs directly related to this course of action cannot be saved by dropping the product. When the company is not committed to this course of action, but is merely considering the impact of various alternatives, total product contribution *after* charging separable period costs is more appropriate.

The type of statement suggested above for the A B C Company is shown in Table 5.3. It will be seen that Products A and B make the same total contribution to period costs and profit, but after deducting separable period costs Product B gives the highest product profit. Product B's contribution as a percentage of sales value (i.e. its profit–volume ratio) is 35 per cent while Product A's is 34 per cent, but the contribution per unit is higher from Product A than from Product B. Product C would appear to be unprofitable. Although it produces a total contribution of £2,125, Product C makes a loss of £375 after charging separable period costs. However, it will be noted that the separable period selling and distribution costs for Product C are far higher than for Products A and B. Product advertising and the company's marketing effort have been concentrated on Product C, and sales of this product are expected to increase to 1,000 units per year. Will Product C then be profitable? This question is answered by the following calculation:

Effect of Advertising on Product C

	£
Sales 1,000 units at £25	25,000
Less Variable Costs at £20.75	20,750
Total Product Contribution	4,250
Less Separable Period Costs	2,500
Product Profit after Separable Period Costs	£1,750

Table 5.3

ABC CO.

Product Profitability 1989

	Product A		Product B		Product C		Total
	Per unit	Total	Per unit	Total	Per unit	Total	
Sales: Units		1,000		2,000		500	
	£	£	£	£	£	£	£
Sales: Value	25	25,000	12	24,000	25	12,500	61,500
Cost of Sales:							
Direct Labour	4	4,000	2	4,000	8	4,000	12,000
Direct Material	5	5,000	4	8,000	5	2,500	15,500
Direct Expense	1	1,000	—	—	2	1,000	2,000
PRIME COST	10	10,000	6	12,000	15.	7,500	29,500
Variable Overhead:							
Production	5	5,000	1.5	3,000	5	2,500	10,500
Selling and Distribution	1.5	1,500	0.25	500	0.75	375	2,375
VARIABLE COST	16.5	16,500	7.75	15,500	20.75	10,375	42,375
TOTAL CONTRIBUTION	8.5	8,500	4.25	8,500	4.25	2,125	19,125
(% of Sales Value)		(34%)		(35%)		(17%)	
Separable Period Costs:							
Production		3,000		2,500		1,000	6,500
Selling and Distribution		550		700		1,250	2,500
Administration		450		300		250	1,000
		4,000		3,500		2,500	10,000
Profit (or Loss) after Direct Product Costs		4,500		5,000		(375)	9,125
Less Common Period Costs:							
Production							3,000
Selling and Distribution							1,000
Administration							1,000
							5,000
NET PROFIT BEFORE TAX							£4,125

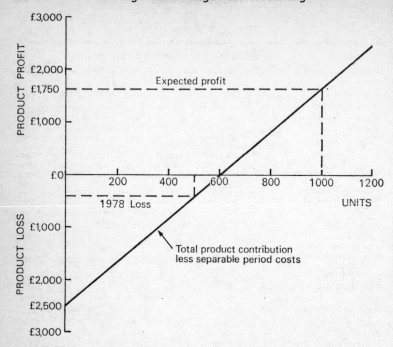

Figure 5.3. *ABC Co. Product profit–volume chart – Product C*

Product C will make a contribution to common period costs next year if the product advertising causes the expected increase in sales. The expected effect of the advertising on the product profit after charging separable period costs is shown graphically in Figure 5.3. It will be noted that Product C will start making a profit after charging direct product costs and, therefore, contributing to the recovery of common fixed costs when sales exceed 590 units. Similar charts could be prepared for Products A and B. The limitations of this type of chart are similar to those of the profit–volume chart for a whole company.

Statements can also be prepared showing total contribution of different markets, sales areas, outlets, classes of customer, and other sub-divisions of overall company operations. The ABC Co. sells in three sales areas and the profitability of each area is shown in Table 5.4. It will be noted that the classification of separable period costs is different in this table from that in Table 5.3. The separable period costs in this instance are those which would be saved if a sales area

Table 5.4

ABC COMPANY

Profitability of Sales Areas 1989

Sales:		Area X Units	Area X £	Area Y Units	Area Y £	Area Z Units	Area Z £	Total Units	Total £
Product A		500	12,500	300	7,500	200	5,000	1,000	25,000
Product B		500	6,000	1,000	12,000	500	6,000	2,000	24,000
Product C		50	1,250	200	5,000	250	6,250	500	12,500
			£19,750		£24,500		£17,250		£61,500
Contribution	per unit								
Product A	£8.5		4,250		2,550		1,700		8,500
Product B	£4.25		2,125		4,250		2,125		8,500
Product C	£4.25		213		850		1,062		2,125
			£6,588		£7,650		£4,887		£19,125
(% of Sales Value)									
Separable Period Costs			(33%)		(31%)		(28%)		
Selling and Distribution Cost			2,000		500		500		3,000
Administration			100		150		250		500
			£2,100		£650		750		£3,500
Profit (or Loss) after Direct Area Costs			£4,488		£7,000		£4,137		£15,625

Less Common Period Costs:

	£
Production	9,500
Selling and Distribution	500
Administration	1,500
	11,500

NET PROFIT BEFORE TAX	£4,125

was dropped, not a product group. Sales Area Y produces the highest contribution before and after charging separable period costs. Sales Area X has the most favourable sales mix in that total contribution is 33 per cent of sales value. It will be seen that the higher advertising on Product C has been concentrated in Sales Area X. If the additional 500 units of Product C are expected to be sold in Sales Area X, the effect on the sales area can be calculated as follows:

Effect of Advertising on Sales Area X

	£
1989 Profit after Direct Area Costs	4,488
Additional Contribution from Product C	
500 units at £4.25	2,125
Expected Profit after Direct Area Costs	£6,613

In this chapter the marginal costing form of presentation has been introduced, and more detailed examples of its application will be presented in the chapters 'Accounting Information for Marketing Management' (Chapter 11) and 'Accounting Information for Selling Price Decisions' (Chapter 12).

Absorption Costing v. Marginal Costing

In Chapter 3 it was emphasized that absorption costing is not suitable to employ when calculating the effects of changes in volume and type of output, and that marginal costing should be used for this type of calculation. The following simple illustration will demonstrate the dangers of absorption costing and the advantages of marginal costing.

The trading results of X Y Z Manufacturers Ltd for the year 1989 were as follows:

	£	£
Direct Materials		240,000
Direct Wages:		
Department A	60,000	
Department B	94,500	154,500
Variable Overheads:		
Department A	75,000	
Department B	189,000	264,000
Fixed Overheads	———	231,750
Total Costs		890,250
Trading Profit		39,750
Sales		£930,000

The company manufactures three products, and details of costs, sales, etc. for 1989 were as follows:

	Product X	Product Y	Product Z
Sales (units)	80,000	100,000	12,000
	£	£	£
Selling Price per unit	3.750	3.600	22.500
Costs per unit:			
Direct Materials	.750	1.500	2.500
Direct Wages			
Department A	.300	.300	.500
Department B	.450	.225	3.000

The company's practice is to absorb departmental variable costs as a percentage on direct departmental wages, and the fixed expenses of the business on the basis of total direct wages.

The management accountant presents the following information on product profitability for 1989:

	Product X £	Product Y £	Product Z £
Direct Material	.750	1.500	2.500
Direct Wages:			
Department A	.300	.300	.500
Department B	.450	.225	3.000
PRIME COST	1.500	2.025	6.000
Variable Overheads:			
Department A	.375	.3750	.625
Department B	.900	.4500	6.000
Fixed Overheads *	1.125	.7875	5.250
TOTAL COST	3.900	3.6375	17.875
SELLING PRICE	3.750	3.6000	22.500
PROFIT/(LOSS) PER UNIT	£(0.150)	£(0.0375)	£4.625
Units sold	80,000	100,000	12,000
PRODUCT PROFIT/(LOSS)	£(12,000)	£(3,750)	£55,000
TRADING PROFIT FOR YEAR		£39,750	

* 150% of Direct Wages

The results for the year are regarded as unsatisfactory, and as a result of a conference between the marketing director and the managing director, with the management accountant's absorption costing information available to them, the following is proposed:

1. As Product X is unprofitable, its sales should be allowed to fall away. It is anticipated that 60,000 units will be sold in the year 1990.

2. Product Y can be sold by additional sales effort and sales can increase by 50 per cent at the same selling price as in the previous year.

3. By reducing the price of Product Z, on which high profits are made, to £18 per unit, sales should be increased by 50 per cent. It is anticipated that these proposals will lead to improved results in 1990. The management accountant is asked to prepare a forecast of the probable results for 1990, assuming no variance in manufacturing efficiency, and no change in the total fixed expenses of the business.

The management accountant asks his newly-qualified assistant to prepare the forecast. The assistant, being familiar with marginal costing techniques, prepares the following schedule:

Forecast of Probable Results 1990

	Product X £	Product Y £	Product Z £
Direct Material	.750	1.500	2.500
Direct Wages:	.750	.525	3.500
Variable Overheads	1.275	.825	6.625
MARGINAL COST	2.775	2.850	12.625
Selling Price	3.750	3.600	18,000
CONTRIBUTION	£0.975	£0.750	£5.375
Units to be sold	60,000	150,000	18,000
Total Product Contribution	58,500	112,500	96,750

	£
Forecast Total Contribution	267,750
Less Fixed Costs	231,750
Forecast Profit	£36,000

The proposals would result in a fall in profit from £39,750 to £36,000. The assistant cannot understand why this is so; the proposals appeared sound in relation to the management accountant's schedule of product profitability for 1989. He decides to recalculate the 1989 product profits on a marginal costing basis, and produces the following schedule:

Revised Results 1989

Product	Units sold	Selling Price per unit £	Marginal Cost £	Contribution £	Total Contribution £
X	80,000	3.750	2.775	.975	78,000
Y	100,000	3.600	2.850	.750	75,000
Z	12,000	22.500	12.625	9.875	118,500
					271,500
				Less Fixed Costs	231,750
				TRADING PROFIT	£39,750

In his calculations the management accountant had absorbed the fixed costs into products as follows:

Product	Total Contribution £	Fixed Costs £	Trading Profit £
X	78,000	90,000	(12,000)
Y	75,000	78,750	(3,750)
Z	118,500	63,000	55,500
	£271,500	£231,750	£39,750

The assistant management accountant now realizes why the proposals had been made and why they result in a forecast of a lower profit. He decides to send his working papers to the management accountant with the following note:

1. Suggest proposals would result in a fall in profit from £39,750 to £36,000.

2. The following comparison of product contributions to fixed costs can be made:

| | Actual 1989 | | Forecast 1990 | | | |
Product	per unit £	Total £	per unit £	Total £	Change £	
X	.975	78,000	.975	58,000	(−)	19,500
Y	.750	75,000	.750	112,500	(+)	37,500
Z	9.875	118,500	5.375	96,750	(−)	21,750
		£271,500		£267,750	(−)	£3,750

3. Would suggest:

(a) Product X is not unprofitable and makes a valuable contribution towards fixed costs and that sales should not be allowed to fall off.

(b) The proposed increased sales effort on Product Y is quite profitable but could possibly be better directed at Product X, which makes a greater contribution per unit, depending upon the limiting factors.

(c) The reduction in selling price of Product Z is not warranted and the present selling price and volume are more satisfactory.

It should be clear from this illustration that the use of absorption costing for providing information to assist management in decision-making can mislead management and result in poor decisions.

Marginal Costing, Stock Valuation, and External Financial Reporting

Marginal costing may be incorporated into the system of recording and collecting costs or it may be used as an analytical tool for studying and reporting the effects of changes in volume and type of output. Accountants in Britain were slow to develop the use of marginal costing techniques for providing management with information for decision-making and control. One possible reason for this delay has been the objection of professional accountants to the use of marginal costing for the external reporting of historical accounting information to shareholders. When marginal costing is incorporated into the system of historical cost recording, stocks are valued at variable cost and fixed costs are charged in the profit-and-loss account as period costs. Traditionally accountants have prepared accounts on an absorption cost basis and have included a proportion of manufacturing fixed costs in their valuation of opening and closing work-in-progress and finished stocks. Differences in stock valuation will arise under the two systems of costing and, therefore, in period profits. This is best understood by studying a simple example. The XYZ Co. manufactures and markets a standard product and the following budget and standard manufacturing cost data was developed for 1989:

	Total		per unit	
	£	£	£	£
Sales (120,000 units)		120,000		1.00
Production Cost of Sales:				
Variable	78,000		0.65	
Fixed Overhead	24,000	102,000	0.20	0.85
Gross Profit		18,000		0.15
Selling and Administration Cost (fixed)		8,400		
Net Profit before Taxation		£9,600		

It was anticipated that production would be equal to sales, i.e. 120,000 units.

Actual production, sales, and stocks, in units for 1989, were:

	Quarters				
	1	2	3	4	Year
Opening Stock	—	6,000	2,000	7,000	—
Production	34,000	28,000	33,000	27,000	122,000
Sales	28,000	32,000	28,000	32,000	120,000
Closing Stock	6,000	2,000	7,000	2,000	2,000

No price or efficiency variances arose during the year. Table 5.5 shows the profit-and-loss accounts for each quarter and for the year on an *absorption costing basis*. Fixed production overhead is absorbed into the cost of the product for stock valuation purposes at the normal level shown in the budget, i.e. £0.20 per unit. It will be noted

Table 5.5

Absorption Costing Approach

			Quarters		
	1	2	3	4	Total
Sales Units:	28,000	32,000	28,000	32,000	120,000
	£	£	£	£	£
Sales: Value	28,000	32,000	28,000	32,000	120,000
Production Cost of Sales at £0.85 per unit	23,800	27,200	23,800	27,200	102,000
	4,200	4,800	4,200	4,800	18,000
Selling and Administration Cost	2,100	2,100	2,100	2,100	8,400
	2,100	2,700	2,100	2,700	9,600
(Under/Over absorbed fixed production overhead – Volume Variance	800	(400)	600	(600)	400
Net profit before Taxation	£2,900	£2,300	£2,700	£2,100	£10,000

that the difference between the fixed production overhead charged to production and the budgeted fixed production overhead for a quarter (£6,000) is the *overhead volume variance*. For example, in the first quarter 34,000 units were produced, and absorbed £6,800 (34,000 × £0.20) fixed production overhead; the budgeted overhead is £6,000 (30,000 × £0.20), and the *overhead volume variance* is £800 (4,000 × £0.20) favourable.

Table 5.6 shows the profit-and-loss accounts on a *marginal costing basis*. The fixed production overhead is not absorbed into the cost of products for stock valuation purposes, but is treated as a cost of the period and charged against sales. With the marginal costing approach stocks are valued at variable cost and there is no volume variance.

The profits produced by the two methods are reconciled in Table 5.7. The difference in the first quarter of £1,200 is represented by the fixed costs included in the closing stock valuation, and in the subsequent quarters by the change in the fixed costs included in the stock valuation.

When a standard absorption costing system is employed, the under/over absorbed fixed production overhead is represented by the

Table 5.6

Marginal Costing Approach

		1	2	Quarters 3	4	Total
Sales Units:		28,000	32,000	28,000	32,000	120,000
		£	£	£	£	£
Sales: Value		28,000	32,000	28,000	32,000	120,000
Variable Cost of Sales at						
£0.65 per unit		18,200	20,800	18,200	20,800	78,000
Total Contribution		9,800	11,200	9,800	11,200	42,000
	£					
Fixed Costs:						
Production	6,000					
Selling and						
Administration	2,100	8,100	8,100	8,100	8,100	32,400
Net Profit before						
Taxation		£1,700	£3,100	£1,700	£3,100	£9,600

volume variance. Students of cost accounting in the 1930s were not entirely satisfied with the techniques of flexible budgeting and the use of volume variances. Volume variances caused confusion, and, while accountants understood their meaning, they had great difficulty in explaining these variances to management. When there were large fluctuations in the levels of stock, the operating management were often very critical of the accountants because of the distortion in reported profits. In the above example sales increased in the second quarter but profit declined under the absorption costing approach (Table 5.5), and in the third quarter sales declined but profit increased. Sales were the same in the first and third quarters, but the profit varied between the two quarters with the absorption costing approach. With the marginal costing approach (Table 5.6) the profits vary directly with the sales and are in the same in the first and third quarters. This type of criticism was particularly valid in highly seasonal businesses with large variations in stock levels from one period to the next and with a high ratio of fixed costs. Wilmer Wright gives the following example of the experience of one large canning company in the United States:

Table 5.7

Reconciliation of Profits

| | | Quarters | | | |
	1	2	3	4	Total
Absorption Costing Profit	£2,900	£2,300	£2,700	£2,100	£10,000
Less Change in fixed Production Costs included in Stock Valuation:					
Units	+ 6,000	− 4,000	+ 5,000	− 5,000	+ 2,000
at £0.2p per unit	+ £1,200	− £800	+ £1,000	− £1,000	+ £400
Marginal Costing Profit	£1,700	£3,100	£1,700	£3,100	£9,600

It was this company's practice to produce and store cans just prior to the packing season because when the season started it did not have the production capacity to meet demand. Under the absorption costing system, standard costs were set on the average planned level of production for the year. Thus, when production was at capacity for inventory, large volume variance gains resulted and were carried directly to profit and loss. As a consequence, net operating profits could, and sometimes did, exceed net sales. The accountants certainly had trouble explaining that to their directors.[2]

The author has had a slightly different experience with a dairy firm supplying milk and orange drink to holiday resorts along the Lincolnshire coast. Not only were sales seasonal because of the nature of the trade, but in the holiday season they depended upon the state of the weather. Although a flexible budget dealt adequately with the variable elements, the volume variance for the fixed elements could fluctuate violently from quarter to quarter. It was difficult to explain to the line management the exact nature of the volume variance.

Direct costing was developed in the United States during the 1930s to overcome the distortion caused by fluctuations in the level of stocks and to eliminate the problem of the volume variance where there are large seasonal variations in the level of sales. Under direct

2 Wilmer Wright, *Direct Standard Costs for Decision Making and Control*, McGraw-Hill, New York, 1962, p. 5.

costing only the variable components of cost are charged to products for inventory and accounting statement purposes and fixed costs are not included in standard product costs. Marginal costing became the term used in Britain to describe the direct costing approach developed in the United States.

Both in Britain and the United States professional accountants have always taken the position that consistency in the method of stock valuation is one of the most important safeguards against the manipulation of the profit reported to shareholders, and rightly so. Unless the method of stock valuation is generally accepted accounting practice, the auditors must qualify their certification of the accounts if such a method results in a material difference in reported profit. 'In the last resort the auditor must decide whether he is prepared to state that in his opinion the accounts give a true and fair view; if all the necessary information is not given the auditor is required to qualify his report accordingly.' [3]

Consistency in the valuation of stocks is one of the well accepted accounting conventions, and professional accountants in Britain have been reluctant to accept a change in the method of stock valuation from a full (absorption) cost to a marginal cost basis unless there has been a material change in circumstances. Direct costing is not accepted in the United States for either financial or tax purposes. In its Statement of Standard Accounting Practice No. 9, 'Stocks and Work-in-Progress', the British Accounting Standards Committee has stated that cost of conversion for valuing stocks and work-in-progress should include production overheads based on the normal level of activity, taking one year with another. The International Accounting Standards Committee has recommended that the historical cost of manufacturing inventories should be based on absorption costing.

Professional accountants have been quite agreeable to the use of marginal costing for internal management control, provided the published accounts are adjusted to coincide with the previously accepted method of stock valuation. The result has been that while many companies have gone over to marginal costing for internal reporting, they have maintained their absorption costing methods for external reporting.

3 *Report of the Company Law Committee*, Board of Trade, Cmnd. 1749, June 1962, para. 334, p. 131.

Summary

Marginal costing is a more useful decision-making technique than break-even analysis in a multi-product, multi-market business. It relies on the calculation of marginal cost and contribution to determine the effects on costs and profits of changes in the volume and type of output in the short run. Contribution is related to the limiting factor when a company's output is restricted by productive capacity or some other factor. Linear programming provides an efficient mathematical search procedure for selecting the optimum plan when there are a number of limiting factors and interacting variables. Marginal costing may also be used as a method of presenting information to management regarding cost–volume–profit relationships in a multi-product business. When it is incorporated into the system of recording and collecting costs this gives rise to stock valuation problems. The professional accounting bodies have recommended that stocks and work-in-progress should be valued on an absorption costing basis. However, marginal costing can always be employed as an analytical tool.

Selected Readings

1. L. R. Amey and D. A. Egginton, *Management Accounting: A Conceptual Framework*, Longman, London, 1973.

2. Robert N. Anthony and James S. Reece, *Management Accounting: Text and Cases*, Irwin, Homewood, Illinois, 1983.

3. John Arnold and Tony Hope, *Accounting for Management Decisions*, Prentice-Hall International, London, 1983.

4. Colin Drury, *Management and Cost Accounting*, Van Nostrand Reinhold (UK), Reading, 1985.

5. Charles T. Horngren and George Foster, *Cost Accounting: A Managerial Emphasis*, Prentice-Hall, Englewood Cliffs, N.J., 1987.

6. C. P. Rickwood and A. G. Piper, *Marginal Costing*, Chartered Institute of Management Accountants, London, 1980.

7. R. Kaplan, *Advanced Management Accounting*, Prentice-Hall, Englewood Cliffs, N.J., 1982.

8. Gordon Shillinglaw, *Managerial Cost Accounting*, Irwin, Homewood, Illinois, 1982.

9. D. Solomons (ed.), *Studies in Cost Analysis*, Sweet and Maxwell, London, 1968.

10. Wilmer Wright, *Direct Standard Costs for Decision Making and Control*, McGraw-Hill, New York, 1962.

6

Profitability – Measurement and Analysis

Among the characteristics of a successful business are expanding sales, a respected household name, accepted products, the Queen's Award for Exporting and/or Technical Innovation, a contented labour force, and many others. All of these are unquestionably desirable achievements and objectives, yet separately or together they are not enough to guarantee the continued existence and growth of a business.

The ultimate measure of the success of any business is whether or not it continues to exist and expand. To achieve this, whatever else a business does or aims to do, it must generate profits and generate them in perpetuity. Of the hundred largest companies in the *Management Today* list of top British companies in 1966, only forty-one remained in that category in 1987. Managerial economists have shown that there is a significant relationship between the rate of profit and the rate of growth. That profits are necessary for growth and growth produces profit is an accepted maxim of modern business. Equally, growth without profits may lead to a company being taken over or going into liquidation. The concept of 'profit maximization' has been extensively qualified by economic theorists to refer to the long run rather than the short run; to refer to the management's rather than to the shareholder's income; and to include non-financial income. They have made allowance for special considerations such as restraining competition, maintaining managerial control, and holding off wage demands. While the concept may have become 'so general and hazy that it seems to encompass most of man's aims in life',[1] and boards of directors may try to 'satisfice' rather than maximize, the fact remains that profitability is the primary aim

1 Joel Dean, *Managerial Economics*, Prentice-Hall, Englewood Cliffs, N.J., 1951; London, 1962, p. 28.

and the best measure of effectiveness and efficiency in competitive business.

In his book *The Practice of Management*, Peter Drucker has pointed out that profit serves three purposes:[2]

1. It measures the net effectiveness and soundness of a business's effort. As will be explained in this chapter, it is the key determinant of growth in earnings per share, in dividends per share, and in share price.

2. It is the premium that covers the costs of staying in business – replacement, obsolescence, market and technical risk and uncertainty. Seen from this point of view, it may be argued that there is no such thing as profit; there are only the costs of being and staying in business. These are the costs of survival. The management of a business has to provide adequately for these costs by generating sufficient profit.

3. It ensures the supply of future capital for innovation and expansion, either directly, by providing the means of self-financing out of retained profits, or indirectly, through providing sufficient inducement for new outside capital in the form which will optimize the company's capital structure and optimize its cost of capital.

Measurement of Profitability

While profitability is the primary aim and the best measure of efficiency in competitive business, a distinction should be made between profits and profitability. Profits as such are of limited value unless related to the equity (ordinary) shareholders' investment in the business. The relationship between the equity shareholders' investment in a company and the profit attributable to the equity shareholders is the *rate of return on equity shareholders' investment*. The ability to earn a satisfactory rate of return on equity shareholders' investment is the most important characteristic of the successful business. Increased sales volume, rising absolute profits, and a satisfactory profit/sales ratio are at best short-term indications of successful growth, and, without additional information, must be viewed as such.

In the long run, increased sales volume may prove a deceptive

2 Peter Drucker, *The Practice of Management*, Mercury Books, London, 1961, pp. 65–9.

guidepost if there is not a proper return on the capital necessary to support these sales. Real growth comes from the ability of management successfully to employ additional capital at a satisfactory rate of return. This is the final criterion of the soundness and strength of a company's growth, for in a competitive economy capital gravitates towards the more profitable enterprises. The company that is merely expanding sales at a declining rate of return on equity shareholders' investment will eventually be unable to attract expansion capital. Thus any measurement of a company's effectiveness must be based on the successful employment of capital. It is vital that the long-run return on equity shareholders' investment should be sufficient to:

1. Give a fair return to the shareholders in the form of dividends and appreciation in share price in relation to the risk and uncertainty attached to their investments;
2. Provide for the normal expansion of the business;
3. Provide, in times of inflation, adequate reserves to maintain the real capital of the business intact;
4. Attract new external capital when required;
5. Satisfy creditors and employees of the likelihood of the continued existence and/or growth of the business;
6. From a management's point of view, deter potential predators from bidding for the company.

As will be seen later in this chapter, the importance of (3) above will depend on whether historical cost accounting or current cost accounting is employed.

Analysis of Profitability

The rate of return on equity shareholders' investment provides a starting point from which to examine influences, make comparisons, and discern trends in the company's performance. It gives rise to a pyramid of subsidiary control ratios based on the factors affecting the return on equity shareholders' investment. These ratios enable a similar process of examination of more detailed aspects of a company's operations to take place.

Rate of return on equity shareholders' investment may be defined as:

$$\frac{\text{Profit after Taxation and Interest and after deduction of Profit attributable to Minority and Preference Shareholders}}{\text{Equity Shareholders' Investment}}$$

or

$$\frac{\text{Profit attributable to Equity Shareholders}}{\text{Equity Shareholders' Investment}}$$

Return on equity shareholders' investment, assuming no minority shareholders and/or preference shareholders, is determined by:

1. The rate of return on net assets employed, i.e. the ratio of profit before interest and tax to net assets employed (total assets less current liabilities);
2. The debt capital/equity capital ratio (i.e. the gearing[3]) of the company; and
3. The ratio of tax to profit before tax but after interest payable. Return on net assets employed may be further analysed into return on operating or trading assets, i.e. net assets employed in the business and return on outside investments.

The analysis of return on equity shareholders' investment for a company with no minority or preference shareholders is illustrated in Tables 6.1 and 6.2. Alpha Ltd's financial statements for the year ending 31 December 1989 are shown in Table 6.1 and the analysis of the 15 per cent return on equity shareholders' investment (ratio 7) in Table 6.2.

It will be noted that:

1. The 40 per cent debt capital to equity capital ratio (the gearing) is reflected in the 'levering up' of the 17.1 per cent return on net assets employed (ratio 3) to give a 25 per cent return on equity shareholders' investment before tax (ratio 5). The net assets

3 The term 'gearing' is used to define the proportions of debt capital to equity capital in the balance sheet of a company. High gearing indicates a high ratio of debt capital to equity capital, and low gearing the opposite. Interest payments on debt capital are chargeable against profits for tax purposes, i.e. debt interest payments reduce the amount of corporation tax payable. Normally loan capital is cheaper than share capital, and it is therefore to the shareholders' benefit if a company is partially financed with fixed interest capital. For example, if a company raises debt capital at 8 per cent per annum interest *after* corporation tax, and invests in a project which produces 20 per cent per annum return after corporation tax, the 12 per cent residual accrues to the shareholders. Financing decisions are examined more fully in Chapter 7 and investment decisions in Chapter 8.

Table 6.1

ALPHA LTD

Profit-and-loss Account Year Ending 31 December 1989	£	Balance Sheet as at 31 December 1989	£	£
		Net Operating Assets		
		Fixed Assets	100,000	
		Current Assets	50,000	
			150,000	
Operating Profit	27,000	*Less* Current Liabilities	20,000	130,000
Investment Income	2,000	Outside Investment		20,000
Profit before Interest payable and Taxation	29,000	*Net Assets Employed*		150,000
Interest payable	4,000	Debt Capital		40,000
Profit before Taxation	25,000	Corporation Tax payable		10,000
Corporation Tax	10,000	*Equity Shareholders' Investment*		
		Ordinary Share Capital	75,000	
Net Profit attributable to Equity Shareholders	£15,000	Capital and Revenue Reserves	25,000	£150,000
		Capital Employed		

employed have been partially financed by loan capital at 10 per cent per annum (ratio 4), the remaining 7.1 per cent return on the assets financed by this loan capital being for the benefit of the equity shareholders.

2. The corporation tax (ratio 6) is 40 per cent of ratio 5 to give a return on equity shareholders' investment (ratio 7) of 15 per cent, i.e. 60 per cent of 25 per cent.

A further illustration is based on the financial statements of the parent company of a large group of companies with minority and preference shareholders. Large Group Ltd's summarized financial statements for the year ending 31 December 1989 are shown in Table 6.3 and the analysis of the 9.2 per cent return on equity shareholders' investment (ratio 10) in Table 6.4.

As in the simplified example of Alpha Ltd, the Large Group Ltd analysis shows:

Table 6.2

ALPHA LTD

Analysis of Return on Equity Shareholders' Investment for year
ending 31 December 1989

---

1. *Return on Net Operating Assets*

$$\frac{\text{Operating Profit}}{\text{Net Operating Assets}} = \frac{£27,000}{£130,000} \times 100 = 20.8\%$$

2. *Return on Outside Investments*

$$\frac{\text{Investment Income}}{\text{Outside Investments}} = \frac{£2,000}{£20,000} \times 100 = 10.0\%$$

3. *Return on Net Assets Employed*

$$\frac{\text{Profit before Interest payable and Taxation}}{\text{Net Assets Employed}} = \frac{£29,000}{£150,000} \times 100 = 17.1\%$$

4. $$\frac{\text{Interest on Loan Capital}}{\text{Loan Capital}} = \frac{£4,000}{£40,000} \times 100 = 10.0\%$$

5. *Return on Equity Shareholders' Investment before Taxation*

$$\frac{\text{Net Profit before Taxation}}{\text{Equity Shareholders' Investment}} = \frac{£25,000}{£100,000} \times 100 = 25.0\%$$

6. $$\frac{\text{Corporation Tax}}{\text{Net Profit before Taxation}} = \frac{£10,000}{£25,000} \times 100 = 40.0\%$$

7. *Return on Equity Shareholders' Investment*

$$\frac{\text{Net Profit attributable to Equity Shareholders}}{\text{Equity Shareholders' Investment}} = \frac{£15,000}{£100,000} \times 100 = 15.0\%$$

---

1. The 'levering up' of return on net assets employed (9.5 per cent) by the 60 per cent debt capital to share capital gearing to give a return on total shareholders' investment of 13.4 per cent (ratio 5).
2. The taxation on profits (ratio 6) is 47.6 per cent of ratio 5 to give a 7.0 per cent return on total shareholders' funds (ratio 7). Table 6.4 also shows an analysis of return on total shareholders' funds (ratio 7) between minority shareholders (ratio 8), preference shareholders (ratio 9), and equity shareholders (ratio 10).

The relationship between the ratios presented in Table 6.4 is shown in Figure 6.1. An analysis of return on net operating assets is presented in Figures 6.2 and 6.3 later in this chapter.

Table 6.3

LARGE GROUP LTD

Summarized Profit-and-loss Account Year Ending 31 December 1989		Summarized Balance Sheet as at 31 December 1989		
	£ million		£ million	£ million
		Net Operating Assets		
		Fixed Assets	243.9	
Operating Profit	31.7	Net Current Assets	89.9	333.8
Investment Income	1.8	Investments		18.9
Profit before Interest payable and Taxation	33.5	*Net Assets Employed*		£352.7
Interest on Loan Capital	7.0	Loan Capital		118.4
Profit before Taxation	26.5			
Taxation	12.6	Taxation payable		12.7
		Tax Equalization and		
Net Profit for year	£13.9	Investment Grants		23.1
Appropriation of Profit:				
Attributable to Minority		Minority Shareholders' Interests		39.2
Shareholders	3.7	Preference Capital		7.4
Preference Dividend	0.4	*Equity Shareholders' Investment*		
Attributable to Equity		Ordinary Share Capital	100.0	
Shareholders	9.8	Capital and Revenue Reserves	51.9	151.9
	£13.9			£352.7

In manufacturing and trading organizations most managers, particularly those employed in subsidiary companies, are concerned with managing operating assets and liabilities to generate operating profits. They contribute to the company's return on net operating assets. In groups of companies, decisions on medium- and long-term financing are normally taken at head office level, not by individual subsidiaries; it is also likely that a tax specialist will be employed at the head office to minimize legally the group's liability; and many decisions relating to outside investments will not be taken by operating managers employed by subsidiaries. *However, if a manufacturing or trading organization does not generate a satisfactory return on its net operating assets it is unlikely that it will generate an adequate return on equity shareholders' investment.* Before examining the pyramid of ratios that can be derived from an analysis of return on net

Table 6.4

LARGE GROUP LTD

Analysis of Return on Equity Shareholders' Investment for year
ending 31 December 1989

1. *Return on Net Operating Assets*

$$\frac{\text{Operating Profit}}{\text{Net Operating Assets}} = \frac{£31.7}{£333.8} \times 100 = \underline{9.5\%}$$

2. *Return on Outside Investments*

$$\frac{\text{Investment Income}}{\text{Outside Investments}} = \frac{£1.8}{£18.9} \times 100 = \underline{9.5\%}$$

3. *Return on Net Assets Employed*

$$\frac{\text{Profit before Interest payable and Taxation}}{\text{Net Assets Employed}} = \frac{£33.5}{£352.7} \times 100 = \underline{9.5\%}$$

4. $$\frac{\text{Interest on Loan Capital}}{\text{Loan Capital}} = \frac{£7.0}{£118.4} \times 100 = \underline{5.9\%}$$

5. *Return on Total Shareholders' Investment before Taxation*

$$\frac{\text{Profit before Taxation}}{\text{Total Shareholders' Investment}} = \frac{£26.5}{£198.5} \times 100 = \underline{13.4\%}$$

6. $$\frac{\text{Taxation}}{\text{Profit before Taxation}} = \frac{£12.6}{£26.5} \times 100 = \underline{47.6\%}$$

7. *Return on Total Shareholder's Investment*

$$\frac{\text{Profit after Taxation}}{\text{Total Shareholders' Investment}} = \frac{£13.9}{£198.5} \times 100 = \underline{7.0\%}$$

Appropriation of Return on Total Shareholders' Investment

8. *Return on Minority Shareholders' Investment*

$$\frac{\text{Profit attributable to Minority Shareholders}}{\text{Minority Shareholders' Investment}} = \frac{£3.7}{£39.2} \times 100 = \underline{9.4\%}$$

9. *Return on Preference Shareholders' Investment*

$$\frac{\text{Preference Dividend}}{\text{Preference Capital}} = \frac{£0.4}{£7.4} \times 100 = \underline{5.4\%}$$

10. *Return on Equity Shareholders' Investment*

$$\frac{\text{Profit attributable to Equity Shareholders}}{\text{Equity Shareholders' Investment}} = \frac{£9.8}{£151.9} \times 100 = \underline{6.45\%}$$

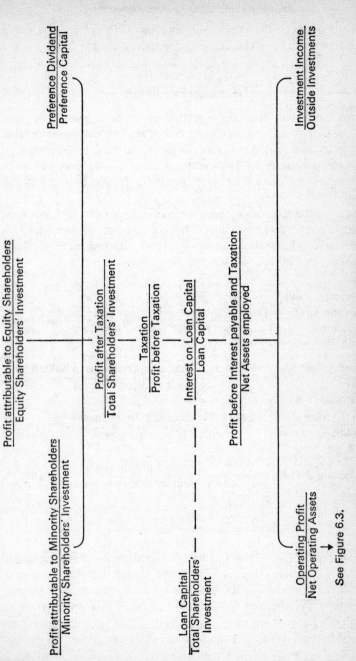

Figure 6.1. *Analysis of return on equity shareholders' investment*

operating assets, the relationship between earnings per share and return on equity shareholders' investment is considered.

Earnings Per Share

Many companies establish objectives in terms of growth in earnings per share; shareholders and financial analysts place considerable emphasis on reported earnings per share and anticipated growth in earnings per share; the financial press calculate and report daily on companies' P.E. ratios, i.e. price per share divided by earnings per share.

What is the relationship between earnings per share and return on equity shareholders' investment? Return on equity shareholders' investment can be analysed to show that it is determined by earnings per share and by equity assets per share. Thus:

$$\text{Return on Equity Shareholders' Investment (R.O.E.)} = \frac{\text{Profit attributable to Equity Shareholders}}{\text{Equity Shareholders' Investment}} \times 100$$

$$\text{Earnings per Share (E.P.S.)} = \frac{\text{Profit attributable to Equity Shareholders}}{\text{Number of Equity Shares}}$$

$$\text{Equity Assets per Share (E.A.S.)} = \frac{\text{Equity Shareholders' Investment}}{\text{Number of Equity Shares}}$$

$$\text{Therefore R.O.E.} = \frac{\text{E.P.S.} \times \text{Number of Equity Shares}}{\text{E.A.S.} \times \text{Number of Equity Shares}} \times 100$$

$$= \frac{\text{E.P.S.}}{\text{E.A.S.}} \times 100$$

For example, if Alpha Ltd has an issued equity share capital of 75,000 £1 ordinary shares, and Large Group Ltd has an issued equity share capital of £100 million £1 ordinary shares, their returns on equity shareholders' investment can be further analysed as in Table 6.5. Because return on equity shareholders' investment is determined by both earnings per share and equity assets per share, it is

Table 6.5

	Alpha Ltd	*Large Group Ltd*
Profit attributable to Equity Shareholders	£15,000	£9.8 million
Equity Shareholders' Investment	£100,000	£151.9 million
Number of Ordinary Shares	75,000	100 million
Earnings per Share	20 pence	9.8 pence
Equity Assets per Share	133.3 pence	151.9 pence
Return on Equity Shareholders' Investment	$\dfrac{20p}{133.3p} \times 100 = 15\%$	$\dfrac{9.8p}{151.9p} \times 100 = 6.45\%$
	per Table 6.2	per Table 6.4

considered to be a relatively more important measure of profitability than earnings per share.

Analysing Return on Net Operating Profits

The rate of return on net operating assets, as well as being the key determinant of return on equity shareholders' investment, provides a starting-point from which to examine influences, make comparisons, and discern trends in a company's operating performance. It gives rise to a pyramid of subsidiary control ratios based on the factors affecting return on net operating assets. These ratios permit a similar process of examination of more detailed aspects of a company's operations.

Rate of return on net operating assets is the percentage operating profit to net operating assets, and can be divided into:

1. *Percentage operating profit to sales*: and

2. *Sales to net operating assets*, i.e. the rate of asset turnover.

Thus:

$$\frac{\text{Operating Profit}}{\text{Net Operating Assets}} = \frac{\text{Operating Profit}}{\text{Sales}} \times \frac{\text{Sales}}{\text{Net Operating Assets}}$$

The essential idea of this division is that low return on net operating assets is due to both/either falling profit margins and/or a low rate of asset turnover. If profit margins in relation to sales income are under pressure because of stronger domestic and international competition, how can return on net operating assets be maintained? Companies have to make more effective use of their assets, both physical and human. They must increase their *productivity*. Rate of asset turnover is one measure of the use of physical assets. However, while the rate of asset turnover is the traditional measure of the utilization of assets, a company's productivity is best measured in terms of *value added*, i.e. sales minus cost of bought-in materials and services, the company's net output. Value added is the wealth the company has been able to create by its own and by its employees' efforts. It is out of the 'value added cake' that a company rewards its various stakeholders – shareholders, directors, managers, employees, Inland Revenue, etc. Value added ratios, such as value added per £ of fixed assets, and value added per employee, can be built into the pyramid of control ratios as determinants of return on net operating assets.

To answer the question, 'Why have the net operating assets in the business not produced the desired level of sales?' or 'Why has the rate of asset turnover declined?', it is necessary to calculate a third tier of ratios. This is attained by splitting up the net operating assets:

$$\frac{\text{Sales}}{\text{Fixed Asssets}} \quad \text{and} \quad \frac{\text{Sales}}{\text{Net Working Capital}}$$

A company may not have made effective use of the fixed assets employed in the business and/or it may have excessive working capital. The fixed assets can be analysed into ratios for different classes of fixed assets together with supplementary value added ratios, such as value added per £ of plant. The net working capital ratio can be further analysed into ratios for stocks, work-in-progress, debtors, trade creditors, etc.

Similarly, to answer the question, 'Why has the operating profit margin on sales declined?', the ratio of operating profit to sales can be analysed into a third tier of cost ratios. Operating profit equals sales minus costs, and costs may be analysed as follows:

$$\frac{\text{Production Cost}}{\text{Sales}} \quad \frac{\text{Selling Cost}}{\text{Sales}} \quad \text{etc.}$$

The production cost ratio can be analysed into ratios for the various components of production cost, that is, materials, wages and overheads. Detailed ratios, including physical and value added ratios, appropriate to the particular industry, can be developed at the lower levels of the pyramid. If profit margins are under pressure from domestic and international competition, percentage profit to sales will be maintained only if management is cost-conscious, exercises cost control, and effects cost reductions.

The relationship of factors affecting return on net operating assets is illustrated in Figure 6.2, and the pyramid of ratios derived from this relationship is shown in Figure 6.3.

Interpretation of Ratios

When interpreting a pyramid of operating ratios, it should be appreciated that:

1.   Individual ratios should not be looked at in isolation; and
2.   The two sides of the pyramid are not independent of each other.

To interpret the ratios it is necessary to work systematically down each side of the pyramid to reveal the cause(s) of unsatisfactory ratios in the higher part of the pyramid. The two sides of the pyramid are interrelated. For example, an increase in the sales of a company at normal prices, without any increase in productive capacity, would not only increase the rate of asset turnover, but also the percentage of operating profit to sales. A company has fixed, semi-variable and variable costs, and an increase in sales would not result in a proportionate increase in costs. A knitwear company undertaking long production runs for Marks & Spencer Ltd could have a lower operating profit/sales ratio than another producing quality knitwear for Bond Street shops; but the rate of asset turnover of the Marks & Spencer supplier may be considerably higher than that of the company supplying Bond Street shops because it is making more effective use of its assets.

Two companies may have the same percentage of operating profit to sales but have different returns on net operating assets. Company A may operate an old plant which it is fully utilizing and, therefore, be achieving a high rate of asset turnover. Company B may have a modern, efficient plant which has a lower variable cost per unit, but

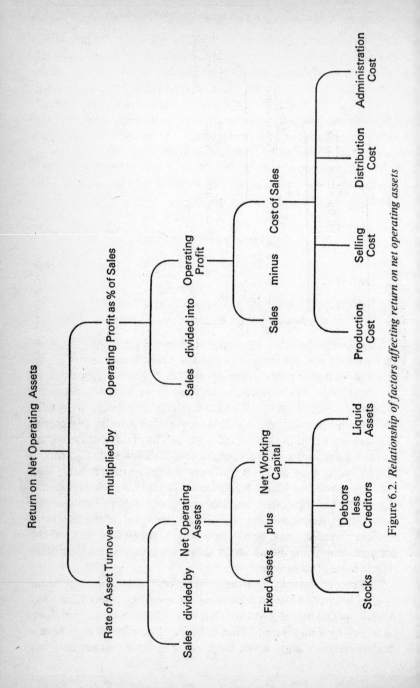

Figure 6.2. *Relationship of factors affecting return on net operating assets*

because it is under-utilizing its capacity, it has a low rate of asset turnover. Its average unit cost is the same as that of Company A because it is working below full capacity. If Company B increased its percentage capacity utilization, both its operating profit to sales ratio and the rate of return on net operating assets would improve.

The point is, one cannot look at one side of the pyramid in isolation from the other. For example, a company with obsolete plant may have a rate of asset turnover which is the median in its industry, but because the plant is obsolete it may have a very low ratio of operating profit to sales and return on net operating assets. Its operating profit to sales ratio may be lower because it has very high production costs. Material costs may be well above average because wastage is high, but the major cause of the high production costs may be the cost of direct labour. Because the plant is obsolete, it may employ more direct employees, have a lower value added per employee, and high rate of labour turnover. Further analysis of the rate of asset turnover may reveal that while the rate of asset turnover is high, the company has a low rate of work-in-progress turnover and a high rate of finished stock turnover. Because the plant is obsolete the work-in-progress cycle is longer than that of its competitors (hence the higher production costs), and its sales are limited by its ability to produce. In analysing this company's case, in addition to working systematically down each side of the pyramid, the two sides of the pyramid must be closely interrelated.

Here is an example of using a pyramid to analyse the performance of the Lincoln Division of the X Y Z Engineering Co. Trade creditors are paid centrally and the division's performance is measured by return on operating assets. The ratios for the Lincoln Division for 1988 and 1989 appear in Table 6.6 and are shown in pyramid form in Figure 6.4. You may wish to make your own interpretation before reading on. It will be noted that the division's return on operating assets (ratio 1) fell from 18.4 per cent in 1988 to 10.6 per cent in 1989. Why did this happen? Primarily because the company's operating profit to sales fell from 18.2 per cent in 1988 to 10.9 per cent in 1989. This reflected a significant increase in production costs (ratio 4) and distribution and marketing expenses (ratio 5). The increase in production costs arose primarily from an increase in cost of materials (ratio 7). There was also a fall in the company's rate of asset turnover (ratio 3) which reflected a significant fall in the turnover

Table 6.6

XYZ ENGINEERING LTD, LINCOLN DIVISION
Comparison of 1988 with 1989

Ratio	1988	1989
1. Operating Profit/Operating Assets (%)	18.4	10.6
2. Operating Profit/Sales (%)	18.2	10.9
3. Sales/Operating Assets (times)	1.01	0.97
4. Production Cost of Sales/Sales (%)	68.3	72.7
5. Distribution and Marketing Expenses/Sales (%)	8.9	11
6. Administrative Expenses/Sales (%)	4.6	5.4
7. Cost of Materials/Sales (%)	43.9	48.5
8. Direct Labour Cost/Sales (%)	10.4	9.2
9. Production Overheads/Sales (%)	14	15
10. Sales/Current Assets (times)	3.35	4.01
11. Sales/Fixed Assets (times)	1.45	1.28
12. Material Stocks/Average daily Sales (days*)	21	18
13. Work-in-progress/Average daily Sales (days*)	8	5
14. Finished Stocks/Average daily Sales (days*)	24	21
15. Debtors/Average daily Sales (days*)	56	48

* Days required to turn the asset over once.

on fixed assets (ratio 11). On the other hand, there was considerable improvement in the turnover of current assets (ratio 10) as a result of falls in the level of material stock, work-in-progress, finished goods stocks, and debtors (ratios 12, 13, 14 and 15). Overall the analysis suggests that during 1989 the division faced falling demand and increasing raw material costs which it was unable to pass on in higher prices, but was able to achieve a significant reduction in stock and debtor ratios.

Departure from Historical Accounts

The use of return on equity shareholders' investment and return on net operating assets for the discernment of trends, and for both internal and external comparisons, can be hindered by the effects of accounting conventions used over past years in the preparation of financial accounts. In Chapter 2 it was emphasized that an over-statement of profit in times of rising prices will occur if any input costs of one date are matched with output revenues of a later date. This particularly applies to the depreciation of fixed assets on the

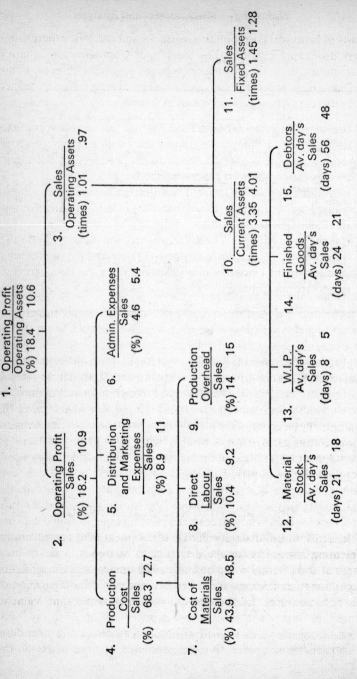

Figure 6.4. *XYZ Engineering Ltd, Lincoln Division — comparison of 1988 with 1989*

1. $\dfrac{\text{Operating Profit}}{\text{Operating Assets}}$ (%) 18.4 10.6

2. $\dfrac{\text{Operating Profit}}{\text{Sales}}$ (%) 18.2 10.9

3. $\dfrac{\text{Sales}}{\text{Operating Assets}}$ (times) 1.01 .97

4. $\dfrac{\text{Production Cost}}{\text{Sales}}$ (%) 68.3 72.7

5. $\dfrac{\text{Distribution and Marketing Expenses}}{\text{Sales}}$ (%) 8.9 11

6. $\dfrac{\text{Admin. Expenses}}{\text{Sales}}$ (%) 4.6 5.4

7. $\dfrac{\text{Cost of Materials}}{\text{Sales}}$ (%) 43.9 48.5

8. $\dfrac{\text{Direct Labour}}{\text{Sales}}$ (%) 10.4 9.2

9. $\dfrac{\text{Production Overhead}}{\text{Sales}}$ (%) 14 15

10. $\dfrac{\text{Sales}}{\text{Current Assets}}$ (times) 3.35 4.01

11. $\dfrac{\text{Sales}}{\text{Fixed Assets}}$ (times) 1.45 1.28

12. $\dfrac{\text{Material Stock}}{\text{Av. day's Sales}}$ (days) 21 18

13. $\dfrac{\text{W.I.P.}}{\text{Av. day's Sales}}$ (days) 8 5

14. $\dfrac{\text{Finished Goods}}{\text{Av. day's Sales}}$ (days) 24 21

15. $\dfrac{\text{Debtors}}{\text{Av. day's Sales}}$ (days) 56 48

basis of historical cost, but also to stocks and work-in-progress in a period of rapid inflation. The Sandilands Committee on Inflation Accounting drew the distinction between *operating gains or losses*, *extraordinary gains or losses*, and *holding gains or losses*. It defined the different type of gains or losses as follows:

> *Operating gains or losses.* The difference between the amounts realized from a company's output (its earnings from goods or services provided) and the 'value to the business' of the inputs used by the company in generating these amounts.
>
> *Extraordinary gains or losses.* The difference between the amounts realized for items which do *not* form part of the company's output and their value to the business at the time of disposal.
>
> *Holding gains or losses.* The difference between the measured value to a company of an asset at any point in time and the original cost incurred by the company in purchasing that asset (less depreciation where appropriate).

In analysing its performance, the management of a manufacturing or trading company will wish to distinguish between the different types of gain, recognizing that its main purpose is to generate operating gains and to make a satisfactory return on net operating assets employed for this purpose. When historical cost accounting is employed, it is not possible to distinguish between operating gains or losses and holding gains or losses; nor is it possible to determine the 'value to the business' of the net operating assets employed to generate the operating gains or losses. Studies by the Bank of England and the Department of Trade and Industry[4] have identified the gap that develops during a period of rapid inflation between historic cost return on assets and real cost return on assets. Table 6.7 illustrates the dramatic fall in the ratio of historic cost return on assets to real return on assets for industrial and commercial companies during the 1970s.

In order to calculate current or replacement cost return on net operating assets, operating assets have to be shown in the balance sheet at their 'value to the business', and operating gains or losses separated from holding gains or losses in the profit-and-loss account. In the latter the charge for 'cost of sales' should reflect the 'value to

4 Published annually in the *Bank of England Quarterly Bulletin*, and each October in *Trade and Industry*.

Table 6.7

Rates of Return on Industrial and Commercial Companies 1965–81

Year	Historic Cost %	Real Cost %	Ratio of Real to Historic Cost
1965	15.8	11.2	0.71
1966	14.2	9.9	0.70
1967	13.6	10.0	0.74
1968	14.8	10.1	0.68
1969	14.9	9.9	0.66
1970	14.4	8.6	0.60
1971	15.2	8.9	0.59
1972	16.8	9.3	0.55
1973	19.7	9.1	0.46
1974	20.0	6.0	0.30
1975	18.4	5.2	0.28
1976	20.4	5.5	0.27
1977	21.1	6.9	0.33
1978	21.1	7.2	0.34
1979	20.4	5.2	0.25
1980	15.6	3.6	0.23
1981	13.2	2.7	0.20

Rates of return are *before* interest and taxation.
(*Source: Bank of England Quarterly Bulletin*, Vol. 22, No. 2, June 1982)

the business' of stock consumed during the period of the account, and the depreciation, the 'value to the business' of the fixed assets consumed during the period. The Sandilands Committee suggested that in the great majority of cases the appropriate basis of estimating the 'value to the business' of a fixed asset will be its written down current replacement cost. S.S.A.P.16 defined value to the business as net current replacement cost or, when appropriate, recoverable amount. The net current replacement cost of an item of plant and machinery is normally calculated by:

(a) determining the asset's gross replacement cost; and
(b) reducing this amount by an accumulated depreciation provision based on:
  (i) the gross current replacement cost;
  (ii) the proportion of the asset's useful economic life which has expired; and
  (iii) the depreciation method adopted for the asset.

Attempts to calculate replacement cost run into the problems of changing technology, and the volume of work involved arising from the quantity and diversity of assets held by companies. In practice, it is not always possible to calculate replacement cost of each fixed asset, and the author prefers the term 'assumed current cost'.

Companies can calculate assumed current cost in a number of ways:

1. By the use of accepted indices such as those calculated by the Economist Intelligence Unit. These are available as a single index for industrial plant or in a number of separate indices for main groups of assets. On the recommendation of the Sandilands Committee, the United Kingdom government's statistical service publishes a wide range of price index numbers in *Price Index Numbers for Current Cost Accounting*.
2. By reference to suppliers' official price lists, catalogues, etc.
3. By formal revaluation undertaken by professional valuers or by competent officials of the company at regular intervals of time.
4. By the substitution of current values as declared for fire insurance purposes.

When technology has changed significantly, a modern asset may be markedly different from the existing asset in respect of initial capital cost, operating cost, life, or output. The simplest, and crudest, way of dealing with this problem is to use a broadly based index (or a general price index if such an index is available) which, because of its wider base, may reflect a gradual change in technology in the industries concerned. Another approach, if the modern asset is in a different index from the existing asset, is to adopt that index as more relevant to the current technology. It may then be necessary to take account of differences in service potential (i.e. capacity) of the modern asset as compared with the existing asset. An example of the type of calculations required to calculate the assumed current cost of the modern equivalent asset is shown in Table 6.8. While none of these methods produces an accurate assessment of the current values of fixed assets, they do go a long

Table 6.8

Calculating the Replacement Cost of Service Potential

Original Cost of each existing asset	£100,000
Price Index for class of assets:	
(a) when existing asset acquired	120
(b) at the accounting date	180
Indexing original cost £100,000 $\times \dfrac{180}{120} =$	£150,000
Current Cost of a modern asset	£220,000
Output of each existing asset	20,000 units p.a.
Output of a modern asset	40,000 units p.a.
Operating Costs per unit and asset lives identical	
Current Cost of existing service potential	
$\qquad$ £220,000 $\times \dfrac{20,000}{40,000} =$	£110,000

Thus the existing asset's current cost would be too high if either the indexed cost (£150,000) or the unadjusted cost of a modern asset (£220,000) is used. The most appropriate figure, that is the current cost of replacing the service potential of each existing asset, is £110,000.

(*Source: Accounting for the Effects of Changing Prices: A Handbook*, Accounting Standards Committee, 1986)

way towards recognizing the problem of changing price levels.[5]

If account is not taken of inflation when determining the ratios described earlier in this chapter, it should not be assumed too readily that a comparison of great accuracy can be made between different companies, factories, or divisions. This does not apply to the same degree to the comparison of a company's performance over a period of time, but considerable caution must still be exercised.

5 A more accurate measure of the 'value to the business' of the assets employed would be the *present value* of all future net cash receipts of the firm. This would require an estimate of future cash flows and an appropriate rate of interest to discount them back to the present. This approach would recognize that the true value to the business of the assets employed is dependent upon their future earning power. However, at this point in time it is extremely difficult to put this concept into practice. Assumed current cost is a practical compromise. Discounted cash flow is explained in Chapter 8.

Using the Ratios

Having calculated the pyramid of control ratios, in what ways can the management of a company use the ratios to measure its efficiency? It can compare its own results roughly or in detail with those of its competitors. It can keep an internal check on the trends of its own overall results. Internal comparisons can be made between one producing division (subsidiary or department) and another, and they can provide an internal check on the comparative profitability of different product or product groups. If long-term plans or short-term budgets are prepared, management can compare actual and planned performance and analyse the variances. The use of return on capital employed to measure the performance of decentralized managements of autonomous subsidiaries and divisions is considered in Chapter 10.

Trend Analysis

By analysing the trends in a company's performance through time, it is possible to isolate causes of profit erosion or improvement. In particular, it is possible to diagnose long-term influences on the company's performance, such as continuing pressure on profit margins. For example, Tables 6.9 and 6.10 form part of the monthly management accounting package of Coloroll Ltd (see Sizer and Coulthurst, *A Casebook of British Management Accounting*, Volume 1). They show key ratios relating to the Coloroll Group Profit-and-Loss Account and Balance Sheet, the basis being moving annual totals from each of the preceding twelve months together with the two preceding financial years. It will be noted from Table 6.10 that profit to capital employed fell from 31.1 per cent in 1981/82 to 17.5 per cent in 1982/83. The turnover of capital employed improved from 2.3 to 2.5 times because of an increase in working capital turnover from 4.4 to 4.7 times, but net profit to sales fell significantly from 13.5 per cent to 6.9 per cent. Table 6.9 shows that a cause of the decline in profit to sales was the increase in materials cost to sales from 45.7 per cent to 49.1 per cent. While materials cost to sales increased, sales per employee and value added per employee (Table 6.10) fell. It will also be observed from Table 6.10 that the steady improvement in moving annual return on capital employed during

Table 6.9

COLOROLL GROUP
Profit-and-Loss Ratios

	81/82	82/83	Period 4 82/83	Period 5 82/83	Period 6 82/83	Period 7 82/83	Period 8 82/83	Period 9 82/83	Period 10 82/83	Period 11 82/83	Period 12 82/83	Period 1 83/84	Period 2 83/84	Period 3 83/84
Sales Value	100.0	100.0	100.0	100.0	100.0	100.0	100.0	100.0	100.0	100.0	100.0	100.0	100.0	100.0
Cost of Sales														
Material	45.7	49.1	47.2	47.3	47.4	47.5	48.0	48.0	48.2	48.3	49.1	49.2	49.6	49.7
Labour	5.4	5.8	6.1	6.0	6.0	6.0	5.9	6.0	6.1	6.0	5.8	5.9	6.0	5.9
Total	51.1	54.9	53.3	53.3	53.4	53.5	53.9	54.0	54.3	54.3	54.9	55.1	55.6	55.6
Gross Margin	48.9	45.1	46.7	46.7	46.6	46.5	46.1	46.0	45.7	45.7	45.1	44.9	44.4	44.4
Overheads														
Origination	5.2	5.8	6.0	6.0	6.0	6.1	6.0	5.8	5.8	5.8	5.8	5.7	5.6	5.4
Works	8.6	9.5	9.4	9.5	9.6	9.6	9.7	9.8	10.0	9.8	9.5	9.4	9.2	9.1
Distribution	4.8	5.6	5.2	5.3	5.4	5.4	5.4	5.4	5.6	5.5	5.6	5.6	5.6	5.7
Selling Expenses	9.5	10.3	10.6	10.9	10.8	10.9	10.8	10.5	10.5	10.5	10.3	10.2	9.9	9.7
Admin. Expenses	5.8	6.2	6.5	6.5	6.5	6.4	6.4	6.2	6.3	6.4	6.2	6.3	6.3	6.3
Other Expenses	1.5	.8	1.6	1.4	1.1	1.2	.9	1.0	.9	.8	.8	.8	.6	.5
Total	35.4	38.2	39.3	39.6	39.4	39.6	39.2	38.7	39.1	38.8	38.2	38.0	37.2	36.7
TOTAL NET PROFIT/(LOSS)	13.5	6.9	7.4	7.1	7.2	6.9	6.9	7.3	6.6	6.9	6.9	6.9	7.2	7.7

All ratios are based on moving annual totals

(Source: John Sizer and Nigel Coulthurst, *A Casebook of British Management Accounting*, Vol. 1, 1984)

Table 6.10

COLOROLL GROUP
Trading Account Key Ratios
Period 3

	81/82	82/83	Period	Period	Period	Period	Period	Period	Period	Period	Period	Period	Period	Period
			82/83	82/83	82/83	82/83	82/83	82/83	82/83	82/83	82/83	83/84	83/84	83/84
			4	5	6	7	8	9	10	11	12	1	2	3
Net Profit on Sales *	13.5	6.9	7.4	7.1	7.2	6.9	6.9	7.3	6.6	6.9	6.9	6.9	7.2	7.7
Profit on Capital Employed *	31.1	17.5	18.9	17.5	17.3	16.0	15.6	17.4	16.2	16.0	17.5	18.2	18.1	19.5
Current Ratio	1.8	1.8	1.7	1.7	1.7	1.7	1.8	1.9	1.7	1.7	1.8	1.7	1.8	1.7
Acid Test	.9	.9	.8	.8	.9	.9	1.0	1.0	.8	.9	.9	.9	.8	.7
Turnover on Capital Employed *	2.3	2.5	2.5	2.5	2.4	2.3	2.3	2.4	2.4	2.4	2.5	2.6	2.6	2.6
Fixed Asset Turnover *	4.7	4.7	4.5	4.5	4.4	4.4	4.4	4.5	4.6	4.6	4.7	4.7	4.9	5.0
Working Capital Turnover *	4.4	4.7	4.5	4.4	4.2	4.0	3.9	4.1	5.1	5.0	4.7	5.0	4.5	4.?
Stock Turnover *	4.2	4.3	3.4	3.4	3.7	3.7	3.9	4.0	4.2	4.3	4.3	4.3	3.6	3.?
Debtor Turnover *	3.7	3.8	4.1	3.6	3.3	3.1	3.1	4.0	4.2	4.1	3.8	3.8	4.2	4.?
Creditor Turnover *	4.4	4.1	4.7	4.7	4.9	4.4	4.3	4.0	5.0	5.2	4.1	4.1	4.0	3.?
Sales per Employee *	54513	53088	50143	50126	50250	50279	50834	52092	52442	52735	53088	53640	54340	5514?
Trading Profit/Employee *	7409	3696	3767	3547	3629	3489	3479	3819	3547	3576	3696	3719	3842	408?
Value Added/Employee *	29592	27042	26459	26428	26454	26405	26426	27108	27178	27237	27042	27228	27405	2776?
Wages/Turnover *	16.6	17.3	18.7	18.5	18.4	18.4	17.9	17.3	17.2	17.2	17.3	17.2	17.4	17.?
Export/Turnover *	17.9	17.2	17.7	17.6	17.2	17.0	16.2	16.8	16.7	17.0	17.2	17.4	17.6	17.?

Figures marked (*) are based on moving annual totals where appropriate. Other figures are based on actual figures at the accounts date
Figures ending (?) not available in full
(Source: John Sizer and Nigel Coulthurst, A Handbook of British Management Accounting, Vol. 1, 1984)

the first three periods of 1983/84 resulted from an improving turnover of capital employed, because of a higher fixed asset turnover.

External Comparisons

The senior management of a company may wish to compare its financial performance roughly, or in detail, with that of its competitors. A comparison with the performance of individual companies or with industry averages may be required. Comparisons with financial accounts of individual companies drawn from the files of the Registrar of Companies may be of limited value for a number of reasons, including:

1. Although the requirements of the Stock Exchange and the Accounting Standards Committee have increased in the past decade, the amount of information which is published is limited.
2. At the present time the accounts are prepared on a historical cost basis, and very few companies take into account the effects of inflation.
3. Although the Accounting Standards Committee has reduced the number of permitted accounting rules for dealing with particular items of revenue, expenditure, assets and liabilities, no two companies are likely to employ exactly the same set of accounting rules, and therefore the rates of return of any two companies may not be intrinsically comparable.
4. If a company is a subsidiary of a large group, it may be difficult to separate the financing of the subsidiary from its trading activities.
5. If the company is a member of a vertically integrated group of companies, where the end products of one company become the raw materials of another company, the *transfer prices* from one company to another may not be market prices and the profits of individual companies in the group may not be meaningful. Transfer pricing is fully discussed in Chapter 10.
6. In a vertically integrated group of companies, one company in the group may accept an export order at a loss, but for the group as a whole the order may be profitable. A comparison with the company accepting the export order at a loss would be of limited value.

7. In a group of companies, a single product line might be produced
    by several subsidiary companies, each of which also produces
    several other products, while the parent company absorbs all
    research and development costs.

A more valuable and meaningful method of comparing the performance of individual companies may be to participate in an interfirm
comparison scheme. Interfirm comparisons are discussed later in
this chapter.

In the United Kingdom there are an increasing number of published sources of return on capital employed by industry groups. Detailed financial information on twenty-two industry groups is contained in the series of annual government publications, *Business
Monitor M3*. Return on capital employed statistics for these twenty-
two industry groups are published at regular intervals in the *Trade
and Industry Journal* and *Economic Trends*. A number of industry
studies have been published by the Economic Development Commit-
tees of the National Economic Development Council. Quarterly
figures analysed under twenty-three industrial groups are published
by the *Economist*, and monthly figures appear in the *Financial Times*
under thirty industrial groups. The triennial government publication, *Company Assets, Income and Finance*, gives the main figures
for each individual large company. Individual company figures
appear weekly in the *Investors' Chronicle*, and annually in *The Times
1000* and *Management Today*. Similar information can be found in
Fortune's directory of the 500 largest U.S. industrial corporations.
Extel cards can also be consulted to obtain individual company
information. Under the Companies Act, 1967, all companies, quoted
and non-quoted, are required to file accounts with the Registrar of
Companies. Inter Company Comparisons Ltd publish industry
sector analysis reports which compare the individual and average
performance over a three-year period of up to sixty leading companies in each of fifty sectors. Their annual publication, *Industrial
Performance Analysis*, contains a three-year detailed comparison of
fourteen average ratios of fifty-four sectors of British industry and
commerce. Clearly there is a vast amount of information available.
These and other sources are fully described in *Sources of British
Business Comparative Performance Data* (Selected Reading 7). Many
data bases are available on-line. However, when comparing company

performance with these published sources, particular attention must be paid to the definitions of profit and capital employed, which vary considerably between sources, and the limitations of unadjusted published financial data must be recognized.

Interfirm Comparison Schemes

Even if it were possible to compare directly with published sources, an external comparison of return on capital employed does not itself tell the management any more than that in a particular year the firm's ratio was higher or lower than that of firm A, B or C. It does not tell the management why the ratios of the firms differ. If it is to provide a basis for judgement, an external comparison should be planned in such a way that management is provided with the detailed ratios in the lower part of the pyramid of ratios that can be derived from an analysis of return on net operating capital. Much of the information required to calculate these detailed ratios is not available in the files of the Registrar of Companies.

A more valuable and meaningful method for a company to compare its performance with individual competitors may be to participate in an interfirm comparison scheme. Participating firms receive anonymous and absolutely confidential comparisons of selected ratios. There are over one hundred industries, trades, services and functions in Britain in which interfirm comparisons have been conducted by the Centre for Interfirm Comparison, and a number of trade associations, such as the British Federation of Master Printers, organize their own schemes. The Centre for Interfirm Comparison undertakes comparisons in the public sector, and it develops and conducts international comparisons. The pyramid of control ratios provides the basis for the majority of schemes, but some schemes are concerned with the analysis of product costs and profitability.

In the operation of such interfirm comparison schemes it is extremely important that the figures for all the firms in a comparison are calculated on the basis of the same definitions and valuation principles. If the data is not strictly comparable, neither the comparison of the supporting pyramid ratios nor the overall return on net operating capital will be useful. It has been argued earlier in this chapter that published accounting data for individual firms can never be of more than very limited value for purposes of comparison. To obtain accurate and meaningful interfirm comparisons it is necessary for a central organization, such as the Centre for Interfirm Comparison, or a trade association, to:

1. Establish detailed definitions and principles of valuation;
2. Agree with each participating company the methods for following them;
3. Collect and check the actual figures;
4. Calculate, tabulate and circulate ratios for the participating firms;
5. Assist the management of the participating firms to interpret the ratios; and
6. Undertake a continuous programme of development of improved comparisons and education in the use of interfirm comparisons.

For example, the Centre for Interfirm Comparison provides participating firms with simple but detailed definitions of terms and instructions on asset values. In particular, they show firms how, by using a price index, they can arrive at comparable current values of plant and machinery. Once the information has been collected, the Centre applies a number of checks: arithmetic, internal consistency, against annual accounts, inherent probability, and consistency with previous years' figures. The control ratios for each form are then calculated, and any ratios that differ substantially from those of other firms are queried. The ratios are tabulated and circulated to the participating firms, each firm being given a code number. The data appear in ratio, percentage, and similar statistical form (rather than absolute figures), which further reduces the possibility of identification. Each participating firm also receives the Centre's observations on its ratios and those of others in the comparison. These observations are made in the light of background information relating to the operating conditions of the industry and the firms in question. The comparative ratios of firms in the Centre's reports will not be the same as those which might be calculated from published accounts, because much of the information is not given in published accounts and because the accounting information has been standardized.

It is important to appreciate that it is *not* the object of interfirm comparisons to arrive at general conclusions about the industry to which a comparison relates. The aim is to provide the top management of each participating firm with a diagnostic tool which may highlight undetected weaknesses in the firm's operating policy and performance. The Centre's confidential reports are designed to show the firm how well their overall performance compares with that of other participants, and possibly *why* it differs. The less efficient the firm, the more it stands to gain from participating in an interfirm comparison scheme. However, the more efficient firms should derive some useful information from the comparison.[6]

It should not be assumed that interfirm comparison schemes overcome all the weaknesses of direct external comparisons. The uniform definitions and valuation problems may not, for example, overcome the *transfer price* problems if a participating company is a member of a vertically integrated group of companies, or the problems of the company accepting an export order which is profitable for the group of companies but not for the company itself. No two companies are strictly comparable in that they market exactly the same products for the same markets. Other difficulties have been examined by Higgins and Jackson, and by Sizer.[7] A scheme should provide a more realistic starting-point in the analysis of a company's past performance relative to that of its competitors than direct external comparisons with published accounts. Even after detailed analysis of the interfirm comparison data, further studies will often be required before recommendations for improving performance can be made. The interfirm comparison should enable the management to determine *where* and possibly *why* its performance was better or worse than that of its competitors, but it will not necessarily tell it *how* to improve it.

6 The Centre for Interfirm Comparison's fee per participating company per annual comparison depends on the scope and content of the comparison; whether firms receive individual reports as well as general results; whether and how often they are visited; and whether it is a U.K. or international comparison project.

7 J. C. Higgins and K. C. Jackson, 'Essential Criteria for Valid Interfirm Comparisons', *Management Accounting*, Vol. 51, No. 6, June 1973, pp. 247–50; and John Sizer, 'Some difficulties facing organisers of interfirm comparison schemes', *Accounting and Business Research*, No. 14, Spring 1974, pp. 116–26. Both reprinted in John Sizer (ed.) *Readings in Management Accounting*, Penguin, Harmondsworth, 1980.

Internal Comparisons

The management of a company may wish to make internal comparisons between one subsidiary and another, one producing division (or department) and another. Some companies also calculate and compare return on net operating capital by product groups. Internal comparisons of this type can assist management in appraising the performance of individual companies in a group, divisions of a company, or product groups from year to year, i.e. by the comparison of performance through time. They are used when measuring the performance of decentralized management in the case of holding companies with a large number of autonomous operating subsidiaries; or individual factories, plants or branches which operate as autonomous units within a large company. Internal comparisons of this type may be of considerable value, but their limitations should be understood. It must be emphasized that the calculation of a separate rate of return for products, departments, divisions, or subsidiary companies frequently involves difficult questions of apportionment, in computing both net operating capital and profit. The problem of transfer prices also occurs in many companies. It is important that management knows how to interpret the rates of return calculated. The case of Bang-Bang Manufacturing Ltd will illustrate the difficulties.

Bang-Bang Manufacturing Ltd manufactures and markets three separate groups of products, Product Groups A, B and C. For the year ending 31 December 1990, the forecast return on operating capital for the company is 15 per cent. Return on capital employed is defined by the company for this purpose as percentage operating profit to net operating assets employed in the business. The chief accountant is asked to calculate the forecast return on capital employed by product groups. The results of his calculations are shown in Table 6.11. It will be seen that Product Group B is expected to produce a return on capital employed of 7.6 per cent during 1990, and its performance in this respect has been consistently below that of Product Groups A and C. What exactly does this mean? How should this information be interpreted? It does *not* mean that:

1. If the company decided to cease manufacturing and marketing

Table 6.11

BANG-BANG MANUFACTURING LIMITED

Forecast Return on Capital Employed for the Year Ended 31 December 1990

| | Total | Product Groups | | | Service Depts | |
		A	B	C	X	Y
	£	£	£	£	£	£
FIXED ASSETS						
Assumed Current Cost	210,000	120,000	20,000	50,000	15,000	5,000
Less Accumulated Depreciation	140,000	90,000	5,000	39,000	5,000	1,000
Written Down Value	£70,000	£30,000	£15,000	£11,000	£10,000	£4,000
NET CURRENT ASSETS						
Stocks	30,000	10,000	6,000	3,000	8,000	3,000
Trade Debtors	40,000	25,000	10,000	5,000	—	—
Less Trade Creditors	(20,000)	(9,000)	(4,000)	(2,000)	(3,000)	(2,000)
	£50,000	£26,000	£12,000	£6,000	£5,000	£1,000
Net Operating Assets Employed	120,000	56,000	27,000	17,000	15,000	5,000
Apportionment of Service Departments	—	11,000	6,000	3,000	(15,000)	(5,000)
Net Operating Assets Employed in Product Groups	£120,000	£67,000	£33,000	£20,000		

Product Group B, the company's net operating assets would be reduced by £33,000 and its operating profit by £2,500 in 1990.

2. £33,000 net operating assets will be realized for investment if the company ceases manufacturing Product Group B.

It has been shown in Chapter 2 that a company's balance sheet is prepared on the assumption that the company is a going concern and will continue trading. The balance sheet does *not* represent the realizable values of the assets. The company would not realize £120,000 if it went into voluntary liquidation. It must also be recog-

Table 6.11 – continued

| | Total | Product Groups | | |
		A	B	C
	£	£	£	£
SALES	173,000	100,000	33,000	40,000
Less Variable				
Cost of Sales	140,000	83,900	25,200	30,900
Total Contribution	33,000	16,100	7,800	9,100
Less Separable				
Period Costs	10,000	4,000	3,500	2,500
Direct Product				
Profits	23,000	12,100	4,300	6,600
Less Apportioned				
Common				
Period Costs	5,000	1,900	1,800	1,300
Operating Profit	£18,000	£10,200	£2,500	£5,300
RETURN ON				
ASSETS				
EMPLOYED				
Forecast 1990	15%	15.2%	7.6%	26.5%
Actual 1989	16.3%	15.0%	9.0%	25.0%
„ 1988	17.0%	14.5%	10.5%	25.3%

nized, in relation to Product Group **B**, that it is not possible to allocate all the period costs of the business directly to product groups. Some of the period costs are clearly related to production and marketing of specific product groups, for example, product advertising and tooling costs. Other period costs are common to the whole organization and have to be apportioned to product groups. They would still be incurred if a product group was dropped: for instance, the managing director's salary would not be reduced. Separable and common period costs were considered in Chapter 5. Similarly, it is not possible to allocate all net operating assets to product groups. Certain capital employed is common to all product groups, e.g. the capital employed in certain service and administration departments, the managing director's car, the company's computer installation, etc.

It will be seen in Table 6.10 that the period costs which are separable are shown separately from those which are common to the whole business. The net operating assets can be analysed in the same way:

	Total £	Product Groups A £	B £	C £
Separable	68,000	37,000	19,000	12,000
Common	52,000	30,000	14,000	8,000
	£120,000	£67,000	£33,000	£20,000

It will now be appreciated that if, on the basis of the forecast return on capital employed of 7.6 per cent for Product Group B, the product group is dropped, the net operating assets will be reduced by only £19,000. On the other hand the operating profit will fall by £4,300, the direct product profit. This would mean that the company would be forgoing a return of 22.6 per cent on the *incremental* net operating assets. In other words, the forecast return on the remaining capital employed must fall:

	£	£
Net Operating Assets		
Separable: Product Group A	37,000	
Product Group C	12,000	49,000
Common		52,000
Total		£101,000
Operating Profit		
Direct Product Profits: Product Group A	12,100	
Product Group C	6,600	18,700
Less Common Period Costs		5,000
		£13,700
Return on Capital Employed		13.6%

What then does the 7.6 per cent return on capital employed for Product Group B indicate? It indicates that the company is not making a satisfactory return on Product Group B in relation to the *total* capital employed in the business. However, unless the company has a better way of keeping the common capital resources employed, there is a case for retaining the product group. Thus, whether the product group should be retained or not depends upon the firm's alternative opportunities. It will be appreciated that the return on capital employed by product groups must be interpreted with considerable caution. The same arguments apply whenever there is an apportionment of common period costs and net operating assets. The difficulties that arise when return on net operating assets is used to measure the performance of decentralized managements of autonomous operating subsidiaries or divisions are explained in Chapter 10.

Setting a Standard

While recognizing the limitations of return on capital employed, increasing emphasis on return on capital employed and attempts to improve it may naturally lead to a number of questions. What rate of return on capital employed should be earned? Is there such a thing as a 'fair' rate of return? What should be regarded as a standard rate of return on capital employed? The establishment of a standard is a difficult and controversial matter and requires careful judgement. Important factors to be considered include:

1. The return on capital employed earned by other companies in the same industry, particularly some of the more successful ones.
2. The return earned by some successful companies in other industries, particularly industries in which the risk and uncertainty faced by the firms in the industry are similar or in which the skills required to be successful are similar.
3. The position of the company in the industry, and the competitive nature of the industry. Is the company a price-maker or a price-taker? What is the company's market share?
4. The likelihood of new companies being attracted into the industry by present high returns. How high are the barriers to new entry?
5. The company's cost of capital, which will be considered in Chapter 8.

6. The risk and uncertainty faced by the firm and the industry. The higher the risk and the greater the uncertainty, the higher the return on capital employed to be expected.

7. The return considered reasonable by crucial outsiders, i.e. the trade unions, the financial press, the investing public, potential competitors, the Monopolies Commission, the Office of Fair Trading, the Price Commission (when in existence), etc. When statutory or voluntary incomes policies are not in operation, the T.U.C. Wage Vetting Committee takes into account the profitability of individual concerns when examining wage claims. The Price Commission, under Labour governments in the 1970s, exercised control over profit to sales margins and undertook investigations into proposed price increases and pricing practices. The wide-ranging inquiry criteria included the earning of profits which give a real rate of return on capital employed sufficient to meet the cost of finance.

The above factors confirm that setting a standard rate of return on capital employed is a difficult matter requiring considerable skill. They also suggest that a standard (or 'fair') rate of return on capital employed *cannot* be applied uniformly to all companies. Return on capital employed is an imperfect tool which must be interpreted against the background circumstances of each individual case. Although they can be useful for the appraisal of long-term performance, profit potentialities and long-term plans, *standard* rates of return may not provide useful criteria for measuring short-term performance. Interfirm comparisons will be more useful for this purpose.

A standard rate of return could be established by the preparation of a business plan covering the normal cycle of, for instance, five years, and reflecting the cyclical nature of earnings. The forecast rate of return for each year of the plan could become the standard for that period. This method would overcome many of the accounting difficulties of setting a standard, such as differences in the age of assets. It would also take into consideration such factors as the competitive position of the company, the cyclical nature of the industry, the risk and uncertainty faced by the industry, and the planned expansion of the company. Alternatively, the long-term plan may be developed to achieve objectives established by the management. This type of planning, *strategic planning*, is considered

in Chapter 7. The basic steps in this type of long-range planning are:

1. *What kind of business should the company be in? What should the objectives of the firm be?* The company will have a whole hierarchy of objectives and constraints, company-wide economic and non-economic objectives. It will have short-term and long-term objectives, individual and institutional responsibilities and constraints. Peter Drucker considers that there are eight areas in which objectives of performance and results have to be set: market standing; innovation; productivity; physical and financial resources; profitability; manager performance and development; worker performance and attitude; and public responsibility.[8] Return on capital employed will form part of the economic or profitability objective of the firm. For example, the economic objectives of a company may be:

Growth per annum	Short-term	Long-term
Earnings per Share	15%	20%
Equity Shareholders' Investment	10%	15%
Operating Profit	15%	20%
Sales	10%	15%
Return per Annum		
Equity Shareholders' Investment	12%	18%
Operating Assets	20%	25%

2. *How should the company pursue its objectives in each kind of business specified in (1) above? What should the company's competitive strategy be?* The long-run sales growth objective of the firm may give rise to a sales and operating profit gap, and the management must determine its strategy to close the gap. However astutely management changes its day-to-day operating strategy there is usually an inevitable fall-off in the rate of growth of existing business, with the result that the company must introduce new products or enter new markets if it is to continue to grow. In order to achieve the desired rate of growth and fill the gap between the momentum line of its existing business and its long-term growth objective, the company may have to rethink its strategy and change its product-market scope. This means the company will have to consider one or more of the following questions:

8 Peter Drucker, *The Practice of Management*, Mercury Books, London, 1961, p. 53.

Can we sell existing products more effectively in existing markets (market penetration)?

Can we sell existing products in new markets (market development)?

Should we introduce new products in existing markets (product development)?

Should we introduce new products in new markets (diversification)?

These questions are examined in more detail in Chapter 7.

3. *How should the events and activities required to accomplish the competitive strategy be programmed? What should the plan of action be?* This step involves spelling out in detail a time-phased schedule of events and activities which will implement the competitive strategy.

4. *When and to what extent should the master plan be changed?* Feedback and reappraisal:

Is a new economic objective indicated?

Is a new competitive strategy indicated?

Is a new programme of action indicated?

Thus, a standard rate of return on capital employed may be the end result of the long-range planning process, or it may be part of the economic objective of the firm in strategic planning.

Summary

Profitability is the primary aim and best measure of efficiency in competitive business. Rate of return on equity shareholders' investment should be the starting-point from which to examine influences, make comparisons, and discuss trends in a company's profitability. It encompasses both earnings per share and assets per share. Assuming no minority and/or preference shareholders, it is determined by:

1. Rate of return on net assets employed;
2. Debt capital/equity capital ratio (i.e. gearing); and
3. Ratio of tax to profit before tax.

Return on net assets employed may be further analysed into return on net operating or trading assets and return on outside investments. Return on net operating assets gives rise to a pyramid of subsidiary control ratios. Departures from published financial statements are justified and advisable. If no account is taken of inflation when determining ratios, caution should be exercised when interpreting ratios and making comparisons. Organized interfirm comparison schemes are the best form of external comparison; internal comparisons can assist management in appraising the performance of subsidiaries, divisions, or product groups. However, while such comparisons may be of considerable value, their limitations should be understood. The establishment of a standard rate of return may be a difficult and controversial matter which may be the result of a long-range planning process or be included in the economic objectives of the company.

Selected Readings

1. P. A. Barnes (ed.), 'The analysis and use of financial ratios', special issue, *Journal of Business Finance and Accounting*, Winter, 1987.
2. The Centre for Interfirm Comparison, publications obtainable from: 8 West Stockwell Street, Colchester, Essex CO1 1HN.
3. Claude Hitching and Derek Stone, *Understanding Accounting*, Pitman, London, 1984.
4. Herbert Ingham and L. Taylor Harrington, *Interfirm Comparisons*, Heinemann, London, 1980.
5. 'Company Profitability and Finance' and 'Performance of Large Companies', annually in the *Bank of England Quarterly Review*.
6. John Sizer, 'Some Difficulties Facing Organizers of Interfirm Comparison Schemes', *Accounting and Business Research*, Spring, 1974.
7. C. A. Westwick and W. J. Westwick, *Sources of British Business Comparative Performance Data*, Accountants Digest 193, Institute of Chartered Accountants in England and Wales, 1986.

7

Long-Range Planning

It is widely accepted that long-range and short-term planning of all aspects of a business should be an integral part of the management of any business. How is long-range planning distinguished from other forms of planning? Long-range planning may be defined as a systematic and formalized process for purposefully directing and controlling future operations of an organization towards desired objectives for periods extending beyond one year. It covers a time period which is long enough to provide management with an opportunity to anticipate future problems, and thus to have greater freedom of action to resolve them in an orderly manner. Management can establish its long-range objectives and then decide its strategy for achieving those objectives. This stage of long-range planning is known as *strategic planning*, and has been defined by Robert N. Anthony as: [1]

. . . the process of deciding on objectives of the organization, on changes in these objectives, on the resources used to attain these objectives, and on the policies that are to govern the acquisition, use, and disposition of these resources.

Management has to translate the agreed strategy into detailed operational programmes for achieving the specified results. This type of planning is called *operations planning*.

Long-range planning is essentially a formalized programme of interrelated actions to achieve desired results. It therefore rests upon the implicit assumption that some planning is better than no planning at all, and that the imposition of a predetermined programme of action upon the future development of the business will favour-

1 Robert N. Anthony, *Planning and Control Systems: A Framework for Analysis*, Division of Research, Harvard Business School, Boston, 1965, p. 24.

ably influence the outcome of future operations. *Short-term planning*, on the other hand, must accept the environment of today, and the physical, human and financial resources at present available to the firm. These are to a considerable extent determined by the equality of the firm's long-range planning efforts. Since *financial planning* is an integral part of the long-range planning process, the accountant should be clearly involved in both strategic planning and operations planning.

Many factors have materially changed the environment in which firms operate: the accelerating pace of technological change; shorter product life-cycles; changing end-use markets; intensified domestic and international competition allied to change in competitive structures; the growing scale and complexity of business; the need for longer lead times; the changing nature of labour cost from variable to fixed; the rapidly changing industrial relations environment, and the shortage of skilled personnel. While the rate of change has accelerated, operations have become less flexible. Specialization within organizations by functional specialists, and highly sensitive and inter-related management processes, raise immense problems of coordination and control. All these developments call for the introduction or improvement of long-range planning. Managements are having to prepare long-range plans against the background of an increasingly uncertain economic environment with technological, ecological, political and sociological unknowns obscuring the horizon, which has necessitated the development of more sophisticated long-range and short-term planning and decision-making techniques.

Discussion in this chapter is concentrated firstly on strategic planning concepts and techniques, secondly on operational and financial planning, and finally on financing a plan.

Strategic Planning: Determining the Long-Range Objectives and Strategy

Long-range planning presupposes *objectives*. A company and its employees will have a whole hierarchy of objectives and constraints: company-wide economic and non-economic objectives, and individual economic and non-economic objectives. It will have short-term and long-term objectives, together with individual and institutional responsibilities and constraints. However, to be useful, a company's objectives should specifically state both the kind of financial performance it wants to achieve and the kind of company it wishes to be.

Strategic planning commences with the specification of objectives towards which future operations should be directed. These long-range objectives will usually be formulated within the framework of a basic company philosophy or broad strategic goals, and are established to specify the results desired during the planning period. For example, the engineering group, TI plc, published the following statement of its broad strategic goals in March 1987:

TI's strategic thrust is to become an international engineering group concentrating on specialized engineering businesses, operating in selected niches on a global basis. Key businesses must be able to command positions of leadership.

The company can then consider the strategic moves required if it is to achieve the desired objectives in the next five or more years.

Objectives should answer a number of fundamental questions about the company's future growth and development. For example:

1. What is the economic mission of the company?
   What kind of business should the company be in?
   What goods and services should be sold?
   What markets should be served?
   What share of the market is desired?
2. What are the profit objectives? (Considered in Chapter 6)
3. What rate of growth is required in sales, profit, assets, and value of equity shareholders' investment? (Considered in Chapter 6)

The establishment of these and other broad direction, growth, and profit objectives leads in turn to the establishment of a strategy to achieve these objectives. It will be appreciated that to some extent strategy flows from primary objectives, and also gives rise to subsidiary objectives in such areas as product development, productivity, management development, employee relations, etc.

When developing its strategy the management of a company has to recognize:

1. Long-term profitability objectives are achieved by a combina-

tion of increasing sales volume; by improving percentage profit to sales by reducing costs, increasing selling prices, or rationalizing product mix; and/or by improving productivity in the use of assets, i.e. improving the rate of asset turnover.

2. However astutely it changes its strategy, there is usually an inevitable fall-off in the rate of growth of existing business, with the result that a company must enter new fields if it is to achieve its growth and profitability objectives.

3. Companies that have a high share of a market tend to be more profitable than their small market share competitors.

4. Relevant strategies which take account of comparative advantages over competitors have to be developed for individual product market segments.

Product-Market Scope

While the product life-cycle, which is examined more fully in Chapter 11, represents a useful idealization rather than a rigid description of all product life histories, it should lead managements to recognize that:

1. Products have a limited market life;

2. Product sales and profits tend to follow a predictable course of introduction, growth, maturity, saturation and decline; and

3. Under conditions of competition and accelerating technological change a new product's life-span is apt to be shorter than those of the past.

Thus, the managements of multi-consumer products companies, and of many industrial products companies, are concerned with managing products or brands over their life-cycles in different markets. If a company concentrates entirely upon its present products and markets, then as an increasing proportion of the company's products enter the maturity, saturation, and decline stages of their life-cycles in different markets, the company's rate of growth will eventually decline and possibly fall away completely. The product life-cycle concept not only illustrates the importance of introducing new products to maintain growth, but also during a recession of life-cycle analysis can help managements to balance the short-term and long-term prospects. Recession accelerates the movement of products towards the saturation and decline stages of their life-cycles. A business area with a high proportion of products in these stages may have an unattractive long-term future.

In order to achieve the desired rate of growth, management needs to identify potential opportunities, threats and problems in its current environment and develop a momentum line for its existing business. It can then consider how to fill in the gap between the *momentum line* and its long-term objectives; this will necessitate a re-think of strategy and a change in the company's *product-market scope*. This means the company should consider one or more of the following:

1. Selling existing products more effectively in existing markets (market penetration);
2. Selling existing products in *new* markets (market development);
3. Developing *new* products for sale in existing markets (product development); and
4. Developing *new* products for sale in *new* markets (diversification).

Figure 7.1 presents the product-market scope in the form of a matrix. Diversification proposals may range from a logical development of new products which are technologically related to existing products for customers that are similar to existing customers, to new products for new types of customers, requiring the use of technology new to the company.

The ability of management to recognize the need to change the product-market scope is vital. In an age of rapid technological change, it is the early recognition of the need to enter new fields that is critical, and this is one reason why companies introduce long-range planning. However, not only must companies recognize the predictable fall-off in the growth rate of their existing business and the need to enter new fields as the expansion of existing business slackens; they must be able to select these new fields correctly. During the 1970s many companies were driven by the desire to achieve ambitious growth objectives into the diversification box, but failed properly to assess their ability to implement such strategies successfully. The success of Japanese companies in international markets has been attributed to their commitment to build long-term market share, to their exploitation of new environmental opportunities, to fast market adaption, as well as to their more aggressive attitude in the market

Product/Service – Market Matrix

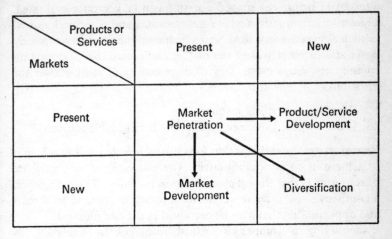

Products or Services Markets	Present	New
Present	Market Penetration	Product/Service Development
New	Market Development	Diversification

Figure 7.1. *Product-market scope*

place. They have a clear view of their customers and of how their products compete in the market place, and as changes occur in the market place they quickly develop new models to exploit not only these changes but also technological developments.

Studies by the Stanford Research Institute into the reasons why certain companies have outstanding growth records have shown that they systematically seek out, find, and reach for growth products and growth markets. Characteristically they have organized programmes to seek out and promote new business opportunities. In order to do this, managements must be able to evaluate correctly two questions:

1. How attractive are the economic characteristics and vitality of the particular field as compared with the existing business in which the company is engaged, especially in regard to the prospects for growth, stability, return on capital employed, degree of risk and size and duration of financial commitment?

2. What marketing, manufacturing, technical and/or financial know-how could existing management contribute to the new business?

It is necessary to undertake an analysis of *corporate strengths and weaknesses* before the second question can be correctly evaluated. The management must decide what resources and skills are required in each alternative new field, and which ones the company currently possesses. In other words, the management must, like the military commander, relate its strategy to its resources. It must answer the questions:

1. What are our critical resources?
2. Is the proposed strategy appropriate for available resources?

Resources are those things that a company *is* or *has* and that help it to achieve its corporate objectives. The essential strategic attribute of resources is that they represent action potential. Taken together, a company's resources represent its capacity to respond to threats and opportunities that may be perceived in the environment.

Identifying a company's critical resources by analysing its strengths and weaknesses will not define a viable strategy for it. It should be accompanied by a creative search for investment opportunities. A first stage in this process should be the preparation of a forecast of the expected future economic, socio-political, ecological and technological environment – not an easy task. Management can then systematically try to identify potential opportunities, threats and problems in the environment to see how they can best develop and exploit the company's distinctive competences.

It has been argued so far that if companies are to maintain a satisfactory rate of growth they need to select new fields of activity, which necessitates a creative search for investment opportunities. In order to select these new fields of activity, they should be aware of their own strengths and weaknesses. They must know their critical resources. Therefore, an analysis of corporate strengths and weaknesses is an essential step in long-range planning. Strengths, weaknesses, opportunities and threats (SWOT) analysis is equally applicable in a recession. However, weaknesses and threats become more important, and the opportunities and search aspects less critical.

It is necessary to develop a *capability profile*. A firm's capability profile is a statement in quantitative and qualitative terms of its resources; factors to be considered include physical facilities, organizational, managerial and technical competence, human resources, financial resources, company reputation, and access to markets. An evaluation is also needed of the products and/or services offered by the company and its shares in different markets. The capability profile developed should indicate where the company's real skills are, whether they are applicable outside the company, and in what way. The capability profile developed can be used:

1. To evaluate any internal strengths and weaknesses within the firm;
2. To derive characteristics which the firm can use in its search for opportunities; and
3. To measure the performance potential between the firm and a possible new field of activity.

Portfolio Models

Let us now consider the relationship between a company's product market scope and *market share strategy* in various markets, including a company's market position in relation to the market share – market growth rate matrix illustrated in Figure 7.2.

Research in the United States by Buzzell, Gale and Sultan [2] suggests that companies that have a high share of the markets they serve are considerably more profitable than their small-share competitors. Economies of scale and the so-called 'experience curve', market power and quality of management are possibly interrelated explanations of the market-share profitability relationship. The authors show that as market share increases a business is likely to have a higher profit to sales margin, a declining purchases to sales ratio, a decline in marketing costs as a percentage of sales, higher quality, and higher-priced products.

Because market share is so strongly related to profitability, Buzzell, Gale and Sultan rightly emphasize that a basic strategic issue for management is the establishment of market-share objectives and strategies, and they classify market-share strategies into three broad groups:

1. *Building strategies* are based on active efforts to increase market

2 Robert D. Buzzell, Bradley T. Gale and Ralph G. M. Sultan, 'Market Share – a key to profitability', *Harvard Business Review*, January–February 1975, pp. 97–106.

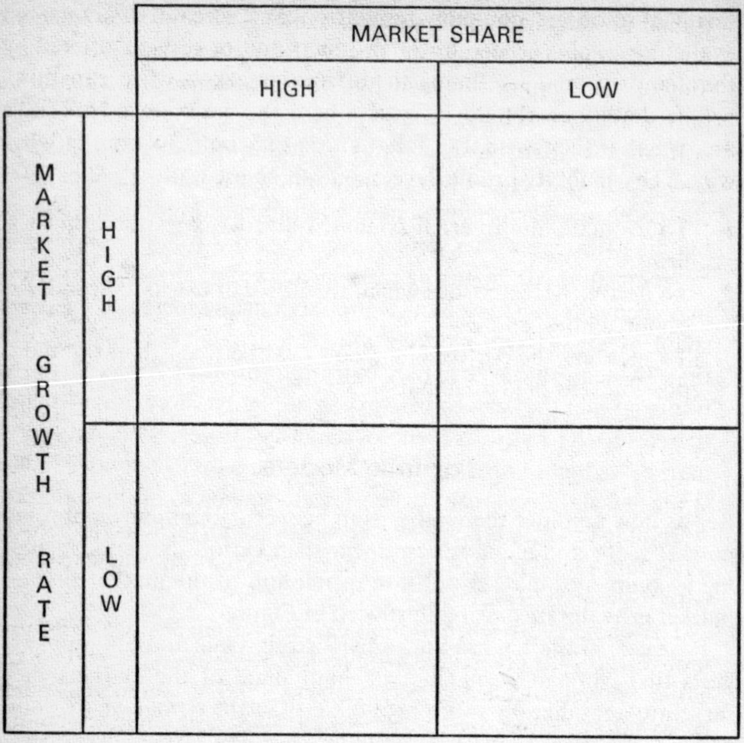

		MARKET SHARE	
		HIGH	LOW
MARKET GROWTH RATE	HIGH		
	LOW		

Figure 7.2. *Market share – market growth rate matrix*

share by means of new product introductions, added marketing programmes, etc.

2. *Holding strategies* are aimed at maintaining the existing level of market share.

3. *Harvesting strategies* are designed to achieve high short-term earnings and cash flow by permitting market share to decline.

The Buzzell, Gale and Sultan data imply that in many cases even a marginally acceptable rate of return on capital can be earned only by attaining some minimum level of market share. If a company's market share falls below this minimum, it can either increase its share or withdraw. Companies with a *low share of a low-growth market* should seriously consider whether to withdraw, particularly if their products are in the saturation and decline of their life-cycles. Such companies can either divest themselves of these so-called 'dogs',[3] i.e. hungry for cash but non-productive, or alternatively pursue a vigorous harvesting strategy.

If, on the other hand, a company has a *medium-sized share of a low-growth market* and there is no dominant firm with a high market share, the management may decide to pursue a holding strategy or a building strategy with a view to becoming the dominant firm, either by acquisition or by an aggressive marketing strategy. However, managements must recognize that significant increases in market share in low-growth markets are seldom achieved quickly, other than by acquisition; that they carry the threat of competitive reaction; and that they can be very expensive in the short run. Generally, therefore, the risk attached to building strategies in low-growth markets is high, and a company would be wise to consider holding strategies and divestment or harvesting strategies in these markets. A holding strategy is a reasonable policy to pursue if a company has a medium share of a low-growth market. It may have to learn to live with the market leader.

The choice between building and harvesting strategies becomes more critical for companies with *low shares of high-growth markets*. These are the so-called 'question marks' (?). Do you increase share, or withdraw, either by divestment to other companies pursuing a building strategy or by harvesting using a premium pricing policy and minimizing marketing expenditure, R & D, and investment in new fixed or working capital? A company that decides to pursue a building strategy in a high-growth market must be convinced that it has the financial, physical and managerial resources to implement its strategy and see it through a period of negative cash flows.

The most common market-share is the holding strategy, and this is particularly appropriate for companies with *high shares in both high- and low-growth markets*. The term 'cash cows' is frequently used to describe companies with high shares of low-growth markets. Market leaders tend to produce and sell significantly higher quality products and services than their lower-share competitors and are therefore able to command premium prices. Unless there is a rapid rate of technological change, low-market growth rate necessitates a

3 The terms 'cash cows', 'dogs', 'question marks', 'stars' and the related concepts of product portfolio were developed by the Boston Consulting Group.

lower level of new investment in fixed and working capital than in high-growth markets, and market leaders in low-growth markets are likely to be high net cash inflow generators. This cash can be used to finance building strategies in high-growth markets (the so-called 'stars'). In the latter the company has to make significant cash investments in research and development expenditure, long-term marketing expenditure to maintain its competitive position, and in new fixed investment and working capital as the demand for products increases. However, care must be taken not to milk 'cash cows' excessively.

Thus, for groups of companies and for large multi-product, multi-market companies, it was suggested during the 1970s that 'cash cows' and divested 'dogs' and 'question marks' should finance holding strategies for 'today's stars' and building strategies for 'today's question marks'. The latter become 'tomorrow's stars', and 'today's stars' become 'tomorrow's cash cows'. What happens to 'today's cash cows'? If the products in the low-growth market are entering the decline and saturation stages of their life-cycles, and because of projected low growth or decline of the market, coupled with a rate of technological change which implies a high level of investment promising relatively low returns, a company may pursue a harvesting or divestment policy with a view to switching its investment into high-growth markets. Alternatively, it may be necessary to harvest because cash requirements of the high-growth markets demand this.

The relationships between product portfolio and market-share strategy developed by the Boston Consulting Group are summarized in Figure 7.3. The areas of the circles are proportional to the turnover of each company or product group within a group's or company's product portfolio.

During the late 1970s there was a growing acceptance of the Boston Consulting Group's model, but also an increasing sensitivity to some of its underlying assumptions and possible limitations. Evidence emerged during the 1980s concerning simplistic use of the model. Questions that arose included:

- How do you define products and markets, including geographical market definition and market segment definition?
- How do you estimate market growth rates, given the difficulties surrounding economic forecasting?

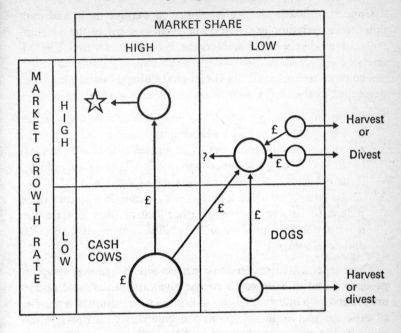

Figure 7.3. *Product portfolio and market-share strategy*

- How do you recognize that international competitors can gain large amounts of experience through acquisitions or licensing, or shift to lower experience curves, i.e. cost curves, by moving production or component sourcing to third world countries?
- What is the impact of foreign exchange rate variations on relative experience curves of international competitors?
- Is relative market share a proxy for relative profit performance, not *absolute* profit performance? Other factors may influence the absolute performance of a market segment.
- Can strategies be implemented? A number of companies may be searching for, and planning to enter, the same growth markets, e.g. leisure and DIY, which places a premium on understanding competitors' actions and responses.
- Does the model over-emphasize cash flow management to the extent that sight may be lost of other critical factors? Cash cows can be excessively milked.

Concerns about excessive emphasis on market share and cash flows, and over-simplistic marketing strategies, led to the development of models which combine the Boston model and SWOT analysis.

The basic technique of the Directional Policy Matrix, which was developed by the Shell Group of companies,[4] is to identify:

1. The main criteria by which the prospects of a business sector may be judged to be favourable or unfavourable (the Shell authors suggest for different sectors of a petroleum-based chemical business these are: market growth rate, market quality, industry feedstock situation, and environmental aspects); and

2. Those criteria by which a company's position in a sector can be judged to be strong or weak (the Shell authors' criteria are: market position, production capability, and product research and development).

These criteria are then used to construct separate ratings of 'sector prospects' and of 'company's competitive capabilities', and ratings are plotted on a matrix. Figure 7.4 displays the position of a number of different sectors in a hypothetical company's portfolio. Alternatively, the matrix can be used to display all the competitors (i.e. A, B and C) in one particular business sector (see Figure 7.5) since the method lends itself to evaluating competitors' ratings as well as those of one's own company.

General Electric[5] (U.S.A.) developed an approach similar to the Shell Directional Policy Matrix. It evaluated each of its businesses in two dimensions: the attractiveness of the industry it was in and its competitive strengths within the industry. Corporate management was given for review a summary of about a dozen factors for each dimension of the matrix (Figure 7.6). They then made a collective judgement based on the importance they attached to each of the factors. As the environment changed, some criteria were changed and new ones added. For example, in 1979 the company gave greater weight than three years previously to such factors as vulnerability to inflation, business cyclicality, or the impact of energy costs. General

4 S. J. O. Robinson, R. E. Hichens and D. P. Wade, 'The Directional Policy Matrix – Tool for Strategic Planning', *Long Range Planning*, Vol. 11, June 1978.

5 Michael G. Allen, 'Corporate Strategy and the New Environment', *Strategic Leadership: The Challenge to Chairmen*, McKinsey and Co. 1978.

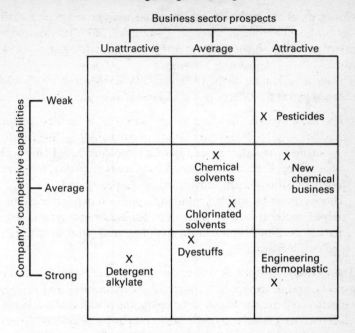

Figure 7.4. *Positions of business sectors in a hypothetical company's portfolio*

(*Source:* S. J. Q. Robinson, R. E. Hichens and D. P. Wade, 'The Directional Policy Matrix – Tool for Strategic Planning', *Long Range Planning*, Vol. II, June 1978)

Electric used the resulting rankings of business investment priorities both for long-term investment allocation and for determining short-term operating performance budgets.

The Boston Consulting Group's market share – market growth rate model was based on a far more logical and quantitative set of relationships than directional policy analysis type models which evaluate the trade-offs between industry attractiveness and competitive strengths, but it was too dependent upon accuracy and precision in defining relevant market segments and evaluation of market shares. Both types of model were overtaken by developments since the late 1970s. High inflation coupled with low growth, increased competition in traditional fields, added regulation, and dramatic growth in

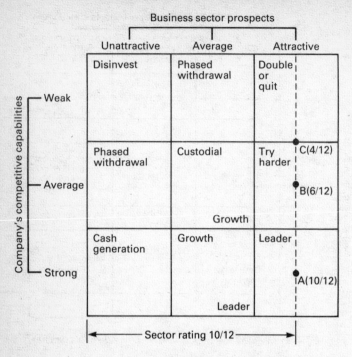

Figure 7.5. *Comparison of competitive capabilities – Product X (note: A, B and C are competitors)*

(*Source*: S. J. Q. Robinson, R. E. Hichens and D. P. Wade, 'The Directional Policy Matrix – Tool for Strategic Planning', *Long Range Planning*, Vol. II, June 1978)

international trade changed the rules of the game. The simplified strategies of the market share – market growth rate and directional policy analysis models became inappropriate to the more complex, low-growth world. Many companies recognized the limitation of cash cow and harvesting strategies and invested substantial sums in core low-growth businesses. General Electric (U.S.A.) recognized the limitations and dangers of the techniques it had employed. It invested £1bn during the mid 1980s in its mature locomotive, lighting and major appliance subsidiaries in an openly admitted catching-up exercise after these areas had been starved of funds in the 1970s.

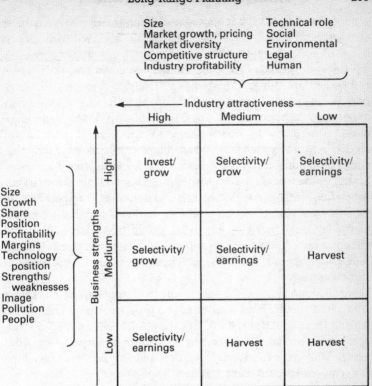

Figure 7.6. *Multifactor assessment*

(*Source:* Michael G. Allen, 'Corporate Strategy and the New Environment', *Strategic Leadership: The Challenge to Chairmen*, McKinsey & Co., 1978)

While portfolio models were extremely valuable in deciding what businesses to sell, they proved less useful in guiding internal growth and business development. They focused on strategy for a group of businesses and gave insufficient attention to strategies for each strategic business unit.

Strategies in pursuit of market share and low-cost position alone met with unexpected difficulty as segmental specialists established strong positions in 'niche' markets, and large numbers of international competitors acquired large volumes and the benefits of economies of scale. The most successful companies – and Japanese companies were paramount amongst these – achieved their success by anticipating market evolution and creating unique and defensible advantages over their competitors in the new environment. Japanese companies are adept at exploiting 'strategic windows', i.e. opportunities created by new market segments, changes in technology or new distribution channels. These success factors led to the development, particularly by Porter (Selected Readings 12 and 13), of models and analytical tools which place emphasis on developing and maintaining competitive advantage for individual businesses. Strategies based solely on growth products and growth markets, which frequently had led in the 1970s to optimism in respect of both growth rates and ability to establish market share, have been replaced by ones based on increased productivity, developing and maintaining competitive advantage, and relevant strategies and differential actions for individual businesses, units and product-market segments.

A full discussion of the development of appropriate marketing strategies for individual businesses and product-market segments is beyond the scope of this book, but the elements of marketing strategy, the information inputs and the decision outputs, are summarized in Figure 7.7. Wong, Saunders and Doyle[6] have argued the key requirements are that a business:

(a) needs a set of *strategic objectives* defining market share, profit or cash flow it is seeking for the product–market segment;

(b) requires a *focus* for achieving these objectives, which may entail stimulating primary demand, winning competitors' customers or improving productivity;

(c) must define the target *customer segments* it is seeking to serve;

(d) should identify its *competitors' strategies*;

(e) must affirm its *competitive advantage* and *market positioning*;

(f) will define its *marketing mix* (considered in Chapter 11);

(g) will audit its *organizational procedures* to successfully implement the strategy.

6 V. Wong, J. A. Saunders, and P. Doyle, 'A Comparative Study of Japanese Marketing Strategies in the U.K., Working Paper No. 153, Department of Management Studies, Loughborough University of Technology, July 1987.

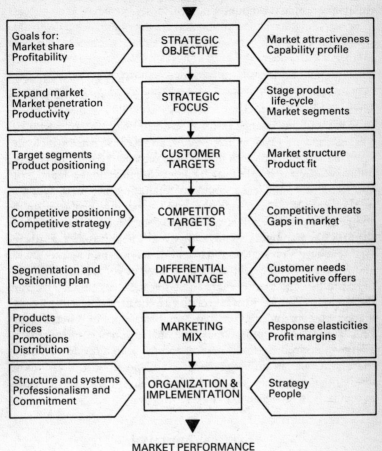

Figure 7.7. *Components of Marketing Strategy*

(*Source:* V. Wong, J. A. Saunders and P. Doyle, 'A Comparative Study of Japanese Marketing Strategies in the U.K., Working Paper No. 153, Department of Management Studies, Loughborough University of Technology, July 1987)

Against the background of this discussion of product portfolio models and the importance of relevant strategies for individual strategic business units and product–market segments, the use of the capability profile is examined.

Internal Appraisal

The capability profile can be used to evaluate any internal strengths and weaknesses of the firm. One of the early stages of strategy formulation will be to assess the firm's capability to meet its objectives without any change in its existing strategy. In order to make this assessment, a *competitive profile* can be constructed which presents the capability pattern of the most successful competitors in the industry in terms of physical facilities, organizational, managerial and technical competence, company reputation, products, access to markets, etc. By comparing the firm's capability profile with the competitive profile it will be possible to determine the areas in which the firm has a competitive advantage and where it is at a disadvantage. The firm's present products and/or services and market shares and strategies can be compared with those of competitors to determine product and market share strengths and weaknesses. These are the strengths and weaknesses relative to the firm's present product-market posture and market shares and strategies in different markets. The internal appraisal may lead, in a group of companies or in a large multiproduct, multi-market company, to a review of market share strategies in different markets and possibly to decisions to *divest* of unprofitable low market-share subsidiaries or activities, particularly in low-growth markets.

External Appraisal

At a later stage of strategy formulation, after the internal appraisal has been made, a broad range of possible fields of new activity should be considered, i.e. possible changes in the product-market scope can be examined. A part of the evaluation of the possible fields of activity will be concerned with determining the inherent potential. The *inherent potential* defines the extent to which a field of activity offers the possibility of achievement in critical performance areas, for example:

1. Growth – both rate of growth and outlook for continuance of growth;

2. Opportunity to establish adequate market share or create a 'niche' market;
3. Flexibility in relation to the uncertainties of technological change;
4. Stability in resisting major decline in economic conditions; and
5. Return on investment and cash flow potential.

The performance of leading firms in each possible field and the current market share structure offer some indication of the potential inherent in the field.

A company must have performance potential in order to take advantage of the inherent potential. A second part of the evaluation measures the *performance potential* or *synergy potential* between the field and the possible new field of activity. The term *synergy* is frequently used to describe the joint effects resulting from a new product–market entry. Synergy is concerned with the desired characteristics of fit between the company and a possible field of activity. It is often referred to as the $2 + 2 = 5$ effect. What is required is a *normative capability profile* for each possible field. A study of the capabilities and resources of strength of the leading firms in each field can provide a starting-point in estimating requirements for success. Relating the firm's capability profile to the normative capability profile for each field of activity will serve to develop a *comparative profile*, which indicates how well the firm's capabilities match the requirements for success in each field and the extent to which it will be able to establish competitive advantages. The firm's *performance potential* in each field may then be derived by matching the comparative capability profiles with the inherent potential in each field with respect to growth, flexibility, stability, size and duration of financial commitment, return on capital employed and cash flow potential. The external appraisal procedure is summarized in Figure 7.8.

Once the firm has decided which fields have the highest *performance potential*, the form of entry into the new field can be considered. The management will have to decide whether to enter by expanding its existing activities, by acquisition, or by establishing an entirely new company. If it is proposed to enter the new field by acquisition, the management, having first decided they want to acquire, can consider which company they want to acquire, how they propose to take it over, and how much they are prepared to pay. At this stage they will have to decide, for example, whether to acquire a small or

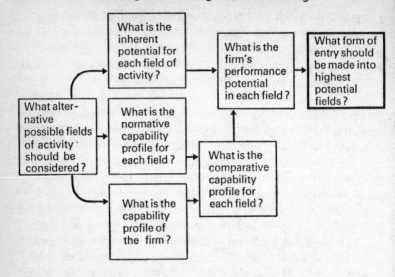

Figure 7.8. *External appraisal procedure*

medium-sized, well-managed company requiring an injection of capital, or a large, badly-managed company requiring an injection of management. They should examine each possible acquisition's capability profile, including its products and position in the markets it serves. The company's capability profile can be used at this stage to measure the synergy potential between the company and the possible acquisition.

With this approach to acquisitions, the diversification strategy is developed first, followed by a decision on the form of entry into the new field, and, finally, if entry is to be made by acquisition, the company to be acquired is identified. However, it should be recognized that no matter how systematic and logical the analysis leading to an acquisition, the risks attached to acquisitions are high. They are difficult and often unsuccessful; a view that has been confirmed by a number of research studies.

Operations Planning

The strategic planning stage of long-range planning, when objectives are established and strategies determined, is similar to strategic military planning. The military commander has his objectives and he has his resources, men, and equipment. He must decide the most suitable strategy to achieve his objectives with the minimum loss of the resources he has available. Strategic planning, like strategic military planning, is followed by detailed operations planning. *Operations planning* comprises the supporting programmes of events and activities required for meeting the planning objectives and implementing the strategy in the areas of research and development, production, marketing, and management development. There will also be plans for the major projects to be implemented during the planning period. Since plans for developing new products, markets, production facilities, acquisitions, etc., will all require finance, there must be planning to determine where the necessary finance is to come from. Management will also require to know whether the plans will achieve their desired profit and growth objectives. The plans must, therefore, be translated into long-range profit, cash flow, and balance sheet forecasts. The relationship between strategic planning and operations planning is further illustrated in Figure 7.9.

Financial Planning

Financial planning is an integral part of the long-range planning process. Not only do plans have to be translated into financial terms and the effect of variations in key assumptions examined; objectives have to be formulated in financial terms, historical financial information has to be provided, and alternatives have to be evaluated. In fact, the management accountant has a central role to play in the long-range planning process. His role was defined some years ago by the National Association of Accountants of the United States in the following terms: [7]

1. Providing background information which serves as a prelude to planning. The accountant can make a valuable contribution in this area of planning by preparing studies covering past performance, product mix, physical facilities and capital expenditures; and by analysing cost–volume–profit relationships, profit margins by product line, cash flows, etc.

7 John D. Simmons, *Long Range Profit Planning*, Research Report No. 42, National Association of Accountants, New York, 1964, pp. 44–5.

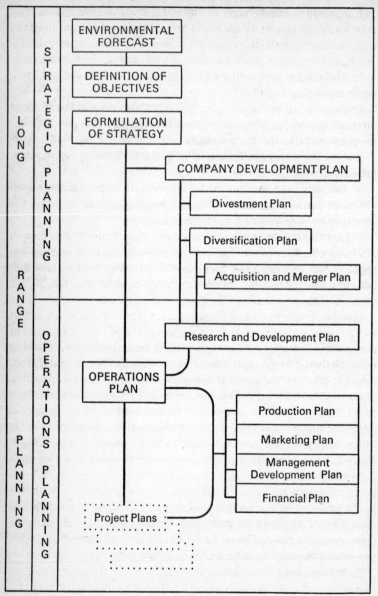

Figure 7.9. *Relationship between strategic planning and operations planning*

2. Assisting management in the evaluation of alternatives and assessing the financial feasibility of proposed courses of action. Relevant data must be analysed and expressed in financial terms, and must constitute a reliable basis for guiding management decisions.

3. Assembling, integrating and coordinating detailed plans into a company-wide master plan.

4. Translating plans into overall schedules of cost, profit and financial condition. These schedules subsequently become the basis for preparing the operating budgets (considered in Chapter 9).

5. Presenting anticipated results of plans for future operations in financial terms.

6. Assisting management in the review, critical appraisal and revision of plans to ensure that they constitute a realistic basis for directing and controlling future operations.

7. Establishing and administering operational controls to help in attaining planned objectives. This vital phase of the planning process requires the integration of long- and short-range profit plans and involves the monitoring of performance against the long-range plans, and the preparation of reports to management.

Space does not permit, in this chapter, a detailed examination and explanation of each of the above activities of the management accountant, though many aspects of these activities are considered in other chapters. The importance of financial information to the planning process, and the types of financial information presented in the plans, will be illustrated in the form of a memorandum to companies which are members of a group. The memorandum concerns the presentation of long-range plans of companies to the group head office. In reading the memorandum it should be borne in mind that the ranking in importance of factors influencing the long-range plans may differ widely according to the nature of each company. It must be recognized that:

1. The planning system has to be tailored to meet the needs of the group and the individual companies in the group. These needs, in turn, should be derived from the opportunities, threats and problems faced both by individual companies and the group as a whole.

2. Problems, threats and opportunities differ from firm to firm depending on its industry, size, stage of growth, management, state of technology, etc. Therefore, each company will require a distinctive and different planning system.

3. On the other hand, there are enough similarities among companies within a group to make it possible to suggest a standard form of presentation which can be adapted to meet the requirements of individual situations. The memorandum should prove a useful guide to companies preparing long-range plans for the first time.

Thus, the relative importance of different factors will be reflected in the plans produced, but individual companies should adhere to the standard layout as far as possible. While the memorandum illustrates the importance of financial information in the planning process, it will be appreciated that planning is not simply an accounting exercise. Note that the memorandum is addressed to managing directors, not financial directors.

To: Managing Directors all Group Companies
From: Group Planning Department

Long-Range Plans

SUBMISSION

1. The Group Board of Directors will consider the long-range Plans of companies annually in October. Plans should be submitted to Group Head Office not later than 30 September.

PERIOD COVERED

2. The Plan will normally forecast five years ahead. Because of the phasing of major developments or for other reasons, it may be appropriate for the future period covered in the Plan to be extended beyond five years.

3. Certain statistics to be provided in the Plan will require previous years' figures and, including forecasts, a total span of ten years is normally requested.

FORM OF PRESENTATION

4. The Plan should be prefaced by a contents sheet and will usually comprise the following sections:
Introduction
Environmental Forecast
Objectives and Strategy
Summary

Product Division Plans (a section for each division)
General Services
Financial Implications
Appendices

SUPPLEMENTARY INFORMATION

5. Certain additional information is required to enable the derivation of figures in the Plan to be followed in detail. This will be required for Head Office use and will not normally be submitted to the Board of Directors.

INTRODUCTION

6. The introduction should briefly describe the recent history of the company, indicate the size and location of its main productive units, define the purpose and scope of its business, its objectives for the current planning period, the strategy it has been pursuing and its success in achieving its objectives. In subsequent years the introduction should provide a link with the previous year's plan by comparing key figures and referring briefly to major developments which have taken place in the interim. Comparison with the previous year's plan and reference to major developments should at this stage be confined to introductory remarks. Developments during the preceding year and such detailed comparisons with previous years' plans as are useful should be dealt with in the appropriate later section of the Plan.

ENVIRONMENTAL FORECAST

7. Companies should make an appraisal of the external influences which affect their activities, including a forecast of the expected economic, socio-political, ecological and technological environment during the next five years. Opportunities and competitive threats should be identified. It would be useful in dealing with the economic influences to make reference to statistics or projections issued by the government or other outside bodies covering the particular business activity. This should not imply that the companies' assessments need to be in conformity with the view of any outside body, but it would be helpful to establish some relationship between them.

OBJECTIVES AND STRATEGY

8. Group corporate financial objectives are formulated in terms of growth in earnings per share, growth in equity shareholders' investment, and return

on equity shareholders' investment. Companies should formulate objectives in terms of:

(a) *existing business* – objectives and strategies for individual product divisions;

(b) *new business* – general areas which the company expects to enter over the next five years and methods of accomplishing entry, distinguishing between market development, product development, and diversification;

(c) *return on net assets employed* – expected return during the next five years;

(d) *growth* – expected company growth of turnover, profits and net assets employed during the next five years;

(e) *cash flow* – expected net cash inflow or outflow.

9. Strategies to be followed in accomplishing the objectives should be discussed in broad terms. An analysis of company strengths and weaknesses should be included, threats and opportunities in the forecast future environment identified, comparative advantages over competitors should be described, and the proposed strategy related to the analysis.

SUMMARY

10. A table summarizing actual and forecast results for the company should be completed for the ten-year period and included in the narrative as follows:

Turnover, Assets Employed, and Profits

Year	Turnover £	Net Assets Employed in Business £	Surplus on Trading £	% Surplus to Turnover %	Rate of Asset Turnover Times	% Surplus to Net Assets Employed %
Actual						
19 ..						
19 ..						
19 ..						
19 ..						
19 ..						
Forecast						
19 ..						
19 ..						
19 ..						
19 ..						
19 ..						

Forecast Growth Turnover 19 .. to 19 .. % per annum
Forecast Growth in Capital Employed 19 .. to 19 .. % per annum
Forecast Growth in Surplus on Trading 19 .. to 19 .. % per annum

11. A table summarizing actual and forecast capital expenditure and working capital requirements for the company should be completed for the ten-year period, and included in the narrative as follows:

Capital Expenditure and Working Capital

	Capital Expenditure			Working Capital		
Year	Total	Already Author- ized	Not Yet Author- ized	Total	Stocks	Debtors less Creditors

12. The table of turnover, assets employed, and profits, and that summarizing capital expenditure and working capital, should show total figures which will be supported by similar figures in tables for each of the main product divisions of the company appearing in the Plan. Observations on the summary tables should be made regarding trends and exceptional items which affect the company as a whole. Comparison between forecast profitability and growth and company objectives should be made. Key assumptions in the forecasts should be identified and the sensitivity of the forecasts to variations in these assumptions discussed. Where necessary, brief references should also be made to trends and exceptional items within product divisions which will receive more detailed examination in the appropriate section.

PRODUCT DIVISION PLANS

13. A Plan for each product division should be produced which should follow a similar sequence to the preceding introduction and summary for the company as a whole. It should commence with brief general and historical information, followed by a statement of the objectives and strategy for the product division, to provide a background leading to tables of actual and forecast figures for the ten-year period in identical form to the earlier summary tables, viz. turnover, assets employed and profits, and capital expenditure and working capital with limits of accuracy clearly indicated.

14. Explanations should be given of any trends or exceptional items apparent from the tables either at this point or in a later section where appropriate. Major capital expenditure schemes (approximately £300,000 or more) should be briefly described, with, if possible, an estimate of D.C.F. rate of return expected from the scheme [8] The effect of capital expenditure

8 Capital investment appraisal, including discounted cash flow (D.C.F.) techniques, is considered in Chapter 8.

schemes on net assets employed, their subsequent effect on profits and the interplay of these two factors on the return on net assets employed should be commented upon.

15. The factors influencing the plans of the product division should be discussed and sections dealing with the following matters should normally be provided.

(a) MARKETS. Details should be given of market size, market growth rate, the division's share of the market, competitors and their share of the market, divisions' and competitors' comparative advantages, marketing objectives and strategies for the division's product-market segments, and market influences on prices and profit margins. Past, present, and forecast future levels should be indicated, trends noted, and the expected impact of the division's strategy commented on. The level of inter-company sales should be stated and mention of special customers should be made. An account could also be given of any special feature of market research undertaken. Exports and the problems of exporting should be considered with particular mention of export markets, price policy, and credit extended.

(b) PRODUCT DEVELOPMENTS. For certain divisions the products and the product strategy may have been sufficiently described in the introduction of the Product Division Plan. More complex product groupings may need to be analysed to indicate their composition. Changes in the range of products, the introduction of new products, and improvements and withdrawals from the existing product range should be indicated and evaluated in terms of effect on turnover, profit levels, and return on net assets employed.

(c) PRODUCTION FACILITIES. The nature, location, area in square feet, capacity in weight or units, utilization and shift working arrangement of production facilities, with mention of recent changes and contemplated changes to meet planned production requirements, should be included. The link between capacity usage and sales achievement, and between forecast sales and planned productive capacity, should be made apparent. The extent to which productive equipment is obtained from Group sources should be mentioned.

(d) TECHNICAL IMPROVEMENTS. Recent and likely future technological developments and technical improvements should be discussed with mention where appropriate of research and development, method study, operational research, etc.

(e) PERSONNEL. The numbers of skilled and unskilled labour, managerial and clerical staff at present employed in the division, and planned future requirements should be stated. Any problems of labour supply, existing or foreseen, should be indicated. Management performance and development and relations with the labour force should also be considered.

(f) MATERIALS. Where significant, the types, qualities, annual consumption and sources of materials should be stated and problems discussed, e.g. licensing and import controls. Purchases from Group suppliers in quantity and quality should be mentioned.

(g) WORKING CAPITAL. The levels of stocks and net debtors should be examined with particular reference to their effect on net assets employed. Past and future trends should be commented upon where appropriate.

GENERAL SERVICES

16. The extent to which general services such as toolroom, welfare facilities, etc., and administrative departments can be treated as part of product divisions will vary with circumstances. In certain cases it may be necessary to deal with them in a separate section. If so, a table of capital expenditure in identical form to that used for product divisions should be provided and the value of assets employed should normally be apportioned to the product divisions concerned, so that the figures shown of total net assets employed in the company will represent the sum of those of the product divisions.

DETAILS OF CAPITAL EXPENDITURE

17. Totals of capital expenditure for the company as a whole and for each product division will appear in the narrative of the plan. Appendices will be required to show analysis of these totals and it is possible that an appendix for each product division will be necessary in addition to an appendix summarizing expenditures for the company.

18. Forecast expenditure yet to be authorized should be analysed in a suitable manner so that projects can be identified from an appendix to the narrative. The analysis should distinguish between projects for:
(a)   replacement, cost reduction, and improving productivity;
(b)   expansion of business; and
(c)   facilities not directly profit-earning such as canteens.

FINANCIAL IMPLICATIONS

19. The financial implications of the Plan will need to be summarized so that the proposed disposition of funds in capital expenditure, additional working capital, taxation and dividend payments, etc., can be examined and set against the expected sources of funds. A standard layout of financial forecast in the form of a funds flow statement is shown as Pro forma A. After arriving at the excess or deficiency of funds internally generated and retained over requirements, provision is made for any expected additional

Pro forma A

LONG-RANGE PLAN

Financial Forecast, 19 . . to 19 . .

19 . .   19 . .   19 . .   19 . .   19 . .   19 . .

(*Current*
year)

Sources of Funds
Profit before Taxation
Depreciation
Sale of Fixed Assets

—   —   —   —   —   —

—   —   —   —   —   —

Disposition of Funds
Capital Expenditure
  already authorized
  not yet authorized
Increase or Decrease in stocks
Increase or Decrease in net Debtors
Taxation paid
Dividend paid

—   —   —   —   —   —

—   —   —   —   —   —

Excess or Deficiency of Funds generated
  and retained over Requirements
Other Funds:

—   —   —   —   —   —

Variation in liquid Resources
Surplus or Deficiency at Commencement
  of Period
Surplus or Deficiency at End of Period

═   ═   ═   ═   ═   ═

sources of finance to be detailed to determine the variation in liquid resources and cumulative surplus or deficiency at the end of each year.

20. A narrative section is required in which the financial implications of
the financial forecast should be discussed and related to the current financial
structure of the company. The sensitivity of the forecasts to variations in
key assumptions should be examined. Where appropriate, present and
future facilities available from banks and financial institutions should be
stated. When additional long-term finance from Group sources is considered
necessary this should be indicated.

21. A further standard form to be provided is Pro forma B, a forecast
profits statement. This form provides a link between the trading surplus
shown in the narrative of the Plan and the cash movements in the financial
forecast.

Pro forma B
LONG-RANGE PLAN
Forecast of Profits, 19 .. to 19 ..

	19 ..	19 ..	19 ..	19 ..	19 ..	19 ..
	(*Current year*)					
Surplus on Trading after Depreciation						
Bank Overdraft Interest						
Loan Interest						
Investment Income						
Profit before Taxation						
Taxation						
Exceptional Income or Charges						
Available Surplus						
Dividends						
General Reserve						

22. Pro forma C, Forecast Trading Account, and Pro forma D, Forecast Balance Sheet, should be completed for each forecast year commencing with the current year. These statements serve the dual purpose of working papers and the provision of supplementary information. The marginal costing form of presentation has been used in Pro forma C to enable variable expenses and fixed expenses to be forecast separately. The statements should not form part of the completed Plan and they will not be submitted to the Board of Directors. They should be submitted to the Group Planning Department to enable the Plan to be followed in detail and so that additional financial information is available to evaluate any proposal made, such as the provision of additional finance.

23. It is appreciated that in arriving at both surplus on trading and net assets employed for product divisions there may be difficulties encountered where apportionments are required. These should be carried out on as realistic a basis as possible.

24. The standard forms should be adhered to as far as possible as this will greatly reduce the number of queries likely to arise. Members of the Group Planning Department will be available to advise companies on all aspects of long-range planning.

A. Fortune-Teller

Head of Group Planning Department

It will be appreciated that the financial evaluation of long-range

Pro forma C
LONG-RANGE PLAN
Forecast Trading Account, 19 . .

Product Division	Turnover	Variable Cost of Sales	Separable Period Costs	Direct Product Profits	Apportioned Common Period Costs	Surplus on Trading
Total						

plans involves the management accountant in some extremely difficult and complex calculations. It has been emphasized that plans are prepared against a background of an uncertain economic environment and increasing international competition, and technological, ecological, political, and sociological unknowns obscure the horizon. Yet if management is to undertake long-range planning, financial estimates of profitability, cash flow, etc., must be attached to proposals. Even when the financial estimates are based on detailed

Pro forma D
LONG-RANGE PLAN
Forecast Balance Sheet, 19 . .

	Total	Product Division	Product Division	Product Division, etc.
Fixed Assets				
Cost				
Less Depreciation				
Written Down Value	___	___	___	___
Current Assets				
Stocks				
Debtors				
Cash and Bank Balances	___	___	___	___
Current Liabilities				
Creditors				
Taxation				
Dividends	___	___	___	___
Net Current Assets	___	___	___	___
Net Assets Employed in Business	___	___	___	___
Investments	___			
Net Assets Employed	___			
Derived from:				
Issued Share Capital				
Capital Reserves				
Revenue Reserves				
Debenture and Fixed Loans				
Deferred Liabilities				
Group Loan Account				
Bank Overdraft	___			

economic forecasting, demand forecasting, and cost analysis, the resulting figures can only be regarded as broad estimates based upon many assumptions about the future environment. Many of these assumptions may be invalidated overnight. Yet, despite the apparent lack of certainty in the estimates, decisions are based on them, individuals and boards of directors are committed to courses of action, and reputations are at stake. The danger is that the company will become too rigid in its approach to the future and inflexible in its attitude to alternative developments. Sticking to the plan can become as meaningless as complying with obsolete rules or reading the news in last week's newspapers. The management accountant must clearly indicate the limits of accuracy to be attached to the financial forecasts.

Many companies employ the new technology of computer-based financial planning models. Such models allow finance directors and management accountants to:

1. Test the sensitivity of financial plans to variations in key assumptions, such as market size, growth rate and share, both when preparing plans and during the planning period. They enable management to ask and obtain answers to 'what if' type questions. For example:

What if raw materials prices increase not by 5 per cent but by 10 per cent in Year 3?

What if market size does not increase by 3 per cent but falls by 2 per cent in Year 4?

What if our market share remains at 15 per cent and does not increase to 18 per cent by Year 4?

The impact of varying rates of inflation on working capital and cash flow can be tested.

2. Quickly update long-term plans and short-term budgets if the key variables do change.

Despite the new technology there is still a high degree of uncertainty attached to long-term planning which computer-based models help to quantify but not dismiss. In preparing and implementing long-term plans management must exercise the right degree of caution and provide for flexibility. The plan must be used as a signpost, not a straightjacket. Long-range planning must be dynamic. The plans require updating:

1. Whenever an event of significant impact takes place to necessitate a change in the company's strategy. The merger of two major competitors, the entry of a Japanese competitor, or a technological breakthrough by a competitor, cannot be ignored.
2. Annually, to take account of the company's actual progress.
3. Every five years or so, to redefine the basic objectives and to revise the strategy.

It must be emphasized that planning is not simply a logical, straight-forward exercise. It is not easy; it is extremely difficult to quantify alternative strategies. Financial evaluation of long-range plans stretches the management accountant to the limits of his ability.

Within the framework of the financial plan, a *budgetary control* system should be operated to ensure that detailed plans are prepared for each year of the financial plan when it becomes current. A budget is a management tool for controlling operations within the scope of the long-range plan. Budgetary control is concerned with short-term planning and control, and is the subject of Chapter 9. Financial planning and control systems employed by groups of companies are described in Chapter 10. A system of budgetary control should ensure that throughout the period covered by the financial plan there are regular accountability budgets prepared to achieve the targets that have been laid down in the plan, including sales volume, price levels, costs, profit, capital expenditure, cash flow, return on capital employed and other ratios of efficiency. At this stage, not only should objectives be established for absolute operating profit and return on operating assets, but also for the detailed ratios which determine return on operating assets. The budgetary control system will add flexibility to the financial plan by making any changes appropriate to the new circumstances at the time the detailed one-year plans are prepared.

An important part of the long-range planning process is the preparation of the *capital expenditure forecast*. Normally, acceptance of the long-range plan by the board of directors does not imply approval of individual capital expenditure projects in the capital expenditure forecast. It merely implies approval in principle, and does *not* constitute authority to proceed on projects or to expend funds. Projects will eventually be included in the annual capital expenditure budget, probably in a modified form to their original proposal in the long-range plan. At this stage projects can be submitted in detail for approval by the board of directors. The merits of the various proposals can be appraised in detail in the light of the current economic environment and the state of technology. The appraisal of capital expenditure decisions is given detailed consideration in Chapter 8.

Financing the Plan

Once the long-term plan has been prepared and approved by the board of directors, the financing of the proposed expansion can be considered. It has been illustrated in Pro forma A how a long-term financial forecast can be prepared. If a computer-based financial planning model has been developed, the key assumptions in the financial forecast can be tested and taken into account in financing decisions. For a group of companies the financial forecasts of individual companies must be consolidated to determine the requirement, if any, of additional finance for the whole group. The consolidated financial forecast may indicate that no deficiency of funds generated and retained over planned requirements is expected. Where a deficiency of internally generated and retained funds is forecast, but is not substantial and is expected to disappear in the later years of the plan, the deficiency may be covered by raising additional short-term finance in the form of a bank overdraft or short-term loan. Alternatively, leasing or hire purchase of specific assets may be considered, or a medium-term loan may be obtained from a finance house.

Bank overdraft and short-term loan finance (up to three years) is not expensive; the interest is allowable as a charge against trading profit for taxation purposes and in the case of a bank overdraft is only payable on the outstanding balance. The effective net of tax rate of interest is usually higher for hire-purchase and leasing contracts, and for medium-term loans obtained from finance houses. It is most suitable for financing transactions which are self-liquidating over a short period. The chief areas are the finance of fluctuations in stocks of materials and components which within a few weeks become saleable goods; an increase in debtors; and the general financing of trade in saleable goods, including seasonal peaks. Investment in vehicles and other short-lived assets may also call for short-term finance. Medium-term finance (three to ten years) is raised by borrowing which is secured against assets with a medium-term life, such as plant and machinery, or to provide general working capital, or to fund hardcore overdrafts. The chief sources are banks, though finance houses and other financial institutions also provide it.

Where a substantial overdraft or term loan for a number of years is required, in making a decision the bank or finance house will probably consider the following characteristics of the customer and his application:

1. The character of the customer.
2. The purpose of the loan.
3. Competence of the customer to implement the project for which the loan is required.
4. The customer's equity stake in the company.
5. The customer's liquidity, in particular his current ratio (ratio of current assets/current liabilities) and his liquidity ratio (liquid assets to current liabilities). If appropriate, creditors : turnover, debtors : turnover, and stocks : turnover ratios may also be considered. Liquidity ratios are considered later in this chapter.
6. The customer's future cash flow. The bank will require a detailed cash flow indicating the rate and period of repayment.
7. Previous behaviour of the account; whether the account has had a 'healthy' swing from debit to credit.
8. Security; whether a legal charge (e.g. mortgage or floating charge) or a guarantee is available. The 'break-up' value of the company's assets, if the company went into liquidation, will also be considered, e.g. debtors at 80 per cent of balance sheet value, stocks at 50 per cent, and plant and machinery at 10 per cent. Liabilities will be taken at the balance sheet figure.

If a company does wish to raise bank overdraft or loan facilities from a bank or finance house at the most attractive terms, it is important that it presents a logical and well-supported request. This is particularly the case when requesting substantial medium-term loans to finance future growth. The request to the bank or finance house should include the following:

1. A statement of the nature of the business, its historical development including an analysis of its financial performance in the previous five years, and its management structure.
2. A statement of the company's long-term objectives and its strategy to achieve these objectives.
3. A statement of the purpose of the loan and its relationship to the company's long-term objectives and strategy. If the loan is to finance one or more capital projects, the pessimistic, optimistic, and most likely D.C.F. rate of return for each project should

be indicated. If the loan is for a major capital expenditure project, the detailed D.C.F. calculations may be presented. (Capital investment appraisal is considered in Chapter 8.)

4. Projected profit-and-loss accounts and balance sheets over the period of the loan, including the current ratios and liquidity ratios.

5. Projected cash forecasts showing rate and period of repayment of the loan.

6. A statement of assets, such as freehold property, which will provide security to the bank.

If the overdraft is required for a shorter period, say up to six months, the annual cash budget should be submitted in place of 2, 3, 4, and 5 above.

It should always be remembered that *banks and finance houses are in the business of lending money*, and they are willing lenders subject to certain minimum requirements. For the bank, the ideal customer is not one who needs no bank finance at all. Frequently, the decision is not whether to lend but how much and at what rate of interest. In fact, where overdraft facilities for working capital are required, the bank's ideal customer is one who has a 'healthy' swing, where the balance swings regularly between a debit and credit position and, given this 'healthy' swing, there may be no ceiling to proposed borrowing. If a company wishes to secure the overdraft it needs at the best terms, it must be able to convince the bank that it is capable of meeting interest charges and of implementing repayments of the overdraft, which means that it must have an effective system of financial planning and control.

Where a continuing substantial cash deficiency, increasing each year, is forecast, the company will probably have to raise additional permanent long-term finance. The basic choice is between *debt* finance and *equity* finance. Decisions regarding the raising of additional long-term finance are not usually the responsibility of the management accountant. Recommendations are made to the board of directors by the finance director after consultation with the company's financial advisers. It is always advisable to seek specialist advice regarding the raising of additional long-term finance. It is not simply a question of what form of finance to raise, but also when to raise and whether to take one or two 'bites at the cherry'.

However, the nature of the long-term financing decision is briefly considered.

Debt capital has always had the advantage of requiring a lower rate of interest than equity capital because it has a prior call on profits and assets, but it is also attractive because the interest payable on it is chargeable against profits as a cost for tax purposes, i.e. debt interest payments reduce the amount of corporation tax payable. Under the Imputation System of corporation tax introduced in the United Kingdom in April 1973, under the Finance Act, 1972, corporation tax is charged at a single rate on all the chargeable profits of a company, whether distributed or undistributed; in the absence of a dividend, the tax is payable on the same dates as before. When a company pays a dividend to shareholders, although it has not to withhold income tax from the payment, it is required to make an advance payment of corporation tax ('ACT') which is then set off against the company's final corporation tax liability on its income for the period. It will be to the equity shareholders' benefit if a company finances part of its growth with fixed interest capital. The effects of gearing on return on equity shareholders' investment were illustrated in Chapter 6, pages 150–54, when the financial statements of Alpha Ltd and Large Group Ltd were analysed. It will be recalled that Alpha's 40 per cent debt capital to equity capital ratio geared up Alpha's 17.1 per cent return on net assets employed to give a 25 per cent return on equity shareholders' investment before corporation tax. In Large Group's case a 60 per cent debt capital to equity capital ratio geared up a 9.1 per cent return on net assets employed to 13.4 per cent return on total shareholders' investment before corporation tax.

The principal sources of long-term loan capital are the institutional lenders, such as insurance companies, pension funds, etc. These institutional lenders' sources of income must be free of risk to either capital or income. They also receive a relatively low rate of fixed interest after tax and the impact of inflation. They are therefore interested in *income cover* for interest payments and *asset cover* for the loan. The standards of creditworthiness they employ are usually expressed in the form of certain financial ratios by which a company's suitability for an issue of loan capital are assessed. The principal financial ratios considered by the institutional lenders are:

1. Ratio of times covered.
2. Ratio of current assets to current liabilities – current ratio.
3. Ratio of long-term debt to net worth.
4. Net tangible assets ratio.

1. RATIO OF TIMES COVERED

This ratio indicates the amount of income cover available to meet long-term interest charges, preference dividends, etc. The Finance Act, 1965, made preference capital very expensive relative to debt capital, and preference capital is now of limited importance. The ratio is of gross income available to the suppliers of long-term capital (both debt and equity) to the interest charges on long-term debt. Gross income is defined as profit *after* allowing for interest due to the suppliers of short-term credit but *before* corporation tax. Loan interest is chargeable as a cost for tax purposes, and the ratio is therefore best calculated gross of income tax. For example, if gross income is £100,000 and debt interest £10,000 the ratio of times covered is ten. The income cover required from a company will depend upon the nature of the industry/industries in which it operates, the company, its past earnings record and future prospects.

2. CURRENT RATIO

The ratio of current assets to current liabilities is an indication of the cover available to short-term lenders of finance such as banks providing overdraft facilities. A current ratio of 2:1 would generally be considered satisfactory and 1.5:1 would be the normal acceptable minimum. The more liquid the current assets the more acceptable is the ratio. The Acid Test Ratio or Liquid Ratio, the ratio of liquid assets to current liabilities, is also applied as a test of liquidity. A liquid assets ratio of 1:1 is considered satisfactory.

3. RATIO OF LONG-TERM DEBT TO NET WORTH

This ratio provides an indication of the extent to which the assets of a company could fail to realize their book value in the event of liquidation, but still realize in aggregate sufficient to meet outstanding debt capital. The net worth is the equity and preference shareholders' investment in the firm at book value, i.e. the total shareholders' interest. In the following balance sheet the ratio is $\frac{1}{4}$, i.e. £200,000 ÷ £50,000. It will be appreciated that the resulting ratio is dependent on the valuation of fixed assets, a problem which has already been considered. Companies sometimes revalue their fixed assets prior to raising debt capital in order to improve their ratio of long-term debt to net worth.

	£		£
Ordinary Share Capital	100,000	Fixed Assets	200,000
Preference Share Capital	25,000		
Capital and Revenue Reserves	75,000	Current Assets	100,000
Total Shareholders' Interest	200,000		300,000
		Less Current Liabilities	50,000
Debenture Capital	50,000		
	£250,000		£250,000

4. NET TANGIBLE ASSET RATIO

This ratio of debt to net tangible assets is also employed to provide some indication of the asset cover available to debenture holders. In the above balance sheet the ratio is $\frac{1}{5}$, i.e. £250,000 ÷ £50,000. The maximum ratio of long-term debt to net worth it is commonly thought practical for a normal manufacturing or distributing company to maintain is about $\frac{1}{3}$ to $\frac{1}{2}$, depending upon the nature of a company's assets. Where this ratio is $\frac{1}{3}$ the net tangible asset ratio will be $\frac{1}{4}$ because:

$$\frac{\text{Debt}}{\text{Net Tangible Assets}} = \frac{\text{Net Worth Ratio}}{1 + \text{Net Worth Ratio}}$$

Taking the above example:

$$\frac{50,000}{250,000} = \frac{\frac{1}{4}}{1 + \frac{1}{4}} = \frac{1}{5}$$

The institutional lenders will appraise a firm's creditworthiness by considering the above financial ratios, together with an evaluation of the firm's past profit record and future prospects. Provided the ratio of debt to net worth did not exceed 1 : 2 and the income cover exceeded five or six times, the institutional lenders would probably find the company an acceptable investment. This statement is subject to the overriding factor that there is no significant element of risk attached to the type of business in which the company is engaged.

As an alternative to raising long-term debt capital, a company may consider 'off balance sheet' the sale and lease-back of freehold property. With sale and lease-back a firm sells its property to an insurance company or pension fund and at the same time takes out a long-term lease on it, thus releasing a capital sum for investment in the business. The liability for future payments is 'off balance sheet', and the gearing of the firm is unchanged. Similarly, instead of using ordinary, medium- or short-term loans, a firm may obtain use of new assets by laying out little or no funds at the outset by leasing or hire purchase.

If a profitable and expanding private company has exhausted available sources of long-term debt capital, long-term and short-term leasing, sale and lease-back, and bank facilities, it might consider approaching an industrial finance company offering venture capital. A growing number of specialist organizations provide venture capital and start-up capital to growing companies by way of minority shareholdings. They take an 'equity stake' in the company. They may do so by subscribing for new ordinary shares to secure a minority shareholding; by way of medium-term lending convertible into ordinary shares at a later date; or by a combination of loan capital and ordinary shares. Many do not provide capital for 'green field' investments, but require companies to have a successful and expanding profit record and proven managerial ability and achievement. The Bank of England and the City Communications Centre have produced a guide, *Money for Business*, which is an excellent source of information and general advice on the types and sources of finance available to small and medium-sized firms.

A public company that has exhausted available sources of long-term debt capital has to consider whether to offer a rights issue of equity capital to existing shareholders to finance its growth. To be successful, the size and price of the rights issue, as well as the timing, must be correctly assessed. Specialist advice from a merchant banker is an essential part of this assessment.

Strategy for Financial Mobility

It has been emphasized that managements are preparing long-term plans against the background of a complex and uncertain external environment. It has become increasingly apparent in the area of liquidity management that more effort must be made to anticipate the unforeseen event and develop a strategy for financial mobility.

Having prepared a long-term financial plan showing their internally generated and retained sources of funds, uses of funds, and proposed sources of external finance during the planning period, management should also prepare an inventory of the resources available to management for meeting an unexpected deficit in cash flow. The inventory of resources should distinguish between availability for use immediately, within one month, three months, six months, etc. The principal objective of the analysis is for the finance director to provide the board of directors with the basis for the development and continuous review of a strategy for coping with any liquidity problems that may occur. The strategy for financial mobility developed by the board of directors should set out not only the sequence in which resources are to be brought into play as unplanned needs emerge, but also take account of the adequacy of resources at the commencement, at each stage, and at the end of the planning period, both in total amount and in distribution among specific resources. A computer-based financial planning model allows management to ask 'what if' type questions and to explore a range of alternatives quickly and accurately.

Summary

The long-range planning process consists of deciding what is to be planned, preparing plans, assuring their acceptance and implementation, and monitoring the firm and its environment for new planning needs. Objectives are established. An appraisal of corporate strengths and weaknesses and a forecast of the future environment are undertaken. Product-market scope, strategies for individual strategic business units, and for product-market segments within business units, are reviewed. Strategies are developed to achieve the objectives, taking account of the available resources, competitive advantages, and the external environment. Operations planning is concerned with the preparation of the supporting programme of events and activities required for meeting planned objectives and implementing strategy. Financial planning is an integral part of the long-range planning process. Plans must be translated into long-range profit, balance sheet, and financial forecasts. The financial evaluation of plans is difficult. The limits of accuracy to be attached to the financial forecasts must be clearly indicated. Computer-based financial models help to quantify but not eliminate the high degree of uncertainty attached to long-term planning. A budgetary control system and financial planning and control systems (the subjects of Chapters 9 and 10) should be operated to ensure that detailed plans are prepared for each year of the financial plan as it becomes current. Acceptance of the long-range plans does not usually imply authorization of individual capital expenditure projects. They will have to be submitted for approval by the board of directors after detailed appraisal (the subject of Chapter 8). Acceptance of long-range plans leads to consideration of the financing of the plan. Bank overdrafts and loans can be raised if limited finance is required for short periods, and medium-term loans can be raised from banks and finance houses. If a substantial deficiency is forecast, additional long-term finance will have to be raised. The basic choice is between debt and equity finance. Debt is cheaper, but limits are set on the amount that can be raised by the standards of creditworthiness imposed by the institutional lenders. Given the increasingly complex and uncertain external environment it is important that companies develop a strategy for financial mobility.

Selected Readings

1. R. N. Anthony, *Planning and Control Systems: A Framework for Analysis*, Harvard Business School, Boston, Mass., 1965.
2. H. Igor Ansoff, *Corporate Strategy*, McGraw-Hill, New York, 1965; Penguin, Harmondsworth, 1968.
3. Bank of England and City Communications Centre, *Money for Business*, London.
4. Richard Brealey and Stewart Myers, *Principles of Corporate Finance*, McGraw-Hill, New York, 1984.
5. J. H. Clemens and L. S. Dyer, *Balance Sheets and the Lending Banker*, Europa, London, 1986.

6. Philip Coggan, *The Money Machine: How the City Works*, Penguin, Harmondsworth, 1986.

7. Terence E. Cooke, *Mergers and Acquisitions*, Blackwell, Oxford, 1986.

8. Gordon Donaldson, 'Strategy for Financial Emergencies', *Harvard Business Review*, November–December 1969.

9. Michael Goold and Andrew Campbell, *Strategies and Styles*, Blackwell, Oxford, 1987.

10. C. W. Hofer and D. Schendel, *Strategy Formulation: Analytical Concepts*, West Publishing, St Paul, Minn., 1978.

11. Kenichi Ohmae, *The Mind of the Strategist*, McGraw-Hill, New York, 1982; Penguin, Harmondsworth, 1983.

12. T. J. Peters and R. H. Waterman, *In Search of Excellence: Lessons from America's Best Run Companies*, Harper & Row, New York, 1982.

13. Michael E. Porter, *Competitive Strategy: Techniques for Analysing Industries and Competitors*, Free Press, New York, 1980.

14. Michael E. Porter, *Competitive Advantage: Creating and Sustaining Superior Performance*, Free Press, New York, 1985.

15. James Brian Quinn, Henry Mintzberg and Robert M. James, *The Strategy Process*, Prentice-Hall, Englewood Cliffs, N.J., 1988.

16. J. M. Samuels and F. M. Wilkes, *Management of Company Finance*, Nelson, Sunbury-on-Thames, 1986.

17. Stuart Slatter, *Corporate Recovery*, Penguin, Harmondsworth, 1984.

8

Capital Investment Appraisal

In Chapter 7 it was explained that an important part of the long-range planning process is the preparation of a *capital expenditure forecast*, and that the projects contained in the forecast will eventually appear in the annual capital expenditure budget. At this stage the merits of the various projects have to be appraised in detail and submitted to a company's board of directors for approval. However, it should be recognized that capital investment appraisal forms only one part of systems of capital expenditure planning and control. The component parts of such systems were summarized many years ago by Joel Dean [1] as follows:

1. A creative *search* for investment opportunities.
2. Long-range *plans* and projections for the company's future development.
3. A short-range *budget* of supply of funds and demanded capital.
4. A correct yardstick of *economic worth*.
5. Realistic *estimation* of the economic worth of individual projects.
6. *Standards* for screening investment proposals that are geared to the company's economic circumstances.
7. *Expenditure controls* of outlays for facilities by comparison of authorizations and expenditures.
8. Candid and economically realistic *post-completion audits* of project earnings.
9. Investment analysis of facilities that are candidates for *disposal*.
10. *Forms and procedures* to ensure smooth working of the system.

1 Joel Dean, *Controls for Capital Expenditure*, Financial Management Series No. 105, American Management Association, 1953.

The main concern of this chapter is the determination of a 'correct yardstick of economic worth', the 'realistic estimation of the economic worth of individual projects', and standards (hurdle rates) for screening investment projects. Reference to the other components of a system of capital expenditure planning and control will be made throughout the chapter, but these will not be considered in detail. Examples of systems employed by large international companies (Unilever and the BOC Group) and in a medium-sized company (Rumenco Ltd), and of the evaluation of a major capital investment project by a large public sector organization (the Post Office) are contained in *A Casebook of British Management Accounting* (see Selected Readings).

The Nature of Investment Decisions

The evaluation of capital investment decisions raises problems which are different from the measurement of past performance. In reviewing (in Chapter 6) the past performance of a business it was found necessary to record the amount of *equity shareholders' investment, net operating assets, profits before and after tax*, and *profit attributable to equity shareholders* (using accounting conventions which combine cash transactions, provisions for depreciation, accruals, and prepayments) for what is in effect the sum total of a vast number of past investment decisions each in a different stage of its life. Various profitability ratios and subsidiary pyramid ratios were calculated, and used to judge the past performance of the business. While these features do not invalidate the return on capital employed concept for measuring past performance, they ignore several considerations which need to be taken into account in assessing future investments.

The basic object of any investment is that in return for paying out a given amount of cash today, a larger amount will be received back over a period of time. This larger amount should not only repay the original outlay, but also provide a minimum annual rate of interest on the outlay. If an individual invests £100 in a building society, he expects to receive back at some later date £100 plus compound interest on the period of his investment. If he borrows £100 from his bank at 6 per cent per annum to invest in shares, he expects to receive back, during the period he owns the shares, and on sale, £100 and compound interest in excess of 6 per cent per annum.

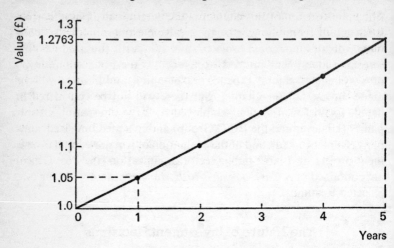

Figure 8.1. *Compounding and discounting at 5% per annum*

When considering an investment decision by a firm, it does not matter whether the *cash* outlay is labelled for accounting purposes 'capital' or 'revenue', nor the *cash* inflows 'profit', 'depreciation', 'taxation allowances', or 'investment grants'. To obtain a true picture of the investment all *cash* outlays and inflows must be taken into account. Furthermore, the value of a cash payment or receipt must be related to the time when the transfer takes place. It must be recognized that £1 received today is worth more than £1 receivable at some future date, because £1 received today could earn in the intervening period; this is the *time value of money concept*. As illustrated in Figure 8.1, if £1 was invested today at 5 per cent per annum compound interest it would accumulate to £1.2763 in five years' time and £1.6289 in ten years' time. Therefore, if income received today could be invested at 5 per cent per annum, £1.2763 receivable in five years' time would be worth only £1 today. It must be *discounted* back to the present at a rate of 5 per cent per annum. Similarly, £1.6289 receivable in ten years' time would be worth £1 today. This statement assumes no inflation; with inflation, £1 today would purchase more than £1 receivable in ten years' time, which reinforces the time value of money concept. The impact of inflation on investment decisions is examined later in this chapter.

The cash and time value of money concepts, although simple in principle, may appear to be difficult to reduce to a single earnings rate for a complex investment project which can be compared with the target rate of earnings. *Discounted Cash Flow* (D.C.F.) produces this single earnings rate. Discounting is a simple concept, being the opposite of compounding. It is best explained by a simple illustration.

On 1 January, Year 1, James Brown borrows £1,000 from a moneylender. Brown repays the moneylender £600 at the end of Year 1, £500 at the end of Year 2, and £55 at the end of Year 3. The moneylender charged 10 per cent per annum interest on the outstanding balance. The transactions can be summarized as follows:

Year	*Balance outstanding 1 Jan.* £	*Interest at 10%* £	*Balance outstanding 31 Dec.* £	*Repayment 31 Dec.* £
1	1,000	100	1,100	600
2	500	50	550	500
3	50	5	55	55
		£155		£1,155

Brown borrowed £1,000 and repaid £1,155 over three years. He paid 10 per cent per annum interest on the outstanding balance. What rate of interest did the moneylender earn on his investment? Clearly, he received 10 per cent per annum compound interest. D.C.F. is concerned with the determination of this 10 per cent.

Discounting is the opposite of compounding. Compounding is used to determine the *future value* of present cash flows; discounting is used to determine the *present value* of future cash flows.

$$\text{Present} \begin{cases} \xrightarrow{\quad \text{Compounding} \quad} \\ \xleftarrow{\quad \text{Discounting} \quad} \end{cases} \text{Future}$$

Compound interest tables are calculated by the formula $(1 + i)^n$ where i is the rate of interest and n the number of years, while discounting tables are calculated by the formula $\dfrac{1}{(1 + i)^n}$. Discounting tables in the form of present value factors are provided in Tables 8.1 and 8.2.

Table 8.1. Present Value Factors – Interest Rates (1% to 14%)

Years	1%	2%	3%	4%	5%	6%	7%	8%	9%	10%	11%	12%	13%	14%
1	.9901	.9804	.9709	.9615	.9524	.9434	.9346	.9259	.9174	.9091	.9009	.8929	.8850	.8772
2	.9803	.9612	.9426	.9246	.9070	.8900	.8734	.8573	.8417	.8264	.8116	.7972	.7831	.7695
3	.9706	.9423	.9151	.8890	.8638	.8396	.8163	.7938	.7722	.7513	.7312	.7118	.6931	.6750
4	.9610	.9238	.8885	.8548	.8227	.7921	.7629	.7350	.7084	.6830	.6587	.6355	.6133	.5921
5	.9515	.9057	.8626	.8219	.7835	.7473	.7130	.6806	.6499	.6209	.5935	.5674	.5428	.5194
6	.9420	.8880	.8375	.7903	.7462	.7050	.6663	.6302	.5963	.5645	.5346	.5066	.4803	.4556
7	.9327	.8706	.8131	.7599	.7107	.6651	.6227	.5835	.5470	.5132	.4817	.4523	.4251	.3996
8	.9235	.8535	.7894	.7307	.6768	.6274	.5820	.5403	.5019	.4665	.4339	.4039	.3762	.3506
9	.9143	.8368	.7664	.7026	.6446	.5919	.5439	.5002	.4604	.4241	.3909	.3606	.3329	.3075
10	.9053	.8203	.7441	.6756	.6139	.5584	.5083	.4632	.4224	.3855	.3522	.3220	.2946	.2679
11	.8963	.8043	.7224	.6496	.5847	.5268	.4751	.4289	.3875	.3505	.3173	.2875	.2607	.2366
12	.8874	.7885	.7014	.6246	.5568	.4970	.4440	.3971	.3555	.3186	.2855	.2567	.2307	.2076
13	.8787	.7730	.6810	.6006	.5303	.4688	.4150	.3677	.3262	.2897	.2575	.2292	.2042	.1821
14	.8700	.7579	.6611	.5775	.5051	.4423	.3878	.3405	.2992	.2633	.2320	.2046	.1807	.1597
15	.8613	.7430	.6419	.5553	.4810	.4173	.3624	.3152	.2745	.2394	.2090	.1827	.1599	.1401
16	.8528	.7284	.6232	.5339	.4581	.3936	.3387	.2919	.2519	.2176	.1883	.1631	.1415	.1229
17	.8444	.7142	.6050	.5134	.4363	.3714	.3166	.2703	.2311	.1978	.1696	.1456	.1252	.1078
18	.8360	.7002	.5874	.4936	.4155	.3503	.2959	.2502	.2120	.1799	.1528	.1300	.1108	.0946
19	.8277	.6864	.5703	.4746	.3957	.3305	.2765	.2317	.1945	.1635	.1377	.1161	.0981	.0829
20	.8195	.6730	.5537	.4564	.3769	.3118	.2584	.2145	.1784	.1486	.1240	.1037	.0868	.0728

Table 8.2. Present Value Factors – Interest Rates (15% to 50%)

Years	15%	16%	17%	18%	19%	20%	25%	30%	35%	40%	45%	50%
1	.8696	.8621	.8547	.8475	.8403	.8333	.8000	.7692	.7407	.7143	.6897	.6667
2	.7561	.7432	.7305	.7182	.7062	.6944	.6400	.5917	.5487	.5102	.4756	.4444
3	.6575	.6407	.6244	.6086	.5934	.5787	.5120	.4552	.4064	.3644	.3280	.2963
4	.5718	.5523	.5337	.5158	.4987	.4823	.4096	.3501	.3011	.2603	.2262	.1975
5	.4972	.4761	.4561	.4371	.4190	.4019	.3277	.2693	.2230	.1859	.1560	.1317
6	.4323	.4104	.3898	.3704	.3521	.3349	.2621	.2072	.1652	.1328	.1076	.0878
7	.3759	.3538	.3332	.3139	.2959	.2791	.2097	.1594	.1224	.0949	.0742	.0585
8	.3269	.3050	.2848	.2660	.2487	.2326	.1678	.1226	.0906	.0678	.0512	.0390
9	.2843	.2630	.2434	.2255	.2090	.1938	.1342	.0943	.0671	.0484	.0353	.0260
10	.2472	.2267	.2080	.1911	.1756	.1615	.1074	.0725	.0497	.0346	.0243	.0173
11	.2149	.1954	.1778	.1619	.1476	.1346	.0859	.0558	.0368	.0247	.0168	.0116
12	.1869	.1685	.1520	.1372	.1240	.1122	.0687	.0429	.0273	.0176	.0116	.0077
13	.1625	.1452	.1299	.1163	.1042	.0935	.0550	.0330	.0202	.0126	.0080	.0051
14	.1413	.1252	.1110	.0985	.0876	.0779	.0440	.0254	.0150	.0090	.0055	.0034
15	.1229	.1079	.0949	.0835	.0736	.0649	.0352	.0195	.0111	.0064	.0038	.0023
16	.1069	.0930	.0811	.0708	.0618	.0541	.0281	.0150	.0082	.0046	.0026	.0015
17	.0929	.0802	.0693	.0600	.0520	.0451	.0225	.0116	.0061	.0033	.0018	.0010
18	.0808	.0691	.0592	.0508	.0437	.0376	.0180	.0089	.0045	.0023	.0012	.0007
19	.0703	.0596	.0506	.0431	.0367	.0313	.0144	.0068	.0033	.0017	.0009	.0005
20	.0611	.0514	.0433	.0365	.0308	.0261	.0115	.0053	.0025	.0012	.0006	.0003

The moneylender made a typical investment decision: he paid out £1,000 on 1 January, Year 1, in order to receive back £1,155 over a period of time. He knows he earned 10 per cent compound interest on his investment; the firm proposing an investment estimates the future cash flows and wishes to determine the rate of interest. How could the moneylender check that he has received 10 per cent compound interest? He could do so by discounting the cash flows as follows:

Years outstanding	Cash Flow £	Discounted at 10%	
		Factor	Present Value £
0	(1,000)	1.0000	(1,000)
1	600	.9091	545.5
2	500	.8264	413.2
3	55	.7513	41.3
		Net Present Value (N.P.V.) £	—

It should be noted that cash outflows are indicated by brackets throughout this chapter. In the above calculation 10 per cent is the rate of interest which discounts the future cash inflows back to the present cash outlay and gives a net present value (N.P.V.) of zero. The discounted cash flow (D.C.F.) or, as it is sometimes called, the 'internal' rate of return, is 10 per cent, because at this rate of interest the *present value* of the future cash inflows is equal to the cash outlay on 1 January, Year 1.

It should be noted:

1. The D.C.F. rate of return is calculated, like repayments of a house mortgage, on the basis that the cash received each year must be apportioned into two parts:
   (a) the amount required to be set aside to provide the given rate of return (in this example 10 per cent) on the amount of cash outlay outstanding; and
   (b) the balance applied to reduce progressively the original cash outlay.

   Ultimately, the sum of all the apportionments under (b) will equal and thus repay the original outlay as shown below:

Year	Uncovered Investment at beginning of year £	Cash Inflow £	(a) Return at 10% per year £	(b) Amount of Investment recovered at end of year £	Unrecovered at end of year £
1	1,000	600	100	500	500
2	500	500	50	450	50
3	50	55	5	50	—
				£1,000	

2. The D.C.F. calculation takes into account the fact that the profits are highest in the early years of the project's life by giving greater weight to these figures in the calculations. Cash inflows received after one year are discounted by a factor of .9091, and in the third year by a factor of .7513, because cash received in the earlier years is of higher value than cash received in the later. Cash received in Year 1 can be re-invested before cash received in Year 3.

It will be recognized that had the above illustration represented an investment by a firm, the 10 per cent D.C.F. rate of return would have been determined by trial and error. If the cash flows had been discounted at 9 per cent and 11 per cent the result would have been:

Years outstanding	Cash Flow £	Discounted at 9%		Discounted at 11%	
		Factor	Present Value £	Factor	Present Value £
0	(1,000)	1.0000	(1,000)	1.0000	(1,000)
1	600	.9174	550.4	.9009	540.5
2	500	.8417	420.9	.8116	405.8
3	55	.7722	42.5	.7312	40.2
	£155	N.P.V.	= £13.8	N.P.V.	= £(13.5)

Discounting at 9 per cent the net present value (N.P.V.) of the future cash flows is *positive*, which indicates that the rate of return is *greater* than 9 per cent, and discounting at 11 per cent it is *negative*, which indicates that the rate of interest is *less* than 11 per cent. By

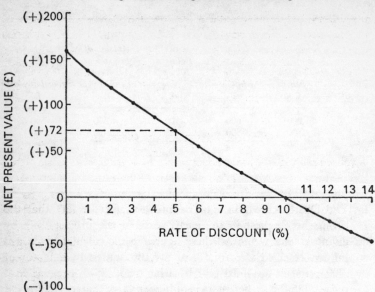

Figure 8.2. *Net present values at various rates of discount and D.C.F. rate of return by interpolation*

interpolation the correct D.C.F. rate of return (10 per cent) can be determined,

$$\text{i.e. } 9\% + \left(\frac{13.8}{13.8 + 13.5} \times 2\% \right).$$

The interpolation can be made graphically as in Figure 8.2.

Net Present Value Method

An alternative application of the D.C.F. principle, which may be used in appraising capital investment projects, is the Net Present Value (N.P.V.) method. This is the converse of the D.C.F., or 'internal', rate of return. A minimum earnings rate is agreed, and this percentage used to discount separately cash inflows and cash outflows to present values. If the total present value of the inflows exceeds that of the outflows, the difference, the net present value, is a surplus yielded by the investment over the minimum earnings rate. For example, if the moneylender could borrow money at 5 per cent per annum, he could discount the future cash flows he expects to receive from James Brown at this rate of interest. If the result is a positive N.P.V., as it is in this case (£72 per Figure 8.2), he knows that the investment will yield a return in excess of 5 per cent per annum. He also knows he will have £72 left after paying the interest on the money he has borrowed.

A More Complex Illustration

A more realistic investment decision is now considered. Traditional 'accounting' measures of profitability are computed and compared with the D.C.F. rate of return for the project.

The Widget Manufacturing Co. has developed in its Research & Development department a new high-technology product far in advance of existing products available to the market. It is proposed to manufacture and market the new product and this will require an investment of £150,000 in plant and machinery, and revenue expenditure of £10,000 during 1989, and a further £20,000 of working capital in 1990. In pricing the new product, advantage is to be taken of its high innovation value. Profits are expected to decline steadily from a maximum in 1990 as substitutes are developed and marketed by competitors and as the product becomes technically obsolete. It is expected that the product will have a fourteen-year life. The plant and machinery will have an estimated residual value of £15,000 in 2003, and the investment in working capital (£20,000) will be recovered in cash in that year. The company accountant prepared in March 1988 the following schedules:

Table 8.3. Details of expected investment outlay and residual receipts, and taxation allowances and reduced corporation tax payments resulting from the investment.

Table 8.4. Estimated profits and corporation tax payable thereon. In these tables cash outflows are indicated by brackets. A zero rate of inflation has been assumed, i.e. money cash flows equal real cash flows. The impact of inflation on capital investment appraisal will be considered later in this chapter. It will be noted that the cash inflows are high in the early years of the project's life. A method of investment appraisal is required that takes account of the pattern of cash flows.

The firm's accountant has prepared the following measures of the project's profitability:

Table 8.3

WIDGET MANUFACTURING CO.
New Product Decision

	Investment Outlay			Residual Receipts
	1989 £'000	1990 £'000	Total £'000	2003 £'000
Plant and Machinery	(150)	—	(150)	15
Working Capital:				
Stocks	—	(15)	(15)	15
Debtors *less* Creditors	—	(5)	(5)	5
Revenue Expenditure	(10)	—	(10)	—
	£(160)	£(20)	£(180)	£35

Taxation Allowances on Plant and Machinery
and Revenue Expenditure

Year		Capital Allowances at 25% Reducing Balance	Revenue Expenditure 100%	Total Tax Allowance	Corporation Tax at 35%
		£	£	£	£
1989	0	37,500	10,000	47,500	—
1990	1	28,125		28,125	16,625
1991	2	21,094		21,094	9,844
1992	3	15,820		15,820	7,383
1993	4	11,865		11,865	5,537
1994	5	8,899		8,899	4,153
1995	6	6,674		6,674	3,114
1996	7	5,006		5,006	2,336
1997	8	3,754		3,754	1,752
1998	9	2,816		2,816	1,314
1999	10	2,112		2,112	986
2000	11	1,584		1,584	739
2001	12	1,188		1,188	554
2002	13	891		891	416
2003	14	(12,328)*		(12,328)	312
2004	15				(4,315)
		£135,000	£10,000	£145,000	£50,750

*Balancing charge being the difference between tax written down value at commencement of Year 14 (£2,672) and estimated residual value (£15,000).

Table 8.4

WIDGET MANUFACTURING CO.

New Product Decision

Profits and Corporation Tax

Year		Profit before Depreciation £	Corporation Tax at 35% £
1989	0	—	—
1990	1	43,800	—
1991	2	42,600	(15,330)
1992	3	39,400	(14,910)
1993	4	36,200	(13,790)
1994	5	33,000	(12,670)
1995	6	29,800	(11,550)
1996	7	26,600	(10,430)
1997	8	23,400	(9,310)
1998	9	20,200	(8,190)
1999	10	17,000	(7,070)
2000	11	13,800	(5,950)
2001	12	10,600	(4,830)
2002	13	8,400	(3,710)
2003	14	5,200	(2,940)
2004	15	—	(1,820)
		£350,000	£(122,500)

Less Depreciation		£135,000	
Initial Revenue Expenditure		10,000	145,000
Profit before taxation			205,000
Corporation Tax			
On Profits		£122,500	
Less Allowances per Table 8.3		50,750	71,750
Profit after Taxation			£133,250

Note: All profits are assumed to generate at year ends and corporation tax payable on profits is paid one year later. Thus all profit in 1990 occurs at end 1990, which is taken as Year 1, and corporation tax on profit in 1990 is payable at end 1991, as Year 2.

Notes to Table 8.3 opposite:
1. A capital allowance of 25 per cent reducing balance can be claimed for each year's use of plant and machinery.
2. It is assumed that all payments occur at year ends, and all taxation allowances on expenditure during 1989 and subsequent years reduce the amount of corporation tax payable one year later. It is further assumed that sufficient taxable profits are made by the company against which the total tax allowances can be offset.

1. Average % profit *before depreciation* to additional assets
   employed   13.9%
2. Average % profit *after depreciation* to additional assets employed 8.1%
3. Average % profit *after depreciation and U.K. taxation* to additional
   assets employed   5.3%

Pay-back periods:
4. Before U.K. taxation   4 years
5. After U.K. taxation   5 years

The accountant's detailed calculations are shown in Table 8.5.

In weighing the financial considerations as an important part of
the process of arriving at a decision on whether or not to recommend
approval of the project, a board of directors would probably:

1. Have in mind a minimum rate of return required after having
regard to the level of taxation, the risk and uncertainty attached to
the project, past returns on capital employed or, possibly, the firm's
cost of capital;

2. Realize that the different ratios calculated by the accountant are
not inconsistent with each other but reflect different stages of profit.

Traditionally many firms compared these 'accounting' rates of
return with past performance for the firm as a whole – 15 per cent
return before tax and 9 per cent after tax were frequently the criteria
employed. On this basis the project under consideration would probably be rejected. If the firm calculates its cost of capital, it would
probably be between 6 per cent and 11 per cent after tax in *real*
terms for normal risk investments depending upon the methods of
financing the firm. With 5.3 per cent 'accounting' return after depreciation and tax, the project would probably be rejected. The cost
of capital concept is considered later in this chapter. The pay-back
periods are relatively short and the project may be considered attractive for this reason. However, pay-back does *not* measure profitability; it merely indicates how quickly the initial investment will be
repaid without taking account of the time value of money. Pay-back
is a useful additional item of information but in isolation is not an
adequate measure of profitability.[2]

2 A project with an infinite life and constant cash flows would have a D.C.F. rate of
  return exactly equal to its pay-back reciprocal. Pay-back reciprocal is a useful tool
  in quickly estimating the D.C.F. rate of return where the project life is at least
  twice the pay-back period and the cash inflows are *constant*. However, after taking
  account of corporation tax and the earnings profile, constant cash inflows are *not*
  common.

In spite of the number of ratios calculated by the accountant, they do not take into account the timing of the receipt of the profits, i.e. the earnings profile, or of the capital allowances. The ratios have averaged the taxation allowances and profits over the life of the project. They are not based solely on cash flows in that depreciation has been included in the calculations.

The D.C.F. approach is fundamentally different to the ratios calculated by the firm's accountant. Firstly, all *cash* outgoings and incomings are catalogued, and secondly, the cash flows are discounted at an annual rate of interest at which the present value of

Table 8.5

WIDGET MANUFACTURING CO.

New Product Decision

Accountant's Calculations

1. Average % profit *before depreciation* to additional assets employed

$$= \frac{£350,000}{14} \times \frac{1}{180,000} \times \frac{100}{1} = \underline{\underline{13.9\%}}$$

2. Average % profit *after depreciation* to additional assets employed

Total profit before depreciation (per Table 8.4)	£350,000
Less depreciation (cost less residual value, i.e. £150,000 − £15,000) and initial revenue expenditure (£10,000)	£145,000
Total profit after depreciation (per Table 8.4)	£205,000

Average % profit after depreciation on additional assets employed

$$= \frac{£205,000}{14} \times \frac{1}{180,000} \times \frac{100}{1} = \underline{\underline{8.1\%}}$$

3. Average % profit *after depreciation and U.K. taxation* to additional assets employed

Total profit after depreciation (as above)		£205,000
Less: U.K. taxation: On Profits	£122,500	
Allowances	(50,750)	£71,750
Total profit after depreciation and U.K. taxation (per Table 8.4)		£133,250

Average % profit after depreciation and U.K. taxation to additional assets employed

$$= \frac{£133,250}{14} \times \frac{1}{180,000} \times \frac{100}{1} = \underline{\underline{5.3\%}}$$

		£'000
4. Pay-back (before Taxation)		
Capital and Revenue Expenditure		160.0
Profit before Depreciation (per Table 8.4)	1990	43.8
	1991	42.6
	1992	39.4
	1993	36.2
Pay-back for first four years		£162.0

Pay-back (before Taxation) = 4 years

5. Pay-back (after U.K. Taxation)		
Capital and Revenue Expenditure		£160.0
Cash Inflows (columns 3, 4 and 5 of Table 8.6)	1990	40.4
	1991	37.1
	1992	31.9
	1993	28.0
	1994	24.5
Pay-back for first five years		£161.9

Pay-back (after U.K. Taxation) = 5 years

---

the future cash inflows equals the original outlay. The D.C.F. calculation is shown in detail in Table 8.6. It will be seen that the project promises a D.C.F. rate of return of 13 per cent after tax compared with an 'accounting' rate of return of 5.3 per cent after tax. If the company's minimum rate of return for this type of project is a D.C.F. rate of return of 10 per cent per annum after tax the project would be acceptable but may still have to compete with other projects. Why is there such a difference on the results shown for this example?

1. The 'after depreciation' and 'after depreciation and tax' ratios are expressed on the original investment. The D.C.F. rate of return is calculated on the basis that the cash received each year must be apportioned into two parts:

(a) The amount required to be set aside to provide the given rate of return (in this example this is 13 per cent) on the amount of cash outlay outstanding.

(b) The balance applied to reduce progressively the original cash outlay.

Ultimately, the sum of all the apportionments under (b) will equal, and thus repay, the original cash outlay.

2. In the conventional ratios the effect of the taxation allowances

Table 8.6

WIDGET MANUFACTURING CO.
New Product Decision
D.C.F. Rate of Return Calculation

1	2	3	4	5	6	7	8
Year	Investment Outlay	*Profit before Depreciation*	*U.K Taxation on Profit*	*U.K. Taxation Allowances*	*Net Cash Flows (Cols. 3 + 5 − 2 − 4)*	*Discounting Factors at 13%*	*Present Values of Net Cash Flows (Cols. 6 × 7)*
Cash Flow	Out £'000	In £'000	Out £'000	In £'000	Net £'000		£'000
1989 0	(160.0)				(160.0)	1.0000	(160.0)
1990 1	(20.0)	43.8		16.6	40.4	.8850	35.8
1991 2		42.6	(15.3)	9.8	37.1	.7831	29.1
1992 3		39.4	(14.9)	7.4	31.9	.6931	22.1
1993 4		36.2	(13.8)	5.6	28.0	.6133	17.2
1994 5		33.0	(12.7)	4.2	24.5	.5428	13.3
1995 6		29.8	(11.6)	3.1	21.3	.4803	10.2
1996 7		26.6	(10.4)	2.3	18.5	.4251	7.9
1997 8		23.4	(9.3)	1.8	15.9	.3762	6.0
1998 9		20.2	(8.2)	1.3	13.3	.3329	4.4
1999 10		17.0	(7.1)	1.0	10.9	.2946	3.2
2000 11		13.8	(6.0)	.7	8.5	.2607	2.2
2001 12		10.6	(4.8)	.6	6.4	.2307	1.5
2002 13		8.4	(3.7)	.4	5.1	.2042	1.0
2003 14	35.00	5.2	(2.9)	.3	37.6	.1807	6.8
2004 15			(1.8)	(4.3)	(6.1)	.1599	(1.0)
	(145.0)	350.0	(122.5)	50.8	133.3	N.P.V.	= (0.3)

D.C.F. Rate of Return = 13%

Notes:
1. All receipts and payments are assumed to occur at year ends. Thus, all expenditure and profit in 1989 occur at the end of 1989, which is taken as Year 0, and corporation tax on profit less capital allowances in 1989 occurs at the end of 1990, as Year 1.
2. The figures in columns 2 and 5 are transferred from Table 8.3, and in columns 3 and 4 from Table 8.4.

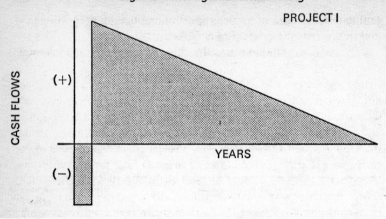

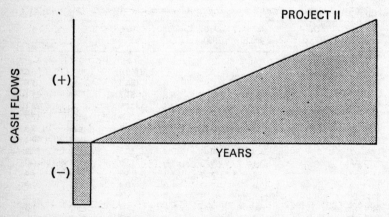

Figure 8.3. *Project I: high profits in early years; Project II: high profits in later years*
Accounting rates of return: Project I = Project II
D.C.F. rate of return: Project I ⩾ Project II

on capital and revenue expenditure is *averaged* over the life of the project. The D.C.F. calculation correctly treats the allowances as reducing the actual amount of tax payable each year. The benefits of the taxation allowances are received in the early years of the asset's life when the discounting effect is less significant.

3. The D.C.F. calculation takes into account the fact that the

profits are highest in the early years of the project's life by giving
greater weight to these figures in the calculations.

The use of conventional accounting ratios will in normal circumstances tend to show a lower rate of return, and this may give a
wrong impression as to whether a particular project is acceptable or
not. For example, in Figure 8.3 two simple investment projects are
illustrated; both projects have the same initial capital expenditure,
and both are expected to generate the same total cash inflow during
the same period of time. However, Project I has high profits in the
early years of its expected life and Project II high profits during the
later years. The D.C.F. rate of returns for the two projects would
reflect the pattern of the cash inflows. Project I would have a far
higher return than Project II. 'Accounting' rates of return would be
the same for both projects, because the initial expenditure and *average* profit are the same for both projects. Similarly, anyone who
fully understands D.C.F principles will also appreciate that if a
project is delayed at the capital expenditure stage, for example by a
strike by the employees of a construction firm building a new factory,
this delay will reduce the D.C.F. rate of return and possibly make a
project unprofitable. Accounting rates of return are not sensitive to
delays of this nature. In the author's experience errors in estimating
the amount and timing of initial capital expenditures are frequently
made by optimistic executives.

Net Present Value Method v. D.C.F. Rate of Return Method

An alternative to the D.C.F. rate of return method is the Net Present
Value method. If the Widget Manufacturing Co. has a minimum
required rate of return for the type of project under consideration of
10 per cent, the project would produce an N.P.V. of £19,300 (see
Table 8.7). The project would be acceptable in that it promises a
yield in excess of 10 per cent, but it may still have to compete with
other projects. Table 8.7 also shows the *discounted pay-back period*
for the project is 9 years. This is the number of years before the
project will repay the initial investment and earn the minimum return
of 10 per cent.

In practice, should the D.C.F. rate of return method or the N.P.V.
method be used? Provided a consistent assumption is made about

Table 8.7

WIDGET MANUFACTURING CO.

New Product Decision

Net Present Value Calculation

	1	2	3	4	5
				Present Values of	
		Net Cash Flow	*Discount*	*Net Cash Flows*	*Cumulative Present*
		per Table 8.6	*Factors*	*(Cols. 2 × 3)*	*Values*
	Year	*£'000*	*at 10%*	*£'000*	*£'000*
1989	0	(160.0)	1.0000	(160.0)	(160.0)
1990	1	40.4	.9091	36.7	(123.3)
1991	2	37.1	.8264	30.7	(92.6)
1992	3	31.9	.7513	24.0	(68.6)
1993	4	28.0	.6830	19.1	(49.5)
1994	5	24.5	.6209	15.2	(34.3)
1995	6	21.3	.5645	12.0	(22.3)
1996	7	18.5	.5132	9.5	(12.8)
1997	8	15.9	.4665	7.4	(5.4)
1998	9	13.3	.4241	5.6	0.2
1999	10	10.9	.3855	4.2	4.4
2000	11	8.5	.3505	3.0	7.4
2001	12	6.4	.3186	2.0	9.4
2002	13	5.1	.2897	1.5	10.9
2003	14	37.6	.2633	9.9	20.8
2004	15	(6.1)	.2394	(1.5)	19.3
		£133.3		N.P.V. = £19.3	

Discounted Payback Period = 9 years

the cost of finance, the D.C.F. rate of return and N.P.V. methods will give the same answer to the relatively simple question of whether a proposal is profitable or not. In practice, the N.P.V. method may occasionally give a different ranking of proposals from the D.C.F. rate of return method. For example, with highly profitable projects the N.P.V. method gives a significantly higher weighting to cash flows in the later years of a project's life than does the D.C.F. rate of return method. This is because the discount factors applied to the cash flows vary in a geometric progression. The N.P.V. approach is superior when choosing between mutually exclusive investments,

Table 8.8

Project	Cash Outlay in Year 1 £	Annual Cash Flow in subsequent 10 years £	D.C.F. Rate of Return	N.P.V. Discounting at 7% £
X	(20,000)	3,986	15%	+7,996
Y	(15,000)	3,220	17%	+7,616
X − Y	(5,000)	766	8.6%	+380

and the D.C.F. rate of return method may produce multiple yields in certain circumstances.

When considering *mutually exclusive investments*, the acceptance of one proposal automatically signals the rejection of all others. The investments under consideration are alternative proposals and only one proposal can be accepted. The alternatives may be ranked in one order by the rate of return method and in a different order by the N.P.V method. Consider the situation in Table 8.8: Project Y offers a higher rate of return than Project X, but a lower N.P.V. when discounted at the company's cost of capital of 7 per cent. Which alternative should be accepted? Provided the company is not in a capital rationing situation, the project which shows the highest N.P.V. is the most attractive, because this project offers the highest surplus after recovering the cost of capital. This can be proved by examining the *incremental* cash flows, the additional cash flows that arise if Project X is accepted. It will be seen that if Project X is accepted it offers a rate of return of 8.6 per cent on the additional investment of £5,000. Of course, it is assumed in this calculation that the degree of risk attached to the two projects is the same. If the risks are different it is a question of deciding whether the rate of return on the additional investment is adequate in relation to any additional risks involved. In a capital rationing situation when a company is not able to finance all the investment opportunities available, the 8.6 per cent return on the incremental investment would also have to be compared with the return promised by alternative projects.

The problem of ranking mutually exclusive alternatives is further

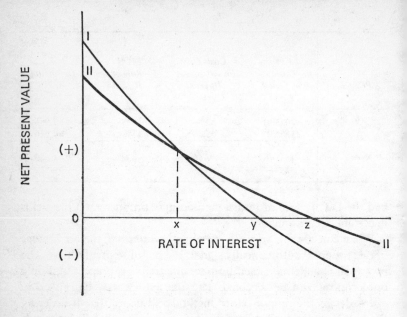

Figure 8.4

illustrated in Figure 8.4. I and II are the N.P.V. curves of two mutually exclusive alternatives. Project II is always preferable using the rate of return method, because it offers a rate of return of Oz compared with Oy for Project I. By the N.P.V. method, however, Project I is preferable if the cost of capital is *less* than Ox. The rate of return method may produce *multiple yields* when a series of cash flows includes multiple sign changes. The subject is primarily of academic interest and the problem rarely arises in practice.[3] However, it should be noted that the N.P.V method will always produce a single N.P.V. for such projects and allow a meaningful economic interpretation to be made. The problem is illustrated in Figure 8.5. It will be seen that the project has two rates of return, Oa and Oc, but only one N.P.V. at a cost of capital of Ob.

Are the theoretical shortcomings of the D.C.F. rate of return

3 Fuller discussion of theoretical problems of the D.C.F. rate of return method, i.e. choosing between mutually exclusive investments and the possibility of multiple yields, is beyond the scope of this book. Readers are referred to *The Management of Corporate Capital*, Ezra Solomon (ed.), Free Press of Glencoe, Chicago, 1959.

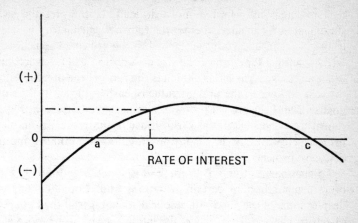

Figure 8.5

method sufficient to outweigh its practical advantages compared with the N.P.V. method? In practice, the D.C.F. rate of return method may be employed for a number of reasons. Management is accustomed to using rate of return as a measure of yield from investment. It is comparatively easy to compare the expected D.C.F. rate of return for a project with the minimum required rate of return based on the cost of capital (discussed in the next section), or with the expected returns from alternative projects. D.C.F. rate of return summarizes expected profitability characteristics into a single percentage regardless of project size. While the D.C.F. rate of return approach may appear difficult and complicated, the trial and error interest calculations are not time-consuming in relation to the main effort of project analysis. A computer can be programmed to do the calculations in a matter of seconds.

N.P.V. is a £ value which depends in part on the size of the project. This may make interpretation difficult; for example, consider the following statements:

1. 'Sir, Project A requiring an investment of £8,000 has an expected D.C.F. rate of return of 15 per cent, and our minimum required rate of return is 8 per cent.'

2. 'Sir, Project A requiring an investment of £8,000 has an expected N.P.V. of £523 after discounting at our minimum rate of return of 8 per cent.'

A manager may find it more difficult to interpret the second statement and consider whether the return is satisfactory in relation to the risk and uncertainty attached to the project. The problem of N.P.V. being a function of the size of a project can be overcome by using a *present value index*, which is the ratio of the present value of the cash inflows to the present value of cash outflows. If the ratio is greater than 1 the project promises a return greater than the required return and the higher the ratio above 1 the more profitable the project. However, it is a spurious method for ranking mutually exclusive projects.

To summarize, the N.P.V. method is superior to the D.C.F. rate of return method in certain situations and should be preferred, despite some of the apparent practical advantages of the D.C.F. rate of return method. In practice, the latter appears to be more widely used.

D.C.F. techniques can be used for any combination of cash outlays and cash inflows, i.e. expenditure on fixed assets and working capital in differing proportions in a single year or over an extended period, and for profits generated evenly or unevenly over a period. The information required for a D.C.F. calculation for a proposed expansion investment is:

(a) The amount to be spent and in which years.
(b) The estimated life of the project.
(c) The proceeds of sale of the asset at the end of its economic life.
(d) Profits before depreciation year by year.
(e) Capital allowances and/or grants, and rates of tax in the country in which the expenditure is to be incurred.

The accuracy of the estimates is likely to diminish for the later years of the project's life, but the discounting procedure gives least weight to these figures; e.g. at 15 per cent, cash flows are discounted by one half after five years and by three-quarters after ten years. With the traditional 'accounting' methods, cash flows in the later years have the same weight as those in the earlier years. D.C.F. techniques should be employed in the appraisal of all long-run decisions which involve cash flows over *time*, and not simply employed in the appraisal of expansion investments. One such decision, lease or buy, is briefly illustrated.

Lease or Buy Decisions

In appraising lease or buy decisions discounting techniques must be employed. If an asset is leased, a greater sum is paid for the asset over a period of *time* than if it were purchased for cash. A simple illustration, which ignores taxation, provides the best method of examining this type of decision.

XYZ Ltd operates in a tax-free world and is considering the purchase of a machine which will save £4,800 per annum in cash operating costs over its useful life of four years. The machine will have no residual value. The company's weighted average cost of capital is 10 per cent. The machine may be bought outright for £13,000; it is also available on a four-year lease at £4,000 annually in advance. Should the company buy or lease?

At the outset it should be recognized that the decision is not simply whether to buy or lease, despite the fact that advertisements for leasing frequently describe the decision this way. There are two decisions to be made:

1. The Investment Decision: whether or not to acquire the asset without regard for how the purchase will be financed. The machine promises a D.C.F. rate of return of 17.6 per cent, calculated as follows:

	£	
Purchase Price	13,000	
Present Value of Future Cash Flows [4]		
Discounted at 17.5% per annum		
£4,800 × 2.7164	13,039	By interpolation
Discounted at 18% per annum		D.C.F. Rate of
£4,800 × 2.6901	12,912	Return = 17.6%

The company's weighted average cost of capital is 10 per cent, and the project is therefore attractive. The means of financing the purchase can now be considered.

2. The Financing Decision: whether to lease the asset or to finance the purchase by borrowing. Leasing is one means of financing the purchase which should be compared with alternative means. By discounting the lease payments back to the cash purchase price of

---

4 Where cash flows are constant, Present Value Factor $= \dfrac{1 - (1 + 1r)^{-n}}{r}$ and this can be obtained from tables.

the asset, the cost of using the finance company's money can be determined. The company would be paying the finance company 15.9 per cent per annum if the asset was leased.

	£	
Cash Price	13,000	
Present Value of Lease Payments		
Discounted at 15.5% per annum		
£4,000 × 3.2644	13,058	By interpolation
Discounted at 16% per annum		Cost of Leasing
£4,000 × 3.2459	12,984	= 15.9%

The company must compare the cost of leasing with the cost of alternative forms of financing. If the company can finance the investment from alternative sources at less than 15.9 per cent per annum, the leasing of the asset may not be justified.

The analysis of lease or buy decisions is more complicated in the real world when investment grants, capital allowances, residual values, and corporation tax rates have to be taken into consideration. Further complications arise when the leasing company offers free maintenance or similar inducements. However, the important point is to recognize that a lease or buy decision is a financing decision and should be appraised separately from the investment decision.

Basic Assumptions: Handling Risk and Uncertainty

It must be emphasized that any method of expressing the financial implications of a proposed investment is dependent upon the soundness of the basic assumptions. The assembly of the relevant estimates takes up the vast majority of the total time devoted to the project appraisal. In the Widget Manufacturing Co. illustration, ninety-five per cent of the work would probably be concerned with such problems as:

1. The assessment of the demand for the product and selling prices, including some estimates of market size, market share, and market growth rate.
2. Estimating and phasing the initial cost of the investment, useful life of the facilities, and working capital requirements.
3. Assessing the rate of output and yield of the plant.

4. Ensuring that the provision of additional services and ancillaries has not been overlooked.
5. Estimating operating costs including assessments of fixed and variable costs.
6. Estimating the rate of corporation tax.
7. Estimating the residual value of the assets.

Many companies have developed check-lists which are applied to all projects to ensure no key factor has been overlooked in a proposal. Usually, there will be imponderables which are hardly susceptible to measurement and evaluation in monetary terms, for example the risk inherent in the particular type of business or in the market to be served. Interpretation and judgement must take over after the calculation stage, however carefully this has been undertaken. Thus, in evidence to the Committee to Review the Functioning of Financial Institutions (the Wilson Committee) in May 1978, Unilever, a large multinational company which employs sophisticated systems of capital expenditure appraisal and control, stated:

It must be stressed that, in modern conditions, the allowance for risk in even an average risk proposal has to be substantial. Moreover, although the formal methods of evaluation of risk can help in a number of cases the overall assessment of risk is mainly a matter of judgement rather than scientific calculation.

Unilever has found from bitter experience that project profitability obtained in the event is on average significantly below project profitability estimated in advance! It is not unusual for capital projects to run late, over-spend and under-earn!

Given the risk and uncertainty surrounding capital projects, it is usually undesirable to present one-answer solutions; it is frequently misleading to give the impression that a project promises a return of x per cent. When making capital investment decisions, management requires to know:

What is the probability of attaining the most likely return?
What is the lowest return we might receive?
What is the highest return we might receive?

How can the management cope with risk and uncertainty? One procedure which recognizes the existence of uncertainty, but does not attempt to evaluate it directly, is to increase the severity of the acceptance/rejection test. For example, a management may decide all projects should give a return at least 5 per cent more than the company's cost of capital. However, this approach assumes the risk is the same for all projects, i.e. two projects with the most likely D.C.F. return of 20 per cent are equally risky. One may be a new project with considerable uncertainty as to market demand and price, a second may be an expansion decision to meet a known demand. Furthermore, it does not distinguish the particular parts of the project which may be risky. The management accountant should evaluate the information that goes into the assessment of the project. The least sophisticated approach to evaluating the information is to calculate three D.C.F. rates of return or N.P.V.s: optimistic, pessimistic and most likely. This gives the management some indication of the range of possible outcomes but no indication of the probabilities of occurrence.

More sophisticated approaches are the use of *sensitivity analysis* or *risk analysis* to determine the impact of fluctuations in the basic data on a project's profitability. Sensitivity analysis is an attempt to show how a project's profitability may be affected by variations or changes in an element of project revenue, operating costs or investment. Risk assessment is concerned with the likelihood of such changes occurring. Frequently in a project there are three or four critical variables and 'what if' type questions are asked in order to test the sensitivity of the project to variations in these key variables. An example of a sensitivity analysis for a project is presented in Table 8.9. The analysis indicates that the project is most sensitive to changes in sales volume and selling prices.

The intent of sensitivity analysis is to present meaningful information to management so that it can make its own judgement of the risks attached to a project and their profit consequences. While sensitivity analysis helps to gauge the effects of changes in key factors, it does not help to assess the likelihood of such changes occurring. There is also a limitation to the number of variations that can be handled simultaneously.

Risk assessment is concerned with assessing the likelihood of changes in the key assumptions occurring. The Unilever Accounting Manual (see *A Casebook of British Management Accounting*, Volume 1) contains the following guidance on sensitivity and risk assessment:

Table 8.9

WIDGET MANUFACTURING CO.
Sensitivity Analysis – New Product Decision
Most likely Net Present Value £19,000

A Difference of 1% in:	Will change Net Present Value by:
Market Growth Rate	£500
Market Share	£630
Selling Price	£950
Direct Labour	£30
Direct Material	£220

1. Project profitability can be assessed by calculating the effect of varying the key assumptions by arbitrary, but stated, amounts (a 'sensitivity' assessment), or by calculating the effect of varying the key assumptions by amounts by which they could in practice vary (a 'risk' assessment).

2. The assumptions/forecasts to be assessed for sensitivity and risk should be the ones where it seems that possible change in them could normally have a significant effect on profitability. The list may include, *inter alia*, volume sold, selling price, cost of fixed assets, cash grants, effect of future exchange-rate changes, life of fixed assets, life of project, level of working capital, production costs and date 'on stream'.

3. An acceptable approach to sensitivity and risk assessment is to determine the degree of adverse variation possible for each crucial assumption on its own (i.e. all other things remaining unchanged) before the project profitability becomes unacceptable, and to express an opinion on the chance of such variation, e.g. how low would selling price have to go (volume, cost and other things remaining the same) before this in itself made the project unacceptable, and how likely is such a variation?

4. Alternatively a two-stage approach can be followed:

 (i) 'Sensitivity'; for example, for a specific project, a drop of 25% in the assumed volume growth (price, cost and other things remaining the same) might cause a 25 per cent drop in the D.C.F. yield (say from 16 per cent to 12 per cent). This result indicates how sensitive the profitability of the project is to the volume growth assumptions, but does not in itself indicate a degree of risk.

 (ii) 'Risk'; for a view on risk it is necessary to test the sensitivity of the yield assuming as great a variation in each key assumption as is considered to be a real possibility and to express an opinion on the likelihood of such variations.

Risk analysis differs from sensitivity analysis and risk assessment in that the possible variations in project factors are not analysed just to see how they might affect the outcomes – they are built into the project evaluation on the basis of their estimated probability of occurrence. Howard Thomas [5] has illustrated the need for this type of analysis with the example of the executives of a food company who must decide whether to launch a new instant potato. They have concluded the rate of return they can expect from the product is a function of five uncertain quantities: advertising expenditure; total market for instant potato; the company's share of the total market; investment costs; and length of life of instant potato as a consumer product. Using the executives' most likely estimates the accountant has calculated a D.C.F. return of 25 per cent. Thomas points out that if the executives assign a 0.5 probability of obtaining correct values for each of the five uncertain quantities there is a 3 per cent chance all five estimates will be correct, i.e. (0.5). This simple illustration shows how the decision-maker needs to know the approximate probability distribution of values for each uncertain quantity and how the combination of values from each probability distribution will interact to form approximate probability distribution for the D.C.F. rate of return or Net Present Value for a project.

Table 8.10

Risk Analysis – Project 125

D.C.F. Rate of Return	Probability of Achievement of Return stated	Probability of Achievement of Return not less than Return stated
13%	5%	100%
14%	10%	95%
15%	25%	85%
16%	35%	60%
17%	15%	25%
18%	10%	10%

In risk analysis, probability factors are attached to sales, costs, and other elements of the proposal, and calculations made of the probability of alternative project outcomes. Graphs or tabulations

5 Howard Thomas, *Decision Theory and the Manager*, Pitman, London, 1972, p. 24.

can be presented which array the probable project outcomes according to a scientific combination of possibilities involved. Management may receive a tabulation as shown in Table 8.10 which indicates the probability of achieving a particular D.C.F. rate of return and the cumulative probability of achieving a D.C.F. rate of return not less than a particular return. Table 8.10 indicates that there is a 10 per cent probability that the project will yield a return of 18 per cent, and a 35 per cent probability that the yield will be 16 per cent. The table also indicates that there is an 85 per cent probability that the project will not yield less than 15 per cent and a 60 per cent probability that it will not yield less than 16 per cent. The information in Table 8.10 is presented graphically to management as in Figure 8.6.

One version of risk analysis is the decision-tree approach which lends itself to simple manual computations. Decision trees are suited to situations with a limited number of possible outcomes. With a large number of outcomes, a Monte Carlo simulation can be performed by computer. All computer manufacturers have developed software packages for this purpose. Decision trees, Monte Carlo simulations, and the use of subjective probabilities are grouped collectively under the head of *decision theory*. A full discussion of the application of decision theory to capital budgeting is beyond the scope of this book and readers are referred to Selected Readings 4, 7 and 8.

It should be remembered that even with a sophisticated probability model, *subjective* probabilities have to be attached to the various elements of the proposal. Decision theory helps management in quantifying and handling risk; it does not erase it.

Although some of the obvious limitations of any mathematical evaluation of the future have been stressed, the method of expressing the economic worth of an investment is an integral part of the assessment. When a great amount of effort has been expended in investigating the many aspects of a project, it must be worthwhile to ensure that all of the financial implications are fairly represented. Although the estimation of future cash flows is at best an inexact science, the data which becomes available should be given its most meaningful expression. The use of D.C.F. and decision theory techniques would seem to be essential if a correct yardstick of economic worth is to be employed, and realistic evaluations of investment projects undertaken. However, it should be recognized that in evaluating an investment project there is a point beyond which financial calculations cannot go and a gap is left which can only be spanned by managerial judgement. The management accountant's responsibility is to reduce as far as possible the area of uncertainty so that managerial intuition is not overworked.

Required Returns or Hurdle Rates

When the D.C.F. rate of return for a project has been calculated, what should it be compared with when deciding whether the project is financially acceptable? If N.P.V method is employed, what rate of interest should be used to discount the future cash flows to arrive at the project's N.P.V.? There are four factors to be considered when determining required returns or hurdle rates for individual capital projects:

1. The firm's cost of capital;
2. The project's risk category;
3. The opportunity cost of investing outside the firm; and
4. The return on alternative investments.

1. COST OF CAPITAL

The minimum acceptable return from any project is the rate of interest that has to be paid for the capital invested in the company, i.e. the cost of capital. A firm draws capital from various sources and each has a different cost. In Chapters 6 and 7 it has been explained that it will be to the equity shareholder's benefit if the company obtains some *gearing* in its balance sheet. The objective should be to develop a financing structure which optimizes the company's weighted average cost of capital. As a standard part of its long-term financial planning and capital budgeting procedure, a company should determine at regular intervals its future financing programme and, on the basis of the proportion of the various forms of finance to be employed, compute the weighted average cost of capital. A full discussion of the determination of cost of capital is beyond the scope of this introductory text, but the basic concepts will be explained and illustrated. Readers seeking a more detailed explanation are referred to Selected Readings 1, 3, 9 and 10.

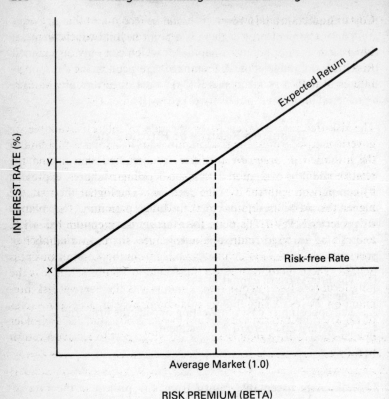

Figure 8.7. *Relationship between risk and expected return*

The Capital Asset Pricing Model can be employed to determine the cost of a company's *equity capital*. It recognizes that the stock market is a 'market' for risky assets, i.e. ordinary or equity shares, and that the pricing mechanism for these assets, i.e. shares, takes account of risk and expected returns. The model hypothesizes that the relationship between risk and return is composed of two parts: A *risk-free rate*, which represents a fixed minimum level of return to investors, and a *premium*, which is proportional to the level of risk associated with the particular asset, i.e. share. This relationship is expressed as follows:

Cost of Equity Capital (%) =

$$\text{Long-term Risk-free Interest Rate(\%)} + \left\{ \text{Average Risk Premium on shares (\%)} \times \frac{\text{Variability of the Company's return in relation to the Average Risk Premium [Beta of 1]}}{} \right\}$$

The risk-free rate is taken to be the rate of interest available on government securities; the risk premium for a share is a function of the *average risk premium* available from quoted shares, and the relative riskiness of a quoted company's ordinary shares, expressed by comparison with the average premium. The higher the risk, the higher the premium relative to the average premium. The relative risk is termed the share's Beta, the average risk premium being 1.0, and can be found for individual companies' shares in a number of specialist reports including one available from the London Business School. These relationships are illustrated in Figure 8.7. If x is the long-term risk-free interest rate, y minus x is the average risk premium on shares. A shareholder in a company with a Beta in excess of 1.0 will expect to receive a return in excess of y, and a shareholder in a company with a Beta less than 1.0 will expect to receive a return less than y.

A SIMPLIFIED EXAMPLE: SIMPLA PLC

The current average yield on long-term government securities is 7 per cent, the average risk premium for ordinary shares is 7 per cent, and Simpla plc's Beta is 0.8. Simpla's equity cost of capital in money terms is:

$$7\% + (7\% \times 0.8) = 12.6\%$$

Debt capital is normally serviced at fixed rates of interest and is allowable for corporation tax. Thus, if the gross rate of interest payable on Simpla plc's debt capital is 10 per cent and the corporation tax rate is 35 per cent, the net *cost of debt capital* is 10% × 0.65 = 6.5%.

If Simpla plc's capital structure is 80 per cent equity capital and 20 per cent debt capital, the company's *weighted average cost of capital* is:

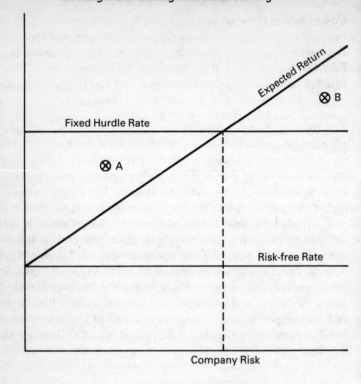

Figure 8.8. *Limitations of fixed hurdle rate*

| Equity capital | 80% of 12.6% = | 10.1 |
| Debt capital | 20% of 6.5% = | 1.3 |

Weighted Average Money Cost of Capital = 11.4%

2. PROJECT'S RISK CATEGORY

The weighted average cost of capital represents a starting-point for the establishment of hurdle rates for appraising individual capital projects. An average hurdle rate for profit-adding projects has to be developed which takes account of the cost of capital but also of the existence of welfare and other non-profit-adding projects. An increasing proportion of many companies' capital investment programmes is in respect of non-profit-adding projects, e.g. improved canteen facilities, safety and environmental expenditure, etc. This has resulted in an increase in the return required from profit-adding projects, and therefore increased the gap between the cost of capital and the minimum hurdle rate. Thus if 80 per cent of Simpla plc's capital projects are profit-adding, its average hurdle rate for profit adding projects is:

$$11.4\% \times \frac{100}{80} = 14.250, \text{ say } 14\%$$

It would be dangerous to use a single hurdle rate for capital investments of differing degrees of risk. For example, consider Figure 8.8. With a single hurdle rate, project A would be rejected and project B accepted. However, A is a low-risk project whose return is in excess of that normally expected for a share of equivelent risk, while B's return may not be high enough to compensate for its higher risk. The use of a single hurdle rate may therefore tend to lead to the rejection of low-risk cost-saving projects offering adequate returns, and the acceptance of high-risk projects, such as new technology and/or new product developments, which do not promise an adequate return in relation to the risk involved. Over the period of time this may result in:

(a) An increase in the riskiness of the company, i.e. its Beta, and therefore its cost of capital, without a commensurate increase in rate of return.

(b) The rejection of cost-saving projects which might weaken a company's overall competitive position.

Recognizing that different profit-adding projects face different degrees of risk, how can a range of hurdle rates be developed? There is no agreed single approach; two are described, both of which involve developing a risk matrix for different classes of project. The Operational Gearing and Revenue Sensitivity matrix is derived from the Capital Asset Pricing Model. We have seen that the outcomes of a capital project are expressed in terms of expected cash inflows and outflows. These cash flows can be analysed into fixed and variable cash flows. Fixed cash flows are those that can reasonably be

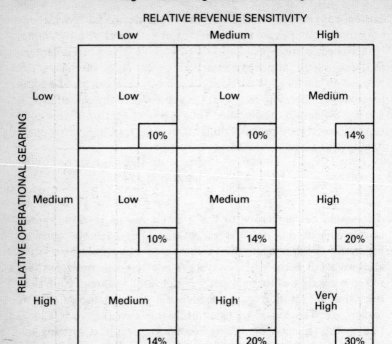

Figure 8.9. *Simpla plc risk matrix and hurdle rates*

expected to occur if the project is undertaken, e.g. initial capital expenditure, incremental fixed overheads, etc. Variable cash flows are those that are subject to uncertainty as to their size, timing, duration or occurrence, e.g. sales volume, raw material costs, etc. The variability of return on a project will depend upon both the proportions of the cash flow that is reasonably certain, called the *operational gearing*, and the potential volatility of the variable cash flows, called the *revenue sensitivity*. Operational gearing is defined as the ratio of variable cash outflows and inflows to total cash flow, and the lower the ratio, i.e. the higher the proportion of fixed cash flows, the riskier the project. Similarly, the more sensitive the variable revenue cash inflows to external factors, the higher the risk of the project. Simpla plc might develop a risk matrix and determine project hurdle rates for each risk class as illustrated in Figure 8.9.

(Cf. average Bowater-Scott)

RELATIVE OPERATIONAL GEARING	Low ½ av. B-S	Medium ½ – 1½ × av. B-S	High 1½ – 2½ × av. B-S	Very High 2½ × av. B-S
Low ½ av. B-S	Low Risk 11%	Low Risk 11%	Medium Risk 17%	High Risk 23%
Medium ½ – 1½ av. B-S	Low Risk 11%	Medium 17%	High 23%	Very High Risk 28%
High 1½ – 2½ × av. B-S	Medium Risk 17%	High 23%	Too High? >34%	Too High? >34%
Very High 2½ × av. B-S	High Risk 23%	Very High Risk 28%	Too High? >34%	Too High? >34%

Figure 8.10. *Risk matrix – relative revenue sensitivity*

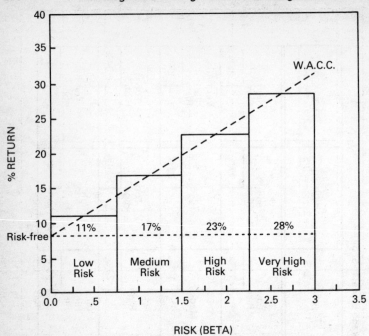

Figure 8.11. *Hurdle rates for risk categories*

A detailed application by Bowater-Scott Ltd of this approach to determining project hurdle rates will be found in Volume 1 of *A Casebook of British Management Accounting* (see Selected Readings). The case study describes how the Capital Asset Pricing Model was employed to determine the company's weighted average money cost of capital (17 per cent), the determination of a matrix of relative operational gearing and relative revenue sensitivity and hurdle rates for each risk class (see Figure 8.10). Project risk (Beta) for each risk class was determined by calculating the relative operational gearing, estimating the revenue sensitivity and applying these to the formula:

| Project Risk (Beta) | = | Relative Operational Gearing | × | Relative Revenue Sensitivity | × | Bowater-Scott Beta (1.1) |

The hurdle rates for each risk class were then derived from Figure 8.11.

Markets Products/Technology	Existing			New	
	Maintain Market Share	Increase Market Share 0–5%	Increase Market Share +5%	Same or similar Type of Customer	New Type of Customer
EXISTING Existing technology	Low	Medium	High	Medium	High
EXISTING Related technology	Low	Medium	High	Medium	High
EXISTING Unrelated technology	High	Very High	Very High	High	Very High
NEW Existing technology	Medium	Medium	High	Medium	High
NEW Related technology	Medium	Medium	Very High	High	Very High
NEW Unrelated technology	High	Very High?	Too High	Very High	Too High?

Figure 8.12. *Risk matrix for profit-adding investments*

Another approach to developing a risk matrix is for a board of directors to classify projects by degree of risk; for example, a replacement project using existing technology to produce an existing product to maintain market share as low risk; a new product using new technology as high risk. A company employing a number of technologies to produce a range of products for a number of markets might develop a *risk matrix* as illustrated in Figure 8.12. The categories of risk in the various boxes should be taken as examples. The board of directors and senior managers would establish the appropriate risk category for each box in the matrix. The number of boxes in the matrix would depend upon the size and diversity of the business. For example, in some companies the new market boxes may be split to separate projects implying high initial market share from those implying low initial market share. The types of risk built into the matrix would vary from company to company. Figure 8.12 is concerned with technological and market risk; in some companies security and reliability of supply of raw materials may constitute a key risk area.

Recommendations can then be made by the finance director for each risk class, but the board should not simply rubber-stamp these; they should discuss their attitudes to risk and uncertainty and their impact on the company. This approach provides a framework within which the board of directors can discuss its attitude to risk and uncertainty surrounding different classes of projects, and in making the inevitable managerial judgements when appraising individual projects within a class. They must decide which portfolio of projects, high and low risk, large and small, etc., is most appropriate in relation to the company's objectives, strategy and operating plans. They may have to accept that their growth and profitability objectives necessitate a strategy that implies the company must be prepared to include in its portfolio of capital projects a limited number of high-risk projects, and reflect this view in the hurdle rates for such projects, recognizing that a change in the company's portfolio may affect its Beta and therefore its cost of capital.

3. OPPORTUNITY COST

Regardless of how the cost of retained earnings is calculated, all projects must compete with the return that the company could earn by investing the available finance outside the business. The risk and uncertainty attached to outside investments must be taken into account.

4. ALTERNATIVE PROJECTS

The ranking of mutually exclusive alternatives has been considered earlier in this chapter. Where the company is in a capital rationing situation, projects will be competing with each other for the limited supply of finance available. Projects may be ranked by magnitude of D.C.F. rate of return as follows:

Project	Capital required £	Cumulative Capital required £	D.C.F. Return %	N.P.V. at 8% £	Net Present Value per £ of Capital required £
504	10,000	10,000	20	5,382	.53
506	50,000	60,000	18	13,764	.28
501	50,000	110,000	17	12,785	.26
502	35,000	145,000	17	10,743	.31
503	25,000	170,000	15	5,645	.23
505	60,000	230,000	12	12,461	.21
	£230,000				

If the company has £145,000 capital available to finance projects, Projects 503 and 505 would have to be rejected, despite the fact that they promise a return in excess of the company's cost of capital of 8 per cent. If the cash flows were discounted at 17 per cent, the return on the marginal project, these two projects would have negative N.P.V.s. A second way of ranking the projects is to calculate the net present value per £1 of capital required, which is the scarce resource. The calculation is similar to relating contribution to limiting factor in a limited production capacity situation, as illustrated in Chapter 5. This ranking also indicates that Projects 503 and 505 should be rejected. If the risk and uncertainty varies between projects, the D.C.F. rate of return or the N.P.V. per £ of capital required may not be the only criterion employed when rationing limited finance to competing projects. The ranking will also become more complex when the projects cover different time periods. Linear programming has been applied to multi-period capital rationing situations, but such approaches sometimes tend to ignore the varying risk and uncertainty attached to the different projects. A full examination of capital rationing will be found in Selected Readings 1, 3, 9 and 10.

Inflation and Capital Investment Appraisal

The persistently high rate of inflation in some Western European countries and North America during the 1970s led accountants to consider more carefully how to take the effects of inflation into consideration when determining a company's cost of capital and evaluating investment projects as well as in the preparation of financial statements.

How does inflation affect a company's cost of capital? In recommending in this chapter the use of D.C.F. techniques for measuring the worthwhileness of investment projects the time value of money concept has been recognized, i.e. that £1 received today is worth more than £1 receivable at some future date, because £1 received today can earn in the intervening period. It will also be appreciated that in a period of inflation £1 received today would purchase more than £1 receivable in one year's time. Therefore, the higher the rate of inflation the greater the value of £1 receivable today compared with money receivable in the future. What is the implication of this statement for the investor's requirement from a company and, therefore, for the company's cost of capital? In theory, the higher the rate of inflation the higher the rate of interest the investor will require if he is to be persuaded not to consume his income today but to invest money today in return for receiving annual dividends or interest payments and the repayment of his investment in the future. (In practice, investors do not always act rationally.) Therefore, *the higher the rate of inflation, the higher the rate of interest the investor requires, and the higher a company's cost of capital in money terms.* How much higher a company's cost of capital in *money terms* will be compared with its cost of capital in *real terms* will depend not only upon the expected future rates of inflation, but also upon the company's gearing and when it raises fixed interest loan capital. In the case of loan capital, once raised, the fixed interest payments in *money terms* remain constant, unless the interest payments are index-linked for inflation, and under conditions of inflation the cost of *existing* loan capital in *real terms* declines over the period of the loan. However, as the inflation rate increases the rate of interest that has to be offered in order to attract *new* loan capital is likely to increase, and the fixed interest payments in *money terms* for new loans will be higher.

Not only does inflation affect a company's cost of capital, it will also affect the cash flows arising from an investment project. When evaluating proposed investments under conditions of inflation a company has to decide whether:

1. To forecast the cash flows arising from an investment project in today's pounds throughout the expected life of the project and ignore inflation, i.e. in *real or constant terms*,
   or:
2. To take account of expected future rates of inflation and to forecast the cash flows in terms of the actual cash receipts and payments that are expected to arise during each year of the project's expected life, i.e. in *money terms*.

If a company forecasts cash flows for a proposed capital project in *money terms* the D.C.F. rate of return or N.P.V. of a project is likely to be higher than the D.C.F. rate of return or N.P.V. in *real or constant terms*. As explained, the higher the rate of inflation the greater will be the difference between a company's cost of capital in *real terms* and its cost of capital in *money terms*. For these reasons it is important that if the cash flows are calculated in *money terms* the D.C.F. rate of return for the project is compared with the company's cost of capital in *money terms*. For example, if a company's cost of capital is 7 per cent per annum in *real or constant terms* and 15 per cent in *money terms*, a capital project promising a 14 per cent D.C.F. rate of return in *money terms*, i.e. after taking into account expected rates of inflation, would be *accepted* if compared with a cost of capital of 7 per cent, but be *rejected* if compared with the appropriate cost of capital of 15 per cent.

It is recommended that companies do take account of expected rates of inflation and determine their cost of capital and evaluate investment projects in *money terms* for two reasons:

1. If a company ignores inflation and determines cost of capital and evaluates investment projects in *real terms*, it is in effect assum-

ing that future rates of inflation will affect equally the cost of different types of finance and all elements of an investment project. In fact this is likely to be an unrealistic assumption; the different elements of a project are likely to be affected by different rates of inflation, and these may change from year to year. For example, the expected rates of increase in wage rates in each year of a project's life may be very different from the expected rates of increase of a key imported raw material in each year of a project's life.

2. Capital projects that are approved have to be incorporated into a company's long-term financial plan and annual budget. As explained in Chapter 7, it is important that these plans are prepared in *money terms* so that the impact of future rates of inflation on a company's financial position can be anticipated and a strategy for future financing developed.

A company may also wish to evaluate a capital project in *real or constant terms*. In Unilever's case (*A Casebook of British Management Accounting*, Volume 1):

> Future cash flows are required to be estimated in 'current' terms (Unilever uses the term 'current' to mean expected future cash flows, i.e. current value of money at the time in question) using as specific as possible rates of inflation, e.g. in so far as specific year-on-year forecasts may be available for the rates of inflation of say, labour, plant and machinery, buildings and energy, these should be used. Cash flows are also assessed in 'constant' terms (i.e. future cash flows expressed in terms of the value of money when the appraisal is carried out) by discounting inflated (i.e. current) cash flows by the forecast year-on-year rates for general inflation.
>
> D.C.F. yields are then calculated in both 'current' and 'constant' terms, i.e. calculated on the net cash flows before and after elimination of the effects of inflation.

Unilever does not set hurdle rates for project acceptability. The acceptability of any project is based on a variety of criteria, including D.C.F. yield. The BOC case study (*A Casebook of British Management Accounting*, Volume 2) contains a detailed description of account taken of inflation when appraising capital projects.

Thus, not only is it recommended that a company evaluates investment projects in *money terms* and compares these with the company's cost of capital in *money terms*, but also that the separate rates of inflation are forecast for the different elements of a project.

It will be recognized that the forecasting of future rates of inflation is a difficult and complex task. Therefore it is important when testing the sensitivity of the profitability of a project to variations in the key assumptions in the evaluation that the assumptions about rates of inflation are treated as key assumptions and included in the sensitivity analysis. Similarly, if risk analysis is undertaken, subjective probabilities should be attached to the forecast range of rates of inflation. This short introduction to the determination of a company's cost of capital and the evaluation of investment projects under conditions of inflation, given a dynamic and uncertain external environment, indicates the difficult and complex issues that arise. A more detailed discussion of these issues will be found in Selected Readings 1, 2, 3 and 10.

Summary

Capital investment appraisal forms one part of the capital budgeting procedure. It raises problems which are different from the measurement of past performance. The basic object of any investment is that in return for paying out a given amount of *cash* today, a larger amount will be received back over a period of time. Furthermore, the value of a cash payment or receipt must be related to the *time* the transfer takes place. Money has a time value. Discounted Cash Flow (D.C.F.) is based on the cash and time value of money concepts. Discounting, being the opposite of compounding, is used to determine the present value of future cash flows. 'Accounting' rates of return do not satisfactorily take account of the cash and time value of money concepts. The D.C.F. or 'internal' rate of return and Net Present Value (N.P.V.) methods are alternative applications of the D.C.F. principle. While N.P.V. is theoretically sounder than the D.C.F. rate of return method, the latter is seen to have practical advantages.

Any method of calculating the prospective return from a proposed investment is dependent on the soundness of the basic assumptions. The assembly of the relevant estimates represents the major time devoted to project appraisal. It is usually undesirable to calculate one-answer solutions; at least 'optimistic', 'pessimistic' and 'most probable' returns should be calculated. More sophisticated approaches employ sensitivity and probability analysis to determine the impact of fluctuations in the basic data on a project's profitability. The D.C.F. rate of return for a project should be compared with the hurdle rate for the project's risk category derived from the company's weighted average cost of capital, the return on alternative projects available, and the opportunity cost of investing outside the firm. It is recommended that account is taken of expected rates of inflation, and that cost of capital is determined and appraised in money terms. There is a point beyond which financial evaluation cannot go and managerial judgement must take over. Sound financial analysis should minimize the gap to be bridged by such judgements.

Selected Readings

1. Richard Brealey and Stewart Myers, *Principles of Corporate Finance*, McGraw-Hill, New York, 1984.
2. Bryan Carsberg and Anthony Hope, *Business Investment Decisions under Inflation*, Institute of Chartered Accountants in England and Wales, 1976.
3. Julian R. Franks, John E. Broyles and William T. Carleton, *Corporate Finance*, Kent, Boston, Mass., 1985.
4. Geoffrey Gregory, *Decision Analysis*, Pitman, London, 1988.
5. London Business School, *Risk Management Service* (quarterly).
6. A. D. McIntyre and N. J. Coulthurst, *Capital Budgeting in Medium-Sized Businesses*, Chartered Institute of Management Accountants, London, 1986.
7. P. G. Moore and H. Thomas, *The Anatomy of Decisions*, Penguin, Harmondsworth, 1976.
8. P. G. Moore, H. Thomas, D. W. Bunn and J. M. Hampton, *Case Studies in Decision Analysis*, Penguin, Harmondsworth, 1976.
9. Richard Pike and Richard Dobbins, *Investment Decisions and Financial Strategy*, Philip Allan, Oxford, 1986.
10. J. M. Samuels and F. M. Wilkes, *Management of Company Finance*, Nelson, Sunbury-on-Thames, 1986.
11. Richard F. Vancil, *The Leasing of Industrial Equipment*, McGraw-Hill, New York, 1962.

CASE STUDIES

In John Sizer and Nigel Coulthurst, *A Casebook of British Management Accounting*, I.C.A.E.W., 1984, 1985.

Bowater-Scott Corporation Ltd (Volume 1) – the use of the Capital Asset Pricing Model for developing hurdle rates for capital investment decisions in a jointly owned disposable paper products business.

Rumenco Ltd (Volume 1) – capital expenditure appraisal and control systems in a medium-sized manufacture of secondary feedstuffs for the agricultural industry.

Unilever (Volume 1) – an outline of the process relating to the planning and control of capital investment and detailed consideration of the appraisal stage of the process in a multinational consumer goods business.

The BOC Group (Volume 2) – a description and illustration of the financial appraisal of major investment projects in a large and diverse group.

The Post Office (Volume 2) – the evaluation of a major investment project.

9

Budgetary Planning and Control Systems

Budgetary planning and control systems are concerned with detailed planning and control in the short term. As explained in Chapter 7, they should be closely integrated with a company's long-term plans. The introduction and operation of budgetary planning and control systems in individual businesses or operating units is considered in this chapter, and financial control in groups of companies and divisionalized businesses in Chapter 10.

There are four aspects of the control process which form the key elements of a system of budgetary planning and control:

1. To *develop* plans to achieve objectives.
2. To *communicate* information about proposed plans.
3. To *motivate* people to accomplish the plans.
4. To *report* performance.

Control involves the making of decisions based on relevant information, which leads to plans and actions which implement the strategy to achieve the company's objectives. It is concerned not so much with the correction of past mistakes as with the direction of the current and future activities in such a manner as to assure the realization of management plans. Thus:

PLANNING is the BASIS for CONTROL.
INFORMATION is the GUIDE for CONTROL.
ACTION is the ESSENCE of CONTROL.

Furthermore, it will be recognized that the plans for and the results of operations should be expressed in terms of *human responsibilities*, not as abstract concepts, because:

People, rather than analyses or reports, control operations and therefore accountability can only be expressed in relation to human responsibilities.

To do their jobs efficiently they will need facts.

Supplying the factual basis for control is an important function of accounting.

The areas of human responsibility represent the various control centres within an organization. As illustrated in Figure 9.1, four types of *responsibility centre* exist in many large companies: investment centres, profit centres, cost centres and revenue centres.

The manager of an *investment centre* is responsible for costs, revenues, and assets employed. Costs and revenues, but not investments, are controlled by the manager of a *profit centre*, such as a product division. *Cost centres* are typified by a production department in a factory, while *revenue centres* and *cost centres* are found in a marketing department where a sales manager generates sales revenue as well as incurring expenses. A system of accounting which produces information by *responsibility centres* has to be developed if effective control information is to be provided to the decision-takers in an organization. Furthermore, as illustrated in Figure 9.2, information should be integrated so that a single figure at one level is analysed in greater detail at the next level. Accountants describe such systems as *responsibility accounting* systems.

Budgetary planning and control employs the concepts of responsibility accounting, and is one of the most useful management tools for planning, co-ordinating and controlling the activities of a business.

What is Budgetary Planning and Control?

Financial planning is part of the overall planning of the firm in the long term and medium term; budgetary planning and control is concerned with planning in the short term. The financial plan projects the long-term plans of the company in financial terms. Within the framework of the financial plan, a budgetary planning and control system should be operated to ensure that detailed plans are prepared for the current year of the long-term financial plan. When a system of budgetary planning and control is in use, budgets are established which set out in financial terms the responsibilities of executives in relation to the requirements of the overall policy of the company. Continuous comparison is made of actual results with budgeted results, either to secure, through action by responsible

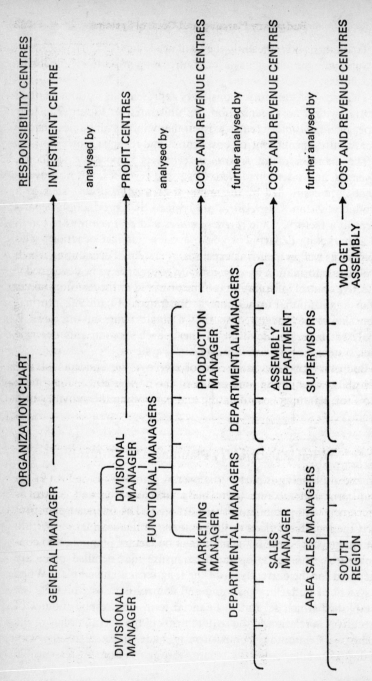

Figure 9.1. Relationship between organization chart and responsibility centres

ORGANIZATION CHART

GENERAL MANAGER

DIVISIONAL MANAGER

DIVISIONAL MANAGER

FUNCTIONAL MANAGERS

MARKETING MANAGER

PRODUCTION MANAGER

DEPARTMENTAL MANAGERS

DEPARTMENTAL MANAGERS

SALES MANAGER

ASSEMBLY DEPARTMENT

AREA SALES MANAGERS

SUPERVISORS

SOUTH REGION

WIDGET ASSEMBLY

RESPONSIBILITY CENTRES

INVESTMENT CENTRE

analysed by

PROFIT CENTRES

analysed by

COST AND REVENUE CENTRES

further analysed by

COST AND REVENUE CENTRES

further analysed by

COST AND REVENUE CENTRES

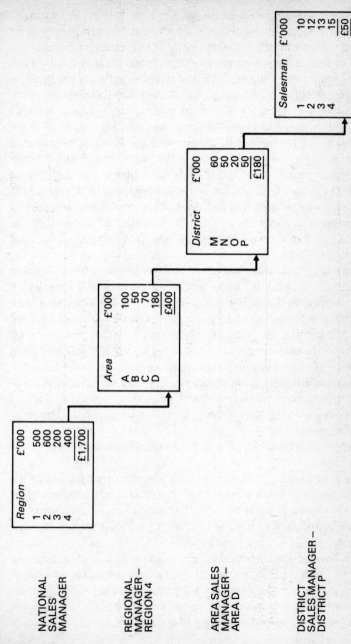

Region	£'000
1	500
2	600
3	200
4	400
	£1,700

Area	£'000
A	100
B	50
C	70
D	180
	£400

District	£'000
M	60
N	50
O	20
P	50
	£180

Salesman	£'000
1	10
2	12
3	13
4	15
	£50

NATIONAL
SALES
MANAGER

REGIONAL
MANAGER –
REGION 4

AREA SALES
MANAGER –
AREA D

DISTRICT
SALES MANAGER –
DISTRICT P

Figure 9.2. Integrated sales budget

executives, the objectives of policy, or to provide a basis for a revision of policy. Financial limits are allocated to component parts of individual enterprises. Accounting for revenues and outlays is done in such a way as to provide continuous comparison between actual results and budgets so that, if remedial action is necessary, it may be taken at an early stage, or alternatively the objectives may be reviewed. A manager within an undertaking agrees a financial limit within which he plans the activities under his command in accordance with the policies of the undertaking. It will be appreciated that a manager should participate in the establishment of the financial limit, since he will be individually accountable both for keeping within the agreed limit and for implementing the plans for which the resources were provided. In fact, the budgetary planning and control system plays an important role in influencing the behaviour of managers in an organization. These behavioural influences are considered later in this chapter.

Thus, the preparation and use of budgets involve the development of a set of estimates of future costs and revenues in a form which will co-ordinate the activities of the company in accordance with selected objectives and strategies, and will serve as a standard for financial control. Budgets are, therefore, financial and/or quantitative statements, prepared and approved prior to a defined period of time, of the policy to be pursued during that period for the purposes of attaining given objectives. They are financial quantifications of action plans to implement strategies to achieve a set of objectives. A budget may include income, expenditure, and employment of capital.

Budgetary control should assist management in three ways:

1. It provides top management with a summarized picture of the results to be expected from a proposed *plan* of operations. This aids management in choosing between a number of alternative plans and in determining whether a particular plan is satisfactory.
2. Following the approval of the plan, it serves as a guide to executives and departmental heads responsible for individual segments of the company's operations. This aids management in *co-ordinating* the operations by clearly defining the responsibilities and objectives of each segment.

3. It serves to measure performance, since budget deviations reflect either the organization's failure to achieve the plan or its ability to better it. This aids management in *controlling* the activities of individuals and the overall performance of the company, as well as assisting managers to measure and control their own performance.

There are a number of basic steps in the design and implementation of accounting systems and procedures which generate financial reports for responsible managers. The responsibility structure of the organization must be determined, and the factors which influence the profitability of the business established. Investment, profit, cost and revenue centres must be created so that responsibility for the control of each item of expenditure and revenue can be assigned to individuals. The next step is to define the specific information needs of each managerial position. Working closely with management, the accountant must determine the information requirements of individual managers. Yardsticks, both financial and non-financial, for evaluating the actual performance of each manager through the budgetary control reporting system must also be agreed with managers. Having established the information requirements and performance yardsticks for each manager, the control reports each manager will receive can be designed in detail. The accounting system must then be established to generate the information necessary for these reports. This requires a classification and coding system which analyses revenue and expense items in relation to the individuals responsible for their control. Procedures for the development of forecasts, and the preparation and approval of budgets, including the design of forms, have to be laid down. The detailed accounting procedures necessary to generate the control reports when and where they are required must be developed. Arrangements have to be made to ensure there is regular advice and explanation to managers from the accounting staff of the control reports which managers receive. Finally, a programme of management meetings to discuss reports and agree courses of action has to be established.

Administering the Budgeting Programme

For a budget to be effective in the accomplishment of its end objective, it must be properly developed and utilized. The budgeting programme must be soundly administered. Budgeting is a management function and not simply an accounting exercise; its success depends in no small way on the support given by top management. It is a management responsibility to plan and control. Managers make decisions, not accountants.

Primary responsibility for the administration of the budgeting programme is frequently delegated by top management to an executive, variously known as the *budget officer* or budget accountant. He is frequently on the staff of the chief accountant, and this is one reason why budgeting may simply be seen as an accounting exercise in some companies. The general duties of the budget officer include:

1. To co-ordinate the efforts of those engaged directly in the preparation of the budgets;
2. To prepare budget reports;
3. To recommend courses of action as may be indicated by the budgets; and
4. To make special studies pertaining to the budgetary planning and control system.

The budget officer is a *staff* officer and as such should exercise no line authority, except over his own staff. Furthermore, the development of the budgets should not be a job delegated to the budget officer but rather one that is supervised and co-ordinated by him. It is a basic tenet of budgetary control that executives develop and accept responsibility for their budgets. The budgets will be the product of the efforts of all levels of management with the budget officer co-ordinating and supervising these efforts.

In some companies a *budget committee*, composed of executives in charge of major functional areas of the business, may be found to be a useful device for co-ordinating and reviewing the budget programme, particularly as related to general policies which affect the budgets. The budget committee is normally advisory in nature and may be charged with the following functions:

1. To establish procedures and timetables for the development of budgets;
2. To receive and review individual budgets;
3. To suggest revisions;

4. To decide general policies affecting the budgets of more than one department;
5. To approve budgets and later revisions;
6. To receive and consider budget reports showing actual results compared with the budget; and
7. To recommend action where necessary.

The budget committee may become a very powerful group in co-ordinating the activities of the firm and in synthesizing, if not developing, corporate policy. The budget officer will normally be secretary of the budget committee.

It is advisable to develop a *budget manual* which sets forth:

1. The objectives of the business;
2. The part which budgetary planning and control plays in the accomplishment of these objectives;
3. The specific procedures to be followed in the preparation of budgets;
4. The reports comparing budgeted and actual performance to be prepared; and
5. The functions of the budget officer and budget committee, and their relationship with the various levels of management in the development of the system of budgetary control.

Development of Budgets

Effective planning of one phase of a business is impossible if all other phases are not planned just as carefully, and all phases co-ordinated into a whole. Therefore, a budgetary planning and control system is made up of many individual budgets, but these individual budgets have to be integrated into a master budget. The following steps are normally taken in the development of the individual budgets and the master budget:

1. Preparation of a statement of the *basic assumptions* on which the individual budgets are to be based, including company objectives for profits, growth, and financial position for the budget period, and strategies and action plans to be implemented during the period.
2. Preparation of a *forecast* of the general economic conditions,

conditions in the industry, and for the firm. If the company undertakes long-range planning, the forecast and objectives, strategies and action plans should flow from the long-range plans.

3. Preparation of a *sales budget* based on the forecast, product-market strategies and plans, and the productive capacity of the firm. The sales budget will be broken down into areas of responsibility, for example, by salesmen or area sales managers. The sales budget will largely determine how much is to be spent on marketing and distribution, and what quality of goods is to be produced.

4. Preparation of a *production budget* based on and set in conjunction with the sales budget, after making necessary adjustments for planned stock changes. It will also include planning the requirement for materials, labour and manufacturing facilities, together with the costs of these items. The production budget will be sub-divided into budgets for each production centre.

5. Within each production centre, preparation of budgets for each area of factory *responsibility*, i.e. budgets for responsible departmental managers based on their authority.

6. Preparation of *marketing and administrative expense budgets* for each area of marketing and administrative responsibility.

7. Preparation of a *research and development budget* analysed into projects by responsible research staff.

8. Where applicable, preparation of *profit budgets* by areas of profit responsibility and by major product groups. Many businesses are organized not on functional lines but into product groups each with profit responsibility.

9. Preparation of a *capital expenditure budget* covering all non-recurring expenditures on fixed assets.

10. Preparation of *working capital budgets* covering all changes in raw material stocks, work-in-progress, finished stocks, debtors and creditors.

11. Preparation of a *cash budget* reducing all activities into cash flows. (This important budget is considered later in this chapter.)

12. Assembly and co-ordination of individual budgets into a *master budget*, that is budgeted profit-and-loss account and balance sheet. If the master budget does not achieve the manage-

ment's objectives for profit, sales growth, return on capital employed and financial position, the budgets will have to be reviewed and revised and, if necessary, strategies and action plans revised.

The interrelationship between the basic assumptions, individual budgets and the master budget in a functionally organized business is illustrated in Figure 9.3.

The primary responsibility for the preparation of the budgets should rest with the heads of the various responsibility centres in a company. For example, the *sales forecast* should be developed by the department charged with the responsibility for market studies. In many firms this may be the sales department, and in others it may be a particular department which specializes in the area, for example the market research department or economics department. However, regardless of the organizational plan, the sales manager should participate actively in the development of the *sales budget*, since he will be individually responsible for the achievement of the sales.

In the Industrial Chemicals Co., whose organization chart is illustrated in Figure 9.4, the annual budgets for the marketing department are developed as follows:

1. Company objectives and strategies flow down from the managing director to the marketing director.

2. The market research manager supplies marketing and customer research information to the marketing director and the sales manager.

3. The marketing objectives and strategy to achieve the company objectives are developed by the marketing director and his senior staff and agreed with the managing director.

4. The marketing objectives and strategy are translated by the marketing director into specific end use market-share objectives, geographical sales objectives by product group, and class of customer.

5. The marketing director develops a sales budget for the customers for whom he is responsible, and passes down to the sales manager objectives for the remaining customers and geographical areas.

6. The sales manager develops a similar budget for the customers for whom he is responsible, and passes to the export sales

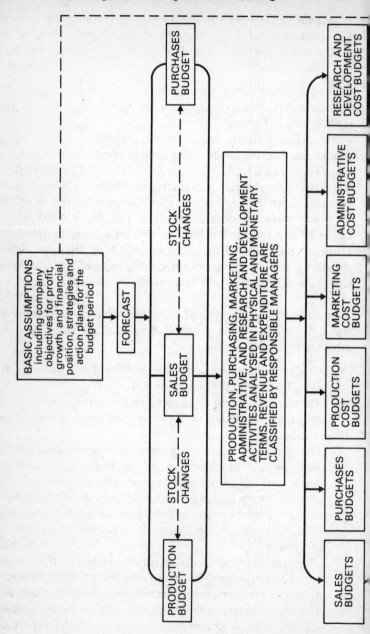

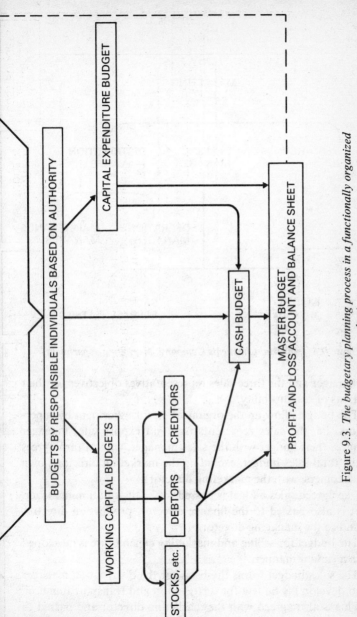

Figure 9.3. *The budgetary planning process in a functionally organized business*

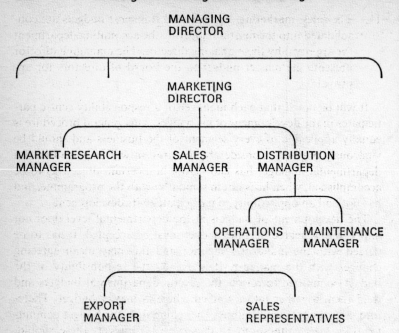

Figure 9.4. *Industrial Chemicals Company. Marketing department*

manager and the three sales representatives objectives for their areas of responsibility.

7. The budgets flow up the organization for agreement by superiors, i.e. the sales representatives and export sales manager agree their budget with the sales manager, who in turn agrees the total sales budget, excluding the marketing director's own customers, with the marketing director.

8. The agreed sales budget is passed to the distribution manager. It is also passed to the finance director, production director, and to the managing director.

9. The budget for selling and marketing expenditure is developed in a similar manner.

10. The sales budget forms the basis for the distribution manager to develop his budget for distribution and transport function. This is also agreed with the marketing director and passed to the accounting department.

11.   The sales, marketing expenses and transport budgets are consolidated into the master budget by the accounting department for approval by the managing director. The managing director presents the master budget to the board of directors for approval.

It will be noted that each manager of a responsibility centre participates in the development of his budget. This general procedure is equally applicable to every segment of the business and should be vigorously pursued. Considerable frustration will be generated if a departmental manager has laid before him certain objectives to be accomplished, when he is not in sympathy with the programme, and has not had an opportunity to participate in its development.

The development of budgets at the departmental level does not imply to any degree that the budget must be accepted. It has to be agreed with the manager's superior and this may mean agreeing changes with the manager. It is usually the responsibility of the budget committee to review the several departmental budgets and weld them together into a unified whole, a master budget. Therefore, adjustments will doubtless be required. If the budget committee does make alterations to departmental budgets these should, as far as possible, be agreed with the departmental managers so that they do feel they have participated in the review of their budgets.

Top-Down – Bottom-Up – Top-Down Budgeting

The steps in the development of budgets that have been summarized in Figure 9.3, and illustrated by the Industrial Chemical Co. example, imply a two-way process of a top-down statement of objectives and strategies, bottom-up budget preparation, and top-down approval by senior management. This process is further illustrated by a discussion with three senior members of the Chartered Institute of Management Accountants on how budgets are prepared and approved in their companies, and the role of the management accountants in assisting managers in the preparation of budgets.

The following is an extract from an edited transcript of an audio cassette which was produced as part of the Open University's

Continuing Education Course P671, 'Accounting and Finance for Managers'.[1]

PROFESSOR JOHN SIZER, a member of Council, discusses the setting and communicating of budgetary objectives with three other members of the Institute's Council;

DAVID ALLEN, President of the Institute and Finance Director of Cadbury Typhoo;

DERRICK WILLINGHAM, immediate past-President of the Institute and Chairman of the Haywood Tyler Pump group; and

RON KETT, Finance Director of the Bath and Portland Group.

PROFESSOR: We are going to discuss how budgets are prepared and approved in your companies, including how managers participate in the development of budgets. In the Open University's course booklet it is stated that the budgeting procedure normally starts bottom-up and for this reason it is valuable for managers at all levels to have a good understanding of the company's overall objectives within which the budget is to be framed, i.e. top-down objective setting and bottom-up budget preparation.

     David, is this the approach you use at Cadbury Typhoo? If so, how do you ensure managers at all levels understand the company's objectives?

DAVID ALLEN: Yes, that is the approach we use at Cadbury Typhoo, absolutely. If I can introduce two more words – tactics and strategy – the budgets represent the financial outcomes of the tactics that are to be adopted over the coming twelve months and the strategy covers the long-term aims of the business.

     To put it into a time context, our financial year is the calendar year, January to December, and round about the spring or summer of each year, in conjunction with the Group, we decide the outline strategy for the Division. So Cadbury Schweppes as a Group will have decided at that time of the year whether, for example, it wants to expand or contract the tea and foods activities of the business, whether it wants to expand the United Kingdom

1 John Sizer, David Allen, Ron Kett and Derrick Willingham, 'Setting Budgetary Objectives', *Management Accounting*, July/August 1984. Further details about Course P671 and other Open University management courses are available from ASCO, P.O. Box 76, The Open University, Walton Hall, Milton Keynes MK7 6AA.

sales of those products, whether it wants to concentrate on overseas markets, and so on. So that by the end of the summer everyone has a pretty clear idea as to where the Group sees the Division going.

And then in the autumn and winter of each year the detailed plans for the up-coming year are developed, as you say, bottom-up. Each of the functional managers, the production managers, the buyers, the marketing managers, suggest what's going to happen in their particular areas of the business. For example, the marketing people will tell us what's going to happen to prices, the buyers will obviously talk about the commodity markets and what impact that's going to have on the business.

Gradually these are assembled so that towards the end of the year we have a detailed budget for the following twelve months, which is compared with the strategy. Now at this stage the easy thing is to say: Provided that agrees with the strategy it has every chance of being approved by the Group as the budget for the forthcoming year. Often, as you might imagine, there are differences between the budget and what was assumed in the strategy and they become the main topics for discussion in, as we call it, negotiating the budget with the parent company.

PROFESSOR: What is the role of the accountants in helping individual managers to prepare their budgets, and then in bringing all these budgets together to ensure that the whole is meeting the overall strategy that has been laid down by the Board and the parent company?

DAVID ALLEN: Well, the management accounting function within our Group is very decentralized, not only to the Division, even within the Division the management accountants are attached to what we call product teams. For example, within the Tea and Foods Division of Cadbury Schweppes there is a business unit which is concentrating on Cadbury's Smash, etc.

There will be an accountant in each of those units and he or she will be making sure, as the budgets are put together, that the functional managers are asking the right questions: asking questions about events within the company, such as what sort of wage awards we are likely to be giving over the next twelve months, and how the various costs respond to changes in volume.

They are also looking outwards and saying what are the latest conditions in the cocoa-growing markets, or the tea-growing countries, and helping to build up a prediction of all those items that are actually outside the immediate control of the business. Probably the main thing that the accountants are doing is making sure that the managers ask the right questions in preparing their budgets.

PROFESSOR: So they are helping the managers to put their budgets into the overall context of the business?

DAVID ALLEN: That's right.

PROFESSOR: So if I went into Cadbury Typhoo and spoke to lower-level managers, middle managers, and other people at lower levels in the organization, I would find that they all have a clear understanding of the overall Cadbury Typhoo strategy, the strategy for their Division, and that they are preparing their bottom-up budgets in the context of this top-down message that has been communicated to everyone in Cadbury Typhoo? You really believe that everybody understands the strategy?

DAVID ALLEN: That is so, but I would add something to that; they are looking out for any danger signals which suggest that the strategy should be reviewed. In other words, the budget is not only a control over the operations of the company, it is actually part of the feedback into the strategic process. For example, we may have said we were going to expand this part of the business because we thought it was a profitable area, but when we came to put the detailed budgets together the responsible managers may have found that it was not as profitable as we had thought. They would feed this back into the strategy process.

PROFESSOR: You said right at the beginning that you distinguish between strategy and tactics; could you just illustrate what you mean by tactics in the context of preparing a budget?

DAVID ALLEN: Yes. The strategy is more or less what sort of business do we want to be in, and are we going to expand certain sectors or not? The tactics tend to be those areas of the business that are responsive to decisions within the relatively short term. We tend to roll our budgets forward on a twelve-month basis, so tactics to us is something that will have a noticeable impact within a twelve-month period. For example, the tactics might be pricing; are we going for a relatively high margin on this product and risk losing the volume, or are we going to go for a relatively low margin to build up our market share?

PROFESSOR: Derrick, David's business is essentially producing and marketing consumer products, very dependent on world commodity prices, particularly the prices of tea and cocoa; is your business more concerned with industrial markets?

DERRICK WILLINGHAM: Very much so – capital goods – and I'm responsible for a group of eight businesses, four of which are based in this country and four overseas, in North America and continental Europe. The output from this country is something like 75 per cent exported throughout the world and the lead times are very long for large pumps for power stations. We have orders now, for example, for delivery in 1990. At the other extreme, with submersible pumps for irrigation, some of the orders there can be two or three weeks ahead, some could be six months ahead.

PROFESSOR: So David's producing consumer products which are standard products that you can buy in the supermarkets, while you are producing to contract specific products to meet specific customer requirements. Is your approach to budgeting similar, or are there factors that make the two businesses different – that lead you to use a different approach?

DERRICK WILLINGHAM: That is one of the interesting things – our approach is very similar. We operate against a background of an overall strategic plan which goes forward three to five years, depending on the particular business. We update that every year in the spring. We then produce in the autumn of every year what we call an operating plan (and this is where we depart from the term 'budget') which concentrates predominantly on the year ahead. But it also contains some detailed financial projections for two or three years beyond. Now the operating plan essentially is a budget in the conventional term, but linked with it are specific detailed action plans against which names are put and people are responsible for implementing them.

PROFESSOR: So those action plans in many ways are the link between the strategy and the tactics that David talked about. Having developed this operating plan, how do you get from that to budgets that reflect the responsibilities of individual managers in financial terms?

DERRICK WILLINGHAM: Well, the budget is really part and parcel of the operating plan. Each of the eight profit centres produces an operating plan including detailed financial projections, and then it is consolidated for the group as a whole. I am slightly amused by this question – bottom-up and top-down and so on – because I believe it is essentially a two-way process all the way through. It is wrong to set too many objectives from the top unless you have adequate feedback from below, and vice versa.

PROFESSOR: How within one of your subsidiaries do you communicate to the managers at the lower levels? Do you have presentations on the action plan, does the top management present to all the levels of the organization, or is it simply a written communication to every manager?

DERRICK WILLINGHAM: We do it by a variety of means. We have management news letters, we have communication meetings, we have a whole series of discussions, trying to make sure that at least each manager knows what his part of the process is. I noticed you asked David if he was 100 per cent sure that everybody understood. I'm 100 per cent sure that I'd *like* everybody to understand, but there is a difference; we try to make sure they do.

The discussion continues in Chapter 10, in particular with Ron Kett, on the role of the parent company in the development and approval of budgets. Detailed descriptions of the developments of budgets in a number of companies are contained in *A Casebook of British Management Accounting*: The Minerals Division of the Bath and Portland Group (Volume 1); the Central Electricity Generating Board (Volume 1); Coloroll Ltd (Volume 1); IPC Women's Magazines Group (Volume 1); Northern Dairies Ltd (Volume 1): The South Wales Electricity Board (Volume 1) and Debenhams Furnishings Ltd (Volume 2). (See Selected Readings, page 347.)

Budget Attainment Levels

It has been argued that it is important that responsibility for the preparation of budgets should rest squarely on those individuals responsible for their achievement. This procedure gives rise to two questions: [2]

1. Does the level of attainment incorporated in the budget influence the motivation of those who are responsible for its achievement?
2. Does the method of determining levels of attainment also affect motivation and consequently the usefulness of the system?

The essential nature of control involves not so much the correction of past mistakes as the direction of the current and future activities in such a manner as to assure the realization of management plans. Therefore, the management control process consists, in part, of inducing people in an organization to do certain things and to refrain from doing others. The control technique may influence both the strength and direction of employee motivation. In particular, the level of attainment incorporated in the budgeting procedure may influence the motivation of individuals responsible for the preparation and achievement of budgets.

An individual normally acts according to what he perceives to be his own best interests. The budgeting procedure should be designed so that the actions of individuals, which are in part determined by their own perceived interests, are also actions that are in accordance with the best interests of the company. Perfect congruence between individual and organizational goals can never be achieved, but the budgeting procedure should be designed to minimize the difference between individual and company objectives, and between departmental and company objectives. It should not encourage the individual to act against the best interests of the company.

It is important that two separate questions are answered regarding this level of attainment incorporated into budgets:

1. What will it motivate people to do in their own personal interests?
2. Is this action in the best interests of the company?

2 These questions were first raised by J. R. Small in 'Developments in Management Accountancy', *Certified Accountants Journal*, November 1966, p. 381.

The answer to question 1 will depend upon the individual and his position in the organization. Clearly, the management accountant cannot fully answer these questions, nor should it be his job to do so. Senior management must consider these questions and may have to consult an industrial psychologist. Budgetary planning and control involves people and, therefore, it is important that the influence of the system on the motivation of individuals is examined. A full discussion of the behavioural aspects of control systems is beyond the scope of this chapter, but they are fully considered in Selected Reading 6. We shall discuss them briefly when considering the reporting stage of budgetary planning and control.

The Cash Budget

The preparation of the cash budget is an important part of the budgetary planning process, particularly:

1. In a rapidly expanding company; and
2. When there is a high rate of inflation.

A rapidly expanding company may budget for and achieve improved profits, but have a deteriorating cash position because the profits generated are not translated into cash inflows. The rise in sales and profits may be accompanied by a disproportionate increase in stocks, debtors, and capital expenditure which more than absorbs the cash flow generated. The company may be *overtrading*. It is referred to by bank managers as 'the dark shadow of the expanding company'. A rapidly expanding company cannot rely solely on a bank overdraft facility; it will normally require an injection of permanent capital. The great danger of relying on short-term bank facilities to finance rapid expansion is that the bank may be forced, particularly in times of credit restriction called for by the Bank of England, to withdraw support, possibly resulting in bankruptcy or liquidation.

Overtrading occurs because insufficient attention is given to the management of the shorter-term fluctuating needs which are associated with the everyday cycle of activities of a company. As explained in Chapter 2, in every business there is a *working capital cycle* which will vary among companies. As illustrated in Figure 9.5, in manufacturing situations it is:

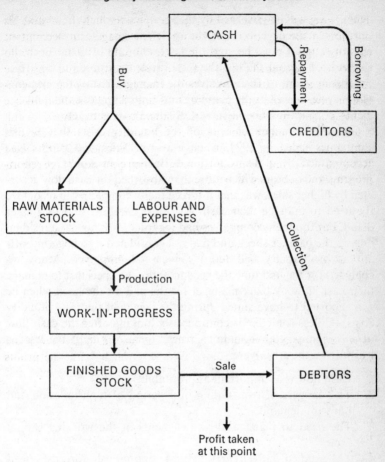

Figure 9.5. *Working capital cycle of manufacturing firm*

CASH → MATERIALS → WORK-IN-PROGRESS → FINISHED
GOODS → SALES → DEBTORS → CASH

In purely retailing organizations the cycle is shortened:

CASH → GOODS → SALES → DEBTORS → CASH

The amount of working capital required and its level at any particular time will be governed by the *speed* with which the cash cycle can be sustained. The faster the cycle the less the investment in working capital must be, and the faster the rate of turnover in the elements of capital the less the total investment needs to be. Thus the management of cash involves the management of the elements of the cycle, as well as the planning and controlling of capital investments, corporation tax payments, dividend payments, etc.

One of the major benefits of the liquidity crisis that British companies faced in 1974, when a rise in sales and profits was accompanied by a disproportionate increase in stocks, work-in-progress and debtors which more than absorbed the cash flow generated by higher sales, was that it forced many companies to recognize the need to manage their cash flow more carefully and in greater detail. Far too many companies had regarded cash flow as a residual item in the balance sheet, and had not considered it to be as important as profitability and return on capital employed. Many recognized for the first time the need to appoint a specialist to manage their cash flow. A bank manager hit the nail on the head when he was reported to have stated during the height of the 1974 liquidity crisis: 'Unless someone is continuously looking after the cash flow of a company, you shouldn't go near them.' Four of the lessons learnt from the crisis were:

1. Cash flow is as important as profitability.
2. The dangers of overtrading in a period of high inflation and buoyant demand.
3. The need to manage all the elements in the working capital cycle.
4. The need to budget carefully and continuously forecast ahead future cash flows, and to test the sensitivity of the forecasts for changes in the key assumptions.

These lessons were reinforced in 1979–80 when British companies faced a liquidity and profitability crisis during a severe recession.

The preparation of an *annual cash budget*, broken down in monthly, or even weekly, budgets is an important aspect of budgetary planning. The need to forecast ahead continuously is considered more fully later in this chapter. The cash budget will indicate whether the company will need additional overdraft facilities, and in which months it will have surplus cash which may be invested in the short-term money market. A company with a seasonal trade may require a bank overdraft facility during certain months of the year, and have surplus cash to invest short term at other times. A bank overdraft may be required to finance the build-up in stocks and debtors in the working capital cycle resulting from the budgeted increase in sales. If a company does require bank overdraft during certain times over the year, as recommended in Chapter 7, the cash budgets should be included in the request to the bank for overdraft facilities.

Control

Having established budgets covering the budget period, budgetary control consists of comparing the estimates of revenues and expenditures in the budgets with the actual revenue received and expenditure incurred. The control embraces every budget, including the working capital and cash budgets. It is all too easy to prepare detailed comparisons of budget versus actual sales and costs, and completely ignore the working capital and cash situation.

The chief value of a budget as a control device will be realized through the effective use of reports, and meetings to discuss the reports. Reports should be compiled showing the annual and monthly budgets, actual revenue and/or expenditure, the variance between actual and budget, and usually the percentage variance. If the comparisons show 'significant' variations, some comment as to their definite or probable causes should be included in order to assist the recipient in taking action. The accountant's reports should highlight the essentials, and point out 'significant' budget deviations and possibilities for improvement. For example, for a cost budget they should:

1. Show the recipient what his costs should have been.
2. Show how closely he came to meeting these costs.
3. Show whether his performance in this respect is improving.
4. Establish a means of explaining the variances so that a knowledge of their causes can be used as a weapon for their reduction.

To be effective, reports must be designed with the different levels and types of responsibility of the organization in mind, and each

LEVEL	SALES MONTHLY	MARKETING COSTS MONTHLY	ROAD TRANSPORT MONTHLY
Managing Director	Budget v. Actual and analysis of variances by product groups for company	Budget v. Actual Total costs by major cost headings	Standard v. Actual Cost and analysis of variances Total
Marketing Director	by product groups for (a) own customers, (b) Sales Manager's customers	Costs by major cost headings (a) controlled personally, (b) controlled by Sales Manager	
Sales Manager	by product groups for (a) own customers, (b) Export Manager's markets, (c) Sales Representatives' markets	Costs within his control analysed by subordinates	by vehicle group
Export Manager	by product group and geographical market		

level of reporting should be interrelated so that reports at one level are analysed in greater detail at the next level. In good and effective reports, each reported fact is in some way related to the authority vested in a single individual or group of individuals. Reports to top management should indicate the overall efficiency of the organization compared with budgeted performance. They should indicate which departments or functions of the organization require attention or praise on account of the success or failure of their efforts. They should also indicate the trend in the performance of the organization. Reports to functional, sectional and departmental managers should indicate which elements of performance require attention. They should also comment on good performance. The content of the reports should be kept simple and limited to data about which the recipient of the report can take action. Regular meetings should take place between budget holders and their superiors to review reports and actions taken.

For example, in the Industrial Chemicals Co., whose procedures for developing annual budgets for its Marketing Department were described earlier in this chapter, the managing director receives monthly a summary report of the overall performance of the company compared with budget; it includes information on the performance of the marketing director. A report is provided to the marketing director showing the performance of the sales manager and distribution managers, as well as comparisons of budget with actual for the sales and costs he controls personally, and each senior manager receives a report on his area of responsibility. As illustrated in Figure 9.6, each level of reporting is interrelated, so that reports at one level are analysed in greater detail at the next level. Monthly meetings take place between the sales manager and his subordinates to discuss their performance and to agree actions. Similar meetings take place between the distribution manager and his subordinates. The marketing director meets with his three senior managers to discuss their performance and review the overall performance of the marketing function, and this forms the basis of the marketing director's report to the managing director. The senior member of the Accounting Department responsible for the preparation of the reports meets each month with the marketing director to discuss the reports, and with the senior managers for the same purpose. He also attends the monthly meetings of the marketing director and his senior managers,

Table 9.1
Operating Costs

	Salaries	Transport and Travelling	Materials and Services	Other	Total Operating Costs	Budget	Variance	
	£'1000s	£'1000s	£'1000s	£'1000s	£'1000s	£'1000s	£'1000s	%
Distribution								
Consumer Service								
Billing and Account Collection								
Admin. and General Expenses								
Training, Safety and Welfare								
Total								

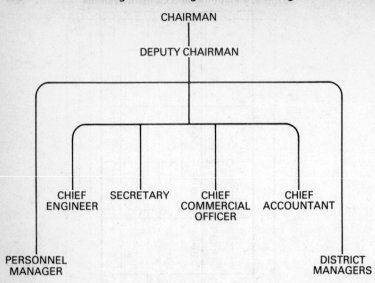

Figure 9.7. *The South Wales Electricity Board, Organization Chart*

when the reports are discussed, to answer any questions and provide further information if required. However, the managers, not the accountant, speak to their reports. Minutes of the meetings summarize agreed actions.

In the South Wales Electricity Board (*A Casebook of British Management Accounting*, Volume 1), whose management structure is shown in Figure 9.7, the monitoring of performance of costs against budget on the revenue expenditure account is carried out at three levels.

Board level

The board produces a full set of financial accounts each quarter for submission to the board members, including a statement showing the operating costs on revenue account (Table 9.1). It shows board totals only and is analysed over the main heads of distribution, consumer service, meter reading, billing and collection of accounts, administration and general expenses and training, safety and welfare expenditure. The total expenditure on each of these heads is further analysed into salaries, transport and travelling, materials and ser-

Table 9.2

BUDGET VARIANCE REPORT

Period Ending .... Management Unit ....

Allocation Code	Description	Total Expenditure to Date	Budget Proportion	± Variance £	%	Explanation of Variance

vices, and other expenditure. A comparison is made with a budget figure for each of these headings and a variance is shown in both cash and percentage terms. Comments are given to explain the variance reported under each heading of expenditure. These comments are derived from the reports submitted quarterly by the unit managers, giving quantified explanations of significant variances to the budget for the year to date (see Table 9.2).

Chief Officer and Senior Manager level

A quarterly report is produced showing expenditure on the main account headings of distribution expenditure, consumer service, meter-reading, billing and collection, administration and general expenses, training, safety and welfare, and general charges. This expenditure is analysed by management unit; for each heading of expenditure within each management unit, figures are shown for the budget to date, actual expenditure to date, and the variance expressed both in cash and in percentage terms. These summary reports are aimed at senior unit managers to give them in easily readable form a summary of performance in their own management units and to enable them to make comparisons of performance with other management units (Table 9.3 is an example).

Operational level

The computer costing system produces a series of printouts analysing expenditure by management unit, by cost centre within management unit, by allocation code within cost centre and by source of expenditure within allocation code. A budget figure is also shown for each allocation code for which budgets are set. A budget variance is also reported both in money terms and as a percentage performance. A number of printouts are available within the management unit expressing this detailed analysis of costing information in a number of different ways for different purposes. The two main variations are:

(a)   A printout showing the district totals of expenditure by detailed allocation code analysed by cost centre. This report enables the unit manager to see which cost centre in his unit has been the

Table 9.3

Expenditure (excl. Direct Capital) Budget Performance for the   months ended   19

	Budget	Actual	Variance		Budget	Actual	Variance		Budget	Actual	Variance	
	£'000	£'000	£'000	%	£'000	£'000	£'000	%	£'000	£'000	£'000	%
Distribution												
Consumer Service												
Meter Reading, Billing												
Administration												
Training												
Safety and Welfare												
General Charges												
(less charged to C & S of A)												
Revenue Expenditure												
OTHER BUDGETED EXPENDITURE												
Non-Trading and Bonus												
Capital Indirects												
Cont. and Sales Indirect												

(This table was originally produced as a computer printout)

major spender and will be used when he is investigating significant variances.

(b) A report showing expenditure of each cost centre analysed in
detail by allocation code and by source. This is available to
enable each cost centre manager to see which activity or which
source of expenditure on an activity has been the major cause
of spending and again will be used by him when he is required
to investigate budget variances.

Departmental cost variances for production departments are
normally reported in the form of *departmental operating statements.*
A statement will be prepared for each department or cost centre.
Costs are divided into *controllable* and *non-controllable* by the individual responsible for that department or cost centre, thus pointing
out to departmental managers the extent of their responsibility for
costs. There is no general agreement as to whether or not departmental operating statements should include non-controllable costs.
This comparison should enable the responsible executive to determine where, how and why actual accomplishment is not equal to the
performance called for in the budget. The comparison should also
assist in determining what corrective measures need to be taken to
achieve budgeted performance in the future. An example of a departmental operating statement for the bottling department of a dairy is
shown in Table 9.4. Further examples will be found in *A Casebook
of British Management Accounting*.

It will be appreciated that accounting controls involving both
budgets and standards rely heavily upon the 'principle of exceptions',
which includes symmetric treatment of favourable and unfavourable
variances and a judgement as to whether they are controllable or
non-controllable. It is important that the management accountant
does satisfy himself that all non-controllable items do in fact lie
outside the firm's control. This means that he must be familiar with
all the controls operating within the firm, and not simply the accounting ones. There is also the danger, which has already been
emphasized in Chapter 3, that with so much attention being focused
on the exceptions, too little attention will be paid to the standards
and budgets. There are important behavioural aspects of reporting
which are considered later in this chapter.

'Significant' Variances

It has been suggested that accountants' reports should highlight the essentials, and point out 'significant' variances from budget and possibilities for improvement. What is a 'significant' variance? The South Wales Electricity Board in 1984 defined a 'significant' variance as one which exceeded 10 per cent of budget, or £1,000.

Inevitably variances of different magnitudes will arise randomly from period to period; it is impossible to budget with absolute accuracy. While the interpretation of variances will take into consideration the level of attainment incorporated in the budgets, it is still necessary to decide whether or not a particular variance is 'significant'. For some costs each budget period can be considered in isolation and the judgement as to whether the budget variance is 'significant' can be made without reference to variances of previous periods. The trend of past variances may enable a 'significant' variance to be anticipated, but with this type of cost the variances of one period do not directly influence the variances of subsequent periods. For example, in the bottling department of a dairy the budget variances of foil used for bottle closures can be considered independently each period, and a decision can be made as to whether the variance for that period is 'significant' or not. The usage of foil for bottle closures in one period does not directly affect the usage in the next period. Of course, there may be a trend in the past variances which enables the management to anticipate a 'significant' variance. Frequently, with this type of cost the significance of the budget variance is measured by expressing it as a percentage of budget. For example, if the variance on bottle closures is in excess of 5 per cent of budget it may be regarded as 'significant' and a detailed investigation made as to the cause. The cumulative variance for the year may not be important.

For many costs the budget will represent the average period cost expected over the whole year, and variances from the budget will arise randomly from month to month. For example, repairs and maintenance costs may be budgeted on the same basis from period to period, but the repairs and maintenance costs incurred will probably be uneven during the year. Adverse and favourable budget variances will probably arise randomly from period to period, but they should offset each other over the year so that the cumulative

Table 9.4

MILKY DAIRIES LTD

Bottling Department Operating Statement

Supervisor:............   Month:............

	This month				Year to Date			
	Budget	Actual	Budget Variance		Budget for Actual Gallons	Actual	Budget Variance	
				%				%
Output								
Gallons bottled								
Labour Hours								
Costs	Budget for Actual Gallons £	£	£		£	£	£	
Controllable Costs								
Bottles								
Closures								
Milk loss								
Labour								
Supplies								
Total								

*Non-controllable
Costs*
Electricity
Fuel and Water
Space Occupancy
Machinery:
  Depreciation
  Repairs

Total

Total costs

* Significant Variances indicated thus
Reasons for Budget Variations:

Prepared by:............

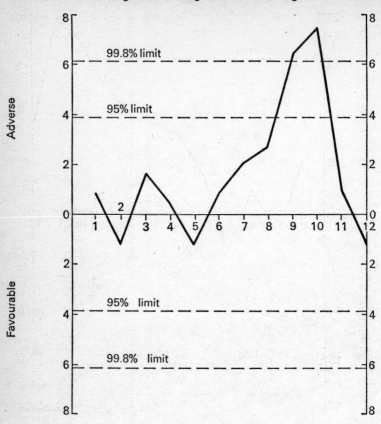

Figure 9.8. *Variance control chart – bottle closures*

variance is not 'significant'. In this situation it is necessary to determine whether the budget variance in a particular period is simply an expected random deviation or a 'significant' deviation from the budget. Similarly, the cumulative budget variance must be examined to decide whether it is 'significant'. A variance will be statistically 'significant' if it is of such a magnitude that it is unlikely to have arisen purely by chance. Statistical techniques, based on applications of probability theory and the normal distribution, are available for determining whether a particular budget variance is statistically 'significant' and worth investigating in detail.

Statistical probability tests based on the normal distribution are

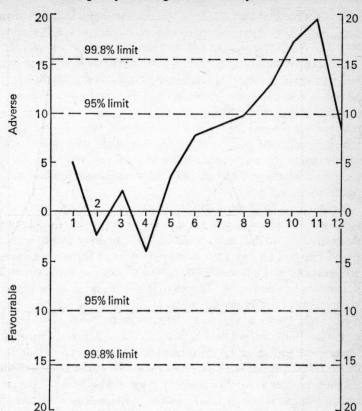

Figure 9.9. *Variance control chart – repairs and maintenance*

employed to verify whether variations from budget are attributable to *chance* and not significant, or to *controllable* causes and 'significant'. It is assumed that:

1. The actual costs which are compared with the budget are drawn from a single homogeneous population.
2. The budget is the mean (arithmetic average) of the population, i.e. it is an attainable budget.
3. Any variations from budget arise from chance and not from assignable causes.

If this is true, the population of actual costs may be assumed to be normally distributed about the mean. The standard deviation measures the spread of the population about the mean. It follows then that if chance alone causes variances from budget, i.e. the variances are caused by non-controllable random causes, 95 per cent of the budget variances should fall within the range of mean (budget) plus or minus 1.96 standard deviations and 99.8 per cent within mean (budget) plus or minus 3.09 standard deviations. On this basis 5 per cent and 0.2 per cent control limits can be established for measuring the significance of budget variances. Statistical probability tables are available for establishing other control limits. The statistical techniques briefly outlined are fully explained in any standard statistics textbook.

Variance control charts can be employed to present the control limits and the actual budget variances. For example, if the standard deviation for bottle closures is calculated to be 2 per cent of budget, the 95 per cent and 99.8 per cent control limits for bottle closures are indicated in Figure 9.8. The actual percentage variances from budget are also plotted in Figure 9.8. It will be seen that 'significant' variances occurred in Periods 9 and 10. For costs of the repairs and maintenance type the magnitude of random fluctuations is likely to be greater, the standard deviation should be higher, and the control limits wider. In Figure 9.9 the control limits are based on a standard deviation of 5 per cent of the budget. It will be seen that in Figure 9.9 there is a trend of unfavourable variances close to the 95 per cent control limits. If this type of control chart had been in use, the upward trend of adverse variances would have been noted and detailed investigations could have been initiated before the 'significant' adverse variances occurred.

The use of this type of variance control chart enables both significant variances to be isolated and possible future 'significant' variances to be anticipated. The principal indications of 'significant' variances are:

1. The variance is outside the control limits as in Periods 9 and 10 in Figure 9.8.
2. Several variances, especially if consecutive, near the control limit, as in Periods 6, 7 and 8 in Figure 9.9.
3. An undue number of variances above or below the budget. In both cases, six of the first eight variances are above budget, but

a 'significant' variance does not occur in both cases until Period 9.

4.   A trend in the variances, as in Periods 5–8 in Figure 9.9.

Different control limits may be established for different costs. A 3 per cent variance from a budgeted cost of £100,000 is more critical than a 10 per cent variance from a budgeted cost of £1,000. The absolute as well as the percentage variance must be considered when establishing control limits. Ninety per cent control limits (1.64 standard deviations) may be established for major items of costs. On the other hand, for small items of cost 100 per cent control limits (3.9 standard deviations) may be considered satisfactory.

The use of the statistical techniques outlined requires the calculation of standard deviations in order to determine the control limits. It has been suggested that this can be done either by analysing records of actual past achievements, provided the causes of deviation from past expected levels have also been recorded, and there have been no changes in such factors as the methods of preparing budgets, plant and equipment, products manufactured, methods of manufacture, organization structure, personnel, managerial policy towards costs, etc. Alternatively such questions as: 'What is the budgeted level of expenditure at which there is an even chance that actual expenditure will be greater because of non-controllable causes?' may be discussed with managers when helping them to develop their budgets.

Statistical variance control charts probably offer their widest application in situations which are similar to quality control applications: for example, in the control of physical quantities for which variances are calculated daily or weekly, such as direct labour hours or material usage. Sampling techniques can be employed to determine the confidence limits.

Recent Developments in Budgetary Planning and Control Systems

In recent years many companies have developed more sophisticated budgetary planning and control systems based on the recognition of the need in a dynamic and hostile external environment to anticipate *future* sales, costs and cash flows, and that control systems which compare actual results with annual budgets are of limited value for this purpose. These developments have been made possible by developments in information technology. However, as Peter Drucker [3] has emphasized, in the absence of effective communication all the information technology revolution can produce is data. There has also been a rapid expansion in the area of study which attempts to synthesize a wide variety of behavioural research, and focus specifically on the nature and functions of large-scale organizations, i.e. organizational theory. It is really an effort to gain new and more realistic insights into human behaviour in organizations.

The development of systems which are more responsive to a dynamic external environment are illustrated in the first instance by reference to their use by marketing management in those companies that employ staff specialists with responsibility for a particular product or group of products. An example of this type of organization is shown in Figure 9.10. In a product management system, such as that developed by many large multi-consumer packaged goods manufacturers, the product manager is responsible for developing marketing plans for individual products. He integrates the planning and marketing effort for his product or group of products. He frequently controls sales promotion, advertising, packaging, pricing, product improvements, and, consequently, product profit. The accounting information needs of marketing management are more fully considered in Chapter 12.

Performance Reporting to Product Managers

A budget is frequently developed for a product against which a product manager measures and controls his performance, and against which his superiors evaluate his performance. If a company's short-term budgeting and long-term profit planning are integrated, annual market share and sales and profit objectives for products should flow from long-term plans. Generally it is accepted that these objectives ought to be agreed with, rather than imposed on, product managers; plans for attaining the short-term objectives being prepared by product managers, approved or amended by top management, and any amendments discussed with the product

3 Peter Drucker, *Technology, Management, and Society*, Heinemann, London, 1970, p. 15.

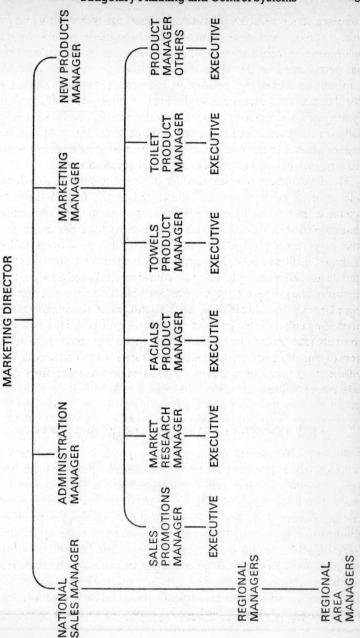

Figure 9.10. *Marketing organization chart: Consumer Division, Paper Products Co.*

Table 9.5

Analysis of Sales and Product Contribution

PRODUCT GROUP 5		PERIOD NUMBER: ENDED:

THIS PERIOD/YEAR TO DATE

	Sales				Product Contribution			
Product	Budget	Actual	Variance		Budget	Actual	Variance	
	£	£	£	%	£	£	£	%
A								
B								
C								
D								
E								
F								
G								
Total	£	£	£	%	£	£	£	%

manager concerned. The planning stage involves the product manager in making decisions about marketing strategy to achieve the objectives, and agreeing to the action necessary to implement the strategy. Thus budgets are the physical and financial quantifications of the agreed course of action.

In order to control his performance against budget during the year, a product manager requires regular reports. He may receive historical 'management by exception' reports comparing actual sales and, possibly, direct profit or contribution with budget. An example of this kind of report is provided in Table 9.5. In looking at this type of performance reporting, it is important to recognize that the purpose of annual budgeting is *not* an attempt to estimate what *actual* sales will be month by month or week by week, but rather to develop a quantified action plan with clearly defined objectives towards which marketing effort is directed. As a *forecast* of actual monthly sales a one-year sales budget very quickly becomes obsolete, but as a set of *objectives* to be achieved normally it is valid throughout the year.

In a dynamic and rapidly changing external environment the product manager will not find *budget against actual* comparisons particularly useful in controlling his short-term performance. The deviations from budget result from so many factors that he is not in a position to determine whether things turned out as he thought they would, and if not, why not. The budget against actual comparison will enable him to see whether he is keeping on the track towards the objectives contained in the annual budget, but as a control comparison it is history: an out-of-date comparison with a budget prepared three, six, or nine months earlier.

The product manager, or any other manager, cannot control the past; his opportunity to do so has passed. In fact because of the time required to implement decisions, he may not be able to control the present or the immediate future. To discover whether he needs to take action, the product manager must have a prediction about the future upon which he can act. Annual budgets may not be useful as predictions of the future, but short-term *forecasts* can be prepared regularly; such forecasts being predictions of the, say, next three months and updated monthly or even weekly. These would be in addition to the equally important rolling annual forecasts and the remainder of financial forecasts that many companies employ for top management planning and control.

Managers have to be properly motivated to produce meaningful forecasts. The manager is being asked to commit to paper what he frequently does intuitively. An atmosphere has to be created in which the managers feel the primary purpose of preparing such forecasts is to produce more effective information for controlling their own performance, and that the forecasts will not simply be used by their superiors as a pressure device. The importance of accurate sales forecasts for production planning purposes, and particularly, in an inflationary environment, for working capital and cash flow management, should also be emphasized. In some cases it may be necessary to state that, from a production planning and stock control point of view, there will be no credits for regularly beating short-term forecasts. Alternatively, a statistical method of forecasting acceptable to both top management and marketing management may be developed. For example, a large British food

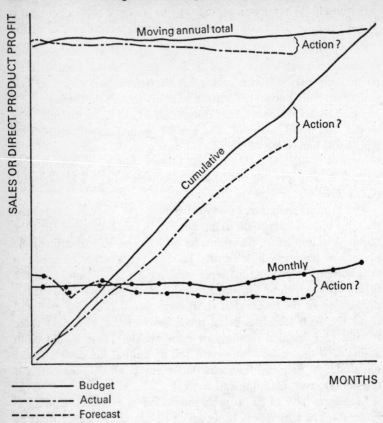

Figure 9.11

product company uses a multiple regression model to produce a projection of future product sales weekly for product managers if no further marketing action is taken.

Once an effective forecasting procedure is developed, *budget against future forecast* comparisons are possible. It will be recognized that while actual against budget comparisons are history, budget against future forecast comparisons provide a basis for short-term planning. They indicate whether direct product profit or product contribution and sales will continue to keep on track if no action is taken, or, as in Figure 9.11, what will happen if no action is taken. The product manager faced with the situation in Figure 9.11 might ask himself: 'What action must I take to get back on budget, and is it worthwhile?' He must evaluate the alternative courses of action open to him. He may conclude that it is not worthwhile taking action to get back on to the budget, but if action is taken he should prepare a *revised future forecast*. Similarly the product manager in the food products company compares the projection he received with budget and evaluates marketing mix alternatives in the context of this comparison. In conditions of falling demand, rising costs and eroding contributions, which many British companies faced in 1979–80, an extremely valuable comparison is *latest forecast v. previous forecast*. This comparison leads to questions such as: Why has the forecast changed? How does it affect our cash flow? What action should we take to improve the situation? Should we review our selling prices? The forecasts can be contrasted with the picture emerging from the monitoring of the external environment which should take place in every company.

Having made his forecast, and if necessary taken action, in subsequent months the product manager can compare *actual against past* forecast to help him see whether he has achieved the kind of performance he thought he would achieve, and if not why not. 'How did I do compared with what I forecast would happen?' This is not an out-of-date comparison with a budget prepared three, six or nine months previously, but a current comparison with a recent forecast. As a result of introducing a forecasting system, the Industrial Chemicals Co. produces a sales variances analysis, as illustrated in Table 9.6. The types of comparison proposed are summarized in Table 9.7. Continually forecasting the future not only forces the product manager to quantify his future expectations, provided he does not see the short-term forecasting as a process of pinning him down, it also provides him with an effective method of planning and controlling his performance.

Corrugated Case Co.

An example of a comparison of actual with previous forecast and of latest forecast with previous forecast developed for each of the operating units of a company producing corrugated cases is shown in Table 9.8. It will be noted that the significant change in the latest forecast is the lowering of the percentage of contribution margin

Table 9.6

INDUSTRIAL CHEMICALS LTD

Sales Variance Analysis

Budget Centre................................   Responsible Manager................................

	PERIOD						PRODUCT		YEAR TO DATE				
		Variance from most recent Forecast			Variance from annual Budget						Variance from annual Budget		
Realization		Price	Volume	Total	Price	Volume	Total			Realization	Price	Volume	Total
£		£	£	£	£	£	£			£	£	£	£

Prepared by ....

Date................................

* Significant variances marked thus
COMMENT:

Table 9.7

TYPES OF CONTROL COMPARISON

BUDGET *v.* ACTUAL	How are we doing? Are we on the track towards our objectives?
BUDGET *v.* FORECAST	Will we remain on track towards our objectives? What will happen if no action is taken? Do we need to take action?
BUDGET *v.* REVISED FORECAST	Will proposed action put us back on track?
LATEST FORECAST *v.* PREVIOUS FORECAST	Why has the forecast changed? Is the situation improving/deteriorating?
ACTUAL *v.* PAST FORECAST	Did things turn out as expected? If not, why not? Are we being too optimistic/pessimistic in our forecasting?

---

and operating expenses forecasts, and that it is expected that selling prices can be improved from Period 6 onwards as compared with the previous forecast. The monthly senior management meetings start with the latest forecast *v.* previous forecast comparisons. The comparisons focus discussions between the managing director and general managers of the operating units on the key assumptions the general managers are making about the future. How is the general manager going to reduce his operating expenses? Why are percentage contribution margins under increasing pressure? Why does he expect to increase selling prices in the second half of the year? At the managing director level, the consolidated actual *v.* forecast, latest forecast *v.* previous forecast, and latest forecast *v.* budget comparisons give a clearer understanding of what the future holds for the company as a whole, direct his attention to areas requiring action, and indicate where actual performance is out of line with expectations. At the operating units the comparisons provide managers with similar but more detailed understandings of areas of activity for which they are responsible. They provide a basis for *action-oriented* discussions between superior and subordinates.

At this time the economy was moving rapidly into recession and other units of the company were forecasting a downturn in demand, with consequent downward pressure on the rate of increase in selling prices and paper and board prices. Discussions between the manag-

Table 9.8

Comparison of Actual and Latest Forecast with Previous Forecast – Period 3

	Actual v. Forecast	Latest Forecast v. Previous Forecast			
	PERIOD 3 £'000	PERIOD 4 £'000	PERIOD 5 £'000	PERIOD 6 £'000	YEAR £'000
Period 2 Forecast Operating Profit/(Loss)	3.0	16.4	34.8	—	200.0
Change in Total Contribution Forecast:					
Output	(−) 1.5	(−) 7.3	—	—	(+) 3.1
Selling Prices	(−) 1.7	(−) 2.7	(−) 3.8	—	(+) 111.0
% Contribution Margin	(−) 9.7	(−) 12.9	(−) 21.2	—	(−) 126.1
Total	(−) 12.9	(−) 22.9	(−) 25.0	—	(−) 12.0
Change in Operating Expenses Forecast	(−) 7.9	(−) 10.8	(−) 18.3	—	(−) 112.0
Change in Operating Profit Forecast	(−) £5.0	(−) £12.1	(−) £6.7	—	(+) £100.0
Period 3 Forecast Operating Profit/(Loss)	£(2.0)	£4.3	£28.1	£20.0	£300.0

ing director and the general manager of the unit on the forecast improvement in operating profit for the year revealed that while the general manager had a good grasp of the short-term position, he had given inadequate consideration to the impact of external economic factors on demand in the second half of the year. These factors have been recognized by general managers of other operating units who had taken actions to reduce further their operating expenses. These discussions and subsequent events brought home to the manager the severity of the recession. By Period 7 he had reduced his forecast operating profit for the year from £300,000 to £65,000. He actually achieved £100,600 profit. As shown in Table 9.9, between periods 3 and 7 he lowered his output forecast, which reduced his forecast total contribution by £234,600, and his increase in contribution from higher selling prices by £46,000. The recession partially held down the pressure of higher raw material costs on percentage contribution margins. He also planned to take further actions to reduce his operating expenses; actions taken earlier in the year by general managers of other operating units. While Table 9.9 shows significant differences between Period 3 forecast and actual for the year, the differences between Period 7 forecast and actual for the year are much smaller, the one significant difference being the improvement in actual percentage contribution margin over Period 7 forecasts. This was because anticipated increases in paper and board prices did not materialize, partly because of the recession in demand in the U.K. and overseas.

An increasing number of companies have introduced forecasting systems as a means of coping with the hostile and uncertain external environment and of encouraging management to look ahead continually, quantify their expectations and take effective action. Most banks require, monthly or quarterly, similar cash forecasts from companies with substantial loans or overdrafts.

Annual Budgets, Rolling Budgets and Forecasts

Some companies choose not to budget annually but to opt for a 'rolling budget' normally for a period of twelve months which is rolled forward quarterly. Others complement their annual budget with a twelve-month rolling budget. While many companies complement budgets with regular forecasts, there is a concern among senior

Table 9.9

Comparisons of Forecasts and Actual Operating Profit for Year

	Period 3 Forecast versus Period 7 Forecast £'000	Period 3 Forecast versus Actual £'000	Period 7 Forecast versus Actual £'000
Forecast Operating Profit/(Loss)	300.0 (Period 3)	300.0 (Period 3)	65.1 (Period 7)
Changes in Total Contribution Forecast:			
Output	(−) 234.6	(−) 256.4	(−) 21.8
Selling Prices	(−) 46.0	(−) 83.0	(−) 37.0
% Contribution Margin	(−) 11.9	(+) 72.5	(+) 84.4
Total	(−) 292.5	(−) 266.9	(+) 25.6
Change in Operating Expenses Forecast	(−) 57.6	(−) 67.5	(−) 9.9
Change in Operating Profit Forecast	(−) 234.9	(−) 199.4	(+) 35.5
Forecast/Actual Operating Profit	65.1 (Period 7)	100.6 (Actual)	100.6 (Actual)

managers that sight will be lost of the original budget if too great an emphasis is placed on latest forecast versus previous forecast, and actual versus previous forecast comparisons. They fear that subordinate managers will no longer regard the achievement of their budget as their primary objective for the budget period, and are concerned that it will be replaced by a moving target which can be manipulated by managers to their own ends. 'They will be released from the discipline of the budget'. This fear would be further reinforced if rolling budgets replaced rather than complemented annual budgets. The forecasting approach should complement and strengthen budgetary planning and control, not replace it, but in some circumstances the original budget is no longer a reasonable strategy and plan, and the forecasting system may have to become the primary system of control. For example, if a company failed to anticipate a recession when preparing its sales budgets, the original budget may become meaningless and the forecasting approach may prove extremely valuable in anticipating, understanding and responding to rapidly changing market conditions.

The use of forecasts and rolling budgets was discussed with David Allen, Ron Kett and Derrick Willingham:

PROFESSOR: What would be interesting, David, is to ask you how long it takes to prepare this budget?

DAVID ALLEN: Well, in a way, the simple answer is that it takes for ever, because it is a continuous cycle. First of all it is important to say the budget is not a discrete, controlled document. It's actually a continuous process, in that we look at it every quarter and roll it a quarter forward. And the other point to make, I think, is that you used the word 'objectives' flowing downwards; I was careful to say 'strategies' flowing downwards, because quite honestly the objectives are not as cast-in-stone as some people might assume. Very often the budget debate is a question of 'here are alternative feasible strategies'.

PROFESSOR: When you say it is a continuous cycle, isn't there a great danger that managers lower down the organization just see it as a ritual, a time-consuming process, and the costs of doing it aren't outweighed by the benefits of having it there.

DAVID ALLEN: Once you've been operating on a cyclical basis for some time the costs are negligible, particularly given what you can do with microcomputers these days. Most people will have a sales forecast built on a microcomputer and will just update it once a month. And they need to, in order to communicate their plans to the other people in the organization. So it is essentially a communications process and a process of evaluating alternative strategies, rather than what it might have appeared to be in the very early literature on budgetary control – that is, keeping tabs on what happened last week.

PROFESSOR: How do you see it, Derrick?

DERRICK WILLINGHAM: I think if it becomes a ritual then it's death, it has to be a tool in management and not an end in itself. Rather like David, I see the budgeting process as a continuous one. We formally go through the business of updating the strategic plan; that may take a couple of months in the spring. We then update the operating plan, which takes two to two-and-a-half months in the autumn, but every month we then do an updated forecast for the following three months. It really is a continuous updating process which we use very much as a management tool, because we have the philosophy that we're looking very critically at forecast profits, return on investment, cash flow. If the forecasts I am getting for the next three months are not giving the sort of answers that I want, then I go back to the management team and say: 'Look, what are we going to do about this? Can we bring this shipment forward? Can we get some extra orders?' It is used very much as part and parcel of the management process, it's not some ivory tower edifice!

PROFESSOR: What you are also illustrating is that these days the budget is not a forecast of what's going to happen; essentially it is a financial quantification of an action plan to achieve objectives and strategies. As a forecast of what's going to happen month by month it very rapidly gets out of date. But what you're doing is complementing that with a system of continually forecasting ahead, and those forecasts really allow you to ask: 'Are we on track towards achieving our objectives, are we on the track to achieving the budget and, if not, what action do we need to get back on to it?'

DERRICK WILLINGHAM: If we're not on track, can we take action to bring us back on track, or we're not going to generate the cash flow; then we've got to cut back on capital expenditure or reduce other cash outflows.

PROFESSOR: Is there a danger that if too much emphasis is placed on forecasts, which are moving targets, the discipline of the budget might be lost?

RON KETT: Well, we don't. You see, unless it is materially in error we will not change the budget for any operating company. We use that as performance measurement, but at the same time the operating companies are required to do three-month rolling forecasts and compare those with budget, both the profits and cash. Because inflation is reasonably under control there's not a great diversion, but where we have marginal variations going forward for the next three or four months we see them in the rolling forecasts. We present to our group Board an aggregation of (a) the actual compared with budget, (b) the budget forward for three months and (c) the rolling forecast for three months.

DERRICK WILLINGHAM: Fundamental to these developments is the advance in information technology. A lot of the things we can do now, with the aid of minicomputers and so on, are the sort of things I was desperately searching for twenty years ago. Of course there was no way you could have done it then.

PROFESSOR: That's right. Twenty years ago, when one was doing budgets manually, it was very difficult to evaluate a number of alternatives. The developments in information technology have also given us that ability to look forward in a much more meaningful way, with the result that the actuals are far less important; we should have anticipated the actuals in the forecasts. David, you have a clear view about whether we're concerned with actuals or whether we're concerned with the future.

DAVID ALLEN: That's right, I think when you've developed this rolling forecast or rolling budget approach, what you find is that there's very little difference between the actuals and the forecasts, and it enables you therefore to concentrate on the difference, as Ron says, between forecast and budget, which throws up the real decision-making parts. Unless we change course we are going to have this problem, if we change course we are going to have this opportunity.

The Impact of Information Technology

If top management is going to act on the three-month budget versus future forecast and latest forecast versus previous forecast comparisons for the firm as a whole, the forecasts must be processed quickly. Usually, manually operated budgetary planning and control systems cannot meet this requirement. Developments in computer-based budgetary planning and control models have enabled companies to forecast ahead with great ease and speed. The National Computing Centre has produced a guide to selecting financial modelling packages.[4]

The development of such models has strengthened both the planning and control aspects of budgeting. At the planning stage budgetary models should enable management to allocate resources more effectively, using (where appropriate) mathematical techniques before and during the planning period. These planning models look across departments and responsibility centres at systems. For example, many chemical and petroleum products companies employ mathematical models to determine the optimal product mix. *Planning budgets* flow from these computer-based models, and are translated into *control budgets* with responsibilities clearly defined by individuals. The sensitivity of the budget to changes in key variables before and during the planning period can also be tested. They should enable management to ask and obtain answers to 'what if' type questions:

What if wage rates increase by 15 per cent from Period 5 onwards?

What if the price of raw material X increases by £5 per ton in Period 7?

What if we fall short by 10 per cent in our sales budget?

The impact of varying rates of inflation on working capital and cash flow can be tested. If the key variables do change, budgets and profit plans can be updated quickly. In fact, developments in

4 P. N. Finlay and T. Servant, *Selecting Financial Modelling Packages*, National Computing Centre, 1987.

information technology have had a significant impact on all aspects of budgetary planning and control, including:

1. Shortening the planning cycle by removing much of the manual calculation.
2. Improving accuracy of forecasts by effectively using the power of the computer.
3. Continuous forecasting being made possible by speed of calculations.
4. Spot analysis capability by questioning results and examining assumptions on input data.
5. Evaluating alternatives by asking 'what if' type questions.
6. Bringing into open view the data and computational procedures and allowing management to question each other's assumptions and decisions.
7. Improving the speed and accuracy of producing control reports.
8. Allowing the production of 'attention directing' reports with 'on request' capability and 'on line' decision support systems.
9. Allowing the generation of more frequent periodic statements, e.g. weekly profit statements.
10. Through the use of PCs, allowing individual managers direct access to the whole or parts of the planning and control system.

At the budgetary control stage, the development of computer models should not only aid accountants in reporting to managers on the significance of reported variances but also to forecast variances unless managerial actions are taken. For example, at I.P.C. Magazines (*A Casebook of British Management Accounting*, Volume 1) a publisher receives during the financial year three formal forecasts for each title he is responsible for publishing: a forecast trading statement (Table 9.10) and a detailed forecast of variances (Table 9.11) against annual profit plan (budget).

A parallel development should be reduced emphasis on routine reporting and the substitution of highly selective *attention directing reports* backed up by an *on request reporting facility*. For example, the management accountant of a medium-sized company producing knitted underwear, leisure-wear and children's outerwear provides a summarized analysis of sales and contribution by product and outlet

Table 9.10

I.P.C. MAGAZINES LTD
Women's Group Forecast 1983/84
(Trading Account Format)

Publication: .... A WOMAN'S MONTHLY
at .... 3 June 1983

	Actual £'000 April	Forecast £'000 May	June	July	August	Sept.	Oct.-Dec.	Jan.-Mar.	Annual
TURNOVER									
Circulation – Publications	109.2	106.0	104.6	104.7	111.5	125.7	364.9	362.8	1389.4
– Currency Benefit									
Advert – Publications	217.6	215.5	143.5	112.1	194.5	339.3	747.1	554.0	2523.6
– Mini Tests									
Other – Publications	3.6	2.9	2.1	1.4	2.6	4.0	8.5	6.5	31.6
Leisure Activities	1.9	1.3	2.5	1.5	2.9	1.4	2.0	2.2	15.7
Syndication	0.5					2.5		2.5	5.5
TOTAL TURNOVER	332.8	325.7	252.7	219.7	311.5	472.9	1122.5	928.0	3965.8
COSTS									
Paper	58.9	60.2	46.2	39.4	54.8	91.8	205.4	168.2	725.4
Printing – Internal	8.9	8.4	8.5	8.4	8.4	9.0	26.4	26.4	104.4
– External	75.9	74.6	60.5	52.2	72.6	116.7	260.4	213.4	926.3

Insetting – Internal	2.8	2.2	0.2	1.5	0.7	3.1		6.0	4.4	20.9
– External	9.5	11.5	9.5	9.2	10.1	12.2		32.5	30.5	125.0
Distribution	(0.2)	(1.5)	(1.6)		(0.1)					(3.4)
Production Costs Contra	13.7	16.2	13.1	12.0	14.4	18.2		46.7	41.7	176.0
Editorial Issue	1.1		1.1		1.2	2.2				3.4
Leisure Activities	0.5					4.0			2.2	4.9
Syndication	3.6									31.6
Other	21.4	3.1	1.8	1.5	2.6	26.6		8.4	6.6	150.0
Publicity	26.3	25.5	26.0	25.9	25.9	25.9		46.0	56.0	311.1
Editorial Staff Costs	13.4	1.9	2.7	2.7	2.6	2.7		77.8	77.8	32.0
Editorial Non-Issue Costs								8.0	8.0	32.0
Editorial Occupancy	7.3	7.2	7.3	7.3	7.3	7.2		21.8	21.9	87.3
Total Costs	233.1	209.3	175.3	160.1	200.5	319.6		739.9	657.1	2694.9
Profit Contribution	99.7	116.4	77.4	59.6	111.0	153.3		382.6	270.9	1270.9
Less: Group Costs										
Publishing Group Profit										
N.B. – Included above:										
1. Mini Tests Costs	18.5	18.5	18.5	18.5	18.5	18.5		55.5	55.5	222.0
2. Salaries* – Direct										
– Group										
3. Occupancy – Group										

* Before Co. Contribs.

Table 9.11

I.P.C. MAGAZINES LTD
Women's Group Forecast 1983/84
(Profit Variance Format – Detailed)

Publication: .... A WOMAN'S MONTHLY
at .... 3 June 1983

	Actual £'000	Forecast £'000							
	April	May	June	July	August	Sept.	Oct.-Dec.	Jan.-Mar.	Annual
TURNOVER									
– Circulation	109.2	106.0	104.6	104.7	111.5	125.7	364.9	362.8	1389.4
– Advertisement	217.6	215.5	143.5	112.1	194.5	339.3	747.1	554.0	2523.6
– Other	6.0	4.2	4.6	2.9	5.5	7.9	10.5	11.2	52.8
TOTAL	332.8	325.7	252.7	219.7	311.5	472.9	1122.5	928.0	3965.8
– Plan	349.8	309.0	255.9	224.2	316.2	474.9	1125.3	937.3	3992.6
– Better/(Worse)	(17.0)	16.7	(3.2)	(4.5)	(4.7)	(2.0)	(2.8)	(9.3)	(26.8)
Profit Contribution	99.7	116.4	77.4	59.6	111.0	153.3	382.6	270.9	1270.9
Profit Variances									
Advert – Net Paging	(7.8)	8.7	3.0						3.9
Quota Rephased									
– Mix	0.8	(2.0)	(1.2)	(1.3)	(1.2)	(1.3)	(3.6)	(5.2)	(15.0)
– Rates	0.4	0.7	(0.4)						0.7
– Insets									
– Recharges	0.5	0.6	(0.2)	(0.6)	0.1	(0.1)	(0.4)	(1.7)	(1.8)
Circulation – Volume									
– Cover Price – home									
– Sales Mix – home									
– Price and Mix – home									

	(3.5)	7.2	0.9	(1.9)	(1.1)	(2.0)	(4.0)	(6.9)	(11.3)
Editorial – bank pages	0.1	(0.1)							—
– Colour	1.3	(1.3)							—
– Issue Costs	(0.7)	0.7							—
– Non-Issue Costs	(0.4)	0.4							
– Staff Costs									4.2
– Occupancy									
Paper – Price	4.2	4.2							
– Waste									
– Rebate									
– Quality									
Printing – Price									
– Extras									
Colour Page Penalty	(0.3)	0.3							—
Distribution	1.1	(1.1)							
Leisure Activities	(0.3)	0.3							—
Syndication									
Other	0.6								
Publicity – Rephased					(0.6)				
– Saved/additional									
Supplements									—
Pan Adjustment									
Previous Year's Business									
Planned not Published									
Published not Planned									
Change of Printer									
Change of Process									
Group Costs									
Provisions									

in the monthly management accounting report for the board of directors. The purpose of the summary is to show changes in the pattern of distribution in the case of outlet and changes in the product mix in the case of product group. More detailed reports are prepared for the departmental directors showing sales by garment, product group and outlet. Because of the computer's ability to store data to which rapid access can be obtained, summarized reports are provided to the board of directors who can then request further analysis. For example, an analysis of sales of athletics garments to multiples by garment size might be requested. The segmental reports produced by the management accountant are of the attention-directing type. Directors can request detailed information when required, using terminals in their offices.

Developments in information technology should reduce the emphasis on routine reporting in the form of comprehensive reports of what has transpired. They should shift the attention of accountants away from the operations associated with the preparation of routine reports and allow them to concentrate on determining managers' information needs. This means they must discuss with individual managers their information needs. (What they must avoid, but what some accountants appear to do, is simply decide what information they would require if they did a manager's job.) They can then think about the data specification for input into the system, the preparation of user-oriented report generation computer programs, the design of attention-directing reports, and 'on request' decision support systems.

Weekly Profit Statements

Developments in information technology have resulted in more frequent periodic reporting of performance. For example, weekly trading summaries of four companies are described in *A Casebook of British Management Accounting*. Coloroll Ltd (Volume 1) produces a weekly provisional profit-and-loss account within two days of the previous weekend, using the 'Insight' model developed by Comshare Ltd. Weekly sales data is keyed into the computer which then prepares the profit-and-loss account by matching the input data with pre-input standard costs and budgeted overhead levels. Table 9.12 shows the weekly trading summary for week ending 12 August 1983.

Similarly, the weekly profit estimate of Northern Dairies Ltd (Volume 1) is one of the basic elements in the company's planning, budgeting and financial control systems. The original system introduced in the 1960s has developed into a sophisticated computer-based system with a central facility for consolidation supported by micro- and mini-computers in the operating areas, which allows parts of the weekly profit estimate to be expanded in greater detail to give, for example, reports to the dairy on an individual roundsman's performance, or a summarized report for area managers and directors. The weekly reporting system of Charcon (ECC) Ltd (Volume 2) provides rapid feedback of information covering the main aspects of the business, i.e. trading summary, sales and production tonnes, variance analysis and stock summary. It is intended to direct attention to significant variances from plans, and enables responsible mangers to obtain, if necessary, the more detailed information that is available to take action on variances. Weekly trading indicators (Table 9.13) form part of the reporting package of Thames Valley Newspapers Ltd (Volume 2).

The Behavioural Aspects of Reporting

As well as determining managers' information needs, accountants must also think carefully about how they are to communicate with their customers. To repeat what Peter Drucker has rightly emphasized, in the absence of effective communication all the information technology revolution can produce is data. The reporting system, whether it be manual or computer-based, can only aim at providing the most useful set of data to each product manager; *responses* to the data or action on the data will be determined by the individual manager. A manager's responses to the reporting system will be influenced by many factors including whether he understands it, whether he considers it meets his information needs, and whether he feels it is for his benefit or for his superior's. Effective communication will only occur if the manager makes *positive* responses and takes *positive* actions.

One of the most important factors in motivating and controlling the performance of individuals within an organization is the ability to encourage 'goal congruence'; to create a situation in which each individual, in attempting to satisfy his own goals, will be making the

Table 9.12

COLOROLL LTD

Weekly Trading Statement

Week Ending 12.8.83
Weeks into Period............2
Week Number 19
Period Number 5
Number Weeks in Period 4

£'000	U.K. W'Coverings Division	% to Sales	Export Division	% to Sales	Textiles Division	% to Sales	Packaging Division	% to Sales	All Divisions	% to Sales
Sales Volume	226.44	59.38	75.81	51.20	16.28	12.85	1.55	4.02	320.08	46.07
Sales Value	381.31	100.00	148.08	100.00	126.72	100.00	38.59	100.00	694.70	100.00
Marketing Rebates	11.00–	2.88–	1.00–	0.68–	3.00–	2.37–			15.00–	2.16–
Net Sales Value	370.31	97.12	147.08	99.32	123.72	97.63	38.59	100.00	679.70	97.84
DIRECT COSTS										
Material Costs	141.71	37.16	69.98	47.26	91.31	72.06	20.17	52.27	323.17	46.52
Labour Costs	31.97	8.38	15.31	10.34			3.53	9.15	50.81	7.31
Total Cost	173.68	45.55	85.29	57.60	91.31	72.06	23.71	61.44	373.98	53.83
Total Contribution	196.63	51.57	61.80	41.73	32.41	25.58	14.88	38.56	305.72	44.01

OVERHEAD COSTS										
Fixed Works Overhead	13.70	3.59	4.30	2.90			4.50	11.66	37.50	5.40
Variable Works Overheads	15.80	4.14	6.20	4.19					22.00	3.17
Origination	32.50	8.52	10.00	6.75	2.68	2.11	1.75	4.53	42.50	6.12
Distribution	22.92	6.01	8.52	5.75	18.89	14.91	1.75	4.53	35.87	5.16
Selling Expenses	41.48	10.88	22.97	15.51	4.50	3.55	3.50	9.07	85.09	12.25
Administration	22.50	5.90	8.00	5.40	0.25	0.20			38.50	5.54
Other Costs	1.75	0.46	0.50	0.34					2.50	0.36
Total Overheads	160.65	42.13	65.49	44.23	26.32	20.77	11.50	29.80	263.96	38.00
Trading Profit	35.98	9.44	3.69 –	2.49 –	6.09	4.81	3.38	8.76	41.76	6.01
VARIABLE COSTS										
Selling Variable Exps.	3.48	0.91	2.97	2.01	2.64	2.08			9.09	1.31
Dist. Variable Exps.	15.92	4.18	5.52	3.73	0.68	0.54			22.12	3.18
% VARIABLE COSTS										
Dist. % Variable	4.30	3.75	3.75	0.55	0.55					
Selling % Variable	0.94	2.02	2.02	2.13	2.13					

Table 9.13

THAMES VALLEY NEWSPAPERS LTD

Weekly Trading Indicator

CENTRE: Reading WEEKLY TRADING RESULTS *Month....... Paper.......*

Reforecast Month		Budget Month	Actual					
			Wk. 1	Wk. 2	Wk. 3	Wk. 4	Wk. 5	Total
	REVENUE							
	Display – London							
	Provincial							
	Local							
	Class'd – Sits. Vac.							
	Property							
	Motors							
	Others							
	Group							
	Total Ad. Revenue							
	Newspapers							
	Other							
	Total Revenue							
	COSTS							
	Newsprint							
	Dep. Costs, etc.							
	Total Costs							
	Result							
	STATISTICS							
	PAGES							
	VOLUME							
	Display – London							
	Provincial							
	Local							
	Class'd – Sits. Vac.							
	Property							
	Motors							
	Others							
	Group							
	Total Ads.							
	Total Others							
	Total Columns							
	CIRCULATION							
	Direct							
	Indirect							
	Total							
	YIELDS							
	Display – London							
	Provincial							
	Local							
	Class'd – Sits. Vac.							
	Property							
	Motors							
	Others							
	Group							

greatest possible contribution to the accomplishment of the goals of the organization. If the reporting system over-emphasizes a single index of performance, i.e. the degree to which a budget has been met, it may cause the manager to concentrate on the index as an end in itself. If, in fact, excessive pressure is applied by the reporting system, the manager may ignore the organizational goals and concentrate upon 'performing well' with respect to the single index at the expense of goal congruence. When evaluating his reporting system to determine whether it aids or inhibits the achievement of goal congruence, the management accountant has to recognize that human beings have complicated goal structures and are motivated by a number of diverse drives: economic rewards, social status, security, sexual needs, etc. Their behaviour is adaptive and the relative importance of these diverse drives will vary from one individual to another, and within the same individual over time. Furthermore, because of the variation in such factors as perception, environment, training and goals, different individuals will react differently to the same stimuli. Therefore, not only must accountants discuss the information they think they would require if they did the manager's job, they must also recognize, for example, that six managers with very similar responsibilities may each require a completely different form of reporting. There is a natural tendency to design and present a standard form of report for managers with similar responsibilities.

If, in fact, computer-based systems are employed to produce comprehensive general purpose reports of what has transpired, and these do not meet the manager's information needs, nor does he understand the information reported, it is unlikely in these circumstances that managers will make *positive* responses to the reports received and, therefore, effective communication will not take place.

Summary

Budgetary planning and control systems recognize that it is the people or employees who should be controlled and that by control of people, and proper control of people through their participation in the control system, resource control will be accomplished more effectively. Budgets are established which set out in financial terms the responsibilities of executives in relation to the requirements of the overall policy of the company. Continuous comparison of actual results and budgeted results is made either to secure through action by responsible executives the objectives of policy, or to provide a basis for a revision of policy. Budgetary control assists management in planning, co-ordinating and controlling activities of individuals and the overall performance of the firm. The administration of the budgeting programme is usually delegated to a budget officer. A budget committee may co-ordinate and review individual budgets. It is advisable to prepare a budget manual. A budgetary plan consists of many individual budgets which are integrated into a master budget. Preparation of the cash budget is an important part of the budgetary planning process. A basic tenet of budgetary control is that executives develop and accept responsibility for their budgets. It is important that the motivational influence of the budgeting system on individuals be examined. The chief value of a budget as a control device will be realized through the effective use of reports. It is necessary to decide whether or not a particular variance from budget is 'significant'. In response to a dynamic and rapidly changing external environment many companies forecast ahead on a monthly basis, some employ rolling annual budgets, and weekly profit statements are also produced. Developments in information technology have had an impact on all aspects of budgetary planning and control. Computer-based models and information systems are employed. It is important that the behavioural aspects of reporting are recognized if the benefits of these systems are to be fully realized.

Selected Reading

1. Lloyd R. Amey, *Budget Planning and Control Systems*, Pitman, London, 1979.

2. R. Anthony, J. Dearden and N. Bedford, *Management Control Systems*, Irwin, Homewood, Illinois, 1984.

3. R. Anthony and D. Young, *Management Control in Nonprofit Organisations*, Irwin, Homewood, Illinois, 1984.

4. D. R. Cooper, R. Scapens and J. Arnold, *Management Accounting Research and Practice*, Chartered Institute of Management Accountants, London, 1983.

5. Jerry Dermer, *Management Planning and Control Systems*, Irwin, Homewood, Illinois, 1977.

6. Clive Emmanuel and David Otley, *Accounting for Management Control*, Van Nostrand and Reinhold (U.K.), Wokingham, 1985.

7. G. A. Hofstede, *The Game of Budget Control*, Tavistock Institute, London, 1968.
8. Charles T. Horngren and George Foster, *Cost Accounting*, Prentice-Hall International, Englewood Cliffs, N.J., 1987.
9. Peter A. Pyhrr, *Zero-Base Budgeting*, Wiley-Interscience, New York, 1973.
10. R. W. Scapens, D. T. Otley and R. Lister, *Management Accounting and Organisation Theory: Three Surveys*, Macmillan, London, 1984.
11. William E. Thomas (ed.), *Readings in Cost Accounting Budgeting and Control*, South-Western Publishing, Cincinnati, 1983.

CASE STUDIES

In John Sizer and Nigel Coulthurst, *A Casebook of British Management Accounting*, I.C.A.E.W., 1984, 1985.

The Minerals Division of the Bath and Portland Group (Volume 1) – a description of management accounting control systems, with particular reference to the quarrying industry.

The Central Electricity Generating Board (Volume 1) – the budgetary planning and control system employed in the electricity supply industry, with particular reference to power station management.

Northern Dairies Ltd (Volume 1) – the development and use of the weekly profit estimate as one of the basic elements of planning, budgetary and financial control systems in a milk processing and distribution business.

The South Wales Electricity Board (Volume 1) – the management accounting system for preparing an electricity distribution board's revenue expenditure budget and for subsequent monitoring of performance against budget.

Charcon (ECC) Ltd (Volume 2) – the weekly trading summary of a precast concrete manufacturer.

Thames Valley Newspapers Ltd (Volume 2) – the management accounting information system in a newspaper printing and publishing company.

10

Financial Control of Subsidiary Companies

Financial control in groups of companies and in divisionalized companies is considered in this chapter in the context of strategic and structural changes that occurred in many British groups of companies during the 1980s. After examining and illustrating the relationship between strategy, structure and financial planning and control systems, and discussing whether recent developments in the United Kingdom have placed excessive emphasis on short-term profit performance, we shall consider the use of return on investment to measure the performance of divisions/profit centres/subsidiaries and the determination of transfer prices for goods and services sold by one autonomous profit centre to another.

From Survival Strategies to Strategic and Structural Change

For the first two to three years of the recession following the election of the Conservative government in May 1979, many groups of British companies were forced to concentrate on the disposal of loss-makers and the elimination of surplus capacity.[1] As noted in Chapter 4, in addition to taking actions to improve the profitability of individual subsidiaries/operating units, groups of companies asked questions such as:

(a) Is the group's organization structure appropriate to the reduced level of activity and anticipated growth? Do we have too many layers of management?

(b) Are we occupying too many buildings and, in particular, too many expensive city-centre properties?

1 See John Sizer, 'Managing Liquidity and Profitability in Recession', I, II and III, *Accountant's Magazine*, September, October and November 1981.

(c)   Are we incurring excessive administrative costs because of the trappings of a large company, e.g. a secretary for everyone?

(d)   Are we incurring excessive selling and marketing costs because we have failed to recognize that we are no longer selling in growth markets?

A C.B.I. survey published in 1985 of interviews with senior executives of seventy-two companies that were successful over the period 1970 to 1984 in terms of growth, earnings per share, and rates of return on capital employed concluded:

It appears that companies are substantially better managed and more profitable than at the beginning of the 1980s.

These improvements have been concentrated in methods of financial control. However, achieving this had led to not only substantial cost cutting but also to a move away from manufacturing, especially that of non-specialized (presumably low value added products) in the U.K.[2]

Following the period of retrenchment more fundamental reviews of policies and strategies were undertaken, often involving significant changes in direction. As explained in Chapter 7, strategies based on growth products and growth markets, which frequently lead to excessive optimism concerning market growth rates and the ability to establish market share, were replaced by ones based on rationalization, efficiency and differentiation, and in some instances short-term cash flow maximization, with greater emphasis on comparative advantage and relevant strategies for different product-market segments. There is evidence that greater attention is being given to product design, product quality, and the requirements of individual product-market segments.

These strategic reviews, together with considerations of whether organizational structures were appropriate to reduced levels of activity and growth prospects, led also to major changes in structure and organizational philosophy involving greater decentralization of profit responsibility. The major structural and philosophical changes that took place in many large groups are well illustrated by those which occurred at I.C.I. under Sir John Harvey-Jones's chairmanship, and were summarized in the following extracts from an article in the *Financial Times* (3 September 1984):

2 Robin Matthews, *Managing for Success*, C.B.I., 1985, p. 15.

. . . a first major step was to reduce the size of the board to manageable proportions. In the 1970s there were a dozen or more executive directors: today, there are eight, including the chairman.

Layers of management have been removed throughout the company, starting at the top with the deputy chairmen, of whom there used to be three. Jobs have been pushed down the hierarchy, with a view to leaving people at the top with room to concentrate on the big picture.

The role of individual directors has been changed substantially. 'We decided that the primary responsibility of board members was for the future of the corporation rather than for the constituent bits . . .'

This means that directors are no longer responsible for the profitability of the businesses in their portfolio, and are not required to act as board-level advocates for them. Instead, chief executives of the operating units and their aides can now present their arguments in person to the executive directors or to the board as a whole.

This puts the operating unit executives in a much more exposed position.

Back at board level, a number of functional responsibilities, such as planning or engineering, have been discarded.

The big difference in practical terms is that the executive directors now spend a great deal of their time talking to each other about where I.C.I. is going.

Strategy, Structure and Control Systems

A key finding of Matthews's study of successful companies for the C.B.I. was the importance of company organization and financial control. The stereotype that emerged from the study was:

- A strategic plan looking three to five years ahead, or more.
- An operational plan setting budgets looking at activities for the next year.
- Reporting on at least a monthly basis to ensure that divisions and departments are on track to achieve their annual budgets.
- The plans are 'rolling plans' in the sense that the operational plan is Year 1 in the strategic plan which in turn is adapted from year to year in the light of circumstances. Sometimes a medium-term plan covering two years or so is produced, linking the operational plan with the strategic plan.
- These plans are generally agreed between senior managers and the relevant operational manager – correspondingly, the operational manager sees the plan as a personal commitment to the senior manager.
- The centre acts as a bank; divisions have to raise finance through the centre and remit profits and cash to the centre.

- The centre co-ordinates decisions – successful executives believe that it is vital that the centre can take decisions quickly and ensure that where decisions are delegated, the responsibility for the decision is clearly assigned. When advice is asked of the centre, it is made clear that responsibility for accepting (or rejecting) this advice rests with the division itself.
- The centre scrutinizes the monthly reports carefully; if performance fails to meet targets, steps have to be taken to put things right or to modify plans. Putting things right can range from advice to changing management or even liquidating entire parts of a business.
- Monthly reports pay at least as much attention to cash as to profits.[3]

Some groups with slimline head offices, such as B.T.R. and Hanson Trust, were less concerned with the strategic planning stage, placing considerable emphasis on short-term performance. They viewed the annual budget as a contract with the management of a subsidiary, concentrated on bottom-line performance, and related rewards closely to performance.

After studying the organizational philosophies, strategies, structures and control systems of sixteen large British companies, Goold and Campbell (see Selected Reading 6) have drawn a useful distinction between three successful styles of managing strategy, which they call *strategic planning*, *financial control* and *strategic control* (see Table 10.1).

In the *strategic planning* companies, senior managers in the corporate head office believe they should be closely involved in the formulation of their business units' strategies rather than leaving them to the business unit managers alone to make them. The strategic planning companies set their individual businesses targets to reach, but they tend to be more understanding if, for reasons beyond their control, their managers find themselves unable to meet them. Corporate head office is more interested in whether the business is moving in the right direction, e.g. achieving market share objectives and successfully implementing long-term manufacturing and marketing strategies. Goold and Campbell consider the strengths of this style are:

1. It builds checks and balances into the process of determining each business unit's strategy.
2. It encourages strategies that are well integrated across business units.

3 Matthews, op. cit., pp. 17–18.

Table 10.1

STRATEGIC PLANNING COMPANIES:
  B.P.
  B.O.C.
  Cadbury Schweppes
  Lex
  S.T.C.
  United Biscuits

FINANCIAL CONTROL COMPANIES:
  Hanson Trust
  B.T.R.
  Ferranti
  G.E.C.
  Tarmac

STRATEGIC CONTROL COMPANIES:
  Courtaulds
  I.C.I.
  Imperial Group
  Plessey
  Vickers

(*Source:* M. Goold and A. Campbell, *Strategies and Styles*, Blackwell, Oxford, 1987)

3. It fosters the creation of ambitious strategies, once the corporate headquarters establishes the direction in which the business is going, and unit managers are free to develop bold plans to achieve whatever goal has been set. Because the strategic objectives come from the corporate headquarters, the units can support these objectives without great concern for the short-term financial impact of their actions.

The strategic planning style also has its drawbacks. It may have negative impacts on business unit managers, both because so many people are involved in planning and because their strategic choices are rejected or changed by head office. The loss of autonomy at the business unit level is particularly a problem when the distance between the headquarters and the market is great. Flexibility may also be diminished because the extensive decision-making process inhibits the company's ability to respond quickly to changing market, technological or environmental conditions. There is also a danger that companies employing this style support losing strategies for too long. Goold and Campbell conclude that the strategic planning style is most effective in organizations that are seeking a broad integrated strategy for developing the business units, where the focus is on long-term competitive advantage.

As will be illustrated later in this chapter, *financial control* style companies tend to have a small corporate head office staff and their central management are not involved in detailed planning with their business units. Responsibility for strategy development is the responsibility of the business unit managers. Headquarters does not formally review strategic plans, but exerts influence through tough, short-term budgetary planning and control systems. The business unit managers are expected to concentrate on tough, but achievable, annual profit targets that will result in both a high return on capital employed and annual profit growth. The financial control companies in the study achieved, on average, higher profitability ratios than the other companies, and were better at rationalizing poor performing businesses quickly and turning around new acquisitions. Goold and Campbell emphasize that the greatest value of this style is the motivation it gives managers to improve financial performance immediately. Other strong points of the style are:

(a) Because corporate management is constantly challenging plans that are producing poor results, it has a way of shaking managers loose from ineffective strategies.

(b) It is good for developing executives, it gives potential high-fliers general management experience early in their careers, and it creates 'winners' psychology' in survivors which improves the quality of the dialogue between headquarters and the business unit general managers.

(c) Because corporate headquarters executives do not need to have an intimate knowledge of each unit's technologies, competitors and markets, it is particularly effective for managing groups with highly diversified portfolios.

One of the shortcomings of this style's emphasis on the short-term, which is examined more fully later in this chapter, is its bias against strategies and investments with long lead times and paybacks. Growth tends to come more from acquisition than from internal development. The decentralized philosophy focusing on a large number of autonomous profit centres also inhibits the exploitation of potential synergies between business units. Excessively rigorous financial control systems may also inhibit flexibility, adaptability, and responsiveness to market opportunities. The control systems can become a straitjacket.

Strategic control companies attempt to balance the difficult task of trying to secure the advantages of the other two styles while avoiding their weaknesses. With this style the corporate head office is involved in helping the business units draw up their strategies but expects them to do more of the work themselves. The role of the central management is to audit the quality of the strategic thinking in the business unit. Strategic control companies attempt to balance long-term and short-term objectives, agreeing with their business unit managers annual financial targets as well as strategic goals such as increasing market share or the introduction of manufacturing technologies and management systems. Goold and Campbell conclude that in practice the tensions involved in balancing control and decentralization make this style of management the most difficult to execute because it creates ambiguity between long-term strategic objectives and short-term financial performance. The strategic plan and the financial targets included in the annual budget may pull in opposite directions. Once the corporate headquarters has approved an annual plan and a budget, it attempts to monitor businesses against strategic objectives, such as market share, as well as budget performance in terms of achievement of financial targets.

The financial control styles of successful companies like B.T.R., Coloroll, G.E.C. and Hanson Trust have become fashionable, with slimline head offices concentrating upon strategy, but with short lines of communication to subsidiaries, and straightforward reporting systems concentrating upon key determinants of profitability – reporting systems designed to provide management control information rapidly and frequently on overall activity, not detailed reporting on all aspects of a subsidiary's operations.

B.T.R. plc, one of Goold and Campbell's financial control companies, is a diversified group of companies with an impressive record of growth and profitability. B.T.R.'s business objectives are expressed in terms of profits with greater emphasis being placed on the ratio of profit to sales than on return on capital employed. Profits consciousness is instilled throughout B.T.R. by a system of de-

Table 10.2
Contents of a Company Profit Plan

A. Managing Director's/General Manager's report

B. Assumptions (Economic and Major Business Changes)

C. Main Schedules:
    1.   Summary of Results
    2.   Profit Analysis by Product
    3.   Sales Change
    3A. Sales Price Movements
    4.   Manpower
    5.   Analysis of Overheads and Associate and Investment Income
    6.   Profit Change
    7.   Capital Expenditure/Approval
    7A. Capital Approvals Analysis
    8.   Balance Sheet
    8A. Cash Flow

D. Supplementary Schedules:
    9.   Principal Cross-references
    10. Added Value Index
    11. Fixed Asset Reconciliation
    12. Inter-Company Trading Analysis

centralization into business units, each with a measure of profit responsibility; short lines of communication from B.T.R. to business units, and small corporate offices. Its ideal is to establish a series of strong positions in 'niche businesses', i.e. activities that have a special sector in a large market, or a large share of a specialized market. A 'niche business' can be shrinking, static or expanding. Consistent with its emphasis on profits, B.T.R. takes an unsentimental view of market share. For example, it gave up a strong position in the belting business because it was reluctant to invest aggressively in new technology. B.T.R.'s straightforward but effective financial planning and control systems, including board reports, are fully described in *A Casebook of British Management Accounting*, Volume 2.

The preparation of annual profit plans is top-down objective-setting for each company, bottom-up preparation of plans, and top-down approval process. By June of each year B.T.R.'s managing director has resolved a profit objective for the following year for each company, which builds up into divisional and regional objec-

Table 10.3

	PROFIT PLAN 1984 – PROFIT CHANGE				SCHEDULE PP 6
	COMPANY				CURRENCY 000s
					( ) = **Profit Decrease**

Line No.		PROFITS	4	Profit change Actual 1982 to Forecast 1983	1 Actual 1982/F'cst 1983		2 F'Cast 1983/Plan 1984	
1	Actual 1982							
2	Forecast 1983		5	Profit change Forecast 1983 to Plan 1984				
3	Plan 1984							
	INFLATION AND PRICE CHANGES							
6	Inc/(dec) Sales Revenues							
7	(Inc)/dec Material Prices							
8	(Inc)/dec Payroll Costs							
9	(Inc)/dec Overheads							
10	(Inc)/dec Depreciation							
11	(Inc)/dec Currency Gains/(Losses)							
12	(Inc)/dec Central Charges							
13	(Inc)/dec Group Royalties/Commissions							
14								
15								
16	*Total Inflation and Price Changes*				%		%	
	PRODUCTIVITY GAINS/DEVELOPMENT COSTS CHANGES							
17	(Inc)/dec Materials, Waste, Rejects							
18	(Inc)/dec Payroll Costs							
19	(Inc)/dec Overheads – brief detail							
20	(Inc)/dec Future Business Development Costs							
21								
22	*Total Productivity Gains/Development Costs Changes*							
	VOLUME AND MIX CHANGES							
23	Inc/(dec) Sales Revenues							
24	(Inc)/dec Material Content							
25	(Inc)/dec Payroll Costs							
26	(Inc)/dec Overheads							
27	(Inc)/dec Depreciation							
28	(Inc)/dec Group Royalties/Commissions							
29								
30	*Total Volume and Mix Changes*				%		%	
	OTHER CHANGES							
31	Subsidiary Company Dividends and Other							
32	Associate/Investment Income							
33	(Inc)/dec Internal Interest on short term monies							
34								
35	*Total Other Changes*							
36	*Increase/(decrease) in Profit*							

tives. Between June and September (Eastern and Western Region) and June and October (European Region) each business unit prepares a profit plan and these are presented to a committee delegated by the B.T.R. board of directors. Revisions to companies' plans are formalized by the end of November and agreed plans are consolidated. A review of the consolidated plan for the calendar year is presented to the early January board meeting at which the board approves the profit plans and capital budgets. Companies submit their profit plans on standard forms which contain only key information. The contents of a company profit plan are shown in Table 10.2, and the detailed schedules are provided in the case study. In reviewing profit plans great emphasis is placed on how much of the anticipated profit stems from inflation, volume movements, cost controls and/or product development (see Table 10.3). As well as examining critical assumptions, the board's committee concentrates on philosophy, seeking commitment and dedication to their profit plans.

The B.T.R. reporting cycle commences with *weekly reports* from each company on sales and orders. Each company reports 'flash results' to the regional financial controller by the *fourth working day* after each month. The '*flash report*' contains year-to-date profit, sales, orders received, manpower, cash balances and interest. The results are fed into a computer and compared with plan and comparative data held in the computer. The company chief executive's commentaries on the 'flash results' are received on the sixth/seventh working day after the month end. Each company submits a *full monthly report* to the regional financial controller by the eleventh working day of each month. The contents of this report are shown in Table 10.4 and the detailed schedules are provided in the case study. The regional financial controller prepares a summary report for B.T.R. plc by the *fifteenth working day*. A series of books is issued on the *tenth working day* of each month which contains summaries of the 'flash results' and management commentaries for the previous month, and the detailed results of the prior month. Regional executive board meetings are held within the *eleventh/fifteenth working day* of each month. At their February meetings the executive boards are concerned with reviewing how the current year has opened up in relation to the profit plan. In subsequent meetings *forecasts* become as important as the position to date. Comparisons

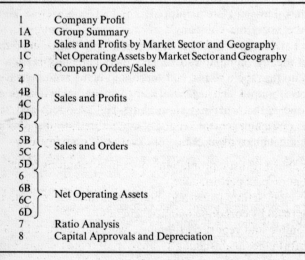

Table 10.4

Contents of Monthly Report

M R 1	Summary of Key Information
M R 2	Graphs – Cumulative Sales, Cumulative P B I T *
M R 3	Profit and Loss Account
M R 3A	Extraordinary Items included in P B I T
M R 4	Balance Sheet
M R 5	Working Capital
M R 6	Provisions
M R 7	Cash Flow and Forecast
M R 8	Capital Expenditure/Approvals

* Profit before interest and tax.

Table 10.5

Contents of B.T.R. plc Board Report

1	Company Profit
1A	Group Summary
1B	Sales and Profits by Market Sector and Geography
1C	Net Operating Assets by Market Sector and Geography
2	Company Orders/Sales
4	
4B	Sales and Profits
4C	
4D	
5	
5B	Sales and Orders
5C	
5D	
6	
6B	Net Operating Assets
6C	
6D	
7	Ratio Analysis
8	Capital Approvals and Depreciation

of actual and planned results are reported to the B.T.R. board meetings. The schedules included in the board package are shown in Table 10.5 and the detailed schedules will be found in the case study.

The key features of B.T.R.'s control systems, which are fully described in the case study, are clearly defined profit responsibility; seeking commitment and dedication to the profit plan; a pyramid system of reporting by responsible chief executives; progressive summarizing of performance by responsible executives; and emphasis on prompt considerations of 'flash results'. The awareness by operating management that results are reviewed quickly by senior management, also a key feature of G.E.C.'s control systems, is regarded as one of the major managerial benefits of B.T.R.'s system.

Hanson Trust's organizational characteristics appear to match closely the U.S. conglomerate's model of a small team of general managers at the centre concentrating upon strategy with specialists in central, legal and financial positions. All functions are present in the operating companies, thus eliminating the need for co-ordination. Corporate divisional interests are co-ordinated through the reward system. Such conglomerates usually pursue more diverse strategies than multi-divisional companies. The resource allocation process is decentralized, but a few sophisticated financial planning and control systems are employed. The budget is viewed as a *contract*; the operating company's management is committed to this contract and is rewarded by comparison with it. Such conglomerates tend to identify companies that need better management, acquire them, and turn them round; this turnabout being accomplished by a corporate group skilled in general management that acts as a consulting group with ownership clout. Financial planning and control systems and management reporting procedures are installed which require the management of the turned-round company to:

1. Establish realistic profitability objectives requiring an improvement on past performance;
2. Develop action plans and budgets to achieve objectives for approval by corporate management; and
3. Monitor and report performance with particular emphasis on performance against budgets, analysis of trends, changes in forecasts and reporting on actions taken.

Rewards are frequently related to bottom-line performance. For example, Coloroll's management style includes not only an 'obsession with financial control' but generous rewards for results, so that divisional managers receive bonuses based on divisional profit, and company directors are rewarded according to earnings per share.[4]

4 Anita van de Vliet, 'The Importance of Coloroll', *Management Today*, January 1987, pp. 42–7 and p. 91.

The relationship between a subsidiary company's budget and the parent and holding company's budget, and the process of approving subsidiary companies' budgets, were discussed with David Allen, Ron Kett and Derrick Willingham. Let us pick up the discussion from Chapter 9, page 298.

PROFESSOR: Let us now consider the next stage in the process of developing budgets, the relationship between the subsidiary company's budget and the parent or holding company's budget. Presumably the parent has some overall objectives, and the question is whether the parent communicates those objectives down to its subsidiaries and allows them to go through the same bottom-up budget preparation and submissions, and then has a look at them and decides whether it is happy with them. Ron, you are finance director of a holding company – a group of companies which could be described as a conglomerate. How do you handle budgeting at your level?

RON KETT: Well, it isn't black and white, it's all shades of grey. It isn't bottom-up, it isn't top-down. We are a conglomerate group with lots of different but not necessarily related activities. We have quarries all over the country, a building activity, a civil engineering activity, an agriculture activity, and so on. We look at our subsidiaries by having a group board member in each of these different companies; so we have the thread already.

For example, if I sit in ten of our subsidiary boards, I see what is going on day by day, month by month, week by week, or whenever we have our board meetings and we have these regularly once a month. We know basically what the subsidiary company is about, in its market and in its activity. So when it comes to July (which is our budget time) we don't necessarily say from the holding company to an operating company: 'You start, that is your parameter, with X amount of cash to use, and do what you can with it.' Nor do we say to the operating company: 'Give us your budget and we will look at it afterwards and see if we can manage it.' It is shades, it is a mixture of bottom-up and top-down.

The operating companies' budgets are all put together, basically in the same way as Derrick and David are saying. The operating company does its production budget, its sales budget, its capital budget; they are all put together in the form of a set of accounts over a year. It's at that stage that they come to the holding company and we aggregate all those budgets for the group; we then see what sort of profit against what sort of funds employed the group as a whole is going to show, and how much finance is needed to fund that kind of activity.

PROFESSOR: When the budgets come to you and you aggregate all the operating companies' budgets, look at the implications on your capital expenditure programme, on your additional investment in working capital and on your cash flow profile, it may well be that they just don't add up. How do you resolve that conflict?

RON KETT: Well, we do that fairly simply. At least, we from the holding company think it's fairly simple – the operating companies may not. My chief executive and myself have a session, then with the executive director team of each subsidiary. We examine their budgets and we say, 'Yes, you can have a £2m. overdraft at that time of the year,' or 'No, you can't have it at another time of the year,' and so we examine each of their activities to see where they can improve their efficiency.

We also look at what additional projects they want to put in, because we say to operating companies, 'You prepare your normal budget.' If they think they want to expand their activity by acquisition or by introduction of new products which they have developed, then we treat that as a separate development or acquisition budget.

PROFESSOR: So we have gone through the process of a top-down view to the subsidiary about the overall framework within which they prepare their budgets. Within the subsidiary the budget is prepared along the lines that Derrick and David have explained: an interactive process within the subsidiary. The subsidiary's board then agrees its budget, it sends the budget to you for your approval; it may well be that you have to say: 'Well, yes, this is a very exciting plan you've put forward and we like it, and though it looks very attractive in financial terms, unfortunately there isn't sufficient cash available to finance everything. You would like to have, say, a £2½m. overdraft in June next year and we really can only allow you to go to two million.' Do you then say to the subsidiary: 'Go back and re-prepare this budget so that we can now see the revised budget,' i.e. some more top-down?

RON KETT: We assist them. We don't just say, 'Go back and do it.' What we try to do is assist them to take the measures which will re-vamp the budget. For example, we have two or three fairly skilled accountants sitting at group headquarters, and we say, 'We will lend you one of these. You go away and discuss with the company how we can financially re-orientate what it is you want to do.' Quite often one finds that that peak cash demand that we are looking for doesn't really occur there at all; it occurs somewhere else. So the company can then have the funding for its budget but at different times of the year.

PROFESSOR: So in the same way that David was explaining how his management accountants in his product groups helped the management to understand and formulate its budget in the most effective way, you're helping your subsidiaries to do the same thing. Derrick, is your relationship with your American parent similar?

DERRICK WILLINGHAM: Yes it is. I present the strategic plan to the board of management early on in the year and then, once we've done the detailed operating plan, the relevant board member and his administrator and other strategic staff come over and we go through it, in some detail. It is then agreed on (or modified, as the case might be) before being finally put to the board of management in Monaco.

PROFESSOR: David, what happens in Cadbury Typhoo? Do you make a presentation to some executive members of the Cadbury Schweppes board, or is it a more informal process?

DAVID ALLEN: Ours is a formal and, I would say, well-prepared programme. There is a particular day in the year, that's established months beforehand, when there will be a presentation of the division's budget to the main board, and they will have had the papers for that presentation a couple of weeks before the actual meeting. The functional specialists in head office, the accountants and marketing advisers, will have advised the group managing director of any problems that the budget appears to throw up, and they will have passed those questions down to the division. So the actual presentation is a very participative process, with the division attempting to answer the questions that the group has raised about the operational side of the budget, and the group explaining any constraints that it might apply on the financing.

As the Goold and Campbell study highlights and the detailed examples illustrate, in considering the appropriateness of the organizational philosophies of financial control style companies such as B.T.R., Coloroll (*A Casebook of British Management Accounting*, Volume 2), G.E.C. and Hanson Trust for other groups, sight should not be lost of the importance of matching organizational structure to corporate strategy, and also of developing an appropriate relationship between organizational philosophy, management style, financial planning and control systems, and incentive payment systems. The organizational characteristics that are appropriate to a successful conglomerate group of autonomous businesses, such as Hanson Trust, may not be appropriate for:

(a)   an interdependent, multi-divisional company with trading relationships between the divisions;
(b)   a vertically integrated group of companies;
(c)   a large, multi-product, multi-market, multinational company, such as an oil company, which requires central co-ordination of exploration, extraction, transportation, refining, distribution and wholesale and retailing operations; or
(d)   companies which have to invest in new high-technology products and new manufacturing technologies in order to maintain their competitive position and sustain competitive advantage in the long term.

The extent to which central co-ordination is necessary will vary in each of these situations, but in the first three situations the profitability of a division, subsidiary or profit centre will be influenced, in some instances significantly, by the prices charged for the transfer of goods and services between one autonomous profit centre/subsidiary/division and another. Transfer pricing is considered more fully later in this chapter. In the fourth situation, the importance of balancing long-term investment and research and development expenditure against short-term profits is crucial. An excessive emphasis on short-term financial performance is likely to undermine long-term competitive survival.

Successful businesses recognize that there is a trade-off to be evaluated between strong corporate leadership and strategic direction on the one hand, and autonomy for business unit managers with clear lines of responsibility and accountability for business unit performance on the other. They also have to trade off the achievement of long-term strategic objectives and competitive strategies against the improvements in short-term performance achieved from an emphasis on short-term financial results and rigorous budgetary planning and control systems. As Goold and Campbell observe, successful corporations make trade-offs between these choices and draw on the combination that best fits the businesses in their portfolios.

Excessive Emphasis on the Short Term?

The organizational philosophies of conglomerate groups such as B.T.R. and Hanson, and the nature of their financial control systems, have led to concern being expressed about their excessive emphasis on short-term financial performance at the expense of longer-term strategic thinking, capital investment, and research and development expenditure. Questions have been asked about whether such systems have a negative impact on long-term investment, reinforce inbuilt conservatism and create risk-averse managers. If a high-technology or science-based company is under pressure to improve short-term financial performance it may reduce research and development expenditure; similarly, a consumer products company may reduce advertising expenditure. In both cases, though this may weaken their competitive position in the long term it has an immediate impact on current year's profit. The contrast between longer-term strategic business logic and short-term Stock Market-driven financial logic was highlighted by the Hanson Trust bid in 1985 for the Imperial Group and the subsequent break-up of Imperial Group, and the proposed merger of Imperial Group and United Biscuits, and also by the B.T.R. bid during 1986 for Pilkington. Companies such as G.K.N. and Rolls-Royce have to invest in advanced manufacturing technologies and flexible manufacturing systems in order to compete internationally, but such investments may depress profitability in the short term even though the reductions in working capital may result in a reasonable cash payback.

At a time when many U.K. groups are placing greater emphasis on decentralized, short-term profit responsibility, it is being questioned by Robert Kaplan of the Harvard Business School and by David Allen, Financial Director of Cadbury Ltd and a past President of the Chartered Institute of Management Accountants. Kaplan[5] has observed that:

> While R.O.I. control and the profit centre organization have contributed greatly to the success of large corporations during the past sixty years, problems have begun to emerge with the excess focus on short-term financial performance.

He argues that these problems arise because managers, being clever, resourceful people, have learnt a variety of ways to meet profit and R.O.I. goals by resorting to three types of short-term behaviour: exploiting accounting conventions, engaging in financial entrepreneurship and reducing discretionary expenditures. The limitations of return on investment as a measure of a division's or subsidiary's performance are considered later in this chapter. Kaplan concludes that financial measures, such as divisional profits, give an illusion of objectivity and precision. They are relatively easy to manipulate in ways which do not enhance the long-term competitive position of the firm, and they become the focus of opportunistic behaviour of divisional managers. He suggests that by de-emphasizing financial performance measures and relying more on multiple measures of performance, including subjective evaluations based on personal communication and observation by superiors, managers will not have a clear target for short-term optimizing behaviour. Kaplan's conclusions are in sharp contrast with the characteristics of the financial control systems employed by what are regarded as successful financial control style groups in the U.K. which many other groups are duplicating. His views are consistent with David Allen's thesis[6] that traditional accounting reports orientated to-

---

5 Robert S. Kaplan, 'The Evolution of Management Accounting', *Accounting Review*, Vol. LIX, No. 3, July 1984, p. 408.
6 David Allen, 'Strategic Financial Management', the Fifth Armitage and Norton Lecture, presented at Huddersfield Polytechnic, 3 December 1986.

wards short-term accounting profits are at best inadequate, and at worst a serious obstacle to proper evaluation and monitoring at the strategic level of planning and control.

The increasing emphasis on the short term is in sharp contrast with the managerial philosophies of major Japanese competitors. As noted in Chapter 7, Japanese companies are more oriented towards exploiting new technologies and long-term market share than towards short-term profits – towards exploiting opportunities to create new market segments and develop new technologies and new channels of distribution. Saunders, Wright and Doyle, and Wong, Saunders and Doyle,[7] found in comparative studies of British and Japanese companies' marketing strategies that, in sharp contrast with Japanese companies, British companies were often production rather than market oriented, and sought short-term profits at the expense of longer-term market position. They failed to recognize that it is necessary to invest in growth markets, that losses of market share not only affect sales but also reduce cost competitiveness, and that periodic repositioning investments are necessary to remain in the growing higher value added market segments. Faced with competitive pressure, British companies tended to focus on cost cutting, range reduction and rationalization; they were willing to allow their market position to erode if necessary to bolster short-term profitability. The Japanese do not favour the detailed standardized planning systems which Western multinationals tend to employ. They rely on continuous informal monitoring; Japanese subsidiaries in the U.K. indicated that reporting was a 'daily' or 'constant' process, with the telephone as the main mode of communication – a control style that is successfully employed by multiple retailers such as Marks & Spencer plc. Saunders, Wright and Doyle conclude that Japanese headquarters/subsidiary relationships appeared to reflect two desiderata of Peters and Waterman's [8] 'excellent companies' – 'operational autonomy to encourage entrepreneurship' and 'simultaneous "loose-

7 J. A. Saunders, L. Wright and P. Doyle, 'A Comparative Study of U.S. and Japanese Marketing Strategies in the British Market', Department of Management Studies, Loughborough University of Technology, Working Paper No. 152, July 1987; and V. Wong, J. Saunders and P. Doyle, 'A Comparative Study of U.S. and Japanese Marketing Strategies in the U.K.', Department of Management Studies, Loughborough University of Technology, Working Paper No. 153, July 1987.
8 Thomas J. Peters and Robert H. Waterman, *In Search of Excellence*, Harper & Row, New York, 1982.

tight" controls'. They support Peters and Waterman's finding that dominance and coherence of culture is an essential quality in 'excellent companies'. Developments in the U.K. during the 1980s suggest that operational autonomy has increased significantly, but that in many groups control tends to be tight and formalized with a short-term emphasis. In many companies the dominant culture is surviving and winning in the short-term financial control environment.

In an address to the World Congress of Accountants in Tokyo in November 1987, Akio Morita,[9] the founder of Sony, contrasted Japanese managers' and engineers' attitudes to risk and to the long term with those of accountants:

I feel that the setting of a clear target to allow an idea to turn into a new product is one of the most important tasks of the manager of a hi-tech industry. My experience with accountants is that when they are told of an idea for a new product they immediately do a cost analysis. Their cost estimates for a new product in most cases are very high and they're reluctant to give their support. Meanwhile, engineers are confident that they will be able to bring down the cost of the product and make back the development cost after the product has hit the market.

All that the accountant can do at this point is to say that the project is going to cost a lot of money. We know this; we don't know how much money exactly but our friend the accountant is unlikely to have a clearer idea than we do. The tension between product developer who is burning with an idea and financial officer whose job is to keep the company from shoving all the chips into the middle of the table at one time is very common in business. The engineer versus the accountant. The spenders versus savers. The good guys versus the bad guys. I'm not saying which is which. The truth is we really need each other and, if an organization is working the way it should be, complement each other.

In my forty years of rough-and-tumble experience with Sony I have learned that the primary function of a manager is to take risks – prudent risks. Risk-taking is the responsibility of the manager. A manager makes his decisions whether or not to take a particular risk by considering several things. First he calculates as best as he can what his chances are of successfully applying a hot new technology to a new product. This is an art in itself. You may be looking five or ten years ahead and trying to make judgement whether a commitment to something called pulse coded modulation can be eventually applied to a commercial product. In this case the commitment paid off and we now have the compact digital audio disc, which is itself spawning a range of new products. We took a risk and it paid off.

9 Shortened version printed in *Accountancy Age*, January 1988, pp. 20–25.

A good manager cannot be a money manager who pushes the short-term financial perspective to the top. Success cannot come in the long run if a manager is concerned just with beating or matching the competitor's record on a quarterly basis.

There is no accounting system in the world that could have justified the decision we made to commit ourselves to an extremely expensive digital recording development programme, for example. What numbers we did see at the time indicated that we were crazy to go on with it, but we didn't seek justification. Management sometimes worries too much about justification through numbers. Instead I tell my people that a good manager develops a sense of intuition, a hunch or sixth sense, when it comes to decision-making. To make a rational decision you have to know all the facts and figures and the environment surrounding those facts. But a person cannot know everything, so in order to run the business I tell them: 'Take risks based on the numbers but also have faith in your sixth sense. Don't let the facts and the figures – the elements of justification – turn you away from a new idea.'

If there is the emphasis on short-term profitability in the United Kingdom at the expense of long-term competitiveness and market position, and there is a willingness to cut discretionary costs at the expense of market share, a further question arises. Does the Stock Market's emphasis on short-term financial-driven logic lead to excessive reliance on growth by acquisition as opposed to long-term investments in new technology, products, markets and channels of distribution, and is this in the national interest? During the 1986 National Conference of the C.B.I., many business leaders expressed concern, and others strongly supported them, that:

1. The perceived short-term orientation of financial investors in stocks and shares was damaging to industrial competitiveness by discouraging companies from undertaking long-term investment in fixed capital, research and development, and training.

2. The number of mergers and acquisitions over the previous few years created an atmosphere that encouraged managers to take a short-term view at the expense of the investment essential to long-term competitiveness.

3. Financial institutions do not understand British industrial companies' problems and opportunities, take decisions affecting a company on superficial evidence, and do not provide the support, either critical or constructive, which is expected from equity ownership.

The strength of feeling expressed led to the establishment by the C.B.I. of a joint City and Industry Task Force to examine the basis of the concerns and the steps needed to correct the situation. A full consideration of the Task Force report[10] is beyond the scope of this book, but surprisingly, on the basis of a survey of 200 U.K. quoted companies, the Task Force concluded that although there has been much concern that short-term pressures from financial markets affect business decision-making, the evidence did not seem to indicate that it is generally warranted. The evidence is summarized in Table 10.6 in response to the request:

Please indicate the significance of certain constraints in preventing you from taking strategic investment decisions in the long-term interest of your company, such as higher spending of fixed investment, research and development, training or marketing.

It will be noted that the survey asked specifically about three possible barriers to investment for financial markets: fear of takeover, weakness of share price or rating, and direct pressure from financial institutions and analysis. Table 10.6 reveals that none of the three were among the most important constraining influences on firms' investment plans, although 41 per cent said short-term price weakness was a constraint of significance or major significance. In contrast, two weeks after the Task Force report was published, the Institute of Directors published a paper, 'Are Equity Markets Short-Sighted?', which argued that the big financial institutions created as a result of the 'Big Bang' in the City make share prices more volatile and encourage a short outlook by industry. Despite the unanimous report of the C.B.I. Task Force, many business leaders are still concerned about pressures to concentrate on short-term financial performance.

Furthermore, despite Allen's and Kaplan's concerns, increasing emphasis has been placed on short-term reporting, including 'flash results', because managements have recognized (for the reasons elaborated in Chapter 9) that it is imperative in today's conditions to employ planning and control systems based on the need, in a dynamic and hostile environment, to anticipate future sales, costs, profits, movements in working capital and cash flows. Hence

10 Report of the C.B.I. City and Industry Task Force, *Investment for Britain's Future*, C.B.I., October 1987.

Table 10.6

Constraints on Long-term Investment
% of Respondents Mentioning

	Of Major Significance	Significant	Not Significant
Shortage of capital	5	10	85
Cost of capital and/or fears of an inadequate rate of return	24	53	23
Exchange rate uncertainties	2	26	72
A lack of confidence in market prospects	9	39	52
Weakness in your share price or rating	7	34	59
Fear of takeover	0	12	88
Pressure from financial institutions/analysts	4	19	77

(*Source:* C.B.I. Survey of U.K Company Chief Executives, 1987)

development of forecasting systems, described in Chapter 9, which encourage management to look ahead continually, to quantify their expectations and to take effective action. However, it will be appreciated that if not properly understood such forecasting systems may increase the pressure on managers to concentrate their efforts on short-term measures of performance at the expense of the long term. John Ashcroft,[11] Chairman of Coloroll, is reported as urging his managers to 'hunger after market share', but to remember that profit is all-important: 'The most heinous crime a sales director, sales manager or sales person can commit is to miss a short-term profit forecast.' When such crimes are linked to bonuses related to short-term profit performance, the pressures to concentrate on the short term, and the dangers of managements simply duplicating Ashcroft's management philosophy and style without fully considering its appropriateness to their businesses, are obvious. Similarly, the trend towards weekly trading summaries (described in Chapter 9), which are only one aspect of rapidly developing real-time information systems, may also increase emphasis on short-term performance.

11 Van de Vliet, op. cit., p. 46.

Before considering in more detail the measurement of divisional or subsidiary profit performance, in particular the use of return on investment for this purpose, and transfer pricing, the following conclusions can be drawn from the consideration of the relationship between strategy, structure and financial control systems:

1. It is important to recognize that in order for organizations to implement structural and strategic changes, such changes have to be matched by appropriate variations in processes and systems, including financial planning and control systems. This is a difficult and complex process and not simply one of observing and duplicating the planning and control systems of successful companies such as B.T.R., Coloroll, G.E.C. and Hanson Trust, but working out the appropriate relationship between organizational philosophy, corporate strategy, managerial style, structure, and planning and control systems.

2. One danger of simple duplication is an excessive emphasis on short-term performance by businesses whose survival in the long term necessitates investment in research and development and in new technologies, products, markets and channels of distribution, if they are to compete in international markets.

3. While sight should not be lost of the dangers of excessive emphasis on short-term profitability, it should be recognized that in a hostile and uncertain external environment there is a need to develop control systems which require managers to look ahead continually, quantify their expectations and take effective action. However, the planning and control system should not place excessive emphasis on short-term forecasting, weekly trading statements, and 'flash results'. They should be seen as elements of a planning and control system.

4. Corporate managements should review regularly the balance between formal and informal modes of communication, in particular whether their control systems are too tight and formalized.

Measurement of Divisional Profit Performance

As Kaplan has observed, accounting rate of return on capital employed (R.O.C.E.) is used by many groups of companies when measuring the performance of decentralized management of autonomous operating subsidiaries and divisions. A full discussion of the measurement of management performance in autonomous subsidiaries and divisions is beyond the scope of this introductory text, but a number of the limitations of R.O.C.E. should be explained. A fuller discussion of the measurement of divisional profit performance will be found in Selected Readings 1, 3, 4, 12, 13 and 14.

While R.O.C.E. has a particular value in analysing the historical performance of a company when it is possible to build a pyramid of ratios and determine why return on capital employed has been improving or declining over a period, it should be recognized that there are important differences between using R.O.C.E. in the measurement of a manager's performance, and in evaluating the worthwhileness of a past investment. A *manager's* performance can only be measured in relation to the assets under his control and a manager may have limited control over inherited fixed assets. However, a *company* must continually view the worthwhileness of fixed assets as an investment. For example, the manager of a supermarket normally will have no control over the value of the property in which his supermarket is situated. He controls stocks, debtors, and possibly fixtures and fittings on the one hand, generates sales and gross surplus and incurs certain expenditure on the other. His performance must be measured in relation to those factors he controls, not the current value of the capital invested in the supermarket. The situation is different when examining the profitability of the supermarket as an investment: it is then necessary to consider whether the supermarket is generating a satisfactory trading profit in relation to the current value of capital invested in it.

We have seen that there are also important differences between the analyses of historical performance using R.O.C.E. (considered in Chapter 6) and the evaluation of investment decisions using discounted cash flow criteria (considered in Chapter 8). D.C.F. calculations are concerned with future cash inflows and outflows, while R.O.C.E. calculations are based on past accounting transactions.

There are three principal reasons why R.O.C.E. may be unsuitable for evaluating the profit performance of the management of an autonomous subsidiary or division:

1. The methods used to measure *capital employed* base can result in misleading rates of return, which may create an inconsistency

between subsidiary or division and parent company profitability. They may lead managers to take actions in the subsidiary or division's interests which are not in the best interests of the parent company.

2. Return on capital employed is *too simple* a decision rule on which to evaluate the appropriate trade-offs between profits and investments.

3. There are implementation constraints which limit its use in practice.

1. THE CAPITAL EMPLOYED BASE

The problems arising from the determination of the capital employed base are caused by the difficulty of valuing fixed assets. The division's fixed assets may be included in capital employed either at *gross book value* (original cost) or at *net book value*, with the consequence that a division with old assets may earn a higher rate of return than a division with newer assets simply because of the impact of lower original cost, i.e. gross book value, or an unrealistically low net book value.

If *gross book value* (original costs) and profit *before* depreciation are used, a manager may increase his R.O.C.E. by scrapping or disposing of perfectly useful assets that are contributing to profits an amount less than the division's R.O.C.E. In deciding whether or not to dispose of an asset, management should be concerned with the market value of the asset and the future cash flows that will be forgone if the asset is disposed of.

Consider the following simplified example.[12] A machine which cost £2,000 is currently earning a profit before depreciation of £300, i.e. 15 per cent return on gross book value, and the division which owns the machine is currently earning £2,500 profit before depreciation on a total gross capital employed of £10,000, i.e. 25 per cent return on gross book value. If the machine costing £2,000 could be disposed of for £400, the division's gross R.O.C.E. would increase to 27.5 per cent (see table, p. 374).

However, the forgone accounting return on the salvage value of the old machine would be 75 per cent, i.e. £300 profit before deprecia-

12 In the simplified example in this chapter it has been assumed there are no taxation or working capital changes.

	Profit before Depreciation £	*Gross Book Value of Capital Employed* £	*Return on Capital Employed* %
Before Sale	2,500	10,000	25
Less Sale	300	2,000	15
After Sale	£2,200	£8,000	27.5

tion as a percentage of the £400 salvage value. If the machine has a remaining useful life of two years at the end of which it would have a zero salvage value, and the forecast profit *before* depreciation for those years is:

Year 1   £300
Year 2   £250

the forgone D.C.F. return if it is sold for £400 would be 25 per cent.

In addition to encouraging the disposition of perfectly good assets, the use of *gross book values* will have an inconsistent effect on the capital employed base when fixed assets are replaced. The gross book value in the capital employed base will *increase* only by the *difference* between the cost of the new equipment and the original cost of the old. The *incremental* investment by the company is equal to the cost of the new equipment minus the salvage value of the old equipment. The salvage value is usually far below the original cost. For example, if the machine costing £2,000 was sold for £400 and replaced by a modern machine costing £2,250, the increase in gross book value would be £250, while the incremental investment would be £1,850, i.e. £2,250 minus £400. If the profit before depreciation on the new machine in the first year is £500, the return on the division's gross book value will increase from 25 per cent to 26 per cent (see table opposite).

However, the accounting return in the first year on the real incremental investment is only 10.8 per cent, i.e. £200 on £1,850 compared with 80 per cent on the incremental gross capital employed. The D.C.F. rate of return on the incremental investment may be below the company's cost of capital. Thus it is possible that replacement

	Profit before Depreciation £	Gross Book Value of Capital Employed £	Return on Capital Employed %
Before Sale	2,500	10,000	25
Less Sale of Machine	300	2,000	15
	2,200	8,000	27.5
Add Replacement Machine	500	2,250	22
After Sale and Replacement	£2,700	£10,250	26%
Change	+£200	+£250	80%

investments offering a D.C.F. return below the company's cost of capital could improve a division's return on capital employed. A manager could improve his R.O.C.E. performance by making a series of marginal replacement investments, none of which offers a satisfactory D.C.F. return.

The use of *net book value* and profit *after* depreciation may have the opposite effects. It does not encourage managers to replace perfectly good assets, but may discourage them from replacing assets that should be scrapped or disposed of. The use of net book value causes an automatic reduction in the capital employed base as the assets age. The rate of return may increase merely by the passage of time. If a division uses the reducing balance method of depreciation, there may be a double effect on profits as well as on asset base. New investments, which offer a satisfactory D.C.F. return, will be discouraged because they may lower a falsely high R.O.C.E. In fact a division could have a rising return on capital employed, and stagnant or falling absolute profits.

Consider the following simplified example. If a machine costing £5,000 is being depreciated on 10 years' straight line depreciation, i.e. £500 per year, after 1 year it will have a net book value of £4,500, after 5 years £2,500, and after 8 years £1,000. If the profit after depreciation earned by the machine has fallen from £1,000 in Year 1, to £600 in Year 5, to a forecast £400 in year 8, the accounting rate of return on year end net book value will have increased as follows:

Year	Profit after Depreciation £	Year End Net Book Value of Machine £	Return on Net Book Value %
1 (Actual)	1,000	4,500	22
5 (Actual)	600	2,500	24
8 (Forecast)	400	1,000	40

If the machine could be sold for £300 at the beginning of Year 8 and be replaced by a more efficient machine costing £6,000, also with a ten-year life, which would generate a profit after depreciation of £1,500 in Year 8, this would result in:

(i)   A first-year accounting rate of return on year end net book value of 28 per cent, i.e. £1,500 profit before depreciation on net book values of £5,400.

(ii) A first-year return on the incremental year end book value of 25 per cent, i.e. an incremental profit before depreciation of £1,100 (i.e. £1,500 − £400) on incremental year end book value of £4,400 (i.e. £5,400 − £1,000).

Given the return on the existing machine is 40 per cent, if the divisional manager's performance was assessed solely on the basis of net book value, the divisional manager would be discouraged from replacing the old machine at the beginning of Year 8 even if it promises a satisfactory D.C.F. rate of return on the incremental investment (£5,700) and £1,100 incremental profit in Year 8.

Some companies have reacted to the above problems by revaluing assets at *assumed current cost* as an approximation to the economic value of assets to the business. The major problem of using economic values is that they are subjective. How do you determine economic values? As explained in Chapter 6, the use of indices of replacement costs produces *assumed current cost* not replacement cost valuations, because one would not replace with the same assets. How do you cope with technological change? Can you look at assets in isolation from maintenance costs, labour costs, raw material usage, yields, etc.? In E.D.18 an attempt was made to take account of these questions by introducing the concept of the *modern equivalent asset* to be employed when there has been a marked technological advance since purchase of the original asset. It is the gross current cost of a modern replacement, adjusted for the *present value* of any material differences compared with an identical replacement of the original asset. The concept came in for considerable criticism in that it was seen to be a complex and subjective calculation. The Hyde Guidelines and S.S.A.P.16 placed considerable emphasis on the use of indices. However, while indices may be adequate for external reporting, managers may argue that they are not sufficient when assessing their performance, and pressurize accountants to employ the concept of the modern equivalent asset. While some accountants may not recognize the delusions of replacement cost accounting based upon indices, many managers and engineers will! On the other hand, while accounting values based on original cost have an appearance of reality to operating management, economic values are subject to argument. The danger is that as one moves away from accounting values based on original cost, a system is developed that seems to many divisional managers to be a 'game of playing at numbers'.

2. OVERSIMPLIFIED DECISION PROCESS

A second important limitation of R.O.C.E. is that it oversimplifies a very complex decision-making process. The use of such a ratio to measure a divisional manager's performance reduces investment decision-making to a simple but unrealistic decision-making model. Since each manager is expected to achieve an R.O.C.E. objective, he will not be likely to propose a capital investment unless it is expected to earn a return at least as high as his objective. Divisions earning a high R.O.C.E. may reject projects which will give a satisfactory D.C.F. return, an increase in absolute profits, but lower R.O.C.E. for the division. Managers, especially those who expect to be moved to another job within a few years, may be reluctant to propose capital investments that do not have a rapid early payback. This may mean that projects offering a satisfactory D.C.F. return and which are in the long-term interests of the division and the company may not be proposed. A failure to understand the limitations of R.O.C.E. may lead managers to assume that different types of fixed assets are capable of earning the same return. It may also encourage managers to resort to financial entrepreneurship, for example to lease assets at excessively high costs compared with alternative forms of financing, because leased assets do not appear in the balance sheet. Thus, over-emphasis on R.O.C.E. may cause seriously inconsistent capital investment actions.

Some of the above difficulties can be overcome by the use of the *residual income method*. With this method a division's profit objective is established and its performance measured in terms of profit less prescribed interest charge on capital employed by the division. After the interest charge the remaining profit is referred to as the residual income, and this is what a divisional manager aims to maximize. This method does make it practicable to require divisional managers to earn minimum rates of interest for different types of assets. It also avoids the problems that occur when a division earns a very high R.O.C.E. on existing assets. For example, if the divisional manager in the previous example was required to maximize residual income after an interest charge of 15 per cent on capital employed, he would replace the old machine at the beginning of Year 8. It would increase his residual income in Year 8 by £440, as follows:

	Retain Old Machine	Replace Old Machine	Change
Profit after Depreciation	400	1,500	+1,100
Interest on Capital Employed @ 15%	(15% of £1,000)	(15% of £5,400)	
	150	810	+660
Residual Income	£250	£690	+£440

Thus, managers are encouraged to invest in assets which will generate a return greater than the interest charge and therefore contribute to residual income. However, it does *not* overcome the problems of the valuation of fixed assets in the determination of the investment base.

3. IMPLEMENTATION CONSTRAINTS

In addition to the technical constraints, there are a number of implementation constraints which have to be overcome when using R.O.C.E. or residual income and which should be recognized. It can be very difficult to set equitable annual profit objectives for different divisions or subsidiaries in terms of R.O.C.E. or residual income.

The *annual* accounting profit can be a poor, and sometimes misleading, measure of what has been accomplished during a relatively short period of time. It does not measure the longer-term benefits of decisions taken by management during the year, but may reflect long-term decisions made by previous managements in earlier years. It is often difficult to assign responsibility for deviations from the return on capital employed objective.

Despite the shortcomings of R.O.C.E. employed as a measure of divisional performance, a number of British and American research studies have shown that most companies with investment centres continue to use R.O.C.E. for this purpose and to make their profit and capital employed definitions and valuations similar to those used in their published financial statements. Reece and Cool (Selected Reading No. 12) have argued that most designers of financial control systems are aware of the shortcomings of R.O.C.E. as a measure of divisional performance, and that these financial managers do not believe that these flows are more than hypothetical. However, they rightly warn that the potential does exist for R.O.C.E. as commonly implemented to motivate some investment centre managers to make decisions which improve their division's R.O.C.E. but which may not be in the best interests of the company as a whole. They conclude that a company's financial managers and its top corporate executives should all be familiar with the shortcomings of R.O.C.E., and should be convinced they are hypothetical and not real in their company. The author's experience suggests this is not always the case.

Some companies have recognized that the control of the investment in the fixed asset base of a division or subsidiary cannot be controlled through either the R.O.C.E. or residual income methods, and that growth in operating profits and the investment in fixed assets should be controlled separately; a division or subsidiary's profit performance being measured in terms of profit earned compared with some absolute profit objectives and after an interest charge for controllable current assets; fixed assets being controlled by capital expenditure appraisal procedures including post-acquisition audits. In *strategic planning and strategic control style companies*, the profit objectives flow from the quantification of the group's long-term objectives and strategy in the form of a long-term operating plan, and are incorporated in the annual profit and financial plan agreed with divisional managers. As the proposed invest-ments in the long-term plan become current they are appraised in detail in relation to the company's investment criteria. In *financial control style companies* the emphasis is on annual profit growth objectives, supported by rigorous investment appraisal and budget-ary planning and control, and responsibility reporting.

Transfer Pricing

One of the principal problems in operating a system of decen-tralized profit centres in larger organizations is to devise a satisfac-tory system of accounting for transfers of goods and services between one autonomous profit centre/subsidiary/division and another. The problems may be compounded when a decentralized organization expands its operations into the international environment. The atti-tude of tax authorities, currency fluctuations, economic restrictions, joint ventures, political stability and public relations are some of the factors than can affect transfer prices in multinational firms. A discussion of multinational transfer pricing is beyond the scope of this introductory text.

A sound system of transfer pricing should accomplish the follow-ing objectives:

1. It should motivate a profit centre manager or subsidiary managing director to make sound decisions, and it should communicate information that provides a basis for such decisions. This will happen when the actions taken by a profit centre manager or sub-sidiary managing director in his own interests and the interests of his division or subsidiary are also in the best interests of the company as a whole.

2. It should result in reported profit centre or subsidiary profits that are a reasonable measure of the economic performance of the profit centre or subsidiary.

It will be appreciated that these objectives cannot be achieved perfectly. Any system of transfer pricing is likely to lead to some dysfunctional behaviour on the part of the profit centre managers or subsidiary managing directors. It is likely that in taking decisions in their own interests and in the interest of their profit centres, managers will take some decisions that are not in the best interest of the supplying/receiving profit centre and, therefore, not in the best interest of the company as a whole. The system for determining transfer prices cannot, and probably should not, eliminate this tendency. It should aim to achieve the right balance between the benefit of decentralized profit centres and decision-making which they imply, and the costs arising from sub-optimal behaviour. Up to a 'point' the transfer pricing system should motivate profit centre managers and subsidiary managing directors to act as if they were managing directors of independent companies; but they should, beyond this 'point', act for the good of the organization as a whole, even at the expense of the reported profitability of their own profit centre or subsidiary.

Development of Transfer Prices

There are two general approaches to the development of transfer prices: the *market-based price* and the *cost-based price*. Anthony and Dearden (see Selected Reading 1) have developed a set of rules for establishing transfer prices based on dividing all products transferred between divisions or subsidiaries into one of four classes, according to the sourcing restrictions.

Class 1: Those products transferred between divisions that are likely never to be produced outside the company. Anthony and Dearden recommend that the most practical method of pricing these products is *standard cost plus a profit allowance*.

Class 2: Those products that management might be willing to purchase from outside sources, but only on a relatively long-term basis because their manufacture requires a significant investment in facilities and skills. Estimated *long-run competitive prices* are recommended for these products.

Class 3: Those products that can be produced outside the company without any significant disruption to present operations. These products are seen to present no problems in pricing as the divisions or subsidiaries deal with each other as outside companies. The transfer prices are therefore *market based*.

Class 4: Those products that are:

1. Sold to both company and outside sources; or
2. Produced from outside sources as well as being produced within the company.

Anthony and Dearden consider these products are easy to price because an *actual competitive price* is always available. In arriving at market prices adjustments may have to be made for cash discounts and for certain selling costs that are not involved in an internal transfer.

Market-based Prices

If a market-based price for the products or services transferred exists it is generally argued that the market price is usually preferable to a cost-based price. The 'buying' responsibility centre should ordinarily not be expected to pay more internally than it would have to pay if it purchased from the outside world; nor should the 'selling' centre ordinarily be entitled to more revenue than it could obtain by selling to the outside world. Problems can arise when the market price is abnormal, as, for example, when an outside supplier sets a low 'distress' price in order to use temporarily idle capacity. While such temporary fluctuations in the market may be ignored in arriving at transfer prices, they may give rise to inter-divisional negotiations and the possibility of conflict. The negotiations may become protracted, consuming scarce management time. If a divisional manager's performance is measured solely in terms of his division's profitability, and he perceives that his rewards and career are closely related to this, he may use such movements in market prices as an opportunity to re-negotiate transfer prices in his favour. For Class 2 products it may prove difficult to obtain competitive long-run market prices because of the unique nature of the product. If it is not possible to obtain quotations from outside suppliers, it may be possible to:

1. Adjust the price of a similar product for which a reliable market price exists for differences in design;
2. Adjust on past market price for changes in product group market price levels since that price became effective.

If no reliable market price can be established, then a cost-based transfer price has to be used.

Once a long-run price for Class 2 type products has been agreed between divisions it may be necessary to agree a procedure for adjusting transfer prices for changes in design, or changes in costs arising from changes in the supplying division's costs so that transfer prices keep in line with the prices an outside producer would charge if he were supplying the product.

Cost-based prices can be grouped into:

1. Marginal cost or variable cost; and
2. Full cost plus profit.

The current *marginal cost* or *variable cost* approach is consistent with the economic model of the firm that assumes the managers make decisions on the basis of complete knowledge of all factors affecting the company, i.e. they make decisions on the basis of the incremental costs and revenues for the company as a whole and *not* solely on the basis of the incremental costs and revenues that will arise in their profit centre/subsidiary; it appears to be rarely used in practice. It is not possible for transferring profit centres to generate a profit if marginal cost is used. In fact, they should always show a loss on internal sales. Many companies prefer to create, when a production division sells wholly to a marketing division, by means of a full cost plus profit transfer price, what are in effect artificial profit centres for at least two reasons.

1. They wish to create a sense of profit responsibility in divisional managers. A psychological advantage is expected to accrue from a manager having a profit objective instead of a cost objective, even though in the case of a production division the divisional manager only controls costs.

2. Central management is interested in establishing some measure of the worthwhileness of its investment in production divisions and therefore prefers profit centres to cost centres.

It is important in these situations to differentiate clearly between the worthwhileness of the company's investment in an artificial profit centre and the measurement of a manager's performance, because the manager of an artificial profit centre normally does not control all the determinants of profit.

If the *full cost plus profit* approach is used, it may be advisable for the method of computing cost and the amount of profit to be added to be laid down by top management in order to lessen arguments that would otherwise occur between buying and selling responsibility centres. If the company operates a standard costing system, the full cost frequently is at *standard cost*. If it is an actual cost, the

selling responsibility centre can pass along its inefficiencies to the
buying responsibility centre, i.e. they may be included in the transfer
price. In some situations, particularly if one is concerned with the
efficiency of the supplying division and the worthwhileness of the
company's investment, the full costs may be neither the standard
nor the actual costs incurred by the selling responsibility centre, but
an estimate of the costs that would be incurred by the most efficient
outside supplier using the latest manufacturing practices and equipment.

Philips (*A Casebook of British Management Accounting*, Volume
1), a major multinational operating in the field of electronics in over
sixty countries, bases transfer prices on *factory standard costs*. A
typical situation relating to the manufacture of television sets by
Philips in the United Kingdom is illustrated in Figure 10.1. The
procedures for calculating transfer prices are fully described in the
case study.

Possible Dysfunctional Behaviour

It is important to recognize that whether transfer prices are *market
based* or *full cost plus profit based*, the existence of transfer prices
and separate profit centres implies the supplying division's fixed
costs become the buying division's variable costs. For example,
assume the *full cost plus profit* transfer price of Product X from
Division A to Division B is determined as follows:

	£
Direct Materials	5
Other Variable Costs	3
	—
Variable Cost	8
Fixed Costs	7
	—
Total Cost	15
Profit 20%	3
	—
Transfer Price	£18
	=

The cost of Product X will be included in Division B's costs as
variable cost (direct material) even though it includes £7 of Division

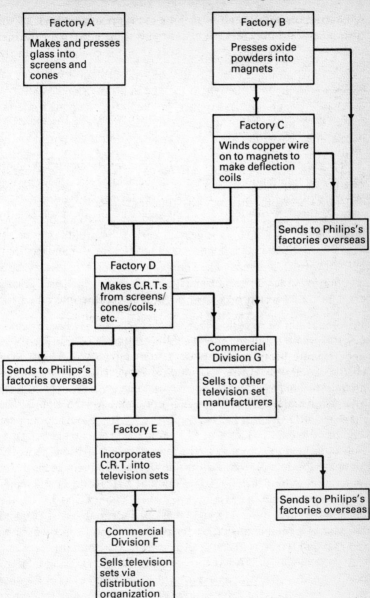

Figure 10.1. *Manufacture of television sets: integrated manufacture of components*

A's fixed costs. As a result of making the supplying division's fixed costs part of the buying division's variable costs:

1. A decision by a divisional manager in his division's interest will have a different impact on the division's profit than it will have on company profit. For example, it may be in his division's interest to purchase from an outside supplier, but be in the company's interest to buy from an internal supplier. A buying division on the basis of its marginal costs may turn away business that does not offer the division an adequate additional contribution, but which, in relation to the company's marginal or variable costs, is worthwhile business. The higher the ratio of fixed costs to total costs in the supplying divisions the greater the risk of dysfunctional behaviour.

2. If a division sells exclusively to other divisions, and an artificial profit centre is created, as suggested earlier, its profits may be affected more by the performance of other divisional managers than by its own performance. The supplying division's sales may be a function of other divisional managers' marketing policies, pricing decisions, etc., which may take no account of the interest of the supplying division's cost structure, capacity utilization, etc.

Consider the following simplified illustrations:

1. Assume Division B purchases from Division A 25 per cent (10,000 units) of Division A's output of Product X at a *full cost plus profit* transfer price of £18 (see breakdown, p. 384). There is no alternative market for Division A's production for Division B. The manager of Division B has been approached by an outside supplier who has offered Product X at £15 per unit. If the manager of Division B decided to act solely in the interest of his division, he would purchase Product X from the outside supplier and reduce his direct material cost by £30,000 (10,000 units at £3). However, the company's costs would increase by £70,000 (10,000 units at £7, i.e. the outside supplier's price £15 less Division A's variable cost £8), and Division A's total contribution to fixed costs and profits would be reduced by £100,000 (10,000 at £10 per unit contribution).

2. Assume Division A has surplus capacity, and Division B has to decide whether to accept an export order for 10,000 units of Product M at a selling price of £80 per unit. Product M contains, as a direct material, Product X which is supplied by Division A. The total cost per unit of Product M is:

	£	£
Direct Material:		
3 units of Product X at £18 per unit	54	
Other Direct Materials	10	
	—	
		64
Other Variable Costs		14
Variable Cost		78
Fixed Costs		24
Total Cost		£102

If the manager of Division B acts solely in the interest of his division, he may not accept the export order because it offers only £20,000 contribution (10,000 units at £2 per unit) towards his fixed costs. However, for the company as a whole the export order offers an additional contribution of £320,000, calculated as follows:

	Per unit of Product M £	Total £
Direct Material:		
Variable Cost of Product X:		
3 units at £8 per unit	24	240,000
Other Direct Material	10	100,000
Other Variable Costs	14	140,000
Total Variable Cost	48	480,000
Selling Price	80	800,000
Additional Contribution	£32	£320,000

Thus, while the order offers only an additional contribution of £20,000 to Division B it would provide, if accepted, an additional £300,000 contribution to Division A (30,000 units at a contribution of £10 per unit).

Given that situations similar to these two simplified illustrations are bound to arise, and that divisional managers may well act in their own interests at the expense of the company as a whole, top management has to evaluate the trade-offs between the benefits of more manageable, profit-oriented divisions and the costs to the company of sub-optimal behaviour. As suggested earlier, they must clearly distinguish between measuring:

1. The worthwhileness of their investment; and
2. The performance of managers.

If divisional managers feel their rewards and career opportunities are strongly correlated to their division's profitability, they may act solely in their division's interests and the costs of decentralized profit centres may outweigh the benefits. If, on the other hand, an atmosphere is created whereby managers do accept the need to take account of the company's overall interests as well as the divisions' and subsidiaries', whereby they do feel top management distinguishes between the worthwhileness of their investment in a division and a divisional manager's performance, and that short-run divisional profit performance is not the sole criterion of success, then the benefits of divisionalization may well outweigh the costs arising from sub-optimal behaviour of divisional managers.

Arbitration Mechanism

Whatever the approach to setting the transfer price, there has to be a procedure for *negotiating* the price of actual transactions between the buying and selling responsibility centres. Such negotiations may give rise to the need for an *arbitration mechanism*. For example, a buying responsibility centre may wish to take advantage of a temporary low outside price, while the supplying responsibility centre is anxious not to lose the business and is willing to negotiate a 'deal'. Unless both responsibility centre managers have complete freedom to act, the negotiations will not always lead to an equitable result because the two managers may have unequal bargaining power. While the buying manager can threaten to take his business elsewhere, the supplying division manager may have no alternative market for the capacity released, nor may he have the power to refuse to supply another division or subsidiary. If the buying division does temporarily place its business with an outside supplier, should the supplying division be required to hold capacity if the outside supplier raises his price at a later date? Negotiations arising from this type of situation can become heated and protracted. There is the need for an arbitration procedure to settle disputes of this type, as well as when cost-based prices have to be negotiated. While the arbitrator's word must be final, he has to be careful to ensure that he is not used by one party to take an advantage over the other or to defend a position which is not tenable. It may well be that he should only make a decision in the last resort.

Summary

Effective financial planning and control systems are a key characteristic of successful British companies. Following a period of retrenchment in the early 1980s, many British groups undertook fundamental reviews of their policies and strategies. It is important to recognize that in order for organizations to implement structural and strategic change, such changes have to be matched by appropriate variations in processes and systems, including financial planning and control systems. A useful distinction can be drawn between strategic planning, financial planning and strategic control styles of relationship between parent companies and their subsidiaries. The dangers of excessive emphasis on short-term performance should be recognized, particularly by businesses whose survival in the long term necessitates investment in research and development, and in new technologies, products, markets and channels of distribution. While return on capital employed is widely used to measure the performance of managements of divisions and subsidiaries, its limitations should be understood. The system of determining transfer prices between divisions and subsidiaries should aim to achieve the appropriate balance between the benefits of decentralized profit centres and decision-making, and costs arising from managers taking some decisions in their own interests which may not be in the best interests of the company as a whole. Corporate managements should review regularly the balance between formal and informal modes of communication, and in particular whether their control systems are too tight and formalized.

Selected Readings

1. R. Anthony, J. Dearden and N. Bedford, *Management Control Systems*, Irwin, Homewood, Illinois, 1984.

2. Ralph L. Benke, Jr. and James Don Edwards, *Transfer Pricing – Techniques and Issues*, National Association of Accountants, New York, 1980.

3. John Dearden, 'Measuring Profit Center Managers', *Harvard Business Review*, September–October 1987.

4. Clive Emmanuel and David Otley, *Accounting for Management Control*, Van Nostrand Reinhold (U.K.), Wokingham, 1985.

5. Jay R. Galbraith and David A. Nathanson, *Strategy Implementation: the Role of Structure and Process*, West Publishing, St Paul, Minn., 1978.

6. Michael Goold and Andrew Campbell, *Strategies and Styles*, Blackwell, Oxford, 1987; and 'Many Best Ways to make Strategy', *Harvard Business Review*, November–December 1987.

7. Akira Ishikawa, *Strategic Budgeting*, Praegar, New York, 1985.

8. Robert S. Kaplan, *Advanced Management Accounting*, Irwin, Homewood, Illinois, 1982.

9. Robert S. Kaplan, 'The Evolution of Management Accounting', *Accounting Review*, July 1984.

10. John Ould, *Controlling Subsidiary Companies*, Woodhead-Faulkener, Cambridge, 1986.

11. Thomas J. Peters and Robert H. Waterman, *In Search of Excellence*, Harper & Row, New York, 1982.

12. James S. Reece and William R. Cool, 'Measuring Investment Center Performance', *Harvard Business Review*, May–June 1978.

13. R. W. Scapens, J. T. Sale and P. A. Tikkas, *Financial Control of Divisional Capital Investment*, Chartered Institute of Management Accountants, London, 1982.

14. D. Solomons, *Divisional Performance: Measurement and Control*, Irwin, Homewood, Illinois, 1965.

CASE STUDIES

In John Sizer and Nigel Coulthurst, *A Casebook of British Management Accounting*, I.C.A.E.W., 1984, 1985.

Philips Electronics and Associated Industries Ltd (Volume 1) – the development and management uses, in a multinational electronics business, of factory standard prices and transfer indices according to replacement value theory.

B.T.R. plc (Volume 2) – the preparation of annual profit plans and system of responsibility reporting in a large, diversified group of companies.

11

Accounting Information for Marketing Management

Dynamic changes are taking place continually in the environment in which companies operate. These changes have their greatest impact in the market place where shifts are constantly occurring in patterns of demand for consumer and industrial products in home and export markets. It is important that a system of accounting is developed which is relevant to these circumstances and satisfies the financial information needs of marketing management. A framework is developed in this chapter for identifying needs. It relates primarily to multi-consumer product, multi-market firms, but it is largely applicable to firms marketing industrial products. The financial evaluation of export opportunities is given special consideration. Accounting information for selling price decisions is examined separately in Chapter 12.

In examining the provision of accounting information for marketing management in multi-consumer product, multi-market firms, it should be recognized that the *marketing concept* focuses decision-making on the consumer:

> The marketing concept is a management orientation that holds that the key task of the organization is to determine the needs, wants, and values of a target market and to adapt the organization to delivering the desired satisfactions more effectively and efficiently than competitors.[1]

Furthermore, marketing management should no longer be viewed as requiring mainly judgement, intuition and experience. Marketing managers employ quantitative analytical techniques and sophisticated data bases when making decisions.

In many multi-product, multi-market companies, product

1 Philip Kotler, *Marketing Management*, Prentice-Hall, Englewood Cliffs, N.J., 3rd edition, 1976.

management is not simply a process of deciding selling prices of products in different markets, but a broader and more complex subject embracing problems of determining characteristics of products to be sold, segmenting markets, choosing sales promotion methods and determining channels of distribution. Increasing competitive pressures and the complexity of the marketing mix lead multi-product companies to develop staff specialists with responsibility for particular products or groups of products with titles such as 'product manager', 'marketing manager' and 'brand manager'. With this form of product management system, the product manager is responsible for developing marketing plans for individual products. He integrates the planning and marketing effort for his product or group of products. He frequently controls sales promotion, advertising, packaging, pricing, product improvements and, consequently, product profit. He seeks guidance and information from various functional specialists in the company when making decisions, or recommendations to senior management, concerning selling prices and changes in the other variables in the marketing mix. Management accountants should provide relevant financial information.

From a financial viewpoint, the management of a multi-consumer-product firm offering products in a number of markets should be concerned with:

1. Managing products or brands over their *life-cycles* in different markets, and, therefore, the sales, total contribution, separable period costs and separable assets employed, and resultant cash flows, associated with the products or brands in different markets.

2. Planning and controlling the manufacture of products to ensure they are produced in their required quantities at a minimum cost for the agreed specification.

3. Planning and controlling the level of *common costs* and *common assets employed* that cannot be associated directly with the manufacture and marketing of products but the level of which tends to increase with growth in product sales in the long term.

Managing Products Over Life-cycles in Different Markets

Many branded products cannot be expected to hold a permanent franchise in the market place. The concept of a product life-cycle has been widely discussed in relation to product classes, product forms and brands during the last decade. It is hypothesized that at the *introduction* stage the product is put on the market; awareness and acceptance is minimal but so may be competition. The product begins to make rapid sales gains at the *growth* stage, because of the cumulative effects of introductory promotion, distribution, and word-of-mouth influence. The competition increases, but by expanding market volume and entering new market segments rather than by fighting for larger shares of the existing market. Eventually the rate of sales growth begins to taper off. There is a diminishing number of potential new customers, some unaware of the product and others not prepared to purchase. This is the *maturity stage* when firms are competing for market shares.

In the *saturation stage*, for some products, consumer resistance to change can be very high. Firm brand loyalties have built up and the last undecided prospects are very difficult to win over. The market becomes flooded with products and crowded by competitors, competition for market shares becomes very tough. For other products, the growth of *private brands* and the successful introduction of new brands suggests lower consumer resistance to change, and indicates brand switching is taking place. *Decline* sets in when sales begin to diminish as the product is gradually edged out by new or better products or substitutes introduced by firms that have left the market. Private brands begin to appear during the growth stage, and their share of the market tends to increase. Rapidly increasing profits as well as booming sales are hypothesized at the growth stage, and that the rate of sales growth increases and reaches its peak in about the middle of the growth stage. Subsequent increases in sales volume are accompanied by a decreasing rate of growth. Usually, it is suggested that profits also will reach their highest level at the middle of the growth stage; a few competitors are operating in a fast-expanding market. Once profits reach a peak they decline more rapidly than sales as a result of both declining prices and rising costs.

The intuitive appeal of the product life-cycle, the existence of a theoretical foundation in the adoption process and the results of empirical tests have led researchers to conclude that the model is valid in many market situations. There is nothing fixed about the length of the cycle, or the length of the various stages of the cycle. These are governed by a number of factors including the rate of market acceptance, the rate of technological change and the ease of competitive entry. Of course, products have been known to begin a new cycle or to revert to some earlier stage as a result of the discovery of new uses, the appearance of new users, the discovery of cheaper sources, or the invention of new features. Television sales have done so on a number of occasions with the introduction over the years of new sizes of screens, commercial television, new channels, colour and teletext systems such as Ceefax. However, while the product life-cycle represents a useful idealization rather than a rigid description of all product life-histories, as noted in Chapter 7, it should lead accountants and product managers to recognize that:

1. Products have a limited market life.
2. Under conditions of competition and accelerating technological change, a new product's life-span is apt to be shorter than those of the past.
3. Product sales and profits tend to follow a predictable course of introduction, growth, maturity, saturation and decline.
4. Products require different marketing programmes at each stage of the cycle.

What are the implications of the product life-cycle for marketing strategy? Different marketing strategies are required for each stage of the product life-cycle, and marketing mixes are the specific combinations of marketing variables which a company uses to implement its strategic decisions. Product managers must be prepared to shift the relative levels and emphasis given to price, advertising, product improvement, product differentiation, etc., during the different stages of the product life-cycle. For example, at the *introductory* stage advertising is instrumental in creating the initial awareness and interest of large audiences. Its main task is to communicate the basic idea of the innovation and to persuade prospective buyers to try it. Product features are usually limited to one or two features at this stage. In contrast, at the *maturity* stage marketing strategy is designed to achieve a competitive advantage by creating customer preference and loyalty. Product features are very important. The competing firms employ all possible means to differentiate their products and segment the market. Product variations are designed to appeal to and fit more closely the needs and desires of specific segments of the market. Advertising is no longer concerned with creating awareness of a new product but with brand appeal and distinguishing the company's product from competitors' products. Product managers require financial information from accountants which they can use when determining the correct combination of marketing variables for each stage of the cycle in different markets, and to help in measuring the effects on product profitability of short-run changes in the marketing mix. They also require segmental reporting on the profitability of products in different markets. Accountants have to recognize that the marketing concept which relates marketing decisions to the customer, requires that data accumulation, budgeting, and performance measurement should focus on market segments.

Long-range Planning and New Product Decisions

How does the concept of a product life-cycle, the management of the variables in the marketing mix over the product's life-cycle in different markets, and the need for segmental reporting, relate to a company's profit planning and control system? In earlier chapters it has been argued that there should be a continuous process of analysing past performance, setting objectives, developing a plan, implementing a plan, and measuring results. The analysis of past performance and the establishment of broad direction, growth and profitability objectives leads in turn to the formulation of a strategy to achieve the objectives. It was recognized that, however astutely management changes its day-to-day operating strategy, there will be an inevitable fall-off in the rate of growth of existing business, with a result that a company must enter new fields if it is to achieve its long-term growth and profitability objectives. In order to achieve the desired rate of growth and fill the gap between the momentum line of its existing business and its long-term objectives, a company must seek, find and reach for growth products and markets. Management must identify potential opportunities, threats and problems in the environment, to see how they can best develop and exploit the company's distinctive competence, create competitive advantage, and achieve its profitability and growth objectives. Product and market share strategies have to be reviewed. It will be recognized that in a product-orientated company one outcome of the planning process is likely to be a new product programme. The new product programme should form part of the company's marketing plan which sets out the company's marketing policy and strategy.

A company's future profit growth, asset growth and cash generation pattern, arising out of the planning process, can be considered in terms of:

1. Sales, direct product profit and separable assets employed, and resultant cash flows, for *existing products* at different stages of their life-cycles in different markets which will decline as these products successively reach maturity and eventually decline.

2. Growth of sales, direct product profit and separable assets employed, and resultant cash flows, arising from the introduction of a flow of *new products* over the planning period.

3. Growth of common period costs and common assets employed, and resultant cash flows, which cannot be directly associated with the introduction of particular new products, but will arise from the expansion of common production and distribution facilities and administrative staff as a result of the planned overall growth of the company. For example, the investment in additional cold storage facilities by a frozen foods producer results from the growth in the firm's total output, and the resulting step in cold storage costs cannot be directly associated with the introduction of a particular new product.

The acceptance of the new product plan by the board of directors, as part of the corporate long-range plan, would not normally imply approval of the individual new product introductions envisaged in the plan. Eventually, each new product proposal will be included in the annual capital expenditure budget, probably in a modified form to the original proposal in the long-range plan. At this stage the proposal can be submitted for detailed approval by the board of directors, and the merits of the new proposal can be appraised in the light of the current situation. The management is concerned with deciding whether the cash investment to be made in Periods 2–6 of Figure 11.1 will produce a satisfactory return as compared with the company's cost of capital and the return on alternative investments.

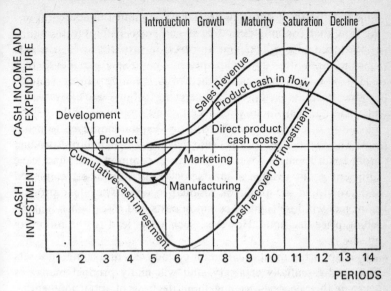

Figure 11.1. *Investment life-cycle of hypothetical new product*

There is considerable uncertainty surrounding the introduction of new products. The cost of launching is large and the likelihood of market acceptance uncertain. Some form of risk or sensitivity analysis is essential. However, many companies that have systematized the new product planning function continue to introduce new products that fail despite considerable market research and careful introduction to the market place. There is in the evaluation of many new product proposals a point beyond which financial calculations cannot go, and managerial judgement must take over.

Short-term Marketing Mix Decisions

Once the new product introduction is approved and the investment made, the company moves to Period 5 in Figure 11.1, product management is concerned with managing the variables in the marketing mix in different markets over a series of short runs which frequently correspond with budget periods. In addition, the growth of common period costs and common assets employed must be controlled through effective capital budgeting procedures and budgetary planning and control systems. Industrial accountants frequently express the view that common period costs and assets employed should be apportioned to products and absorbed in product costs to ensure that they are reflected in selling prices. They also argue that there is a lack of information as to whether in the long run in a multi-product business each product is carrying its fair share of overheads and making a satisfactory return on assets employed, if there is no allocation of common period costs and capital employed to products. They are concerned to ensure that the growth in direct product profit is sufficient to cover the growth in common costs, and leave sufficient profit to give a satisfactory return on assets employed and growth in net profit or residual income. They fear product managers will lose sight of common costs and assets when making selling price decisions. However, such views lead to the following questions:

1. Is apportionment of common period costs and common assets employed essentially arbitrary, and will many product managers dissipate their energies arguing about the basis of apportionment?

2. Are apportioned costs and capital outside the manager's control?

3. Will the inclusion of apportioned sunk costs lead to incorrect decisions when evaluating changes to non-price variables in the marketing mix?

4. Is the long run frequently irrelevant when managing the variables in the marketing mix over a product's life-cycle?

5. Should top management plan the growth of common facilities, which give rise to the common period costs and assets employed, as part of the long-range planning process, and control the level of these costs through an effective system of capital budgeting for additional investments, and budgetary planning and control for current costs?

As explained and illustrated in Chapter 4, in providing information to product managers and marketing managers for decision-making, the accountant should recognize that the relevant concepts to employ are future incremental costs and revenues and opportunity cost, not full costs which include past or sunk costs. These concepts will be employed when the evaluation of export opportunities is considered later in this chapter, and when selling price decisions are examined in Chapter 12.

Segmental Reporting

The marketing concept requires data accumulation, budgeting and performance measurement to be focused on market segments. In a multi-product, multi-market company the accountant should establish a system of periodic reporting of segment profitability which recognizes that profit contribution is the relevant measure of a segment's performance. An N.A.A. Research Team reported in 1971 that:

Marketing management's number 1 priority information need is the identification by segment of incremental profit (plus or minus) which might result from changes in volume and/or marketing effort. Most marketing managers are not receiving this information now, either regularly or in answer to special requests. Often accounting will provide analyses based on averages of product manufacturing costs, delivery costs, and selling costs, but since these are not broken down by specific segments of the business, marketing management is unable to relate them to the profit impact of a particular area of marketing effort.[2]

Marketing managers require financial information on the implications of the shifting patterns of consumer demand on product and market profitability in both home and export markets. When a company is faced with deciding relevant marketing strategies and marketing mix decisions for individual product-market segments in rapidly changing market conditions, segmental reporting becomes even more relevant. However, there is evidence that such information is not available in many British companies. For example, in their comparative study of Japanese and British companies' marketing strategies in the U.K. market, Wong, Saunders and Doyle[3] found that:

Few of the British companies had budgeting or information systems showing performance at the market or product line level. Rather, these were designed to show factory or production profitability. So, market or product performance were often obscured and with them the individual commitment and responsibility for overall results. By contrast, organization, re-

2 National Association of Accountants, *Information for Marketing Management*, New York, 1971, p. 14.
3 V. Wong, J. A. Saunders and P. Doyle, 'A Comparative Study of Japanese Marketing Strategies in the U.K.', Department of Management Studies, Loughborough University of Technology, Working Paper No. 153, July 1987.

Table 11.1

UNDERWEAR AND LEISUREWEAR DEPARTMENT

Sales Analysis: Period 6, 1971

	Month of June 1971		Cumulative to June 1971		% Standard Contribution	Contribution per £mu lab.[b]	% Increase/ Decrease in Sales since last year
	% of Total	£	% of Total	£			
By Product							
Leisurewear	55	37,968	42	159,049	23	2.2	—
Children's Knickers	7	4,605	8	30,293	17	1.7	+ 19
Athletic	12	8,409	9	33,359	23	2.2	+ 12
Heavy	—	170	—	993	—	—	−158
Women's	26	18,121	41	156,057	29	3.8	+ 6
	100	£69,273	100	£379,751	25	2.9	+ 4
By Outlet							
Manufacturers	—	—	—	813	8	0.8	− 51
Mail Order	24	16,372[a]	20	75,695	24	2.7	− 12
Wholesale	18	12,611	19	73,847	27	3.2	+ 31
Multiples	48	33,085	50	187,562	24	2.6	− 7
Export	10	7,205	11	41,834	28	4.0	+ 41
	100	£69,273	100	£379,751	25	2.9	+ 4

[a] See Table 11.2

[b] £mu lab. = £ of making-up labour.

sponsibilities and systems in the Japanese subsidiaries generally centred around the product or market. The usual explanation was that 'the parent company in Japan is set up this way – every division is a profit centre'.

In the past, accounting and data-processing systems in many companies were not capable of producing the segmental analysis required. With today's information technology it is no longer a problem, provided the marketing managers and accountants recognize and act upon the information needs. In Chapter 9, the segmental reports produced by the management accountant of a medium-sized knitwear company were cited as examples of 'attention-directing' reports, backed up by an 'on request' reporting facility allowed by the computer's ability to store data to which rapid access

Table 11.2

UNDERWEAR AND LEISUREWEAR DEPARTMENT

Outlet 2

Sales and Contribution Analysis: Period 6, 1971

Size	Quantity (dozens)	Sales	Production Cost	Distribution Cost	Selling Cost	Contribution	% Contribution	Contribution per £mu lab.	% Sales
Product Group 1*	4,228.3	10,077.10	7,077.95	177.588	604.39	2,217.18	22	1.90	14
Product Group 2	391.0	1,806.87	1,296.37	39.100	108.39	363.01	29	1.38	3
Product Group 5	386.6	4,488.30	2,664.54	38.560	269.32	1,515.88	33	4.19	6
Outlet Total	5,005.9	16,372.27	11,038.86	255.248	982.10	4,096.07	—	2.29	—

* See Table 11.3.

Table 11.3

UNDERWEAR AND LEISUREWEAR DEPARTMENT
Outlet 2 Product Group 1
Sales and Contribution: Period 6, 1971

Style no.	Size (in.)	Quantity (dozens)	Sales	Production Cost (standard)	Distribution Cost (standard)	Selling Cost (standard)	Contribution	% Contribution	Contribution per £mu lab.	% Sales
e.g. 5,003	36	63.0	118.20	85.05	2.646	7.09	23.42	20	2.17	
Each style has a number		No. of dozens sold	Actual value of sale	This is standard and comes from the file i.e. labour cost + material + make-up material + folding material	Carriage + packing (standard). Again this is on file	This is a proportion of the standard cost and is a recovery. This is on file also	Sales – (production + distribution, + selling)	Contribution as a % of sales	Contribution as a multiple of make-up labour in garments	This column refers to group totals only. Group totals' sales as a % of total sales
		4,228.3	10,077.10	7,077.95	177.588	604.39	2,217.18	Weighted average 22 for group	Weighted average 1.90	14

— Totals for group —

Table 11.4

INDUSTRIAL CHEMICALS COMPANY

Contribution Analysis

PRODUCT/MARKET ....

Product/Market	PERIOD				YEAR TO DATE			
	Tonnes	Contribution		% of Sales Value	Tonnes	Contribution		% of Sales Value
		Per unit	Total			Per unit	Total	
		£	£			£	£	

Prepared by ....

Date ....

COMMENT:

Table 11.5

B.T.R. plc

Sales and Profits by Market Sector and Geography   Schedule 1B
weeks ended   £ mn.

	Plan			*Actual*		
	Sales £	*Pbit* £	*Ros* %	*Sales* £	*Pbit* £	*Ros* %
Construction						
U.K., Europe, Middle East						
North and South America						
S. Africa, Australasia, Far East						
Energy and Electrical						
U.K., Europe, Middle East						
North and South America						
S. Africa, Australasia, Far East						
Industrial						
U.K., Europe, Middle East						
North and South America						
S. Africa, Australasia, Far East						
Consumer-related						
U.K., Europe, Middle East						
North and South America						
S. Africa, Australasia, Far East						
Financial Services						
U.K., Europe, Middle East						
North and South America						
S. Africa, Australasia, Far East						
Total						
U.K., Europe, Middle East						
North and South America						
S. Africa, Australasia, Far East						
Investment Income						

can be obtained. Table 11.1 shows an analysis of the underwear and leisurewear department sales by product and by outlet. An example taken from the segmental reports prepared for departmental directors is shown in Table 11.2. It will be noted that total sales in Period 6 to mail order companies in Table 11.1 of £16,372 is analysed by product groups, as well as the contribution of each product group. The factor that frequently limited Wilson's capacity to manufacture additional garments was making-up labour. For this reason, Wilson's segmental reports show contribution per £ of making-up labour. The product group totals by outlet were further analysed by garment, and the garment totals by size of garment. Thus, for each size of garment, the computer printed out the information in Table 11.3.

Incoming orders can be analysed to obtain a sales mix and contribution analysis for future sales, sales and contribution budgets prepared on a segmental basis, and sales and contribution variances reported by segments. Thus the Industrial Chemicals Co., whose budgetary planning and control system was described in Chapter 9, analyses profit contribution by product and market, which indicate in summary for the managing director, and in more detail for the marketing director, sales manager and market research manager, which products and markets are most profitable. The form of presentation used by the company is illustrated in Table 11.4. An example of a holding company board-level report of sales and profits by product-market segments taken from the B.T.R. case study (*A Casebook of British Management Accounting*, Volume 2) is shown in Table 11.5. This report is built up from detailed product-market segment analyses at the operating company level.

An interesting and useful approach to examining profitability of products and markets, of products within a market, and customers within markets, which can also prove effective in communications with marketing managers, is the use of contribution graphs or pictures as illustrated in Figure 11.2. By assuming constant marginal cost over the relevant output range, equi-contribution curves are derived by multiplying unit contribution on the vertical axis and units. For example, in Figure 11.2, a total contribution of £1,200 can be generated by any of the following combinations: 1,200 units at £1.00 per unit; 2,000 units at £0.60 per unit; 2,400 units at £0.50 per unit; 4,000 units at £0.30 per unit; etc. The graphs can be segmented to show high and low unit and total contribution areas, and high and low volume areas. Products shown in the bottom left-hand corner, i.e. numbers 1, 6 and 10, are candidates for withdrawal from the market. The most profitable products are shown in the top right-hand segment, i.e. products 11, 2 and 8. They have high unit contributions and high volume, and, therefore, generate a high total contribution. As will be illustrated in Chapter 12, contribution graphs or pictures can be used not only to contrast the relative profitability of products and markets, but also when examining the trends in product and market profitability, alternative marketing strategies, and changes in price and non-price variables in the marketing mix.

Detailed descriptions of management accounting systems which generate segmental information for marketing managers and senior management in a large magazine-publishing company (I.P.C. Women's Magazines Group) and a large milk-processing and distribution business (Northern Dairies Ltd) are contained in Volume 1, and in a retail furnishing company (Debenhams Furnishings Ltd) and a newspaper printing and publishing company (Thames Valley Newspapers Ltd) in Volume 2 of *A Casebook of British Management Accounting*.

Financial Evaluation of Exporting Opportunities

Companies contemplating entering export markets for the first time, and those successfully competing in export markets, require a framework for decision-making which can be used to evaluate exporting opportunities in terms of their impact on profitability. A framework for decision-making has been developed by the author jointly with W. A. Atkins & Partners Ltd and H. R. Windle (see Selected Reading 2).

It is possible to identify three different positions or 'postures' from which a company may export. They represent three different levels of commitment and phases through which a company will normally proceed on the way to developing a large-scale international marketing activity. They also involve increasing levels of risk. The three phases are:

Phase One: The 'no change' posture. In this posture exporting is regarded as a secondary or marginal activity in which the company

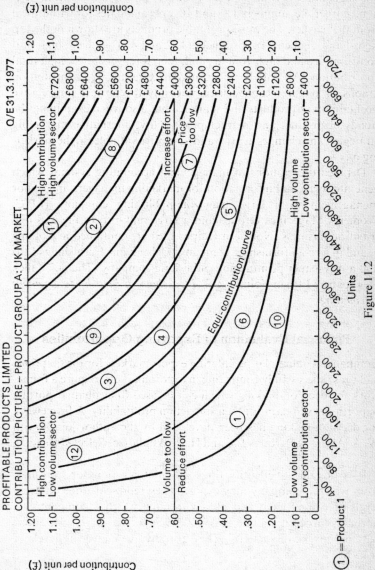

PROFITABLE PRODUCTS LIMITED
CONTRIBUTION PICTURE – PRODUCT GROUP A: UK MARKET

Q/E 31.3.1977

Contribution per unit (£)

Units

Figure 11.2

① = Product 1

engages when it has limited surplus capacity it wishes to utilize. The company is accepting one-off orders which it fulfils by using temporary surplus capacity or by temporary overtime working. This type of exporting activity requires no additional production facilities or major change in method of operation, no increase in marketing staff, and limited additional working capital, so only limited risk is involved. The company is a 'price-taker' rather than a 'price-maker' and therefore pricing strategy and pricing decisions are not important.

Phase Two: The 'production change' posture. As a result of its marginal exporting activities a company may identify continuing export opportunities and decide to export on a regular basis. It moves into the second stage of exporting, regards it as a regular activity, and makes deliberate changes to its production methods to increase its capacity. It undertakes such changes as extra shift-working, changes in plant layout, employee training to improve productivity, and recruitment of additional design staff. The company is increasing its productive capacity without any major investment in fixed assets, but will require additional working capital. Unlike marginal exporting postures, changes of this type cannot be implemented overnight, and the company will require continuing export opportunities before it implements such changes. In order to identify the export opportunities and translate them into firm orders the company will probably have to employ additional marketing staff. It will move from being a 'price-taker' towards being a 'price-maker' in export markets. While pricing decisions will become more important, the scale of activity may not require the company to develop market share and price strategies for export markets. There is a greater degree of risk involved in this type of exporting activity because it results in a higher level of fixed costs. It might be some time before the volume of export orders is sufficient to compensate for the higher level of fixed costs and provide a satisfactory profit.

Phase Three: The 'production and capital change' posture. In the third stage of exporting the company has become well established in export markets and is receiving large volume orders from overseas buyers on a continuous basis. It decides to invest substantial amounts of capital in plant replacement and modernization, or in expanding its range of machinery and production capacity, and in additional working capital, to supply its customers at home and abroad more effectively. It is undertaking a major investment decision with long-term consequences. This is clearly a decision involving a significantly higher level of risk and uncertainty as compared with the first two postures. It requires a careful assessment of the company's long-term marketing prospects at home and overseas. Before embarking upon a major development of this type a company must have acquired considerable experience in exporting. It must have marketing resources to create and maintain a high level of export business at satisfactory prices. Not only will the company be a 'price-maker', it will have to develop market share and pricing strategies either for different export markets or global strategies, and study its international competitors' strategies and price structures. As explained in Chapter 7, in the third phase the concepts of critical mass, competitive advantage and selectivity become central to export market strategy formulation.

While the three postures can be different stages in the growth of a company's exporting activities, it will be recognized that a company may decide to restrict the scale of its exporting activities by adopting a 'no change' or 'production change' posture, and that different companies faced with the same export opportunities may adopt different postures. For example, a large firm might handle an order in the 'no change' posture, while a much smaller firm would need to adopt a 'production capital change' posture to enter the same market.

The financial evaluation of export opportunities under the three postures is now considered.

1. *Financial evaluation of 'no change' posture opportunities*. When a company has decided a price to quote to secure an export order, or receives an export inquiry to supply products at a stated price, it is faced with two questions:

How much will it cost to produce and deliver the order?

Is the margin between the additional cost to the company and the income that will be received sufficient to justify quoting for or accepting this order?

It must consider whether the export order offers an adequate additional profit. Consider the following example.

A high-quality outerwear manufacturer, Knitted Garments Ltd, is currently selling in the home market 25,000 dozen knitted garments per annum at an average selling price of £36 per dozen

Table 11.6

KNITTED GARMENTS LTD
Budgeted Profit-and-loss account

	£	£
Gross Sales		
25,000 dozen Garments at £36 per dozen, ex-works		900,000
Carriage		13,500
		913,500
Less Discounts		22,500
Net Sales		£891,000
Direct Production Costs		
Materials		360,000
Labour		207,000
Consumables		45,000
		612,000
Indirect Production Costs		
Staff and Indirect Labour	66,000	
Indirect Expenses	40,000	106,000
Selling and Distribution Costs		
Salesmen's Remuneration	45,000	
Selling Expenses	18,000	
Distribution Costs	13,500	76,500
Administration Costs		
Staff Salaries	15,000	
Office and Administration Expenses	5,000	20,000
Total Costs		£814,500
Profit before Taxation		£76,500

ex-works, which results in an annual turnover of £900,000 and a budgeted profit of £76,500. Knitted Garments Ltd's budgeted profit-and-loss account is shown in Table 11.6. Knitting production, while quite flexible, is normally on a two shifts per day basis. The ancillary making-up functions are carried out largely by female labour operating on piece work rates during the day. Making-up and finishing capacity could be expanded by overtime working, sub-contracting, or by a temporary increase in staff.

The company has received an inquiry from Scandinavia for some 2,000 dozen garments. The retail selling price of the garments in Scandinavia is some 50 per cent higher than the corresponding U.K. price, but higher retail mark-ups mean that a selling price ex-works of £37 per dozen garments must be quoted, which is only a little higher than the price in the U.K. Should the company pursue the order? The additional costs which will be incurred if the order is accepted need to be calculated and deducted from the additional sales income to determine the additional profit. The management needs then to decide whether the additional profit is satisfactory. The calculation of the additional profit is shown in Table 11.7. The net sales income has been determined by adding carriage and deducting discounts and agents' commission from the ex-works sales. The variable production costs are calculated in a similar manner to those in Table 11.6. The additional selling, distribution and administration expenses that would result from the export order are added to the variable production costs. These headings include the costs involved in securing the order and arranging delivery in Scandinavia; the transport, freight and insurance costs recoverable from the customer; additional office salaries, transla-tion expenses, etc; and the E.C.G.D. charge. It will be noted that there will be no increase in the company's indirect production costs and home selling costs, and only a small increase in administration costs, because these are primarily fixed costs which will not be affected by the acceptance of this export business. The export opportunity offers a profit of £11,250, and if the order is obtained, the company's budgeted profit-and-loss account will show a total profit of £87,750.

The steps involved in evaluating an export opportunity with a 'no change' posture are summarized in Figure 11.3. This is a logic dia-gram in which oblongs represent events, or calculations to be made, and diamonds represent questions to be answered. Figure 11.3 is a marginal costing approach to evaluating exporting opportunities. With this approach the encouragement to take on export orders which make only a small contribution towards fixed costs and profit may be so strong that when an opportunity for more profitable export business arises, such business may have to be forgone because of inadequate free capacity, unless there is an expansion in capacity with an attendant increase in fixed costs. In choosing between export

Table 11.7

KNITTED GARMENTS LTD
Evaluation of Export Opportunity

	£	£
Sales Income		
2,000 dozen Garments at £37 per dozen, ex-works		74,000
Carriage		4,000
		78,000
Less Discounts	1,850	
Agents' Commission	7,400	9,250
Net Sales Income		£68,750

	Variable Cost per unit £	
Additional Costs		
Valuable Production Costs		
Materials: yarn and dyestuffs	14.40	28,800
Labour: additional knitting, making up and finishing, wages and related social security contributions	8.30	16,600
Consumables: additional packing materials, needles, etc.	1.80	3,600
Marginal Cost of Production	£24.50	£49,000
Additional Selling, Distribution, and Administration Overheads		
Overseas Selling Expenses		1,500
Carriage		4,000
Administration Salaries		2,000
Administration Expenses		1,000
Total Additional Costs		£57,500
Additional Profit before Taxation		£11,250

orders in a limited capacity situation the management must know its markets and customers, and be able to forecast future demands on production capacity.

2. *Financial evaluation of 'production change' posture opportunities.* If a company's export opportunities are in excess of its present production capacity it may adopt a 'production change' posture, and introduce extra shift-working, changes in plant layout, employee training to increase productivity, and/or recruitment of extra design staff. If

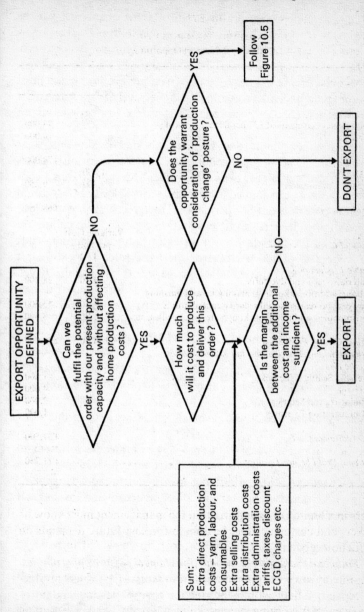

Figure 11.3. *Logic diagram for 'no change' posture*

a company undertakes one or more of these changes it will be redeploying its productive resources and committing itself to a new strategy and cost structure. Changes of this type are likely to give rise to additional fixed costs. The company will have to achieve a permanent increase in sales to maintain its present profit, and must therefore be confident of a continuing higher level of export business. A 'production change' posture is a higher risk strategy than a 'no change' posture.

Let us now consider further the case of the high-quality outerwear manufacturer exporting to Scandinavia. Knitted Garments Ltd has the opportunity of higher export business to Scandinavia on a continuing basis. It can immediately increase its sales to 4,000 dozen garments per annum at £37 per dozen. However, it cannot meet this business unless it increases its production capacity. The unions are agreeable to the introduction of an extra Saturday morning shift at a wage rate of 150 per cent of the basic rate. The extra shift could produce an extra 2,500 dozen garments per annum, which would enable the company to export 4,500 dozen garments per annum. To maintain a higher rate of export orders from Scandinavia, additional design and sales staff would have to be recruited, and permanent links established with agents in Scandinavian markets.

In deciding whether to introduce the extra shift and increase its export sales to 4,000 dozen garments per annum, the company is faced with two questions:

What additional costs and revenues would result from this strategy?

Is the margin between additional cost and income sufficient to justify the change in production methods, and the resulting higher level of fixed costs and additional investment in working capital? Table 11.8 is a calculation of the additional costs and revenues. It will be noted:

(a) The marginal production cost per dozen would increase to £26.70 with the introduction of the Saturday morning shift.
(b) There would be an increase in the company's fixed production costs of £1,500 with the introduction of the extra shift.
(c) There would be an increase in the company's fixed selling costs resulting from the recruiting of additional sales staff.

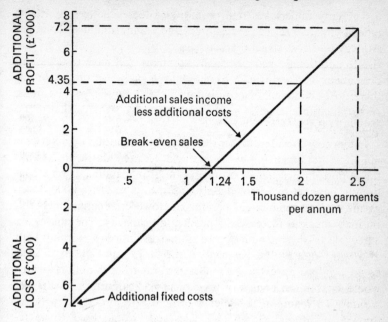

Figure 11.4. *Knitted Garments Ltd. Profit-volume chart for extra shift*

(d) There would be an increase in the fixed administration costs with the introduction of additional design staff.

(e) Additional working capital is estimated to be equivalent to one month's sales for debtors and six weeks' sales for stocks to give an additional investment of £15,000 for 2,000 dozen and £18,750 for 2,500 dozen additional garments, which would be financed in the first instance by a bank overdraft at 15 per cent per annum.

If the company increased export sales to 4,000 dozen garments per annum, the additional 2,000 dozen garments would generate an additional profit before bank interest of £4,350, compared with a profit of £11,250 on its present export sales of 2,000 dozen garments. The additional export sales are not so profitable because of the increase in fixed costs. If the additional sales staff could increase total export sales in Scandinavia to 4,500 dozen garments per annum at the same selling price per dozen, the additional 2,500 dozen garments produced by the extra shift would generate an additional

Table 11.8

KNITTED GARMENTS LTD
Profitability of Extra Shift

	2,000		2,500	
	£	£	£	£
Sales Incomes at £37 per dozen, ex-works		74,000		92,500
Carriage		4,000		5,000
		78,000		97,500
Less Discounts	1,850		2,300	
Agents' Commission	7,400	9,250	9,250	11,550
Net Sales Income		£68,750		£85,950

	Marginal Cost per unit £		
Additional Variable Costs			
Variable Production Costs			
Materials: yarn and dyestuffs	14.40	28,800	36,000
Labour: additional knitting, making up and finishing, wages and related social benefits	10.50	21,000	26,250
Consumables: additional packing materials, needles, etc.	1.80	3,600	4,500
	£26.70	£53,400	£66,750

Additional Fixed Costs		
Fixed Selling, Distribution, and Administration Overheads		
Overseas Sales Staff	2,500	2,500
Overseas Selling Expenses	500	500
Design Staff	2,000	2,000
Administration Expenses	500	500
Indirect Production Costs		
Staff and Indirect Labour	1,000	1,000
Indirect Expenses	500	500
	£7,000	£7,000
Carriage (recoverable from customer)	4,000	5,000
Total Additional Costs	£64,400	£78,750
Additional Profit before Interest and Taxation	£4,350	£7,200
Interest on Bank Overdraft	£2,250	£2,800

profit of £7,200 before bank interest and tax. On the other hand, the company must sell an extra 1,240 dozen garments to break even on the extra shift before bank interest (see Figure 11.4). At this point management judgement must take over.

To summarize, the adoption of a 'production change' posture gives rise to a higher level of fixed costs, and is therefore a higher risk strategy than a 'no change' posture. A company must therefore identify continuing export opportunities before it adopts such a strategy. The steps in evaluating a 'production change' posture are illustrated in the form of a logic diagram in Figure 11.5.

3. *Financial evaluation of 'production and capital change' posture.* The demand for a company's products in export markets may expand to the point where it cannot satisfy this demand by making changes in production methods, but must contemplate the investment of additional fixed and working capital to increase its production capacity. An evaluation of alternative additional investments must be undertaken on the basis described in Chapter 8. Figure 11.6 is a logic diagram for the evaluation of a production and capital change. The adoption of a 'production and capital change' posture is a significantly higher risk strategy requiring a major commitment of company resources. Before embarking upon a major development of this type a company should have acquired considerable expertise in exporting, and in the assessment and exploitation of marketing opportunities.

It is vital to know whether in the long term it can expect to compete on a profitable basis with manufacturers abroad. Initial guidance can be derived from the prices being obtained in prospective export markets by local manufacturers and by existing exporters to the country. It may be difficult to find comparable goods. Differing price levels may be due to varying material content, different methods of manufacture, or products may be designed for different segments of the market. However, without a knowledge of competing manufacturer's costs, current price levels do not indicate current profit margins earned by each producer, and it is not possible to make any assessment of whether they will reduce prices if faced with increasing competition. Not only is one concerned with competitors' short-term reactions to increased competition, but also with an assessment of the long-term trends of prices and profit margins in the various export markets. For long-term decision-

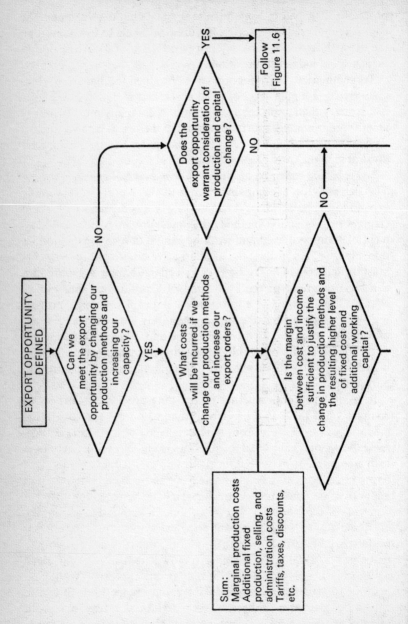

EXPORT OPPORTUNITY DEFINED

Can we meet the export opportunity by changing our production methods and increasing our capacity?

NO

What costs will be incurred if we change our production methods and increase our export orders?

YES

Is the margin between cost and income sufficient to justify the change in production methods and the resulting higher level of fixed cost and additional working capital?

NO

Does the export opportunity warrant consideration of production and capital change?

YES → Follow Figure 11.6

NO

Sum:
Marginal production costs
Additional fixed production, selling, and administration costs
Tariffs, taxes, discounts, etc.

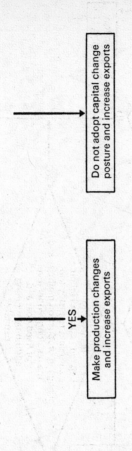

Figure 11.5. *Logic diagram for 'production change' posture*

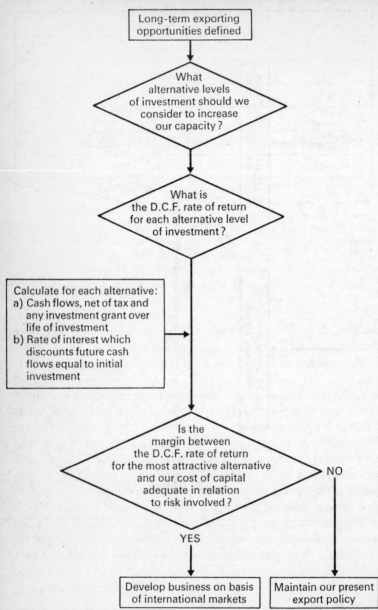

Figure 11.6. *Logic diagram for 'production and capital change' posture*

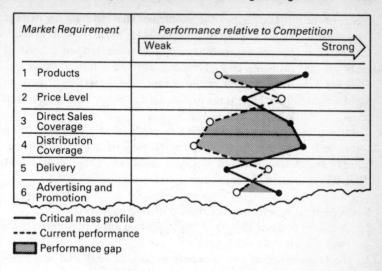

Figure 11.7. *A critical mass profile*
Source: Attiyeh and Wenner, op. cit.

making, an evaluation of the basic cost competitiveness of foreign firms is desirable.

The concepts of *critical mass*, *competitive advantage*, *market segmentation* and *selectivity* are central to the evaluation of long-term export opportunities, and to the successful development and implementation of export market strategies. It has been explained in Chapter 7 that if a company is to maintain a profitable position in most markets, it must achieve a minimum level of size and effectiveness. Attiyeh and Wenner[4] have argued that to achieve this minimum level involves meeting a number of individual requirements of the market place, what they call achieving *critical mass*. As illustrated conceptually in Figure 11.7 the required capability levels in these various areas, based on performance standards set by the leading established competitors, constitute a critical mass profile for the market, as represented by the solid line. They suggest that once the critical mass is reached, profitability takes a marked upturn as the exporter starts to benefit from meeting the competitive require-

4 Robert J. Attiyeh and David L. Wenner, 'Critical Mass: Key to Export Profits', *McKinsey Quarterly*, Winter 1981.

ments of the market. Part of the problem is that defining the market requirements for achieving critical mass is far more difficult in overseas markets. It does necessitate extensive researching of individual markets, and investing enough resources to be a leader; hence the need for *selectivity*. It is a resource-intensive, longer-term task to build a competitive advantage and sustain a competitive position in an export market.

Attiyeh and Wenner argue that *selectivity* must be the governing principle for any effective export marketing strategy, and this requires careful research and vigorous analysis. They suggest that three things are usually needed:

1. A method of selecting the right portfolio of markets.
2. A means of developing and implementing appropriate strategies within each individual market.
3. Techniques for helping the company decide when and how business opportunities should be pursued.

They adapt directional policy matrices (described in Chapter 7) for selecting the portfolio of markets as illustrated in Figure 11.8, and discuss how to assess a company's position relative to critical mass and market attractiveness. They emphasize, as with other applications of directional policy matrices, that in estimating where the critical mass threshold lies in a particular market involves a 'heavy dose of old-fashioned business judgement'. However, the matrix forces the exporter to undertake a careful and rigorous analysis, and provides a starting-point from which to judge how best to focus market development resources and in which markets detailed business plans are warranted.

Once priorities have been established, it is important that a development plan is prepared based on a sound analysis of *market segmentation*. The preparation of such a plan should ensure that adequate thought and analysis underlies the export development programme, and minimizes the risk that the programme will be subverted by short-term pressures. It should contain clear financial and non-financial objectives, and subsequent financial reports should measure progress against these objectives. Not only should investment decisions be evaluated in the context of this development plan, but price strategies and individual pricing decisions should

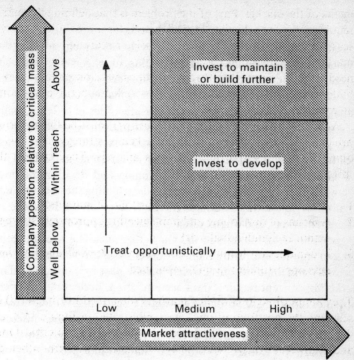

Figure 11.8. *Setting development priorities*

Source: Attiyeh and Wenner, op. cit.

flow from market share strategies for each market segment contained in the plan.

Having developed clearly defined long-term objectives and strategies for individual export markets based on the concepts of critical mass, market segmentation and selectivity, and evaluated and undertaken investment decisions in the context of these plans, it is important that the preparation of annual budgets and periodic performance reports, as well as short-term pricing and other decisions, is related to the same concepts, i.e. a system of budgeting, periodic segmental reporting and short-term decision analysis which recognizes profit contribution as the relevant measure of a segment's performance. In key export markets, it may be wise to prepare such reports in both £ sterling and in local currency.

Summary

A system of accounting should be developed which satisfies the financial information needs of marketing management, and recognizes that the marketing concept focuses decision-making on the consumer. Multi-product, multi-market firms are concerned with managing products or brands over their life-cycles in different markets, and, therefore, the sales, total contribution, separable period costs and separable assets employed, and resultant cash flows, associated with the products or brands in different markets. This should be recognized in long-term planning and decision-making. Financial information is required when determining the correct combination of marketing variables for each stage of the life-cycle in different markets, and when evaluating the effects on product profitability of short-run changes in the marketing mix. The relevant concepts to employ are future incremental costs and revenues and opportunity cost, not full costs which include past or sunk costs. The marketing concept requires data accumulation, budgeting, and performance reporting to be focused on market segments. When evaluating exporting opportunities it is useful to recognize three different postures involving increasing levels of risk from which a company may export: 'no change', 'production change' and 'production and capital change'. The concepts of critical mass, competitive advantage, market segmentation and selectivity are central to the third posture.

Selected Readings

1. American Accounting Association, 'Report of the Committee on Cost and Profitability Analysis for Marketing', *Accounting Review*, Supplement to Vol. XLVII, 1972.
2. Hosiery and Knitwear Economic Development Committee, *Exporting is for Profit*, National Economic Development Office, 1970.
3. Philip Kotler, *Marketing Management*, Prentice-Hall, Englewood Cliffs, N.J., 1980; or *Principles of Marketing*, Prentice-Hall, Englewood Cliffs, N.J., 1983.
4. National Association of Accountants, *Information for Marketing Management*, New York, 1971.
5. Charles H. Sevin, *Marketing Productivity Analysis*, McGraw-Hill, New York, 1965.
6. Benson P. Shapiro, V. Kasturi Rangan, Rowland T. Moriarty and Elliot

B. Ross, 'Manage Customers for Profits (not just sales)', *Harvard Business Review*, September–October 1987.

7. R. M. S. Wilson (ed.), *Financial Dimensions of Marketing: A Source Book*, Macmillan/Chartered Institute of Management Accountants, London, 1981.

8. R. M. S. Wilson and A. L. Bancroft, *The Application of Management Accounting Techniques to the Planning and Control of Marketing*, Chartered Institute of Management Accountants, London, 1983.

CASE STUDIES

In John Sizer and Nigel Coulthurst, *A Casebook of British Management Accounting*, I.C.A.E.W., 1984, 1985.

I.P.C. Women's Magazines Group (Volume 1) – the management accounting system employed to assist the management of the magazine group to prepare a business plan, and to control performance.

Northern Dairies Ltd (Volume 1) – the development and use of weekly profit estimates as one of the basic elements in planning, budgetary and financial control systems in a milk-processing and distribution business, including segmental information for marketing management.

Debenhams Furnishings Ltd (Volume 2) – a description of the mainframe and mini-computer-based accounting systems employed by a retail furnishing company.

Thames Valley Newspapers Ltd (Volume 2) – a computerized system for the accurate and timely provision of relevant monthly management accounting information, including newspaper profitability information for marketing management.

12

Accounting Information for Selling Price Decisions

The determination of selling prices for sales to third parties are important decisions in most companies. The accountant should make a major contribution to the decision-making process by providing management with cost and revenue information relevant to the pricing decision at hand.

It was recognized in Chapter 11 that in many multi-product, multi-market companies pricing is not simply a process of setting figures at which the company's products are to be offered to customers, but rather it is part of a broad and complex field also embracing problems of determining characteristics of products to be sold, segmenting markets, choosing sales promotion methods, determining channels of distribution and obtaining a satisfactory volume of business. While selling price is an important variable in the mix, there was until relatively recently a general reluctance to review selling prices more than once or possibly twice a year. Altering prices can be a very expensive and complicated business. Silberston [1] concludes that 'nearly all the evidence supports the view that the home market price of manufactured products tends to be stable for months or even years at a time'. Reviewing selling prices frequently tended to form part of the annual preparation of the budget. Between price reviews product managers manipulated the non-price variables in the marketing mix. The high rate of inflation in the 1970s increased the importance of pricing decisions. The continuous pressure on profit margins forced companies to review prices more frequently and systematically in the context of a company's pricing and marketing policy, and in many cases continuously.

An essential first stage in the pricing decision is a comprehensive

1 Aubrey Silberston, 'Surveys of Applied Economics: Price Behaviour of Firms', *Economic Journal*, September 1970, pp. 511–76.

Table 12.1
Price Monitoring System

---

1. Sales, in units and value:
   (a) previous year comparisons
   (b) different markets/channels comparisons
   (c) budget *v.* actual comparisons
   (d) forecast *v.* budget comparisons
   (e) forecast *v.* actual comparisons
   (f) latest forecast *v.* previous forecast comparisons
2. Competitors' prices and conditions of sale
3. Inquiries from potential customers about a product
4. Sales at 'below list' prices:
   (a) measured as a percentage of total sales
   (b) revenue as a percentage of sales at full list price
5. Types of customers getting the most and largest price reductions
6. Market shares in individual markets
7. Present and forecast product costs:
   (a) production, marketing, etc.
   (b) fixed, variable
8. Product unit and total contributions in different markets
9. Price complaints:
   (a) from customers
   (b) from salesmen
10. Stocks of finished goods at different points in distribution chain
11. Customers' attitudes to company's prices, packaging, etc.
12. Number of lost customers (brand switching)
13. Inquiries and subsequent purchases

---

monitoring system that signals the need for a price review. Such a system might collect some or all of the information contained in Table 12.1.[2] This type of monitoring system is forward-looking and is likely to identify some of the shifts in demand that are occurring in the market place and future trends in costs and product profitability. In this respect it is important that the management accountant recognizes that the marketing manager requires a system of periodic reporting of current and forecast segment profitability, i.e. the profitability of different products in different markets, as described in Chapter 11. When making price and other marketing mix decisions, marketing managers require financial information on the implications of these shifting patterns of consumer demand on product and market profitability, which implies *segmental reporting*.

2 Adapted from Alfred R. Oxenfeldt, 'A Decision-Making Structure for Price Decisions', *Journal of Marketing*, Vol. 37, No. 1, January 1973, pp. 48–53.

The product cost changes since the last price review and product cost forecasts are an important part of a systematic price monitoring system. Marketing management at Shapland and Petter Ltd (*A Casebook of British Management Accounting*, Volume 1), manufacturers of high-quality wooden doors to customers' specifications, are provided with information on the costs of approximately forty products which are thought to be representative of the output of the company. The quarterly review draws upon cost information and cost forecasts available from within the company, and this information itself is monitored on a regular basis. An example of the layout of the cost review for one product is shown in Table 12.2. A detailed description of the sources of the information and its uses in reviews of selling price lists and for specific pricing decisions and new product decisions is contained in the case study, and is referred to elsewhere in this chapter.

The monitoring system advocated, including product cost reviews, segmental reports and contribution pictures, should signal the need for price reviews as well as providing vital information. It is important to keep in mind that estimated costs should be used only as a reference point in determining selling prices. Failure to recognize the complex nature of pricing decisions, and the role of costs in such decisions, is often reflected in claims by marketing executives that accountants do not fully understand the importance of competitive pricing; while accountants frequently contend that marketing executives disregard costs in setting selling prices.

At the root of this conflict is the use of conventional absorption costing (described in Chapter 3) under which the volume of output is fixed or set at an assumed *normal* level, usually for one year, and the product costs are based on that volume. Product costs based on *normal* volume and a *normal* mix of facilities do not provide a direct answer to questions which arise in making short-run pricing decisions, because the point at issue is how costs will be changed by differing volumes and mixes of output. It has been illustrated in Chapter 3 that costs which are based on a *normal* volume concept are only valid when the actual volume is the same as the assumed *normal* volume. In making selling price decisions it must be remembered that volume is one of the most important variables. There is very rarely a rigid relationship between selling prices and product costs because competition and the elasticity of consumer demand enter into selling price decisions, as well as product costs. Profits are the result of a satisfactory combination of a number of factors, including price, volume and product mix, and for this reason volume must be viewed as a variable in assembling cost data to guide management when making selling price decisions.

Absorption or Full Cost Pricing

When absorption costing is used and product costs are based on a normal volume concept, unit product costs cease to be a helpful guide in making pricing decisions when the management requires an answer to such questions as:

1. How much more will it cost to produce and sell an additional 1,000 units of Product A?
2. What will this order for 1,500 units of Product B add to the company's overall profit?
3. If the estimated demand curve for Product C is:

Selling Price	Demand
£15.0	1,500
£16.5	1,400
£17.0	1,250
£17.5	1,100
£18.0	900

which price should I charge?

The total costs of conventional absorption costing will not give a correct answer to these questions, because they do not represent the *incremental cost*, the additional cost which would result from the change in volume, and they include some fixed costs which are historical *sunk costs* in relation to these changes in volume.

With the conventional absorption costing or full-cost method of fixed selling prices, the usual procedure is for the manufacturer to calculate the cost of producing a unit of each product at the normal capacity level of his existing plant, and then add to this unit cost what he regards as the most satisfactory profit margin in relation to his competitors' prices. This procedure is illustrated in Table 12.3. It will be noted that the fixed costs have been charged to products

Table 12.2

SHAPLAND & PETTER LIMITED
Door Cost Review, October–December 198–

Door Type – Cellcor

Raw Material	Quantity	Rate	Ply for Paint £	Sapele Veneer £	White Melamine £
2 Cedar Stiles	0.005 m³	@ £100 per m³	0.50	0.50	0.50
2 Cedar Rails	0.004 m³	@ £100 per m³	0.40	0.40	0.40
2 Cedar Lock Blocks	0.006 m³	@ £100 per m³	0.60	0.60	0.60
2 Sheets Hardboard	2	@ £2.50 each	5.00	5.00	5.00
1 Honeycell Core	1	@ £0.50 each	0.50	0.50	0.50
2 Sapele Veneer Lay-ons	2	@ £3.00 each	—	6.00	—
2 Sheets White Melamine		@ £8.50	—	—	17.00
2 Meranti Lippings		@ £1.00	1.00	1.00
plus Sundries, glue etc.	0.005 m³	@ £2.00 per m³	1.00	1.00	1.00
Total Raw Materials			9.00	15.00	26.00

	Paint Hrs.	Veneer Hrs.	Melamine Hrs.			
Direct Labour						
Veneer Jointing	—	0.5	0.1			
Saw Lipping	0.1	0.1	0.1			
Frame Making	0.2	0.2	0.2			
Pressing	0.5	0.0	0.5			
Sizing and Lipping	0.5	0.5	—			
Sanding	0.2	0.2	—			
	1.5	2.5	3.0	@ £2.00/Hr.	3.00	5.00	6.00

	Paint	Veneer	Melamine
PRIME COST	12.00	20.00	32.00
Works Overheads (£ per hour) @ £4.00/Hr.	6.00	10.00	12.00
General Overheads (% on Prime Cost) 25%	3.00	5.00	8.00
TOTAL COST	21.00	35.00	52.00
Previous Total Cost (July/September 198–)	20.00	33.00	50.00
% Cost Increase/Reduction	+5%	+6.1%	+4%

Table 12.3

MARKUP LTD

Determination of Selling Prices by Absorption Costing

	Production	Fixed Costs Selling and Distribution	Administration
Annual Cost	£30,000	£5,000	£2,000
Basis of Absorption	60,000 Direct Labour Hours	£100,000 Cost of Production	£100,000 Cost of Production
Absorption Rate	£0.5 per direct labour hour	5% of Cost of Production	2% of Cost of Production

Suggested Selling Prices

	Product A £	Product B £	Product C £
Direct Labour	4.00 (10 hours)	2.00 (5 hrs)	8.00 (20 hrs)
Direct Material	5.00	4.00	5.00
Direct Expense	1.00	—	2.00
PRIME COST	10.00	6.00	15.00
Production Overhead:			
Variable	5.00	1.50	5.00
Fixed	5.00	2.50	10.00
COST OF PRODUCTION	20.00	10.00	30.00
Selling and Distribution Cost:			
Variable	1.50	0.25	0.75
Fixed	1.00	0.50	1.50
Administration Overhead:			
Fixed	0.40	0.20	0.60
TOTAL COST	22.90	10.95	32.85
PROFIT MARGIN	2.30 (10%)	1.65 (15%)	6.55 (20%)
SELLING PRICE	£25.20	£12.60	£39.40
MARGINAL COST	£16.50	£7.75	£20.75

using the various overhead absorption rates as explained in Chapter 3.

There is an evident danger that if Markup Ltd uses these average total costs as the benchmark for price-making or price-taking actions, business which is going at a price which is less than total unit cost, but which nevertheless would cover its marginal cost (or incremental cost) and make a contribution to fixed costs, may be rejected. This argument is particularly pertinent when a business has surplus capacity, for in conditions such as these, marginal costs will nearly always be *lower* than average total cost, whether the latter is determined in relation to normal output or not. For example, if Markup Ltd based selling prices on total cost at normal capacity, had surplus capacity, and received the following inquiry:

20 units of Product A at £20

50 units of Product B at £10

75 units of Product C at £25

they would reject the inquiry because the prices are in each case below the total cost which they have calculated. However, if they accepted the order it would make the following additional contribution towards fixed costs:

Product	Order Price £	Marginal Cost £	Contribution per Unit £	Number of Units	Total Contribution £
A	20.00	16.50	3.50	20	70.00
B	10.00	7.75	2.25	50	112.50
C	25.00	20.75	4.25	75	318.75
					£501.25

On the other hand, it may be that when a consumer product is offered to a market at a price, the selling price which will maximize a product's total contribution towards fixed costs and profits may be higher than the selling price determined by the cost plus pricing procedure. Rigid cost plus pricing fails to take account of price-demand relationships. As explained in Chapter 4, in many industries fixed costs have been rising in relation to variable costs. This means that the variable item of unit cost is being replaced by fixed costs which have been allocated to products on the basis of an assumed volume of sales. Total unit costs become increasingly dependent upon the volume of sales assumed, and, in so far as different prices give rise to different sales volumes, unit costs themselves become a function of prices. The increase in the ratio of fixed to variable costs gives the manufacturer far more room to manoeuvre in fixing his selling prices than when variable production costs are high in relation to fixed costs.

Rate of Return Pricing

If a standard rate of return on capital employed is established, as explained in Chapter 6, for a group of companies, a single company, or for individual divisions of a company, this may lead to the introduction of rate of return pricing. As a guide in making pricing decisions, management may wish to know what selling price would be required to produce a given rate of return on capital employed. With this method, pricing commences with the establishment of a planned rate of return on capital employed. To translate this rate of return into a percentage mark-up on costs, i.e. to find the profit margin, it is necessary to estimate a 'normal' rate of production, averaged over the business cycle. Total costs of a year's normal production are then estimated, and this is taken as the total annual cost in the computation. The ratio of normal capital employed to the year's total annual cost is then computed, i.e. the rate of capital turnover. Multiplying the rate of capital turnover by the planned rate of return on capital employed gives the mark-up percentage to be applied to total unit costs for pricing purposes. The basic formula for this calculation is:

$$\frac{\text{Capital Employed}}{\text{Total Annual Cost}} \times \frac{\text{Profit}}{\text{Capital Employed}} = \frac{\text{Profit}}{\text{Total Annual Cost}}$$

Therefore:

$$\text{Percentage Mark-up on Cost} = \frac{\text{Capital Employed}}{\text{Total Annual Cost}} \times \text{Planned Rate of Return on Capital Employed}$$

For example, if the capital turnover ratio is 0.5 and the planned rate of return is 20 per cent on capital employed, the mark-up is 10 per cent on total cost. In other words, the required mark-up percentage can be obtained by multiplying the desired rate of return on capital employed by the capital turnover ratio, with the latter computed on normal total annual cost.

Illustration of Rate of Return Pricing

The Domestic Appliance Co. manufactures and markets a consumer durable. The company's sales volume is strongly influenced by external economic conditions which are outside of the control of the management. The company, over the long run, desires a rate of return of 15 per cent on capital employed. In pursuing this objective, the company has based selling prices on normal production. The existing product is being replaced by a new model, and management need to know the selling price per unit which will produce the desired rate of return on capital employed. The following estimates have been made:

Variable Costs	£40 per unit
Fixed Costs	£1,000,000 per year
Normal Production	50,000 units
Normal Capital Employed:	
Variable	£10 per unit
Fixed	£1,500,000

The percentage mark-up on cost is calculated as follows:

$$\frac{\text{Capital Employed}}{\text{Total Annual Cost}} \times \frac{\text{Desired Rate of Return}}{\text{on Capital Employed}}$$

$$= \frac{(50,000 \times £10) + £1,500,000}{(50,000 \times £40) + £1,000,000} \times 15\%$$

$$= \frac{2,000,000}{3,000,000} \times 15\% = \underline{\underline{10\%}}$$

The selling price per unit which will produce the desired rate of return of 15 per cent on capital employed is calculated as follows:

	£
Variable Costs per unit	40
Fixed Costs per unit	
(£1,000,000 ÷ 50,000)	20
Total Cost	60
Mark-up on Cost (10%)	6
Selling Price	£66

The calculation of the selling price can be checked by calculating the rate of return on capital employed for 50,000 units:

		£
Sales	at £66 per unit	3,300,000
Variable Costs	at £40 per unit	2,000,000
Fixed Costs		1,000,000
Total Costs		£3,000,000
Profit		£ 300,000
Capital Employed:		
Variable	at £10 per unit	500,000
Fixed		1,500,000
Total		£2,000,000

Return on Capital Employed:

$$\frac{30,000 \times 100}{2,000,000} \qquad \underline{15\%}$$

The long-run base price that is obtained by applying the percentage mark-up to total unit cost will be altered with short-run changes in costs, such as increases in wage rates or when material prices change significantly, but not for fluctuations in the 'normal' rate of production. During periods when production is in excess of normal, profits will produce a higher than planned rate of return on capital employed, because actual unit costs will be lower than the normal unit costs used as the mark-up base. The fixed costs will be averaged over a greater volume of production, and the unit fixed costs will be lower than at normal production. Similarly, the capital employed will not increase in proportion to the increase in production. It can

Table 12.4

	Per unit £	
Selling Price	66	
Variable Cost	40	
Contribution	£26	
Number of Units	40,000	60,000
	£	£
Total Contribution	1,040,000	1,560,000
Fixed Costs	1,000,000	1,000,000
Profits	£40,000	£560,000
Capital Employed		
Variable at £10 per unit	400,000	600,000
Fixed	1,500,000	1,500,000
Total	£1,900,000	£2,100,000
Return on Capital Employed	2.1%	26.7%

be seen in Table 12.4 that if the Domestic Appliance Co. produces 60,000 units of the new model at a selling price of £66 per unit the rate of return on capital employed increases to 26.7 per cent. In periods of low production the reverse will occur: actual profits and return on capital employed will be lower. If 40,000 units are produced the rate of return on capital employed falls to 2.1 per cent. Thus, as with absorption cost pricing, costs and prices which are based on a *normal* volume concept are only valid when the actual volume is the same as the assumed *normal* volume.

In a multi-product business the percentage mark-up is an average, both among products and through time. Actual prices of specific products will vary from the base price, derived from the long-run mark-up on cost, to meet varying demand conditions and competition for each product. However, if the planned rate of return on capital employed is to be attained over, say, a five-year period these variations must be made to balance so that the weighted average of mark-ups remains close to the planned overall mark-up. The planned mark-up thus provides a bench-mark for controlling short-run price-making and price-taking actions, and appraising the extent to which these actions direct profits away from the planned return on capital employed.

Rate of return pricing is thus a refined variant of absorption pricing. It does build on cost that is 'normalized' for fluctuations in the rate of output, and it develops a profit mark-up that is related to a planned rate of return on capital employed. However, these refinements do not necessarily remove the arbitrary element in setting the mark-up percentage. It may simply transfer the arbitrariness to the planned rate of return. The method does have the advantage of directing pricing at some planned rate of return on capital employed, despite the fact that there is no guarantee that this planned rate of return will be achieved, except when demand and competitive conditions are as anticipated when the mark-up was established.[3] While it might guide short-run pricing decisions there is still the danger that average total costs will be regarded as the rock-bottom price for price-making and price-taking, and business which is going at a price which is less than total unit cost, but which nevertheless would cover its marginal cost and make a contribution to fixed costs, will be rejected. If the profit margins in Table 12.3 were based on a planned rate of return, the order which gives £501.25 contribution to fixed costs could still be rejected.

A Case Study

Consider the following case study which provides an illustration of three variants of cost-plus prices and considers their limitations.

Mr Hawkeye, the management accountant of James Wilson & Son of Milchester, whose segmental reporting system was described in Chapter 11, calculated three possible costed selling prices for a garment. Wilson's was an old-established company producing knitted underwear, leisurewear and children's outerwear. They had premises in Bridge Street and South Street, Milchester, and had recently opened a new factory in North Ashfleet, ten miles south of Mil-

---

3 Varying degrees of sophistication can be introduced into the calculation of the percentage mark-up. In a multi-product business separate mark-ups can be calculated for individual products, but this necessitates the apportionment of common fixed costs and common capital employed. The time value of money can be introduced into the calculations. Space does not permit a full examination of these approaches, but, regardless of the degree of sophistication, the fact remains that there is no guarantee that the planned rate of return will be achieved.

chester. Underwear and leisurewear were produced at Bridge Street, and knitwear at South Street and North Ashfleet. The company had an annual turnover of £1,300,000 and some 500 employees.

The three methods Mr Hawkeye employed to calculate costed selling prices for a garment are illustrated in Table 12.5. The weight of yarn per dozen garments was determined from production samples and a fixed percentage was added for waste. Yarn costs were obtained by multiplying the yarn weight by the standard cost per pound of yarn (standard cost is the normal cost under acceptable levels of efficiency). For needles, cost was estimated on the basis of past experience, and trimmings were charged at standard cost. Labour-time standards and piece rates were established by the work-study engineer, and the allowances were multiplied by the standard wage rates. If times or piece rates had increased in a department since the standards were established, separate allowance was made for the increase. Overheads were included by multiplying the total labour cost by the overhead recovery rate for the factory in which the garment was to be produced (i.e. by assuming that overheads were incurred in proportion to labour costs). The sums of the two columns in the table represent total cost and variable cost. For example, the total cost of the boy's jersey was £16.08 and the variable cost £12.66.

The three costed selling prices were determined by the following additions to total or variable cost:

1. Total cost plus 8.5 per cent gave a costed selling price of £17.45 for the boy's jersey.
2. Variable cost plus 43 per cent gave a costed selling price of £18.10 for the boy's jersey.
3. Variable cost plus three times making-up labour gave a costed selling price of £17.50 for the boy's jersey.

The mark-ups of 8.5 per cent and 43 per cent were calculated by Mr Hawkeye in the following manner:

Knitwear Division Budget

Budgeted Sales	£510,000
Estimated Capital Employed, with fixed assets valued on an assumed current-cost basis	£270,000
Required Return on Capital Employed	15%
Required Profit	£40,000
Fixed Overheads	£112,000

Table 12.5

Illustration of Calculation of Costed Selling Prices

	Boy's Jersey size 26 in.		Baby's Cardigan size 18 in.		Maxi-cardigan size 36 in.	
Yarn Usage per dozen	(lb)		(lb)		(lb)	
Weight	8.88		2.26		16.44	
Waste	0.56		0.16		1.03	
	9.44		2.38		17.47	
	£	£	£	£	£	£
Cost per dozen						
Yarn cost	7.08		1.93		14.15	
Draw thread and Swatches	0.02		0.02		0.02	
		7.10		1.95		14.17
Needles		0.06		0.06		0.06
Buttons	0.13		0.03		0.50	
Sewing/Tabs/Tapes	0.26		0.25		0.30	
Plastic	0.90		—		—	
		1.29		0.28		0.80

Bags/Boxes		0.15			0.13			0.30
Knitting Labour	0.66			0.46			2.80	
Making-up Labour	1.62			0.89			2.29	
	2.28			1.35			5.09	
Holiday Pay/Increase (24%)	0.55	(24%)		0.25	(24%)		0.56	(11%)
Carriage/Packing		2.83			1.60			5.65
		0.18			0.16			0.18
	11.61	11.61		4.18	4.18		21.16	21.16
Overheads	3.42		(121%)	2.03		(121%)	7.63	(135%)
	15.03		(121%)	6.21			28.79	
Commission Discount (7%)	1.05	1.05		0.43	0.43		2.02	2.02
Total Cost/Variable Cost	16.08	12.66		6.64	4.61		30.81	23.18
+8.5%/43%	1.37	5.44		0.56	1.99		2.64	9.97
	£17.45	£18.10		£7.20	£6.60		£33.45	£33.15
Costed Selling Price per dozen	£17.50			£7.30			£30.50	

Variable Cost + 3 × making-up labour

$$\begin{aligned}
\text{Mark-up on} \\
\text{Total Cost} \quad &= \quad \frac{\text{required profit}}{\text{total cost}} \quad \times 100 \\[6pt]
&= \quad \frac{\pounds40,000}{\pounds(510,000 - 40,000)} \quad \times 100 \\[6pt]
&= \quad 8.5\% \\[6pt]
\text{Mark-up on} \\
\text{Variable Cost} &= \quad \frac{\text{required total contribution}}{\text{total variable cost}} \quad \times 100 \\[6pt]
&= \quad \frac{\pounds152,000}{\pounds358,000} \quad \times 100 \\[6pt]
&= \quad 43\%
\end{aligned}$$

The factor that frequently limited Wilson's capacity to manufacture additional garments was making-up labour. The making-up capacity involved a labour cost of £50,000. To achieve the budgeted contribution of £152,000, the company had to obtain a little over £3 of contribution for every £1 spent on making-up labour. Therefore the third pricing rule was to take variable cost plus three times making-up labour.

Mr Hawkeye used his costed selling prices in the following manner:

I recommend to Mr Simpson, the sales manager, the highest costed selling price produced by the three methods. Everyone's criterion is then met. Mr Simpson cannot always negotiate the highest selling price and sometimes has to come down below the lowest costed selling price, but I am very unhappy with any selling price below total cost. For example, as you are no doubt aware, maxi-cardigans are very fashionable at the present time, and last month we introduced them to our knitwear range. For the maxi-cardigan in Table 12.5 I recommended a selling price of £33.45 per dozen to Mr Simpson and, in the event, he has sold twelve dozen at £40 per dozen. Business is hard to come by at the moment and our North Ashfleet factory, which produces the maxi-cardigans, is working on short time. I could not recommend the price of £30.05 based on making-up labour; the total cost per dozen is £30.81 and we would not recover our overheads.

Each quarter I produce an analysis of sales which distinguishes between:

(i) Sales below total cost;

(ii) Sales between total cost and lowest desirable selling price;

(iii) Sales between desirable selling price on labour and desirable selling price on variable cost;

(iv) sales above highest desirable selling price.

Analysis of Case Study

This is an interesting case study in that Mr Hawkeye appears to use a 'belt and braces' approach to pricing. He employs three methods to determine recommended 'costed' selling prices for garments: the full cost plus, the rate of return on capital employed variant, and a third variant derived from marginal costing but which is also designed to recover overheads at normal capacity.

Mr Hawkeye calculates separate overhead rates for each of Wilson's factories, even though two of the factories appear to be capable of producing the same knitwear. The result is that in Table 12.5 an overhead rate of 121 per cent is applied to the boy's jersey and the baby's cardigan, and a rate of 135 per cent to the maxi-cardigan. Furthermore, a single overhead rate is applied for each factory. Mr Hawkeye appears not to recognize that there are two distinct parts to a knitwear factory – the capital intensive knitting operation and the labour intensive making-up operation. It will be noted that in Table 12.5 the ratio of knitting labour to making-up labour varies significantly between the three garments. There should, perhaps, be separate overhead rates for each operation, e.g. one rate for the knitting operation and another for the making-up operation.

Mr Hawkeye sees the costed selling price he recommends as the starting-point from which Mr Simpson, the sales manager, arrives at the final selling price. He does not object to Mr Simpson's negotiating a higher price, but is 'very unhappy with any selling price below total cost'. However, Mr Hawkeye's system fails to take formal account of price-demand relationships. Mr Hawkeye would have been unhappy to recommend the maxi-cardigans at a selling price of less than £33.45 and appears to be happy that Mr Simpson has sold twelve dozen at £40 per dozen. He appears not to have taken into consideration that, for example, at a lower price of £30 per dozen Mr Simpson might have sold not twelve dozen but fifty dozen when business is 'hard to come by'. Twelve dozen at £40 per dozen gives a total contribution of £201.84 (i.e. $12 \times (£40 - £23.18)$), whereas fifty dozen at £30 per dozen would give a total contribution of £341.00 (i.e. $50 \times (£30 - £23.18)$).

The strength of Mr Hawkeye's system is that it is directed towards achieving clearly defined objectives, namely £40,000 profit and 15 per cent return on capital employed; and it also takes account of making-up labour, the factor that frequently limits Wilson's capacity. When the company achieves or exceeds budgeted sales, provided Simpson achieves the 'costed' selling prices, the profit and return on capital employed objectives should be achieved. Furthermore, Hawkeye directs management's attention to the relationship between his recommended pricing decisions and actual prices, highlighting those prices which appear to fall short in their contribution to the profit and return on capital employed objectives; no doubt this leads management to consider price–demand relationships.

The weakness of the system is that it does not provide Simpson with guidance on how to take account of price–demand relationships when arriving at the final selling price, particularly when the company is working below capacity. Hawkeye and Simpson may have developed a good working relationship which encourages Simpson to request the information he needs and allows Hawkeye to provide informal advice on price–volume relationships.

Criticisms of Full Cost Pricing

Thus, the James Wilson case study and the earlier examples illustrate why critics of full cost pricing argue that:

1. It tends not to take account directly of demand, and assumes prices are simply a function of costs.
2. It fails to reflect competition adequately.
3. It is not based on the incremental costs and revenues relevant to alternative selling prices being considered, but includes past costs which are not relevant to the decision at hand.
4. It overplays the precision of allocated fixed cost and possibly capital employed in a multi-product business.
5. The allocation of common fixed costs to product groups is a crude measure of the opportunity cost of directing managerial effort at particular products, because opportunity costs should be measured in terms of profits forgone, not costs incurred.
6. It is based on a long-run pricing concept and it is doubtful whether it is useful to think in terms of the long run, given the rapidly changing external environment in which companies operate.

7. Selling price is one of a number of variables in the marketing mix and, if selling price decisions are based on full cost data, there is danger that decisions about variations in the non-price variables are incorrectly evaluated.

While cost-plus pricing tends not to take account directly of demand, and assumes prices are a function of costs, a price decision-maker may do so indirectly by varying mark-up percentage on total costs, but such a procedure may be a poor substitute for price-demand information. For example, a manufacturer of fully-fashioned knitted outerwear calculated the total cost and selling price of a garment as illustrated in Table 12.6.

The managing director of a fully-fashioned knitted outerwear company maintained that he was happy so long as he was getting a $12\frac{1}{2}$ per cent mark-up on total cost, and he did not like to see any of his products falling below this mark-up. On investigation it was found that frequently he did not fix the selling price of a style at total cost plus $12\frac{1}{2}$ per cent, but increased it to a slightly higher level. The final selling price appeared to be based on the managing director's subjective judgement. He explained that he did this where he believed that there had been some extra input of skill in making-up or design, and the market could bear the extra price. However, his variation of the mark-up percentage was based on 'extra input' and not on any systematic assessment of price-demand relationships.

Baxter and Oxenfeldt[4] have neatly summarized the major criticism of cost plus pricing:

On the other hand, inability to estimate demand accurately and in time scarcely excuses the substitution of cost information for demand information. Crude estimates of demand may serve instead of careful estimates of demand but cost gives remarkably little insight into demand.

Nevertheless, 'full cost' appears to be used by many firms as a starting-point in selling price decisions, while managerial judgement determines the size of the 'plus'. For example, at Shapland and Petter the cost reviews illustrated earlier in Table 12.2 are discussed with the marketing director:[5]

4 W. T. Baxter and A. R. Oxenfeldt, 'Costing and Pricing: the Cost Accountant versus the Economist', in *Studies in Cost Analysis*, D. Solomons (ed.), Sweet & Maxwell, London, 1968, p. 299.

5 J. Sizer and N. J. Coulthurst, 'Shapland and Petter Ltd', *A Casebook of British Management Accounting*, Volume 1, I.C.A.E.W., 1984, pp. 167–8.

Table 12.6

Cost Sheet

Style No. 7317
Type: Long line halter polo with belt

Department	Overhead (%)	Direct Labour (£)	Overheads (£)	Yarn (£)	Trim and Packaging (£)	Yarn: matt tricel bonde	
						Dye and Print (£)	Total (£)
Flat-knit ribs	304	0.04	0.12	—	—	—	0.16
Run on steam iron, etc.	110	0.26	0.28	—	—	—	0.54
F F knit	128	0.62	0.79	4.13	—	—	5.54
Pre-dye make-up	145	0.29	0.42	—	0.11	—	0.82
Flat-knit trim	304	0.09	0.26	1.54	—	—	1.89
Dye/Scour	—	—	—	—	—	2.13	2.13
Print							
Post-dye make-up	121	1.04	1.21	—	0.07	—	2.32
Press and counter	287	0.19	0.53	—	0.20	—	0.92
		£2.53	£3.61	£5.67	£0.38	£2.13	£14.32

Cost Summary

	£
Factory cost brought down	14.32
Seconds allowance	0.34
Pack and dispatch	0.44
Sub-total	14.70
Profits 12½%	1.83
Total per dozen	£16.53
Cost per garment	£ 1.38

The review shows the marketing director the changes in total costs which have occurred since the last review, and is accompanied by the management accountant's recommendation of the price increase necessary for the company to achieve its net profit target. If, for example, the cost increases comprise, entirely, increases in labour, materials and variable overheads, then an equivalent percentage increase in selling prices would be required.

If there has been a major improvement in labour productivity, and consequent reductions in prime cost, the effect of this would be noted separately. The marketing director may wish to pass only a part of this saving on to the customer in the form of reduced prices. If there has been a reduction in budgeted volume and budgeted profit, resulting in an increase in overhead rates and of total product costs, again, the effect of this would be noted separately. The accountant would advise that the profit target should be achievable without a price increase in this case. If there has been a change in product specification, the management accountant would normally point this out, and recommend that prices be adjusted to allow for it.

The marketing director prepares his recommendations for discussion with the managing director, and any resulting price change decision has to be made in sufficient time to allow for the re-calculation and re-typing of price lists.

MARGINAL PRICING

Clearly, the use of conventional absorption costing or the rate of return variant for pricing decisions has shortcomings, at least in the short run. Is the marginal cost and contribution towards fixed costs approach a satisfactory alternative? The marginal cost approach to pricing decisions recognizes that decision-making is essentially a process of choosing between competing alternatives, each with its own combination of income and costs; and that the relevant concepts to employ are future incremental costs and revenues and opportunity cost, not full costs which include past or sunk costs.

With the marginal approach the question is not 'Shall we raise or lower our selling prices?' but 'What will happen to our total profits if we raise or lower the selling prices of particular products?' In a highly competitive industry where demand for an individual firm's products is correspondingly elastic, and the ratio of fixed to variable costs is high, it is possible to make a wide range of prices which are all economically possible, i.e. each price generates sufficient total sales revenue to cover total costs and provide some profit. In deciding these prices, advocates of marginal cost pricing suggest that fixed costs must be omitted from unit costs and selling prices determined on the basis of marginal cost. A pricing decision involves planning into the future, and as such it should deal solely with the anticipated, and therefore estimated, revenues, expenses, and capital outlays. All past outlays, it is argued, which give rise to fixed costs are historical and unchangeable. They are inescapable, 'sunk costs', regardless of how they may be 'costed' for financial accounting purposes, for stock valuation or distribution of profit through time.

With *marginal pricing* the firm seeks to fix its prices so as to maximize its total contribution to fixed costs and profit. Unless the manufacturer's products are in direct competition with each other, this objective is achieved by considering each product in isolation and fixing its price at a level which is calculated to maximize its total contribution. At this point it may be useful to illustrate the discussion with four examples of marginal pricing decisions and use of marginal product cost information.

1. CHOICE OF CONTRACTS

The Bettermade Electronic Company operates in an area where there is little prospect of increasing its labour force. The firm employs twenty direct operatives whose working week is forty hours and whose average rate of pay is £0.15 per hour. No overtime is worked. On 1 September the company has to choose between two contracts, with AB Ltd or with CD Ltd, each commencing on 1 January and lasting until the end of March. Either contract would fully utilize the company's productive capacity and therefore they cannot be undertaken at the same time. Standard direct costs for each contract, and the best prices that can be obtained, are:

	AB Ltd Contract £	CD Ltd Contract £
Per dozen:		
Direct Materials	4.50	1.50
Direct Wages	1.50	3.00
Selling Price	10.75	13.50

The company's standard overhead per week is £300, of which £200 is variable and £100 fixed. Overhead is absorbed by a standard rate per direct labour hour. The managing director asks his management accountant to:

(a) calculate the total cost per dozen for each contract;
(b) calculate the percentage profit to sales for each contract; and
(c) state which contract he would recommend the company to undertake. There are no reasons of special policy which favour one contract or the other. The management accountant's calculations are shown in Table 12.7.

On the basis of percentage profit to sales and profit per dozen the contract with CD would appear to be more profitable. However, it will be seen that when the two contracts are examined more closely AB Ltd gives the higher total profit and contribution per direct labour hour.

2. RAISING OR LOWERING PRICES

The Bang Bang Manufacturing Co. is reviewing the selling price of Product X, a consumer durable, and after carrying out extensive market research has estimated the following annual demands for the product at varying prices.

Price	Estimated Annual Demand
£17	8,000
£17.5	7,800
£18 (existing price)	7,600
£18.5	7,200
£19	6,600
£19.5	5,700
£20	4,200

It is anticipated that each of these demands can be manufactured and marketed with existing capacity. The average variable cost per unit over the relevant output range is constant at £12 per unit, i.e. marginal cost equals average variable cost. The *separable* fixed costs are £25,000, i.e. the fixed costs associated with the product, such as a product manager's salary, as opposed to the *common* fixed costs, such as the managing director's salary.

Table 12.7

BETTERMADE ELECTRONIC CO.

Comparison of A B Ltd and C D Ltd Contracts

		A B Ltd Contract	C D Ltd Contract
		£	£
(a)	*Total Cost per dozen*		
	Direct Material Cost	4.50	1.50
	Direct Wages	1.50 (10 hrs)	3.00 (20 hrs)
	PRIME COST	6.00	4.50
	Overhead at 37½p per direct labour hour*	3.75	7.50
	TOTAL COST	£9.75	£12.00

* Overhead rate $\frac{£300}{800 \text{ hrs}}$ = £0.375 per direct labour hour,

		£	£
(b)	*% Profit to Sales*		
	Selling Price	10.75	13.50
	Total Cost	9.75	12.00
	Profit per dozen	£1.00	£1.50
	% of Selling Price	9.3%	11.1%

(c) *Recommendation*

Would recommend the acceptance of contract with A B Ltd. Although the profit percentage on sales is higher in the case of C D Ltd, the total profit for 13 weeks ended 31 March would be more in the case of A B Ltd.

	A B Ltd Contract	C D Ltd Contract
Production for 13 weeks	1,040 doz	520 doz
	£	£
Direct Material Cost	4,680	780
Direct Wages	1,560	1,560
PRIME COST	6,240	2,340
Overhead 13 × £300	3,900	3,900
Total Cost	10,140	6,240
Sales	11,180	7,020
PROFIT	£1,040	£780

Table 12.7 continued

Another way of looking at the problem is to recognize that direct labour is the factor which limits production and that the objective must be to maximize *contribution per direct labour hour*. In this situation, where the company is operating at full capacity, all costs are fixed costs other than material. The only differential cost in the above calculation is material. The contribution per direct labour hour should therefore be calculated as follows:

	A B Ltd Contract	C D Ltd Contract
	£	£
Selling Price per dozen	10.75	13.50
Direct Material per dozen	4.50	1.50
Contribution per dozen	£6.25	£12.00
Direct Labour Hours	10	20
Contribution per direct labour hour	£0.625	£0.6

The additional profit on A B Ltd in 13 weeks would be 10,400 hrs at £0.025 per hour = £260.

With the marginal costing approach the company determines which price will make the greatest contribution towards fixed costs and profit. The type of calculation the accountant could make is shown in Table 12.8. It will be noted that the greatest profit improvement would result from raising the selling price of Product X from £18.0 to £18.5.

The information in Table 12.8 is presented in the form of a Profit-volume Chart in Figure 12.1. CC′ is the *Contribution Curve* for Product X. It shows the relationship between demand in units, direct product profit, total contribution, and break-even units for each price. For example, a selling price of £18.5 would result in a demand for Product X of 7,200 units, a total contribution of £46,800, a direct product profit of £21,800, and a product break-even at 3,846 units. In establishing the contribution curve and determining the price which promises the highest contribution, the demand function has been taken into consideration and the cost function is based upon a concept of cost (marginal cost) that is relevant to the pricing decision at hand.

Table 12.8

BANG BANG MANUFACTURING CO.
Review of Selling Price of Product X

	£	£	£	£	£	£	£
Selling Price	17.0	17.5	18.0	18.5	19.0	19.5	20.0
Marginal Cost	12.0	12.0	12.0	12.0	12.0	12.0	12.0
Contribution	5.0	5.5	6.0	6.5	7.0	7.5	8.0
Estimated Demand (units)	8,000	7,800	7,600	7,200	6,600	5,700	4,200
	£	£	£	£	£	£	£
Total Contribution	40,000	42,900	45,600	46,800	46,200	42,750	33,600
Separable Fixed Costs	25,000	25,000	25,000	25,000	25,000	25,000	25,000
Direct Product Profit	15,000	17,900	20,600	21,800	21,200	17,750	8,600
Product Break-even							
Sales (units)	5,000	4,545	4,167	3,846	3,572	3,333	3,125
Percentage of Demand	62.5	58.3	54.8	5.34	54.1	58.5	74.4

The Shapland and Petter case study [6] contains the third and fourth examples of the use of marginal product cost information.

3. EXPORT CONTRACTS

The export market is very competitive, with British, Continental and Far Eastern companies competing for business in the Middle East.

The marketing director here is concerned to know what the contribution of the prospective job would be at different price levels. In other words, he needs to know how much of the cost of the job comprises variable costs (i.e. raw materials, direct labour and variable overheads), and how much is allocated fixed overheads which will be incurred in any case. He needs to know the contribution of the job as a whole, and also of each of the principal items within the job. Each item is costed, using cost review data, but allowing for any special savings which may be obtainable if the job is large, e.g. bulk purchase prices of raw materials, savings on setting-up time in the factory, etc. The availability of fixed and variable overhead rates enables the contributions on each of the important items in the contract to be calculated readily. In the case of export contracts, there are additional costs which have to be taken into account before arriving at a selling price, i.e.

6 Sizer and Coulthurst, op. cit., Volume 1, p. 168.

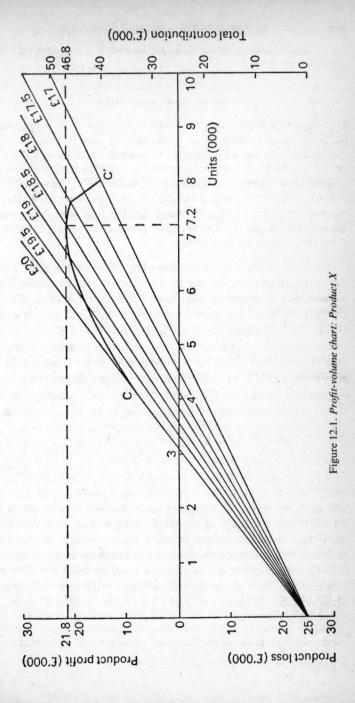

Figure 12.1. *Profit-volume chart: Product X*

export credit insurance cover, agent's commission, if any, and the cost of crates or containers.

4. MAKE OR BUY DECISIONS

The company sometimes has the option of buying in door components of the more common kinds, or of manufacturing them in house. The cost review data provides a uniform basis on which to make such decisions. Only where the bought-in component shows a substantial saving compared with the prime cost (material and direct labour only) of the manufactured product, will the bought-in component be seriously considered. This can happen where components are made in the Far East, near the sources of hardwood timber, thus saving transport costs on the waste timber, as well as utilizing cheaper labour supplies.

It is usually assumed in examples of marginal cost pricing that the firm has surplus capacity, and that additional sales can be produced without any increase in fixed costs. It may be argued that if a company is operating at full capacity in the short run, it cannot always take full advantage of demand elasticity and short-term contracts, and that it can therefore rely on the conventional method of fixing its price on the basis of normal cost at full capacity. Is this necessarily so? It is probable that many manufacturers in a highly competitive industry will be working below full capacity and have L- rather than U-shaped marginal cost curves, i.e. they will be operating below the level at which marginal cost starts to rise. In any case if any manufacturers are working below full capacity, they may well be the price leaders when it comes to price fixing. Even if the company is working at normal capacity, it can usually increase the output of the existing plant by working it more intensively. This may give rise to higher marginal costs, but this can be taken into consideration when fixing prices. It may be that prices resulting from costs based on normal capacity are too low. Even when it is necessary to increase plant capacity and pricing becomes a long-run problem, the additional contribution resulting from the difference between the short-run marginal cost and price can be compared with the additional investment and fixed costs which will result from the increased capacity.

Advantages of Marginal Pricing

What then are the advantages claimed for marginal pricing; is it to be considered superior to pricing under absorption costing? It is argued in favour of marginal pricing:

1. Marginal costs more accurately reflect *future* as distinct from present cost levels and cost relationships. When making a pricing decision you are interested in the changes in cost that will result from that decision. Marginal cost represents these changes, while total costs developed by absorption costing include fixed costs which are not incurred as a result of the pricing decision.

2. When the demand for a product is highly elastic, the price which maximizes contribution, and therefore profits, may be less than (or more than) the total cost plus normal profit margin developed under absorption costing. Some of the prices determined by marginal costing would probably be considered uneconomic if they were simply compared with total costs including fixed overheads based on normal capacity.

3. When making pricing decisions, firms have to consider the costs potential competitors would face if they are, or were to commence, producing the firm's products. Will the total costs developed under absorption costing or marginal costs give the best estimate of these costs? In many instances, when the competitor is a multi-product firm with existing production facilities it is the marginal or incremental cost which the competitor will incur.

4. Will a policy of rather rigid and uniform pricing, such as absorption costing can bring about, be more or less discouraging to actual and potential competitors than a policy which tends to make prices more differentiated and more flexible through time? Marginal pricing permits a manufacturer to develop a far more aggressive pricing policy than does absorption costing. However, before entering into a more differentiated and a more flexible pricing policy it would be necessary to consider the impact of unstable prices on customer goodwill.

5. While marginal pricing is essentially a short-run concept it is probably more effective than absorption costing because of three characteristics of modern business:

(a) *The prevalence of multi-product, multi-process, and multi-market concerns which makes the absorption of fixed costs into product costs absurd.* The total costs of the separate products can never be estimated satisfactorily, and the optimal relationship between costs and prices will vary substantially both among different products and between different markets. If markets are to be segmented successfully, it is necessary to know the variable costs and specific fixed costs attributable to each segment. In this type of business one is constantly considering proposals for changing selling prices or terms of sales, for segmenting the market to gain advantage of the different layers of consumer demand, and for selecting the most profitable business when capacity is limited. These are usually short-run problems because the underlying conditions are always changing, and marginal pricing is the most suitable method of short-run pricing.

(b) *In many businesses the dominant force is innovation combined with constant scientific and technological development, and the long-run situation is often highly unpredictable.* There is a series of short runs and one must aim at maximizing contribution in each short run. When rapid developments are taking place, fixed costs and demand conditions may change from one short run to another, and only by maximizing contribution in each short run will profit be maximized in the long run. To argue that the normal capacity absorption costing approach is more satisfactory for long-run pricing is to miss the point, for it is doubtful whether it is useful to think in terms of the 'long run' in view of these characteristics of modern business.

(c) *Once a new product introduction is approved and the investment made, a product manager is concerned with managing the variables in the marketing mix over a series of short runs.* It was recognized in Chapter 11 that many branded products cannot be expected to hold a permanent franchise in the market place; that they will proceed through the *product life-cycle* of introduction, growth, maturity, saturation, and decline; and marketing management requires cost information to assist in determining the correct combination of price, advertising, product improvement, product differentiation, etc. They require short-run marginal cost and separable fixed or period cost data relevant to that stage of the cycle.

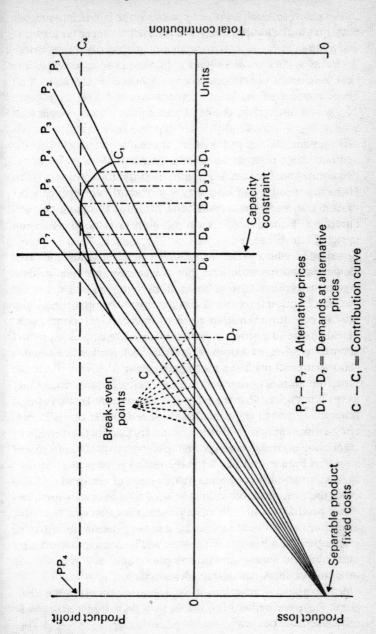

$P_1 - P_7$ = Alternative prices

$D_1 - D_7$ = Demands at alternative prices

$C - C_1$ = Contribution curve

Figure 12.2. Product profit-volume chart—Product A

For example, contrast pricing policy at the *introductory stage* with that at the *maturity stage*. A product manager may adopt a *skimming policy* or a *penetration policy* towards selling price decisions at the *introductory stage*. Limited production capacity may rule out a penetration policy. A capacity limitation has been imposed in the product profit-volume chart in Figure 12.2 which restricts the choice of selling price. P_6 may be chosen with a view to successfully reducing prices as

(i) the price elasticity of demand increases;

(ii) additional capacity becomes available; and

(iii) competitors are attracted into the market.

If the new product introduction is successful, with the growth of demand, both the *position* and *shape* of the contribution curve (CC′) change. Alternatively, if there is no production capacity constraint, a penetration price, such as P_3 or P_4, may be adopted which yields early high volume accompanied by slow competitive imitation, but lower unit product profit. Again, with the growth in demand, the position and shape of the contribution curves will change, but a company may be relying on the penetration price to maintain the company's market share in a growing market, without having to resort to successive price reductions. It is likely to have lower variable costs as it proceeds down the learning curve.

At the *maturity stage* the firm will have far less discretion over selling prices. Prices probably will have fallen in real terms during the growth stage as a result of economies of scale and competitive pressures. Prices decline further in the maturity stage, but eventually may stabilize. The profit-volume chart shows in Figure 12.3 that P_4 is the selling price promising the highest direct product profit. At this stage of the product life-cycle the firm probably would be wise to maximize short-run direct product profit. The management may, for what usually are described as 'long-run policy reasons', decide upon some price other than P_4. If they do, they will be consciously deviating from the short-run optimal price, and will be able to measure the short-run cost of such a policy.

In the above illustrations it has been assumed that the firm either is a price maker or, if it follows a price leader, has some choice around the price leader's price. Situations in which the

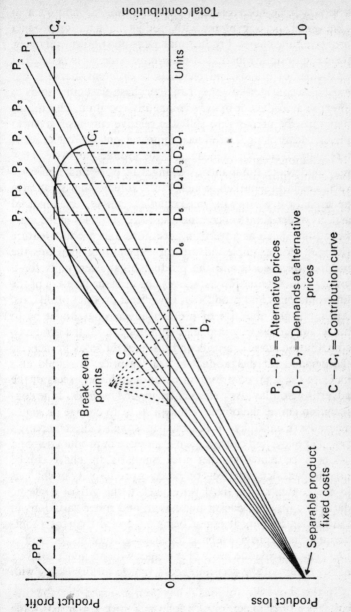

Figure 12.3. *Product profit-volume chart - Product A*

$P_1 - P_7 =$ Alternative prices

$D_1 - D_7 =$ Demands at alternative prices

$C - C_1 =$ Contribution curve

firm is a price taker or adopts a 'price-minus'[7] approach to pricing can also be explored with product managers on product profit-volume charts. Product managers must not merely view their responsibility as that of determining the various demand elasticities of brands and products in different markets, but must also consider how they can alter these elasticities so as to improve a product or brand's competitive position. This means they must be prepared to shift the relative emphasis given to price, advertising, product improvement, product differentiation, etc., for each stage of the product life-cycle. They may undertake simultaneous changes in price and non-price variables in the marketing mix. Profit-volume charts can also be used to explore with marketing executives, the financial aspects of decisions concerning non-price variables in the marketing mix, such as advertising decisions and product feature changes. For example, advertising expenditure increases the product fixed costs and the product break-even units for a given price. Alternatively, it moves upwards the position of the horizontal axis and produces a new direct product profit axis. An important objective of product advertising should be to move, not necessarily in one accounting period, the product's contribution curve upwards and to the right so as to increase the demand for the product at a given price. It should also increase the total contribution by an amount in excess of the advertising outlay. As well as changing the *position* of the contribution curve, the objective may also be to change its *shape*. The advertising may be designed to support the company's pricing policy, and cause a greater increase in product demand at one price than at another price. Similarly, the charts can be used to consider the effects on product profitability of changes in the contents of a fixed price packet, the gift of a plastic daffodil with each packet purchased, and other variations in the marketing mix. It is not being suggested that the profit-volume charts provide a basis for making decisions, but rather that they provide the product manager with an understanding of the nature of the decision, and a vehicle for discussing with

---

7 With the 'price-minus' approach the company works backwards from a market price to alternative quality-cost-volume relationships.

the management accountant the financial information needed to evaluate the alternatives available.

While it has to be admitted that marginal pricing is essentially a short-run concept, this is not to say it has no part to play in long-run pricing policy. On the contrary, the consideration of marginal cost and contribution is an essential part of an intelligent long-range pricing policy, especially for multi-product firms. In the long run, cost recovery may be best attained on an overall basis by varying the rates at which 'fixed' costs are reflected in sales prices of different products, or in the sales prices of a product at different stages of its life-cycle or in different market segments. In the multi-product firm a variety of possible combinations must be considered and some products are able to contribute a wider margin over marginal cost than are other products. Products will make different contributions at the various stages of their life-cycles in different markets. This means setting prices which will maximize contribution in the particular situation, and marginal costs may then be more useful guides. It may be that a range of interrelated products are manufactured and they appeal to the consumer or distributor as a whole range, i.e. there is a demand curve for the range rather than for individual products in the range. In such a case each product cannot be considered in isolation, and it will not be possible to think in terms of maximizing the contribution from each separate product. It will be necessary to develop the prices of the products in relation to each other so as to maximize the contribution from the entire range of products. The demand for the whole range of products must be considered rather than the demand for individual products. For example, the Gillette Safety Razor was marketed at very low prices in order to create a market for the more profitable razor blades. In this situation the objective must be to maximize the combined contribution from the safety razor and the razor blades.

Advocates of absorption costing suggest that with marginal pricing there is a lack of information as to whether in the long run in a multi-product business each product is carrying its fair share of overheads, since there is no allocation of fixed costs. With marginal costing the fixed costs can be allocated to products or product groups at least once a year for profit planning purposes. Separable and common fixed costs can be distinguished, but allocated in total for the planned volume and sales mix and never unitized. It is the unitizing of fixed costs on the product cost sheets as in Table 12.3 that makes absorption costing confusing to operating management, because these unit costs are valid only at the assumed *normal* volume and the assumed *normal* mix. By showing the allocation of fixed costs to product lines in total, along with the forecast volume and sales mix, this confusion is avoided. Operating management can see clearly the true interrelationship of sales prices, costs, and volume. This form of presentation has been discussed in detail in Chapter 5. Table 12.9 shows in summary the type of presentation that can be made.

Disadvantages and Special Considerations of Marginal Pricing

Having considered the arguments put by those in favour of marginal pricing, are there any disadvantages and special considerations to be taken into account when deciding whether to employ marginal pricing? While marginal costing may be superior to absorption or full costing when generating cost information for selling price decisions, it is a more efficient technique to employ.

The importance of fixed costs
It is important that fixed costs should not be ignored to the extent that they are not covered by contribution. Total contribution from all products must be sufficient to cover fixed costs and leave a balance which is at least a normal profit for that type of business. It is *not* essential that each separate product or market should produce a contribution which is sufficient to cover allocated fixed costs and provide a normal profit. The contribution from an individual product should at least cover the separable fixed costs attributable to that product. Contribution to common fixed costs will vary from one product to another and from one market to another. Another danger in over-emphasizing the contribution to fixed overhead approach is that the encouragement to take on business which makes only a small contribution may be so strong that when an opportunity for higher contribution business arises, such business may have to be forgone because of inadequate free capacity, unless there is expansion in organization and facilities with the attendant increase in

Table 12.9

HIGH QUALITY PRODUCTS LTD
Product Profits Forecast 1989

Product Group	Sales Units	Sales Value	Variable Cost of Sales	Total Contribution	% of Sales	Separable Fixed Costs	Direct Product Profits	Common Fixed Costs	Trading Profit
		£	£	£	%	£	£	£	£
A	2,000	10,000	5,000	5,000	50	1,000	4,000	1,000	3,000
B	4,000	25,000	16,000	9,000	36	4,000	5,000	2,500	2,500
C	3,500	22,000	17,000	5,000	23	2,000	3,000	2,200	800
D	5,000	31,000	24,000	7,000	23	3,000	4,000	3,100	900
E	8,350	42,000	30,000	12,000	29	3,000	9,000	4,200	4,800
		£130,000	£92,000	£38,000	29	£13,000	£25,000	£13,000	£12,000

Note: Common fixed costs have been allocated to products on the basis of sales value

fixed costs. *The management must know its markets and customers, and be able to forecast their future actions.*

Marginal pricing and price stability

Assuming a low level of inflation, is there a danger that with marginal pricing, where prices are fixed at a level calculated to maximize contribution, there will be constant price variations with changes in demand. (The impact of a high rate of inflation on pricing decisions and price stability is considered later in this chapter.) Will marginal pricing militate against price stability? When there is a temporary expansion of demand will manufacturers raise their prices to maximize short-run contribution and when there is a decline in demand will they lower prices? If a firm is constantly making short-run price changes to exploit changes in demand it may prejudice its long-term interests. In a period of business recession firms using marginal pricing may lower prices in order to maintain business and this may lead other firms to lower their prices. Cut-throat competition might in fact develop. With the existence of idle capacity and the pressure of fixed costs, firms may successively cut prices to a point at which no one of them is earning sufficient total contribution to cover its fixed costs and earn a fair return on capital employed.

With regard to the use of marginal pricing during a business recession two situations can be considered:

1. When there is a short-run recession in the industry, i.e. when there is unused capacity in the industry caused by a temporary fall in demand.
2. When the industry is contracting and there is excess capacity in the industry, i.e. the capacity which if withdrawn from production would bring a rise in prices sufficient to restore normal profits to the industry.

In the first situation, the short-run recession in the industry, the firm can lower its price to take account of the new shape of the demand curve and set a new price which will maximize the total contribution, given this new demand curve. But if the firm considers the recession is only temporary, it may not wish to risk the possibility of a price war with its competitors when there is likely to be a recovery in business in the near future. It may not employ an aggressive marginal pricing policy because of the fear of retaliation. Non-price competition in the form of special offers, gifts, etc., may be more attractive than price cuts, particularly when it is extremely difficult to forecast the new demand curve. However, it may still be possible to engage in an aggressive marginal pricing policy in differential markets, e.g. in export markets, where retaliation is less likely to occur because the firm may not be in direct competition with its usual competitors.

In the case of a contracting industry it is a question of the 'survival of the fittest'. The contraction adjustments will tend to take place by means of cut-price competition. The more efficient firms will have lower marginal cost curves and/or lower fixed costs than their less efficient competitors. As the more efficient firms lower their prices to maintain business, their weaker competitors will be eliminated from the industry. Prices should eventually be restored to a level which maximizes total contribution at a figure which provides a normal profit margin. As the more efficient firms lower their prices they attract trade from their weaker competitors, thus increasing their total contribution. Then, as the weaker firms are eliminated, the industry supply curve will rise and so will the price which maximizes total contribution. An aggressive marginal pricing policy by the efficient firms may well speed up the process of contraction.

In the past there appears to have been a widespread feeling amongst accountants, which many still hold, and which some text-books tend to promote, that marginal costing is a technique which can be used most advantageously only in periods of business recession. Thus, when business is buoyant and output is high, average total costs based on absorption costing will be preferred to the marginal cost as cost data for pricing decisions. The accountant may assume that marginal cost is always lower than average total costs; that prices should be a function of cost; that there is a 'price' the market will bear rather than a range of price-demand relationships, and he may tend to ignore the fact that prices are also a function of demand. When business is buoyant, he chooses the cost which he believes will give the higher price and therefore higher profits. It may be argued that the accountant is in fact honouring the idea that prices are also a function of demand if he considers marginal cost only in recession, and he thinks of the highest price at other times. It is true that by using marginal cost data the accountant does tend to recognize the demand function in a recession, but the use of the total cost data of absorption costing in a buoyant period is not full recognition of the demand function. It does not recognize the fact that profits are maximized at that price which gives the highest total contribution in the short run, and that this is not necessarily the highest price. The price developed by absorption costing will probably not be the price which would maximize total contribution and profits. In the higher ranges of output average total cost may be superior, if the accountant assumes that marginal cost is constant in the higher output ranges. But true marginal cost may exceed average total cost as the limit of short-run productive capacity is approached, and marginal cost accurately determined will always be superior to average total cost for short-run pricing decisions.

Will marginal pricing in fact give rise to price instability? It is doubtful in the majority of firms. There are a number of reasons why many firms would be ill-advised or reluctant to change prices during short-term cyclical fluctuations, particularly lowering prices during cyclical recessions, regardless of the method of pricing employed:

1. In many industries in the short run it is a very expensive and complicated business altering prices—involving the calculation, printing, and circulation of price lists. The benefit to be derived from a small alteration in prices will often be outweighed by the cost of making the price changes. If prices are lowered during a cyclical recession it may be difficult to raise them again.

2. In most, if not all, industries some form of imperfect competition exists. If there is price leadership, all the firms large enough to cause the leader concern will probably follow the price leader. Price leadership tends to dampen down the amplitude of cyclical fluctuations. In an imperfect oligopoly the firms will have, or will think they have, a kinked demand curve. They will be reluctant to raise their prices because they think their competitors will not do likewise, and they will lose customers to their competitors. They think that if they lower their prices their competitors will do likewise and no advantage will be gained. Companies marketing industrial products have to recognize that they are selling to professional buyers who often possess a high degree of countervailing power. Thus, if advantage is taken of limited industry capacity to maximize contribution by increasing prices to industrial buyers, these same buyers may squeeze their suppliers when excessive capacity appears during a recession.

3. Another important factor is the relationship between quality and price in the eyes of the customer. A marketing economist has pointed out:

It has been suggested that to the consumer price is an important indicator of product quality and the satisfaction he can expect from the relevant purchase. The housewife and the industrial buyer like, at least socially in the purchasing side of a trade transaction, to 'know where they stand'. Steady price implies steady product quality, makes advance budgeting possible and buying simpler. It reduces the need for 'haggling' or shopping around which tend to be unwelcome chores to the busy Anglo-Saxon purchaser. The seller in the organised market, selling mainly on reputation, his 'brand' image perhaps, in a field where product sophistication makes comparison testing on any scale prohibitive, has no desire whatever to upset his customers in the social activity of buying, or to upset their preconceived notions about the product's quality associated with price.[8]

If one accepts the above arguments, then, in the absence of a high rate of inflation, the pricing of consumer goods and mass-produced capital goods will tend to be stable in the short run. Such firms would tend to restrict their aggressive short-run pricing to *secondary* pricing decisions, such as export orders, sub-contracting, supplies to institutions, etc. On the other hand, in a jobbing undertaking, where it is unlikely that any significant degree of repetition of orders for similar products will occur, the objective of maintaining full capacity working and maximizing contribution to fixed costs may only be achieved consistently if the price fixing policy is flexible.

In a competitive industry marginal pricing is more likely to produce price stability by discouraging manufacturers from using every increase in costs as an excuse for raising prices in order to safeguard unit profits. A manufacturer who fully understands the principles of marginal pricing will never increase his selling price simply because his fixed costs have risen. Any attempt to safeguard profit by raising selling prices because fixed costs have risen will be self-defeating if there has been no change in the demand function and the selling prices have already been fixed at a level calculated to maximize total contribution. Existing selling prices should be yielding a maximum

8 T. E. Milne, 'Price, Investment Scale and Resource Allocation', in *Essays in the Theory and Practice of Pricing*, Institute of Economic Affairs, London, 1967, pp. 223–4.

total contribution in present demand conditions, and if a manufacturer raises his selling prices because his fixed costs have increased, he will find himself earning a smaller total contribution than before he increased his prices. The increase in price will be offset by the fall in demand.

Pricing Decisions with a High Rate of Inflation

When there is a high rate of inflation the price monitoring system advocated should signal the need for price reviews. Let us consider the impact on a product profit-volume chart of:

1. A high rate of inflation in a sellers' market; and
2. A high rate of inflation during a recession.

With a *high rate of inflation in a sellers' market* the product profit-volume, period costs, variable product costs, and break-even volume for existing prices are increasing continuously, but it is likely that the income elasticity of demand effects will allow the higher costs to be passed on in higher prices. The contribution curve is likely to move upwards and to the left to compensate for the increase in variable costs and period costs. The company is likely to generate a higher total contribution and direct product profit in money terms at the optimal price. These effects of inflation are illustrated in Figure 12.4. While increases in costs and break-even volume can be forecast with a reasonable degree of accuracy, the move in the contribution curve cannot. An effective monitoring system should assist in this direction.

Consider now the situation in a period of a *high rate of inflation during a recession*. Period and variable costs rise continuously, but as real disposable incomes fall the income elasticity effects no longer compensate for the increase in costs. The contribution curve may move *downwards* and to the left as consumers move on to lower indifference curves. The shape of the contribution curve may change as demand switches to cheaper products and to substitutes, or as some consumers stop purchasing the product. As real disposable incomes fall it becomes increasingly difficult for companies to pass on higher costs in the form of higher prices and at the same time maintain demand for their products. As illustrated in Figure 12.5, companies are faced with rising costs, falling demand and disap-

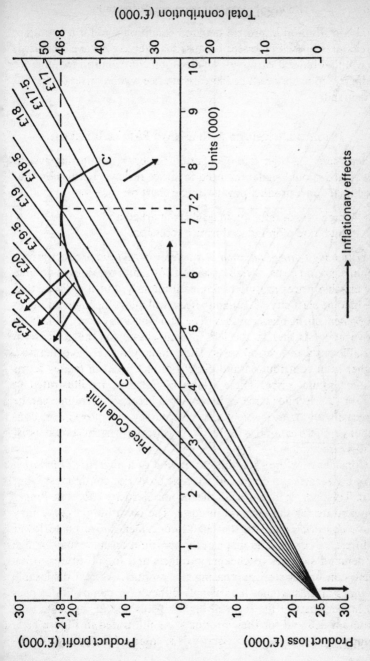

Figure 12.4. *Effect of inflation in a sellers' market*

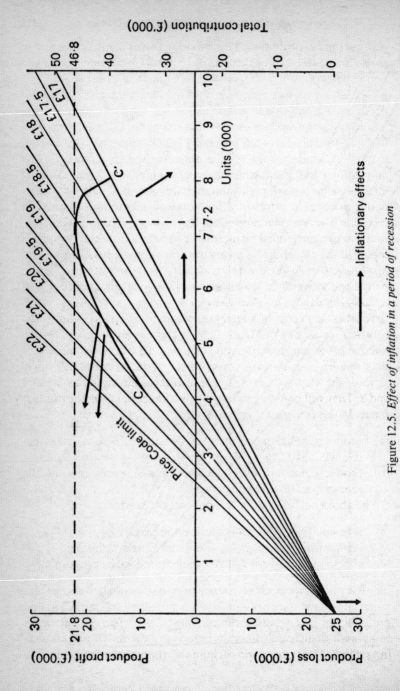

Figure 12.5. *Effect of inflation in a period of recession*

pearing total contribution. This situation forces many companies to take a long, hard look at their costs, both variable product costs and period costs.

A similar analysis can be hypothesized for producers of industrial products. An important difference is that the customers in these markets are professional buyers. In a recession, companies marketing industrial products can very quickly find themselves in a buyers' market. A similar profit-volume chart can be developed, for example, for a firm producing industrial components, by substituting alternative percentage contribution margins or P.V. ratios for alternative prices. The effect of a high rate of inflation in a period of recession is very similar. Period costs are rising, percentage contribution margins are eroded by increasing variable costs, and demand is falling at the same time. It is very difficult to raise prices in a buyers' market, and if losses are to be avoided it is necessary to reduce period costs. See the discussion and example of the impact of cost inflation on pages 113–19 of Chapter 4.

What is the impact of a high rate of inflation and recession on the contribution picture in Figure 12.6? If variable costs are increasing, and therefore unit contribution is falling, demand is falling and it may not be possible to increase prices; then products will move towards the left-hand corner of the picture, as illustrated by Styles 4 and 8. They will become candidates for withdrawal from the product range. In this respect it is important to distinguish between:

(a) products whose move into the withdrawal box has been accelerated, and
(b) products that are likely to recover their position when the economy starts expanding again.

The above analysis not only highlights the need for:

(a) segmental reporting and contribution picture analysis;
(b) comprehensive forecasting and monitoring systems; and
(c) effective cost control systems and cost reduction programmes,

but also the importance of recognizing that normally margins are more important than volume when a company has liquidity and profitability problems in a declining market. A company that attempts to maintain or increase volume by reducing prices and cutting margins in a period of rising costs and declining market size may suddenly find

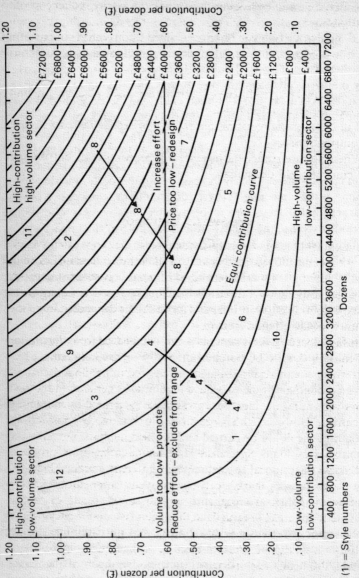

Figure 12.6. *James Wilson & Son: Contribution picture for men's knitted briefs in the British market*

(1) = Style numbers

it has no margins. Management accountants should explain to their non-financial colleagues their company's price–volume–profit relationships and how inflation changes the relationship between price changes and volume changes. Contribution pictures are helpful for this purpose – for example, when considering such questions as:

What will be the impact of alternative price changes on unit contribution and demand?

Will the possible reduction more than offset the increase in unit contribution?

Where do we envisage the product will appear on the contribution picture after the decision?

Forecasting Demand

An important factor which militates against the more extensive application of marginal pricing is the lack of accurate demand information. A forecast of total contribution for any given price depends upon a knowledge of demand at that price. The determination of the contribution curve in Figures 12.1 to 12.5 is dependent upon the accuracy of the demand forecast.

In fact, locating the position of the demand curve is the major difficulty in the use of marginal pricing. Forecasting demand is a field where commercial judgement is required in the final decisions. Some accountants argue they have had bitter experience in the past with over-optimistic 'most likely' estimates generated by marketing executives. However, the large firm can remove a considerable amount of the doubt by careful and detailed analysis, reducing the error to narrow limits. Specialists can examine competitors' products and assess their appeal to customers in different markets. Penetration trends in each market can be analysed. Competitors' pricing policies, marketing arrangements, and discount structures can be evaluated. The effect of tariffs and the general economic background of the various overseas markets can be taken into account. Econometric models can be built. Subjective probabilities can be introduced. Although these specialists can remove much of the doubt from demand forecasting there still remains the problem of drawing a demand curve with any great precision.

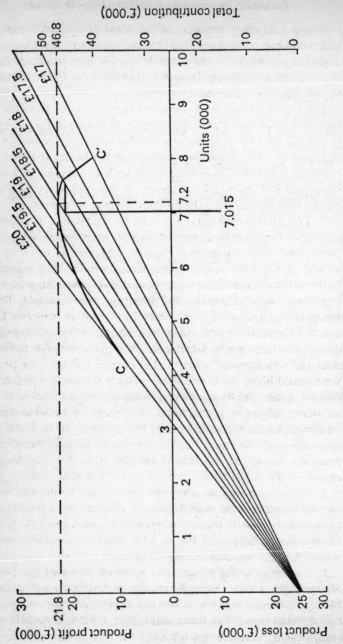

Figure 12.7. Product profit–volume chart

When conducting seminars on marginal pricing with marketing executives it is pointed out that the analysis is dependent upon their ability to provide a demand curve. Invariably they agree they cannot provide precise estimates. However, after some discussion the following conclusions are frequently reached:

1. It is possible to answer sensitivity analysis type questions from the product profit-volume charts or from the contribution graphs (see Chapter 11). For example, if the price of Product X was increased to £18.5, how far can demand fall before the total contribution falls below that forecast for the current price (£18.0)? As illustrated in Figure 12.7 the answer to this question (7,015 units) can be read directly from the product profit-volume chart.

2. The contribution curve CC' can be drawn as a band and for each price there will be a range of possible units demanded, product profit, and total contribution outcomes. Marketing has long been viewed as requiring mainly judgement, intuition, and experience, but marketing researchers are increasingly combining scientific techniques with judgement and intuition. For example, Pricing Research, a company set up jointly by Kraushar Andrews Eassie and the University of Nottingham, undertakes demand curve studies. It produces graphs which reveal the optimum price for a product and which predict what the fall in sales will be if the product were priced higher or lower. While market researchers cannot predict accurately the shape of the demand curve, they should be able to attach subjective probabilities to a range of possible demand outcomes for each possible price. The accuracy of demand curve estimates could be improved, but the cost of refining the estimates generally outweighs the benefit derived from the improved accuracy.

3. There are many assumptions underlying the product profit-volume chart, and the analysis is only relevant over a limited range of output. It is more realistic to present to management a product profit-volume chart as in Figure 12.8, which takes account of the uncertainty surrounding the pricing decision.

4. Normally, at the growth and maturity stages of the product life-cycle, the product manager should be concerned with choosing between a limited number of alternative prices on the crown of the contribution curve. The lower and higher prices on the tails of the contribution curve are not normally relevant except in a severely

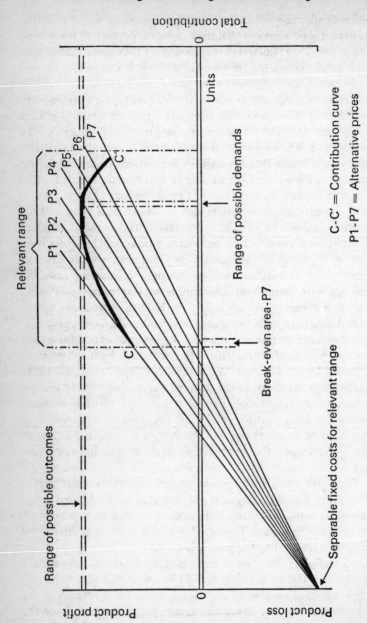

Figure 12.8. *Product profit-volume chart under uncertainty*

limited capacity or when considering a skimming policy or penetration policy at the introductory stage. One of the interesting things that emerges from the studies undertaken by Pricing Research is that low prices can deter consumers just as much as high.

5. The subjective probabilities attached to demand curve estimates by market researchers can be incorporated into probability diagrams to determine alternative outcomes, and graphs or tabulations can be presented which array the probable price-contribution outcomes according to a rational combination of possibilities involved. Risk profiles can be developed, as illustrated in Tables 12.10 and 12.11,

Table 12.10
Review of Selling Price of Product X

Selling Price £	Most likely Outcome		Expected Value		Range of Total Contribution	
	Units	Total Contribution £	Units	Total Contribution £	Minimum £	Maximum £
18	7,600	45,600	7,676	45,288	35,910	54,340
18.5	7,200	46,800	7,344	47,001	37,260	55,440
19	6,600	46,200	6,534	44,995	37,125	54,450

Table 12.11
Review of Selling Price of Product X

Price: £18		Price: £18.5		Price: £19.0	
Probability %	Total Contribution not less than: £	Probability %	Total Contribution not less than: £	Probability %	Total Contribution not less than: £
100	35,910	100	37,260	100	37,125
96	39,900	98	41,400	94	41,250
86	41,040	86	42,120	84	41,580
72	43,890	79	45,360	63	44,550
66	44,460	78	45,540	60	45,375
64	45,600	72	46,800	56	46,200
29	49,400	30	50,400	21	49,500
24	50,160	24	51,480	16	50,820
3	54,160	3	55,440	2	54,450

for each alternative price indicating the likelihood of achieving various total contributions.[9]

It will be noted that while the most likely total contribution at a selling price of £18.5 is only £600 greater than that at £19.0, after taking into account the subjective probabilities, the expected value is over £2,000 higher and the minimum and maximum outcomes are more attractive. The range of possible outcomes may also be presented in the form of a cumulative probability distribution, as in Table 12.11. This table shows the probability of achieving not less than a certain total contribution for a given price. The management is now in a position to choose between the alternative prices with a clearer picture of the possible outcomes.

In a jobbing or contracting undertaking, where there is unlikely to be any significant degree of repetition of orders for similar products, the firm is also a price-maker, but is bidding for specific jobs rather than offering a product to a market at a price which will generate a certain demand. Model-builders have also been active in the area of competitive strategy in situations where a company is bidding for a limited number of large jobs or contracts. Decision trees can be used to evaluate the uncertainties involved in the establishment of a pricing policy for a new product.

It may well be argued that while the results of this type of analysis look impressively neat and infallible, they are based on purely subjective judgements. It is true that no one has yet developed a completely reliable method to measure precisely the price elasticity of demand of any brand or product, particularly where there are cross-elasticities of demand affecting a number of brands. The product manager must intuitively estimate the effects of a proposed price change. He will rarely find precisely comparable circumstances in either his own or his firm's experiences. However, as Baxter and Oxenfeldt[10] have emphasized, crude estimates of demand may serve instead of

9 For a simple risk analysis procedure using a discrete probability density function, see John Sizer. 'A Risk Analysis Approach to Marginal Cost Pricing', *Accounting and Business Research*, No. 1, Winter 1970, pp. 30–38.

An alternative and more sophisticated approach is to use a continuous probability distribution function. For example, see R. Jaedicke and A. A. Robichek, 'Cost Volume Profit Analysis under Conditions of Uncertainty', *Accounting Review*, October 1964, pp. 917–26; and J. F. Flower, 'A Risk Analysis Approach to Marginal Cost Pricing: A Comment', *Accounting and Business Research*, No. 4, Autumn 1971, pp. 335–7.

10 Baxter and Oxenfeldt, op. cit., footnote 4.

careful estimates of demand, but cost gives remarkably little insight into demand. Similarly, subjective judgements of the range of likely outcomes based on the cumulative experience of executives are better than subjective 'most likely' estimates based on the same cumulative experience. As management becomes more accustomed to attaching subjective probabilities to its demand forecasts and cost estimates, its ability to make such judgements will improve. It is simply formalizing something it has always done in decision-making: weighing the odds.

Costs for Pricing Decisions in Practice

Despite the apparent advantages of marginal pricing as compared with product prices based on total costs derived from absorption costing, full costs appear to be used by most firms when developing product prices. The results of recent research studies do not cast doubt on the impression obtained from the several empirical studies of product pricing, that the accountant's advice to management is invariably based upon full cost at normal capacity in the first stage of price fixing. It appears that in many firms marginal cost pricing principles are not employed, or are restricted to what might be called 'secondary' pricing decisions, e.g. tenders, by-products, unusual work, export orders, sub-contracting, etc. These secondary pricing decisions are not seen as long-run decisions. Why is this? All decisions which deal with the future involve risk and uncertainty, and the attitude of the decision-maker is conditioned by the degree of risk and uncertainty involved. Accountants, by tradition and training, are conservative and cautious in their attitude to the future. They anticipate losses before they are incurred, but never gains before they are realized. The full cost or cost-plus approach to pricing decisions is attractive to the accountant under conditions of uncertainty; it provides a *starting-point* from which the process of fixing selling prices can begin. Managerial judgement can then enter into determining the size of the plus factor. The accountant knows that the product cost covers the full cost of production, selling, distribution and administration at normal capacity. Marginal cost, on the other hand, provides him, not with a starting-point, but with a rock-bottom price, and not one which will cover the 'full' cost at normal capacity.

Organizational theorists[11] have argued that firms develop a number of simple operating rules, and the organization's rules permit the transfer of past learning. Full cost pricing procedures provide such simple operating rules:

> The main attraction of cost plus is, of course, that it offers a means by which plausible prices can be found with ease and speed, no matter how many products the firm handles. Moreover, its imposing computations look factual and precise, and its prices may well seem more defensible on moral grounds than prices established by other means.[12]

Full cost pricing appears to offer a procedure which enables the complex problem of pricing, which involves considerable uncertainty, to be reduced to a rather simple problem with a minimum of uncertainty.

Furthermore, there may be little pressure by managers on accountants to provide more relevant cost information for pricing decisions. Unless the managers have sufficient understanding of their information needs, so that they can ask the right questions and know whether they have received the right answers, accountants may be content to continue to provide the full cost information they have always provided.

The probable reason why the full cost basis is used in 'primary' pricing decisions is because these are considered to be long-run decisions. They will in the first instance be long-run prices although they may be increased or decreased in the future to accord with existing short-run conditions. But when initially deciding on the price of standard 'bread and butter' products, firms are thinking in terms of a price which will cover all their costs and give a satisfactory return on capital employed in the long run. Hence the increasing use of the rate of return variant of absorption pricing. Seen in these long-run terms, all costs are variable. Therefore, once commitments which entail continuing fixed costs have been entered into, management wants unit costs for pricing decisions which include a provision for recovery of total outlay according to some systematic plan. The use of conventional absorption costing with fixed costs included in product costs on the basis of normal capacity appears to offer such

11 R. M. Cyert and J. G. March, *A Behavioural Theory of the Firm*, Prentice-Hall, Englewood Cliffs, N.J., 1963, p. 104.

12 W. T. Baxter and A. R. Oxenfeldt, op. cit., footnote 4.

a 'systematic' plan. Marginal costing offers no equally obvious plan for the recovery of fixed costs; it merely gives, if the demand curve can be forecast, the optimum short-run price–output combination which will yield the largest possible total contribution out of which fixed costs and profit can be provided in the long run. It does not guarantee that all costs will be met and a normal profit will be provided in the long run. On the other hand, full cost pricing only provides this guarantee *if sales volume is equal to or more than normal capacity output on which the plus for overhead absorption and profit is based.*

Furthermore, the accountant may persuasively argue that:

1. His system of providing full cost estimates for pricing purposes is quick and cheap to operate.
2. It enables top management to delegate the complex decision of pricing by devising a number of simple costing rules which it can keep within its control.
3. Marginal cost pricing relies heavily on demand forecasts which marketing executives are unable to estimate accurately.
4. If the large firms offering a limited number of products to a market still find forecasting their demand curves a major problem, what of the smaller firms who cannot afford to employ specialists and the firms, both large and small, that produce large numbers of products for many different markets?

For these and other reasons many progressive, as well as less enlightened, accountants are prepared to rely on the total costs of conventional absorption costing for pricing purposes when the firm is a *price-maker*. Thus, while the mechanics of 'full-cost-plus' pricing may be emphatically and repeatedly rejected in economic theory, for long-run as well as short-run pricing policy, in practice it still forms the basis of the accountant's contribution to the majority of 'primary' pricing decisions.

Summary

Selling price decisions are difficult and complex and the accountant should provide financial information relevant to the decision at hand. In many multi-market companies pricing is not simply a process of setting figures at which the company's products are offered to customers, but selling price is one of a number of variables in the marketing mix. An essential first stage in individual pricing decisions is a comprehensive monitoring system which signals the need for a price review. The principal methods of determining cost-based prices are full cost or cost-plus pricing, the rate of return on capital employed variant, and marginal cost pricing. The major criticism of full cost-plus pricing is that it fails to take direct account of demand and assumes prices are a function of costs. On the other hand, while being sound in theory, the principal problem associated with marginal cost pricing is that of forecasting price–demand relationships in different markets. A high rate of inflation increases the importance of pricing decisions. Period costs, product variable costs, and break-even volumes for existing prices are increasing continuously, and management has the difficult task of deciding to what extent higher costs can be passed on in higher prices. Full cost appears to be used by most firms as a starting-point in 'primary' pricing decisions; managerial judgement on price–demand relationships entering into the size of the plus.

Selected Readings

1. T. Bruegelmann, G. Haessly, C. Wolfgangel and M. Schiff, *The Use of Variable Costing in Pricing Decisions*, National Association of Accountants, Montvale, N.J., 1986.

2. Joel Dean, 'H B R Classic: Pricing Policies for New Products', *Harvard Business Review*, November–December 1976.

3. Andre Gabor, *Pricing: Principles and Practice*, Heinemann, London, 1977.

4. D. C. Hague, *Pricing in Business*, George Allen & Unwin, London, 1971.

5. D. Lund, K. Monroe and P. Choudhury, *Pricing Policies and Strategies: an Annotated Bibliography*, American Marketing Association, Chicago, 1982.

6. Robert N. Scapens, Mohamed Y. Gamael and David J. Cooper, 'Accounting Information for Pricing Decisions', in David Cooper, Robert Scapens and John Arnold, *Management Accounting Research and Practice*, Chartered Institute of Management Accountants, London, 1983.

7. John Sizer, 'Pricing Policy in Inflation: A Management Accountant's Perspective', *Accounting and Business Research*, Spring 1976; or 'Pricing

Policy and Decisions in Inflation', in *Perspective in Management Accounting*, Heinemann/I.C.M.A., London, 1981.
8. D. Solomons ed., *Studies in Cost Analysis*, Sweet & Maxwell, London, 1968.

CASE STUDY

In John Sizer and Nigel Coulthurst, *A Casebook of British Management Accounting*, I.C.A.E.W., 1985.

Shapland and Petter Ltd (Volume 2) – a system designed to provide marketing management of a medium-sized, high-quality door manufacturer with information on product costs and product profitability for selling price reviews.

Index